# The Thief of Time

# The Thief of Time

Philosophical Essays on Procrastination

EDITED BY
Chrisoula Andreou &
Mark D. White

Oxford University Press, Inc., publishes works that further
Oxford University's objective of excellence
in research, scholarship, and education.

Oxford   New York
Auckland   Cape Town   Dar es Salaam   Hong Kong   Karachi
Kuala Lumpur   Madrid   Melbourne   Mexico City   Nairobi
New Delhi   Shanghai   Taipei   Toronto

With offices in
Argentina   Austria   Brazil   Chile   Czech Republic   France   Greece
Guatemala   Hungary   Italy   Japan   Poland   Portugal   Singapore
South Korea   Switzerland   Thailand   Turkey   Ukraine   Vietnam

Copyright © 2010 by Oxford University Press, Inc.

Published by Oxford University Press, Inc.
198 Madison Avenue, New York, NY 10016
www.oup.com

First issued as an Oxford University Press paperback, 2012.

Oxford is a registered trademark of Oxford University Press

All rights reserved. No part of this publication may be reproduced,
stored in a retrieval system, or transmitted, in any form or by any means,
electronic, mechanical, photocopying, recording, or otherwise,
without the prior permission of Oxford University Press.

Library of Congress Cataloging-in-Publication Data
The thief of time : philosophical essays on procrastination / edited by Chrisoula Andreou
and Mark D. White.
    p. cm.
Includes bibliographical references and index.
ISBN 978-0-19-537668-5 (hardcover); 978-0-19-991737-2 (paperback)
1. Procrastination.  I. Andreou, Chrisoula. II. White, Mark D., 1971–
BF637.P76T45 2010
128'.4—dc22         2009021750

9  8  7  6  5  4  3  2  1

Printed in the United States of America
on acid-free paper

To
Mike and Kaemon
and
Paul and Ree

# Acknowledgments

We owe special thanks to the Centre for the Study of Mind in Nature for funding a workshop in New York City in the summer of 2008 for the contributors to gather and share ideas; Jennifer Hornsby and Olav Gjelsvik, the research directors of the Rational Agency section of CSMN, played an integral role in arranging this tremendous collaborative opportunity. We also thank the philosophy program at the Graduate Center of the City University of New York for hosting the workshop.

We are very grateful to Peter Ohlin and Brian Hurley at Oxford University Press for their support and encouragement of this project. Most of all, we would like to thank the contributors, who not only developed insightful analyses of procrastination but helped prove wrong everybody who heard about this book and joked, "Oh, but you will never get it done."

# Contents

Notes on the Contributors, xi
Introduction, 3
*Chrisoula Andreou & Mark D. White*

## PART I

1. Procrastination: The Basic Impulse, 11
   *George Ainslie*
2. Economic Models of Procrastination, 28
   *Don Ross*
3. Is Procrastination Weakness of Will? 51
   *Sarah Stroud*
4. Intransitive Preferences, Vagueness, and the Structure of Procrastination, 68
   *Duncan MacIntosh*
5. Bad Timing, 87
   *Jon Elster*

## PART II

6. Prudence, Procrastination, and Rationality, 99
   *Olav Gjelsvik*
7. Procrastination and Personal Identity, 115
   *Christine Tappolet*
8. The Vice of Procrastination, 130
   *Sergio Tenenbaum*
9. Virtue for Procrastinators, 151
   *Elijah Millgram*
10. Procrastination as Vice, 165
    *Jennifer A. Baker*

## PART III

**11** Overcoming Procrastination through Planning, 185
*Frank Wieber & Peter M. Gollwitzer*

**12** Coping with Procrastination, 206
*Chrisoula Andreou*

**13** Resisting Procrastination: Kantian Autonomy and the Role of the Will, 216
*Mark D. White*

**14** Procrastination and the Extended Will, 233
*Joseph Heath & Joel Anderson*

**15** Procrastination and the Law, 253
*Manuel A. Utset*

Bibliography, 275

Index, 293

# Notes on the Contributors

**George Ainslie** is a behavioral economist who has used several different methods to explore the basic determinants of choice. His modeling of higher mental processes from the motivated interaction of simple reward-seeking interests has been published in journals of psychology, philosophy, economics, and law; in many book chapters; and in two books: *Picoeconomics: The Strategic Interaction of Successive Motivational States within the Person* (1992) and *Breakdown of Will* (2001). Ainslie is a research psychiatrist at the Veterans Affairs Medical Center in Coatesville, Pennsylvania.

**Joel Anderson** studied philosophy at Princeton, Northwestern, and Frankfurt Universities and taught at Washington University in St. Louis for nine years before becoming a research lecturer in 2004 at the philosophy department of Utrecht University in the Netherlands. He specializes in moral psychology and social theory and focuses especially on issues of autonomy, agency, mutual recognition, and normativity. He coedited, with John Christman, *Autonomy and the Challenges to Liberalism* (2005) and is currently writing a book entitled *Scaffolded Autonomy: The Construction, Impairment, and Enhancement of Human Agency*.

**Chrisoula Andreou** is Associate Professor of Philosophy at the University of Utah. She completed her Ph.D. at the University of Pittsburgh. Her research areas are theoretical and applied ethics, action theory, practical reasoning, and rational choice theory. She is especially interested in dynamic choice problems, analyses of temptation, and Humean conceptions of practical reason. Her earlier publications on procrastination include "Understanding Procrastination" (2007) and "Environmental Preservation and Second-Order Procrastination" (2007). Her articles on closely related topics have appeared in *American Philosophical Quarterly*, *Bioethics*, *Philosophical Studies*, *Philosophy and Public Affairs*, and *Ratio*.

**Jennifer A. Baker** is in the philosophy department at the College of Charleston. She earned her Ph.D. in philosophy at the University of Arizona and has taught at Duke University and the University of North Carolina at Chapel Hill. Her research is focused on virtue ethics; she promotes a traditional, practical, rationality-based account of virtue against contemporary accounts that attempt to do without a final end. In her paper "Operationalizing Virtue," she presents her own data on moral reasoning and reports on other means of gathering empirical support for the traditional accounts of practical rationality. In "Virtue and Meaning," she attempts to distinguish an integrated moral psychology from meaning in a life. Her most recent publications include "Money Is the Product of Virtue" and "Virtue and Behavior: The Intersection of Ethics and Economics."

**Jon Elster** is the Robert K. Merton Professor of Social Science at Columbia University. He also holds the Chaire de Rationalité et Sciences Sociales at the Collège de France. He has previously taught at the Universities of Oslo, Paris (XIII), and Chicago. Among his recent books are *Alchemies of the Mind* (1999), *Closing the Books: Transitional Justice in Historical Perspective* (2004), *Explaining Social Behavior* (2007), *Le Désintéressement* (2009), and *Alexis de Tocqueville: The First Social Scientist* (2009). His main current research interests fall within philosophical psychology and the study of collective decision making.

**Olav Gjelsvik** is a professor of philosophy at the University of Oslo since 1994. He earned his D.Phil. at Oxford University in 1986 and has since published articles and papers in metaphysics, epistemology, philosophy of science, philosophy of mind, philosophy of action, and philosophy of language. He participated from 1994 to 1998 in an international and interdisciplinary project on addiction, organized by Jon Elster. Since 2002, Gjelsvik is a member of the Norwegian Academy of Science and Letters; he is currently head of the group that includes psychology, philosophy, and history of ideas. He is presently working mainly on a general account of human agency, and he codirects, with Jennifer Hornsby, the Rational Agency project within the Centre for the Study of Mind in Nature at the University of Oslo.

**Peter M. Gollwitzer** holds the Social Psychology and Motivation Chair at the University of Konstanz in Germany and is Professor of Psychology at New York University. His research focuses on the willful pursuit of goals. He is coeditor, with John A. Bargh, of *Psychology of Action: Linking Cognition and Motivation to Behavior* (1996) and, with Ezequiel Morsella and John A. Bargh, of *The Oxford Handbook of Human Action* (2009).

**Joseph Heath** is Professor in the Department of Philosophy and the School of Public Policy and Governance at the University of Toronto. He is the author of *Communicative Action and Rational Choice* (2001), *Following the Rules* (2008), and a number of scholarly articles on the subject of practical rationality.

**Duncan MacIntosh** is Professor of Philosophy at Dalhousie University. Lately, he has been working in decision theory, the theory of practical rationality, meta-ethics, metaphysics, political philosophy, and epistemology. He has published in *Analysis, The Australasian Journal of Philosophy, The Journal of Philosophy,* and elsewhere.

**Elijah Millgram** received his Ph.D. from Harvard in 1991 and held positions at Princeton and Vanderbilt before joining the faculty at Utah in 1999. His current research is focused on theory of rationality, particularly on practical reasoning and on inference in the face of partial truth. He is the author of *Practical Induction* (1997), *Ethics Done Right: Practical Reasoning as a Foundation for Moral Theory* (2005), and *Hard Truths* (2009). His historical research interests include John Stuart Mill and Friedrich Nietzsche. He is editor of *Varieties of Practical Reasoning* (2001) and a former fellow of the Center for Advanced Study in the Behavioral Sciences and of the National Endowment for the Humanities.

**Don Ross** is Professor of Economics at the University of Cape Town and Professor of Economics and of Philosophy at the University of Alabama at Birmingham. His research concentrates on impulsive consumption, game theoretic modeling of personal development and socialization, and trade and industrial policies in Africa. Recent books include *Economic Theory and Cognitive Science: Microexplanation* (2005), *Midbrain Mutiny* (with C. Sharp, R. Vuchinich, and D. Spurrett, 2008), and *Every Thing Must Go* (with J. Ladyman, 2007). He is coeditor, with H. Kincaid, of *The Oxford Handbook of Philosophy of Economics* (2009).

**Sarah Stroud** is Associate Professor of Philosophy at McGill University in Montreal. Her research interests range across moral psychology, moral and practical reasoning, moral theory, and metaethics; she is currently working on partiality in moral psychology and moral theory. With Christine Tappolet, she coedited *Weakness of Will and Practical Irrationality* (2003/2007), and she recently contributed the entry on weakness of will to the *Stanford Encyclopedia of Philosophy*. Her work has appeared in *Ethics* and *Philosophy and Public Affairs*, among other journals. She is one of two associate editors of the *International Encyclopedia of Ethics*, now under preparation for Wiley-Blackwell with Hugh LaFollette as editor-in-chief, to be published in 9 to 12 volumes in 2012.

**Christine Tappolet** is Canada Research Chair in Ethics and Metaethics and full professor in the philosophy department at the Université de Montréal. She has coedited several volumes, including, with Sarah Stroud, *Weakness of Will and Practical Irrationality* (2003/2007) and, with Luc Faucher, *The Modularity of Emotions* (2008). She has written articles in metaethics and moral psychology and is the author of *Émotions et Valeurs* (2000) and, with Ruwen Ogien, of *Les Concepts de l'éthique* (2009).

**Sergio Tenenbaum** is Associate Professor of Philosophy at the University of Toronto. He is the author of *Appearances of the Good: An Essay on the Nature of Practical Reason* (2007) and various papers on ethics, practical reason, and Kant's practical philosophy. He is also the editor of a collection of papers in moral psychology for the series *New Trends in Philosophy* (2007), and he is currently editing a volume of original work on the relation between desire and the good, entitled *Desire, Good, and Practical Reason* (forthcoming).

**Manuel A. Utset** is the Charles W. Ehrhardt Professor at the Florida State University College of Law. He is a leading scholar on applying behavioral law and economics to issues in corporate, securities, and criminal law. His recent work has examined how people's preference for immediate gratification can lead otherwise rational actors to engage in repeated misconduct and how the content and operation of different types of legal rules help reduce or exacerbate people's self-control problems. Before joining Florida State, he taught at the Boston University and University of Utah law schools.

**Mark D. White** is Professor in the Department of Political Science, Economics, and Philosophy at the College of Staten Island, City University of New York, and the economics doctoral program at the CUNY Graduate Center. His edited books include *Theoretical Foundations of Law and Economics* (2009) and *Economics and the Mind* (with Barbara Montero, 2007), and he is the author of several dozen journal articles and book chapters in the intersections of economics, philosophy, and law. He is currently writing a book collecting and expanding on his work on economics and Kantian ethics.

**Frank Wieber** studied psychology at the universities of Jena, Louvain-la-Neuve, and Canterbury before accepting a research associate position at the University of Konstanz in 2006. He has published several journal articles and chapters on the impact of self-regulatory strategies on the goal attainment of individuals as well as groups, and is the editor of an interdisciplinary special issue of *Social Psychology* on the limits of intentionality, to be published in 2011.

# The Thief of Time

# Introduction

*Chrisoula Andreou & Mark D. White*

Procrastination is familiar and interesting but also puzzling. Although it is generally perceived as harmful and irrational, recent studies suggest that most of us procrastinate occasionally and many of us procrastinate persistently.[1] Not even saints are immune: Saint Augustine records in his *Confessions* how, after years of sexual hedonism, he vowed to return to Christianity and prayed for chastity and continence—"only not yet." Although he "abhorred" his current way of living and "earnestly" wanted to change his course, he kept deferring any change until "tomorrow."[2]

What, exactly, is procrastination? According to one simple and familiar characterization, procrastination involves simply putting things off until the last minute. But some people do this intentionally, maintaining that they do their best work under pressure. Taking the simple, familiar characterization of procrastination as their starting point, some psychologists have explored the question of whether procrastination improves or reduces quality of work and quality of life. Prominent studies suggest that, in general, the strategy of leaving things until the last minute is not a good one—the agent pays a steep price in the form of reduced well-being and shoddy work.[3]

But does this really get to the core of the problem of procrastination? In a unique classic essay on procrastination, psychologists Maury Silver and John Sabini suggest that the answer is no.[4] According to their view, we do not *discover* that procrastination is a problem by discovering that it has bad consequences. Rather, proper analysis of the concept reveals that delay does not count as procrastination unless it is "irrational." Taking this as their starting point, they then look into the factors that prompt or support irrational delaying.

1. Steel, "Nature of Procrastination."
2. Book VIII.
3. Tice and Baumeister, "Longitudinal Study."
4. Silver and Sabini, "Procrastinating."

Here, philosophical distinctions and debate concerning reason and rationality become relevant. Presumably, a person does not count as a procrastinator simply because she performs an action later than it should have been performed. For instance, given the information available, she may have had very good reason to believe that she should act later rather than sooner. In this case, she need not count as irrational, even if she failed to do what she had most reason to do.

Drawing on a common philosophical conception of irrationality, one might characterize procrastination as acting later than one *thinks* one should. Before accepting this characterization, one must carefully think through the following questions: Is there room for a subtle form of procrastination that works precisely by influencing one's thinking about when something ought to be done? For example, can procrastination take the form of discouraging one from forming any clear judgment about the need to act promptly, perhaps by distracting one's attention away from certain inconvenient truths (or possibilities), such as that one will be even more tired tonight than one is now? What if one is not only distracted from inconvenient truths but also develops a rationalization for delaying (for example, "I really must watch this DVD so that I can return it to Maria promptly")? Can this still count as procrastinating? If so, must the rationalization be interpreted as self-deception? Otherwise put, must it be true that, on some level, one thinks delaying is uncalled for? Another thing to consider in relation to the idea that procrastination involves acting later than one thinks one should is the possibility of procrastinating with respect to an action that one commits to against one's better judgment. Suppose someone forms the intention to tell a lie even though he believes he should not do so. He can, it seems, procrastinate with respect to his akratic intention, but it is not clear that procrastination of this sort can be squared with the idea that procrastination involves acting later than one thinks one should.

Perhaps more promising is the idea, taken for granted by some psychologists, that procrastination involves irresoluteness, which is possible even with respect to an akratic intention. In being irresolute, one violates a prior intention. But this alternative characterization of procrastination might also be too restrictive. For it seems that there could be a form of procrastination that works precisely by discouraging one from forming any specific intention about when to act.[5] Evasiveness of this sort is particularly easy to get drawn into when vagueness concerning when one must get started on goal-directed actions makes it possible to interpret oneself as having a goal (such as retiring with enough funds to live comfortably), though one has not acted on the goal or even yet formed any plan for realizing it.

---

5. According to Sarah Stroud (chapter 3), procrastinating with respect to X may be possible without even a vague intention to X at some point (let alone a specific intention regarding when to X).

The possibility of vague goals raises questions concerning the connection between procrastination and hypocrisy, as well as questions concerning procrastination and self-management problems associated with the fact that our choices are spread out over time. Based on the idea that actions speak louder than words, it might be suggested that procrastination is nothing but hypocrisy, understood as mere lip service to a goal one does not genuinely have. Traditional economic models of choice suggest that preferences (broadly construed so as to capture all of the agent's values) are revealed in (informed) choice. This suggests that when an agent puts off an action too long relative to her proclaimed preferences, this betrays a mismatch between her proclaimed preferences and her true preferences. Recent quasi-economic models have made room for genuine procrastination by showing that there are ways in which global preferences (preferences over extended courses of action) can fail to be revealed in choice. If, for example, an agent experiences preference reversals as a result of discounting, or has intransitive preferences, her preferences concerning her current options can lead her to follow a course of action that she finds unacceptable and invariably ranks below another available course of action that she finds acceptable. Consider an agent who values saving for a comfortable retirement but also values the goods she can get from current spending. At every point in time, the agent may rank never saving below saving every week and rank saving every week below spending this week and saving next week. Given these preferences, the agent can be led to constantly put off saving and so end up having never saved, which she invariably ranks below having saved every week.[6]

The introduction of preference reversals and intransitive preferences raises issues concerning the challenges associated with effective self-management in the face of fragmented and temporally extended agency. As such, a deep understanding of procrastination will require some reflection on personal identity and on what it takes to be a functional enduring agent. Is procrastination the product of compromised agency, involving a breakdown of will? Does it betray a lack of identification with one's future self? If the latter, does the assumption that procrastination is irrational involve a commitment to the normative force of the dictates of prudence and a rejection of pure instrumentalism about practical reason? Is procrastination just a manifestation of the vice of imprudence? Are there dimensions of procrastination that can be illuminated by (or that can illuminate) ethical theory, particularly virtue theory?

Like questions about the nature of procrastination, questions about coping with the problem are both interesting and important. Consider the following: If procrastination involves a breakdown of will, is the

---

6. Regarding procrastination and preference reversals, see, for example, O'Donoghue and Rabin, "Doing It Now or Later," "Incentives for Procrastinators," and "Choice and Procrastination." Regarding procrastination and intransitive preferences, see Andreou, "Understanding Procrastination" and "Environmental Preservation and Second-Order Procrastination."

solution the building of greater willpower or, instead, less reliance on the will in achieving one's long-term goals? Are social and legal pressures aimed at reducing procrastination unacceptably paternalistic? Do we have a right to access legally enforceable precommitment devices that can keep us on course, and do those in power have the right to provide or impose upon us these devices at our expense and for our own good?

We pose these questions without expecting to work through every one of them in this volume. The aim of this project is to take the first major step toward integrating the problem of procrastination into philosophical debate. The mix of theoretical models, empirical data, and critical argument in these chapters reflects our sense that philosophical questions concerning the nature of procrastination are illuminated by a wide range of methods of inquiry. Our hope is that this exploration of procrastination will spark novel ideas about both familiar and newly emerging philosophical issues.

We have divided the volume into three parts. The chapters in the first part are primarily concerned with analyzing procrastination or uncovering its sources. In "Procrastination: The Basic Impulse," George Ainslie presents procrastination as the purest illustration of our propensity to disproportionately value the immediate future. Given his definition of impulses as temporary preferences for smaller, sooner rewards over larger, later rewards, procrastination figures in Ainslie's view as the most basic impulse. Don Ross's "Economic Models of Procrastination" relates the leading psychological account of procrastination, which is tied to Ainslie's work on impulses, to economic models of procrastination and other self-control lapses. According to Ross, economic modeling illuminates features of self-control lapses that would otherwise remain obscure. In "Is Procrastination Weakness of Will?" Sarah Stroud considers the hypothesis that procrastination is a species of weakness of will—a practical failing that has received a great deal of philosophical attention. She argues that while there are important affinities, procrastination does not fit seamlessly with either the classic or the revisionist account of weakness of will but, instead, is distinctive enough to require an analysis of its own. In "Intransitive Preferences, Vagueness, and the Structure of Procrastination," Duncan MacIntosh resists the idea, mentioned above, that procrastination can be fostered by intransitive preferences and argues that procrastination is more closely tied to familiar explanations of weakness of will. Part I ends with Jon Elster's "Bad Timing," which embarks on the task of cataloguing the causes of irrational delay. Elster's discussion covers a range of mechanisms that can generate procrastinating behavior, including perfectionism, wishful thinking, and self-deception.

The chapters in the second part of the book explore the connection between procrastination and imprudence or vice. In "Prudence, Procrastination, and Rationality," Olav Gjelsvik picks up on the idea, mentioned above, that procrastination is tied to preference reversals that result from discounting the value of future well-being and argues that recognizing external reasons is the key to a solid defense of the idea that rationality precludes discounting-induced preference reversals. Christine Tappolet's "Procrastination and Personal Identity" ties procrastination to a lack of concern for one's future self and suggests that, so understood, the phenomenon of procrastination undermines certain objections to psychological continuity accounts of personal identity, since many of the objections assume that we invariably have a special concern for our future selves. Sergio Tenenbaum's "The Vice of Procrastination" casts procrastination as a failure of instrumental rationality and, more specifically, as the "vice of deficiency" corresponding to the virtue of "practical judgment," which allows for the successful implementation of long-terms plans and policies. Based on his reasoning, Tenenbaum questions the influential view that a purely instrumental conception of rationality is incoherent. In "Virtue for Procrastinators," Elijah Millgram connects procrastination with the fact that the value of many important human goods is not simply the sum of the goods they provide at each moment. He then sketches a picture of the "fallback virtue" procrastinators sometimes use to overcome their problem and, building on this picture, challenges the Humean idea that instrumental reasoning is all there is to figuring out what to do. Finally, Jennifer A. Baker's "Procrastination as Vice" suggests that procrastination cannot be understood independently of a rich ethical theory concerning virtue and vice and that ethical theorists can benefit from exploring the complexities of procrastination, which are often papered over for the sake of clean analysis.

The chapters in the third part of the book are concerned primarily with strategies for coping with procrastination. In "Overcoming Procrastination through Planning," Frank Wieber and Peter M. Gollwitzer recommend forming detailed implementation intentions (plans concerning when, where, and how one will perform goal-directed actions) as an easily applicable planning strategy that can help automate goal-directed behavior. Their discussion reviews and draws on their extensive empirical research in this area. Chrisoula Andreou's "Coping with Procrastination" focuses on a puzzling but familiar coping strategy that has not yet been analyzed in the literature on procrastination. The strategy involves leveraging control, and, according to Andreou's reasoning, in employing the strategy, we take advantage of the possibility that poor self-control can be a local trait rather than a robust character trait. Mark D. White's "Resisting Procrastination: Kantian Autonomy and the Role of the Will" explores procrastination in the context of a volitionist economic model of will and character that he developed in previous work. White represents procrastination as a type of akratic behavior, reflecting weakness of will, and warns against weakening the will further via heavy reliance on external coping devices. In "Procrastination and the Extended Will," Joseph Heath and Joel Anderson argue that an overly internalist conception of the will has biased discussion toward coping strategies focused on changing one's thinking and has obscured the strength and significance of the environmentally scaffolded will. In the final chapter, "Procrastination and the Law," Manuel A. Utset considers how lawmakers can help us cope with procrastination or, alternatively, can take advantage of our procrastinating ways. In this chapter, the social significance of procrastination—an often neglected but important issue—is made apparent.

# Part I

# 1

# Procrastination

The Basic Impulse

*George Ainslie*

Webster's defines *procrastinate* as "to put off until tomorrow, or from day to day"; it generally means to put off something burdensome or unpleasant and to do so in a way that leaves you worse off. By procrastinating, you choose a course that you would avoid if you chose from a different vantage point, either from some time in advance or in retrospect. Thus, the urge to procrastinate meets the basic definition of an impulse: temporary preference for a smaller, sooner (SS) reward over a larger, later (LL) reward. I will argue that it is the most basic impulse, the one in which the disproportionate value of the immediate future can be seen without confounding factors.

The motives we think of as impulses usually involve an impending thrill, a vivid sensation that is hard to resist. Examples include eating rich food, drinking, taking recreational drugs, having sexual encounters, and making purchases. Often, impulses are focused on a physical activity or consumption good, which makes them easier to understand in terms of conventional utility theory. But many impulses involve no consumption. It could be argued that gambling is the most basic impulse, because it requires no physical stimulation, only surprise. The emotions occasioned by play in an addicted gambler are as strong as those provoked by drugs and are followed by the same physical symptoms on sudden discontinuation.[1] But gambling also creates a thrill in the short run. More basic still must be the simple temporary preference for less cost in the present over the greater cost that leads to a better deal in the long run. Procrastination needs no great pleasure to drive it and no activity to instantiate it. It is just the venerable sin of sloth.

Most impulses have definable boundaries. Sometimes the impulsive act itself is naturally demarcated—you take a drug, or you do not. Even where no line divides the harmful from the benign, there is usually a definable topic that can be subjected to rules—diets to define overeating

---

1. Wray and Dickerson, "Cessation of High Frequency Gambling."

and budgets to regulate spending and gambling. But the impulse to procrastinate is diffuse, seeming to grow pervasively from the way we experience time. It always feels better to defer costs. We put off going to our workroom; in our workroom, we put off cleaning it; when cleaning it, we put off the grungy or monotonous parts. However small the unit of activity, we are drawn from the more tedious parts to the less tedious. This is not to say that we always do the work in that order; we are apt to make a rule to do just the opposite and follow the rule so habitually that it becomes second nature. But the rule is our response, not the original impulse. Where the impulse comes from a reward that is too imminent, too variable, and/or too vague to control with a rule, it simply prevails. When cleaning the workroom, our attention wanders in undefined ways that reduce our efficiency. At the most microscopic level, the more interesting parts of a picture "jump out" ahead of the less interesting. To give a personal example, whenever I have a choice regarding the order in which I add columns of figures, I add the ones that look as if they will produce round numbers first, even though a systematic approach would probably be more efficient. It is hard to be sure, when each competing behavior takes fractions of a second.

## HYPERBOLIC DISCOUNTING AS A MECHANISM OF PROCRASTINATION

There is debate about what causes impulses. Sometimes they are attributed to naiveté or inability to estimate the values of the contingencies involved. But impulses, including procrastination, persist despite the person's great familiarity with the outcome. A popular explanation is to say that the "viscerality" of an SS reward—its emotional evocativeness—can make it preferable to an LL alternative when it is close but not when it is distant.[2] But procrastination can occur at such a low level of interest that viscerality would have to imply only the quality of being marginally more attractive than some alternative, that is, nothing more than rewardingness itself. Instead, I would argue that the occurrence of procrastination among even the most mundane alternatives is evidence for a pervasive tendency to perceive value as a hyperbolic function of delay, an instance of the Weber-Fechner law by which most psychophysical quantities are perceived.[3] Mathematically, the discount function is

$$\text{Present value} = \text{Value}_0 / [1 + (k \times \text{Delay})]$$

---

2. Bernheim and Rangel, "Addiction and Cue-Triggered Decision Processes"; Laibson, "A Cue-Theory of Consumption"; Loewenstein, "Out of Control."
3. Gibbon, "Scalar Expectancy Theory." For the possibility that hyperbolic discounting is based in the elementary dynamics of receptor saturation by neurotransmitters, see Berns, Capra, and Noussair, "Receptor Theory."

where Value$_0$ = value if immediate, and k is degree of impatience. A plot of this function against delay shows that for some combinations of SS and LL rewards with a constant lag between them, SS rewards will be temporarily preferred when they are close. This pattern contrasts with the prediction of the exponential curve that is necessary to produce consistent choice over time:

$$\text{Present value} = \text{Value}_0 \times \delta^{\text{Delay}}$$

where Value$_0$ = value if immediate, and $\delta = (1 - \text{discount rate})$.

A general tendency for both humans and nonhumans to discount prospective rewards hyperbolically has now been widely documented.[4] Hyperbolic discount curves describe conflicts between short- and long-range motives. Short-range motives are based on the spike of value that occurs as a reward gets closer. Long-range motives are based on the values described by the tails of the curves that describe value at a distance, which are much lower but have the tactical advantage of governing first. Each may survive in competition with the others as long as it sometimes gets its goal. A motive and the behaviors that have been learned on the basis of this motive can be called an interest, by analogy to economic interests in the larger world.[5]

If procrastination is defined broadly as temporary preference for early reward at the expense of greater reward later, it becomes the same thing as impulsiveness, which has been extensively reported in the above experiments. It will be more useful to follow common usage and define procrastination negatively, as a preference for deferring aversive experiences rather than just a preference for SS rewards. However, the shape of its discount curve in this case has been little studied. With human subjects, there has been only a Dutch survey in which undergraduates were asked to rate their motivation to study in the face of five kinds of temptation, such as social invitations or favorite TV shows, as a function of the delay before an exam.[6] Although both the exam and the delays were hypothetical, subjects estimating their likely motivation produced a hyperbolic curve for all five temptations. This shape might seem to predict that the relative values of partying and passing an exam will shift over time, but the experiment was not designed to elicit changes in relative value; this

---

4. Ainslie, *Breakdown of Will*; Green and Myerson, "A Discounting Framework"; Kirby, "Bidding on the Future"; Mazur, "Hyperbolic Value Addition."

5. Any reward that is sometimes chosen could be seen as giving rise to an interest, but the term is useful only when one interest includes motivation to interfere with another interest. A student who feels like watching TV would not increase her prospective reward by controlling a desire to play Frisbee; there is no point in calling these separate interests. But both may be included in a short-range interest in relaxing, which succeeds to the extent that it evades a long-range interest in doing well on her exams.

6. Schouwenburg and Groenewoud, "Study Motivation."

would have required a constant lag between partying and exam and evaluation at a variable distance before both.

The nonhuman literature is not much fuller. If pigeons are given the choice between interruption of intermittent noncontingent reward by an obligatory five-response task (FR5) after six seconds or a harder task after a longer delay, they will accept harder and harder tasks as the delay before they have to perform them is lengthened. They will often accept tasks that are more than three times as hard (FR > 15) if the task is delayed by only a few seconds more.[7] However, this design, too, fails to demonstrate preference reversal as a function of delay. Analysis of preference as a function of delay in a similar experiment where the longer, later task was a duration of required pecking (FI 7.5 or FI 15 vs. FI 5) showed that the discount *rate* varied with delay, implying a curve like a hyperbolic one that could produce temporary preferences.[8] This finding confirmed the implication of an earlier concurrent interval study in which rats preferred a schedule that intermittently delivered LL shocks instead of SS ones when the delays to the SS shock were small.[9] However, all of the criteria for impulsive procrastination—preference for an LL pain over an SS one in discrete trials, if and only if the SS pain would be immediate—have been met only by Deluty et al.[10] Rats were given repeated trials in which they could spare themselves an eventual 5.0-second foot shock by accepting a much briefer, 0.5-second shock a few seconds earlier. When the brief shock would occur immediately, subjects rarely accepted it; when the brief shock would not occur for a period varying from 20 to 60 seconds, subjects' rate of accepting it varied from 50 percent to 95 percent, respectively. Thus, the rats preferred a few seconds of comfort to a brief shock that would prevent a much longer shock but only if this comfort was nearby—*temporary preference*.

Experimental analysis of procrastination is still in its infancy. Nevertheless, we can predict that ways of controlling procrastination will not be as simple as in the control of a single, clearly demarcated behavior. The kit of tools that work against discrete impulses will not be as effective against procrastination. A short catalogue shows their limitations.

Best understood are forms of precommitment. Pigeons can learn to peck a key, the only effect of which is to prevent a tempting option from being offered subsequently.[11] The latter rat experiment just described found that subjects would choose an option that committed them to get the SS shock but only if they chose while the SS shock would still be

---

7. Mazur, "Procrastination by Pigeons: Preference for Larger, More Delayed Work Requirements."
8. Mazur, "Procrastination by Pigeons with Fixed-Interval Response Requirements."
9. Deluty, "Self-Control and Impulsiveness."
10. Deluty et al., "Self-Control and Commitment."
11. Ainslie, "Impulse Control in Pigeons."

distant.[12] The choices in these experiments were predicted by the discounted value of the alternative outcomes at the time the subject chose and did not require awareness of a need for commitment. Subjects who are aware of the problem, presumably only we humans, can actively arrange for external controls such as deadlines or, even better, series of subdeadlines.[13] Or we can associate with people who share our long-range interests and exert pressure, directly or by example. This kind of external control may or may not be available and may have undesirable costs—excessive restrictiveness, say, or side demands by the other people. Alternatively, we can avoid information on the availability of distractions—keep the TV off, do not call friends to ask what's happening—or we can avoid toying with appetites that may grow to be overwhelming, such as fantasizing about resentments, romances, or favorite kinds of thrills. However, plans maintained by such controls on our attention or emotions will be unstable, vulnerable to reweighings of options that may give a short-range interest an opening. Furthermore, the exploration of possible information or emotion will be tempting in itself, and some incentive will be needed to maintain our plan of not exploring. As with other kinds of impulse, the most effective control for procrastination is usually willpower.

## A THEORY OF WILL

Will has been an elusive concept, partly because of multiple meanings but more importantly because it has lacked a clear mechanism of action. The term *will* has been applied to the process of connecting thought with behavior (a holdover from philosophical dualism, found superfluous by Gilbert Ryle)[14] and to your sense of ownership of your actions (shown to be often misleading by Daniel Wegner)[15] as well as to a faculty for controlling impulses such as procrastination. The nature of the impulse-controlling faculty has been variously depicted as resembling a muscle,[16] as an application of attention control,[17] as a learned loss of taste for short-term rewards ("molecular" vs. "molar" rewards),[18] as a function that in principle cannot be analyzed,[19] and, again, as a concept that is superfluous, because people always maximize prospective reward.[20] However, the

12. Deluty et al., "Self-Control and Commitment."
13. Ariely and Wertenbroch, "Procrastination, Deadlines, and Performance." See also chapter 14 in this volume.
14. Ryle, *Concept of Mind*.
15. Wegner, *Illusion of Conscious Will*.
16. Baumeister and Heatherton, "Self-Regulation Failure."
17. James, *Principles of Psychology*, 562–565; Bratman, *Faces of Intention*; McClennen, "Pragmatic Rationality and Rules."
18. Rachlin, *Science of Self-Control*, 108–129.
19. Pap, "Determinism, Freedom, Moral Responsibility, and Causal Talk."
20. Becker and Murphy, "Theory of Rational Addiction."

discovery that reward discounting is an innately hyperbolic function permits an explicit hypothesis about how will operates. Hyperbolic discount curves predict a relationship of limited warfare among successive motivational states, which can be stabilized along truce lines by the person's perception in each state that her current choice will function as a test case of the relevant truce (or *personal rule*). That is, a self-aware person notices that her current choice of an SS or LL reward is evidence about whether she will pick SS or LL rewards in similar situations in the future and thus finds that her expectation of a bundle of prospective rewards is at stake in a choice that literally determines only one.[21] This perception supplies the force that the Victorian psychologist James Sully said was added to an otherwise weaker alternative to give the will its strength.[22]

This hypothesis about the mechanism of will has two parts. The first is that bundling prospective rewards into series increases the present value of LL rewards relative to their SS alternatives, contrary to what exponential discounting predicts.[23] This effect has been shown experimentally in both people and rats,[24] the latter finding being proof that the effect is not an artifact of cultural suggestion. The second part is that the very perception of the present choice as a test case for similar choices in the future puts at stake a bundle of the expected rewards for those choices. This part has intuitive appeal but is only tangentially available to empirical test. Kris Kirby and Barbarose Guastello found that students who made choices weekly were more apt to choose LL rewards if it was initially suggested to them that a current choice had predictive value,[25] but this is not definitive proof. More substantial evidence comes from a tightening of introspection by means of thought experiments, which, I have argued, can be interpreted conservatively to test hypotheses, just as controlled experiments can.[26] Simplest is Monterosso's problem: Imagine that you are trying to stop smoking, and an angel tells you that you will never smoke after today, whatever you do now. Do you smoke a cigarette now? (Why not?) Now, imagine that the angel says you will always smoke after today, whatever you do now. Do you smoke a cigarette today? (Again, why not?) These and other intuitions can be interpreted as demonstrating that the way you are motivated to forgo a current indulgence is by how it affects your expectation of your own future choices.[27]

21. Ainslie, *Breakdown of Will*, 90–116.
22. Sully, *Outlines of Psychology*, 669.
23. Summed *exponential* curves from pairs of SS and LL rewards have no more tendency to cross than curves from a single pair (Ainslie, *Breakdown of Will*, 78–85).
24. Kirby and Guastello, "Making Choices" (people); Ainslie and Monterosso, "Building Blocks" (rats).
25. Kirby and Guastello, "Making Choices."
26. Ainslie, "Can Thought Experiments Prove Anything?"
27. Monterosso and Ainslie, "Beyond Discounting."

## THE USE OF WILL AGAINST PROCRASTINATION

From here on, I will assume that the mechanism of willpower is the perception of current choices as test cases for bundles of prospective reward, as I have just described. This is *recursive self-prediction*, which can change your prospects of reward several times before you make a single choice. When dealing with procrastination, the will's maneuver is to ask, "If not now, when?" Unfortunately from the viewpoint of your long-range interests, this is not a rhetorical question; a short-range interest will readily answer it with, "Tomorrow, when I'm rested," or "In that empty time slot I'll have next week." The will's great vulnerability is to rationalization. Although an expected sequence of LL rewards may have more present value than the sequence of their SS alternatives, the sequence of SS now and LL thereafter, if believable, has the most present value of all. To the extent that a person relies on willpower, the success of impulses will depend not on the imminent availability of gratification but on the existence of a credible excuse that lets her expect to be, as in Saint Augustine's prayer, "chaste and continent, but not yet."

The credibility of the excuse is the pivotal factor. If you start to accept waiting until you are rested as an excuse, your estimate of whether you will get the task done at all may fall. That is, you may expect your future selves to interpret it as a lapse and decide to lapse themselves, thereby reducing the credibility of your resolutions in this area. The threat of this fall may move you to reject that excuse and do the job—or find a better excuse. As you survey the possible excuses and your likelihood of buying one, your predictions of getting your long-range reward may seesaw violently, variations that are fed back recursively over a period of mere seconds until you actually behave in one way or the other. The sensitive dependence of choice on self-prediction is arguably the source of enough introspective opacity to account for the experience of free will in a mechanism that is strictly determined by incentives.[28] In order for will to operate, the summed, discounted value of the bundle of prospective rewards at stake must be more than the discounted value of the present impulse, and resisting the impulse must seem both necessary and sufficient for eventually obtaining this bundle. If a credible excuse is available, resisting the impulse will not seem necessary. Conversely, if you have given in to too many similar impulses in the past, resisting this one may not seem sufficient to reverse the trend. As Roy Baumeister's muscle model also predicts, exercise gives the will more strength;[29] but unlike the prediction of the muscle model, the strength is somewhat specific to particular temptations—perhaps to procrastinating but not to smoking—and is

---

28. Ainslie, *Breakdown of Will*, 129–134.
29. Muraven, Baumeister, and Tice, "Longitudinal Improvement."

affected asymmetrically by exercise and lapse: "Every gain on the wrong side undoes the effect of many conquests on the right."[30]

To be credible to a sophisticated decision maker, an excuse must be unique, one that holds only for today or at least infrequently enough that neither it nor similar excuses occur too frequently to preserve adequate value in the bundle. Perhaps you forgot that your son's piano recital was today. That would be a credible excuse, one that you would not later see as a rationalization and thus evidence against the credibility of your resolve. But by its very nature, a credible excuse has to be a stroke of luck, not something that you can find by looking for it. It also has to stand out from other excuses that would be too available, such as your nieces' and nephews' recitals, and their soccer games, and your favorite team's soccer games, and so on. A property that elevates a credible excuse above any old pretext is distinction by a *bright line*: your own children versus other children, recitals versus mere lessons, championship games versus others. In inter*personal* bargaining, bright lines have long enabled opposing parties in legislatures to reach stable compromises. In inter*temporal* bargaining, they form a major determinant of how much impulsive motivation can be resisted by willpower. Most smokers manage to quit, as do about half of alcoholics, aided by the bright line between some consumption and no consumption at all.[31] By contrast, 5 percent of overweight dieters manage to achieve long-term weight reduction, presumably because there is no unique threshold that defines overeating.[32] Where temptation is both strong and dangerous, a bright line may make it possible to renounce all excuse making and follow a 12-step program in declaring, "I am powerless against [the relevant impulse]." Far from abdicating self-control, as some have feared,[33] the perception that your will is naked against temptation makes it strong, albeit rigid. It offers a more effective alternative than "controlled drinking." However, there is no obvious alternative to controlled eating or controlled spending; to declare yourself to be powerless over food or purchases would dictate no safe course of conduct.

Even less is it possible to give up procrastination. "Never put off until tomorrow what you can do today" is a brave slogan, but it is literally impossible not to put off most of what you actually can do. You have to continually make selections, not just among big alternatives but also among a continuum of middle-sized, small, and tiny ones. Not only are potential boundaries between categories of choices often lacking, but impulsive incentives also are often inextricably mixed with rational ones. Colorably rational reasons to put off a task include:

---

30. Bain, *Emotions and the Will*, 440. See Monterosso, Ainslie, Toppi-Mullen, and Gault, "Fragility of Cooperation," for an experimental model.
31. Garvey et al., "Smoking Cessation Patterns"; Helzer, Burnham, and McEvoy, "Alcohol Abuse"; Smart, "Spontaneous Recovery."
32. Garner and Wooley, "Confronting the Failure."
33. Levy, "Self-Deception and Responsibility."

1. To take advantage of an exceptional present opportunity.
2. Not to squeeze it into a busy schedule when you will have more time later.
3. To dispose of a potential distraction.
4. To commit yourself not to devote more time to the task than it deserves.

1. Alternative opportunities can be evaluated according to many rationales. For instance, the hypothetical examples presented to students in the Dutch survey on reasons to put off studying used these examples:

- Friends call with an invitation.
- A favorite TV show is on.
- A temporary employment agency calls offering a job.
- You walk past a party in a nearby room.
- A fellow student comes to your door.[34]

A student must make a fresh evaluation each time about how rare and how valuable the opportunity is, at a time when motivation to take it is strongest, that is, when it is imminent. How many invitations come; would she miss this show more than others; how good a job is it and how much does she need it; how many parties happen in nearby rooms? Without information about these properties, the subjects imagined similar answers for all five cases but showed a trend toward putting off studying more for the fellow student at the door. This result makes sense, since on the face of it, this occasion is more special. Still, the judgment of being special will be determined by which fellow student it is, how often people come to the door, what this one wants, whether she could reasonably be put off, how much social obligation there is, and so on—all reasons that potentially affect whether the individual will feel the need to count this as a test case for her resolution not to procrastinate. Where an occasion is predictable, such as a TV show, she could be more objective by resolving in advance to see it or not, thus avoiding having to decide during the hyperbolic surge of temptation that precedes an imminent opportunity, but such advance warning is often not available. Where a temptation is recurrent, past judgment calls become a factor as well: "This TV show isn't very special, but I've been letting myself see it before I study, so I might as well go on doing so." A baggage of old compromises and sheer happenstances provide historical boundary lines that offer themselves as excuses.

2. A sparser future calendar suggests that spacing out tasks might be objectively efficient. However, people are poor at estimating what will arise to fill it as a time gets closer and regularly expect to be less busy

---

34. Schouwenburg and Groenewoud, "Study Motivation."

despite having been wrong about this repeatedly.[35] Sometimes a task really would be better assigned to a future slot, but such cases are hard to discriminate from wishful thinking.

3. Likewise, it seems rational to dispose in advance of distractions that might interrupt a task. However, cases where advance preparation is clearly called for, such as assembling necessary files, shade over into cases where you are just taking advantage of technicalities in your rules for authenticating productivity. To procrastinate while staying compliant, you can give yourself credit for preparing your worksite, collecting relevant information, checking your mail and e-mail, forestalling people who might call you by calling them first, taking action on any problem that might worry you while you try to work, getting food so you will not be hungry, adjusting the thermostat, and so on. The blocked author who sharpens dozens of pencils has become a cliché. It is possible to catch yourself at this activity and stop it in individual instances but probably not to avoid trying a new version next time—pushing the edge of justifiable preparations.

4. I have argued elsewhere that personal rules do not necessarily maximize long-range reward, because the risk that a person may interpret choices as lapses may motivate her to become compulsive—prone to adopt concrete rules over subtle ones and to forgo opportunities unnecessarily.[36] This consideration creates a long-range incentive to sometimes limit the scope of a personal rule. In the midst of performing a task, personal rules may hinder judgment calls about how thorough or painstaking to be and prevent cutting corners where an objective appraisal of efficiency would call for it. If you are aware of a tendency in yourself toward misplaced perfectionism, a rational tactic may be to commit yourself to jettison unnecessary parts of a task by making time so short that you have to. Of course, this is a crude tactic and apt to be misjudged, especially if adopted when the urge to procrastinate is strongest.

Another way to look at the limitations of personal rules is to see them as creating a principal-agent problem.[37] A long-range interest (principal) can be regarded as supervising successive motivational states of the person (agents) by means of personal rules. The purpose of personal rules is to organize enough incentive to keep the long-range interest continuously dominant over many successive states. However, an individual agent (the person at a given moment) may increase her discounted expected reward by following a short-range interest to a limited extent, stopping short of violating a rule and thereby reducing the expected reward that depends on this rule. This is an *intertemporal* variant of the *interpersonal* situation where an employer (principal) tries to accomplish a task by hiring an employee (agent) who does not have an interest in the outcome of that

35. Zauberman and Lynch, "Resource Slack."
36. Ainslie, "Dangers of Willpower," and *Breakdown of Will*, 143–160.
37. Mirrlees, "Optimal Structure"; Ross, "Economic Theory of Agency."

task, paying her as long as she follows the principal's instructions. The agent may then maximize her personal welfare by looking busy, being passive where an instruction does not require action, focusing on the letter of the instructions rather than on any personal sense of what will bring results, and making her work as opaque to the supervisor as her instructions allow—the classic pattern of command economies.

Within the person, the principal-agent relationship leads to maximization of the welfare of the current moment, which may entail a similar passivity, doing good-sounding, easy tasks before genuinely productive ones and not auditing her choices too closely. The result will be not frank impulsiveness but stealthy procrastination. The agent of a given moment does have an interest in the long-term outcome but may find many small ways to pilfer from this outcome without reducing its discounted, expected value as much as she increases her current, undiscounted reward.[38] As in interpersonal economies, the best strategies will give individual agents the greatest possible interest in the long-term outcome, that is, make the necessary steps rewarding in the short run as well as the long run. However, opportunities to do this are limited, and personal rules remain an imperfect approach to controlling procrastination.

## PROCRASTINATION IN EMOTIONAL REWARD

We humans notoriously live inside our heads. That is, *reward*, which selects among our options, does not depend strictly on the environmental *rewards* that shape the choices made by most animals.[39] Most of our reward comes from expectations we construct of the future, our rehearsal of the past, and occasions for emotion that we have in the present, which are not necessarily connected to physical rewards. And to shape current choices, all of these categories must boil down to just the third: occasions for present emotion. Our choices have no intrinsic momentum, so even the greatest of long-term projects must be chosen and chosen again, whenever a possible alternative is imagined, according to how we currently feel about it.[40] Likewise, the past matters to us only to the extent

---

38. To the extent that the agents find these evasions by trial and error, without being aware that they are imperiling the long-term goal, this process may be described by Andreou's intransitivity model (see her "Understanding Procrastination"); but eyes-open impulsiveness requires the person additionally to be a hyperbolic discounter.

39. The use of "reward" for both the internal selective process and an event that occasions it invites confusion, but there seem to be no simple alternatives. When I use "reward" without an article, I am referring to the internal process, the one that makes the choices it follows more likely to be made again; "a reward" or "rewards" means the events that occasion this internal reward. "The reward" is ambiguous, and I will avoid it.

40. There is a way that we can avoid subjecting plans to reweighing for short periods of time—just to direct our attention away from alternatives—but our ability to avoid reexamining a plan in the face of temptation is limited.

that it is the occasion for present feelings; there are people who are largely successful in discarding this option, who report that they never revisit their histories, who "live only in the present." We conjure so much that is not in our current sensory fields that we live as if in a video game, cultivating some virtual scenarios and trying to avoid others, able to prevent the intrusion of even physical reality in many cases but unable to prevent the intrusion of imagined horror in other cases. Much (I would say most) reward that modern people experience from goods of various kinds is inducible ad lib, within our psyches, and what we buy from the world is only some kind of sheet music that lets us pace it well. There has been no good term for reward that does not require an association with physical occasions; it could be called mental reward, self-reward, or process reward, but these terms all have extraneous connotations. I will use *emotional reward*, since emotions are its best examples, even though *emotion* connotes an intensity that many examples do not have.

Even reward from a concrete commodity such as food, ostensibly released by specific turnkey stimuli, can be partially summoned in imagination by the people who read cookbooks for pleasure; the fantasy-prone are said to be able to get the same satisfaction as from a meal.[41] Similarly, even reward from an instrumental device such as money includes a component that is independent of its instrumental value, that is, independent of what the money can buy.[42] And what we buy is more apt to be ways of occasioning emotion—fiction, vacations, sports tickets, fashions, aids to the companionship or admiration of others or to the assuaging of guilt, and investments to make us feel that we will be able to buy more of them—than ways of assuaging hunger, thirst, cold, and pain. The point of these virtual games is just to occasion emotions that we supply from the inside, but the games have constraints as binding as those on getting substantive goods. There are the pains that come when you excite but do not physically satisfy appetites for food, sex, and some drugs, in addition to the disappointment inherent in not getting an expected pleasure. There are addictive appetites that can be provoked by some fantasies. There are negative emotions that get occasioned along with the positive ones, often, like them, independently of factual rationales—the extreme example being the clinical phobias, which only rarely arise from painful experience with the phobic object.[43] Most important is the wasting of potential reward caused by suboptimal pacing, a major example of which is procrastination in its subtlest form.

## Emotions as Reward-Seeking Processes

The requirements for pacing emotional reward are introspectively familiar and well predicted by hyperbolic discounting, but analysis has been

---

41. Lynn and Rhue, "Fantasy Proneness."
42. Lea and Webley, "Money as Tool."
43. Lazarus, "Phobias"; Murray and Foote, "Origins of Fear of Snakes."

hindered by two oddities in conventional motivational theory that have received little attention—call them the problem of pain and the problem of pleasure. I will here summarize an exposition made elsewhere.[44]

The problem of pain is how aversive events and their prospect can lure attention but deter motor behavior. Conventional theory says that attention to aversive events is hardwired, a kind of reflex, and attention to their prospect is a conditioned reflex. But alternatives to experiencing fear and pain can often compete with them on the basis of reward, such as during sports or combat. Minor chronic pains can be suppressed even by routine daily activities, to prevail again when you are trying to go to sleep. Furthermore, not entering into many aversive emotions (panic, anger, even the emotional component of physical pain) is a learnable skill. Finally, all stimuli that can induce conditioning have a motivational valence as well, an association that is unlikely to be mere coincidence. However, theoretical attempts to make all mental selection depend on motivation have been stymied by the problem of how to attract attention with a negative valence. An unmotivated process such as conditioning has seemed necessary. Hyperbolic discount curves offer a solution: just as addictive binges are driven by a cycle of temporarily preferred, transient reward and a consequent hangover of nonreward, a more rapid cycle of urges that reduce ongoing reward can drive itches, symptoms of obsessive-compulsive disorder, tics, and other "wanted but not liked" behaviors;[45] and a still more rapid cycle, more rapid than our flicker-fusion threshold, may let aversive urges be irresistible, such as to panic or to invite the emotional (protopathic) component of pain, despite an almost instant plunge in reward—"given in to but not wanted."[46]

The problem of pain cannot be solved on a motivational basis without some mixture of reward and nonreward. The cyclical mechanism just described remains speculative but is consistent not only with hyperbolic discounting but also with recent brain imaging, which has found areas responding to the unexpected occurrence of both pleasure and pain but not to their unexpected nonoccurrence.[47] As one neurophysiological commentator has said, "If reward is defined to include all motivating factors, then there may be no differences between attention and expectation of reward."[48] The risk of aversive emotions constrains the pacing of emotional reward—not in that some stimulus will impose them on us but in that either external or internal contingencies will provide occasions for them, luring us into the rapid cycle just described.

---

44. Ainslie, *Breakdown of Will*, 48–70, 161–197, and "Précis of *Breakdown of Will*"; only references subsequent to *Breakdown of Will* will be given here.
45. See Berridge, "Motivation Concepts."
46. Ainslie, "Pleasure and Aversion."
47. Becerra et al., "Reward Circuity Activation"; O'Doherty, "Reward Representations."
48. Maunsell, "Neuronal Representations," 264.

The problem of pleasure is that positive emotions are clearly accessible without physical stimulation and can even be trained to occur at will, as in actors; but people still depend largely on external events to occasion these emotions. As with aversive emotions, conventional theory invokes an automatic, unmotivated response of emotions to certain innately programmed stimuli and a transfer of these emotions by conditioning to other stimuli. It has seemed only common sense that pleasure has to be released by external events—otherwise, people could sit and reward themselves ad lib, short-circuiting the adaptive reward contingencies by which the environment motivates behavior. But people do have a great capacity to experience imaginary scenarios emotionally; some "fantasy-prone personalities" do so to a maladaptive degree. The constraint on this process seems to lie not in a limited evocativeness of imagination but in the decreased emotional impact of a scenario with repetition (apparently less in the fantasy-prone).

Again, hyperbolic discounting suggests a motivational model. To evoke strong, positive emotion, scenarios must include periods of deprivation, in which suspense or longing builds up. A hyperbolic discounter will temporarily prefer lesser, earlier payoffs to the more intense ones that entail initial deprivation and so will be lured to harvest emotional reward as soon as it becomes even slightly available. She will thus stay at a high level of satiety, just as someone who feeds herself by continual grazing will not get much pleasure from food. In response to this tendency, we learn to cue our emotions by relatively infrequent occasions that are outside our control. Even so, when these occasions recur predictably, our attention jumps ahead to their high points, and any suspense component is lost. Since attention cannot be restrained by personal rules,[49] the most effective occasions will have to be surprises. Thus, we learn to optimize emotional reward by some form of gambling. To the extent that we gamble on challenging jobs, unpredictable relationships, and even our own creativity, the outcomes reward us more intensely than assured attainments. The motivational constraint on pacing emotional reward arises from our intrinsically poor ability to surprise ourselves.

### Application to Procrastination

The ever-present availability of emotional reward creates an obvious potential for procrastination. Cultivating such reward brings continual choices about how to allocate it over time, decisions that must themselves be based on discounted prospective reward and that are thus subject to temporary preferences for SS over LL indulgences. We know very little about how such choices are made, but hyperbolic discounting may at least help define the problem. The fundamental constraint on mental

---

49. Monitoring a rule not to think about X entails thinking about X; see Wegner, *White Bears*.

reward is your capacity to be rewarded in a given modality,[50] your *appetite* for that reward.[51] The occurrence of reward almost always reduces this appetite as it happens.[52] The combination of reward and using up your appetite in that modality can be called the *consumption* of reward. Most consumption patterns use up appetite faster than it regenerates. Activity in a modality thus tends to divide into consumption and regeneration phases. In the regeneration phase, there is little reward from that source—you have to find other sources while waiting for the potential in this modality to regenerate, which entails some changeover cost whether or not a good alternative is available. Even when the returns from consumption are all but exhausted, a hyperbolic preference for small, immediate over larger, delayed amounts of reward creates a temptation to defer the regeneration phase. In sum, the cost of emotional reward is the wait for its regeneration; deferring that cost in return for inferior current reward is a form of procrastination.

The most concrete example of deferring regeneration is the choice of bedtime. For many people (perhaps all young children and most college students), it always feels better to stay up a little longer, until pleasure is seriously marred by fatigue. Choices about timing are also evident in the consumption of fiction. We learn in childhood that daydreams habituate, even after we have learned to reduce premature satiety by inventing challenges to be overcome. Surprise must be supplied by another person, such as the author of a book, and we make personal rules not to cheat on the pacing the author supplies by reading ahead. Still, some styles of fiction require more patience than others and offer greater long-range impact in return for their greater short-range cost. In buying fiction, and in creating it for sale, there are choices about how frequently to have emotional payoffs occur. Over the last century, more frequent payoffs seem to have increasingly won out over less frequent ones, so that earlier works seem slow; and publishers require books to have an increasingly high "flip value," the frequency with which emotional payoffs occur from page to page. Play or movie audiences hedge their gambles on satisfaction for their next few hours by relying on the predictability of a style, an author, or a

---

50. A modality comprises the varieties of reward that satiate together. Meat and cheese are in the same modality; meat and water are not. There are an unknown number of modalities that satiate separately (Herrnstein, "Evolution of Behaviorism"), and the divisions may be only partial: you can still have an appetite for sugar when satiated for cheese, although both also contribute to a common satiety. Divisions among purely emotional rewards are even less clear. Satiation with comedy may leave some appetite for tragedy, but the underlying substrates that define such modalities are almost entirely unknown.

51. More strictly speaking, your *capacity* for appetite, or "drive" (see Ainslie, *Breakdown of Will*, 166).

52. The only exceptions to have evolved seem to be the brief rewards that command your attention to pain or panic, which lead to sufficient aversion (obligatory nonreward) such that they are not in danger of keeping your behavior fixated on repeating them; but even aversive stimuli have some tendency to habituate with repetition.

performer, thus often settling for a familiar but somewhat habituated work over a greater gamble. Eventually, any of these may become so stale that we are driven to search for untried sources; but until then, we are apt to fall into this form of procrastination.[53]

To some extent, the conflict between SS emotional rewards and LL ones affects not only our make-believe but also our construction of beliefs. Events that we really expect to happen have potentially more pacing power than fictions, because we cannot arbitrarily substitute one expectation for another—or, at least, must not catch ourselves doing so. In the short run—over hours or minutes or certainly seconds—we may be inescapably motivated to prepare for them: to become tense and vigilant when we expect danger, to thrill to breaking good news, or to wince as we fall toward a cold lake. However, more distant events are subject to interpretation. Here we are tempted to authenticate the most desirable scenarios as expectable; but abject surrender to this temptation would make our expectations no better emotional pacing patterns than fictions, just wishful thinking by which we prematurely satiate our appetites. We learn early to subject expectations to conventions, personal rules. "Testing reality," as the psychotherapists say, produces a limited set of expectations that somewhat prevent us from putting off the lean, boring experiences that restore appetite. However, even defensibly realistic expectations permit evasions. It may be possible to believe that a bad investment has hope until you actually sell it, leading to the sunk-cost fallacy. You may enjoy feeling the possession of money until you actually pay bills with it, a consideration that leads to irrational delays. You can somewhat expect each of two or more incompatible goals to be realized until you commit yourself to one of them, fostering indecisiveness. And you can believe that the infinitesimal chance of winning the grand lottery is possible and thus in a different category from a pure daydream.

The conflicting motives of currently consuming reward versus building appetite shape rules for testing reality that differ among individuals in their permissiveness toward wishful thinking. These differences have never been analyzed but might be said to loosely correspond to the conventions for writing fiction that are shaped by the same conflict—on a continuum from naturalistic to realistic to somewhat contrived ("well made," in the case of plays) to farce. Expectations must compete with remote possibilities and even outright fantasies according to the same determinants of current rewardingness,[54] which include the incentive to put off the less productive parts.

---

53. Since risk is required for emotional renewal, this procrastination could also be classed as risk aversion, but putting off necessary renewal should be distinguished from the usual application of this term. Conventional risk aversion is a way of defending wealth and is often rational; because your wealth is finite but opportunities for gain are infinite, the value of a potential loss should not be the symmetrical opposite of the value of a potential gain.

54. See also Ainslie, "Motivation Must Be Momentary."

## CONCLUSION

Procrastination is one aspect of the universal tendency to discount future events hyperbolically. Temporary preference for accelerating benefits is called impulsiveness; temporary preference for deferring costs is called procrastination. Procrastination is the "tragedy" half of "tragedy tomorrow, comedy tonight." Although the timing of benefits and the timing of costs are just flip sides of the same phenomenon, focusing on people's preference to defer costs lets us realize how pervasive the phenomenon is. What we call impulses are often intensely rewarding choices, such as getting a thrill or consuming an addictive substance, giving intuitive appeal to the suggestion that they win out because of a special, "visceral" quality.[55] Procrastination, by contrast, may offer very little reward up front and win out just because the prospect of effort or deprivation feels better if deferred. Here, plain and simple, we can see the warp in the way we experience the future. And while conspicuous temptations can be identified and subjected to personal rules, a preference for deferring effort, discomfort, or boredom can never be entirely controlled. It is as fundamental as the shape of time and could well be called the basic impulse.

---

55. See Ainslie, "Core Process in Addictions and Other Impulses"; Laibson, "A Cue-Theory of Consumption"; Loewenstein, "Out of Control."

# 2

# Economic Models of Procrastination

*Don Ross*

Almost all people procrastinate, some to the point of suffering severe welfare losses.[1] This fact has recently become a prominent topic at the interface between academic and popular discussion of economics, as attested by a wave of briskly selling books.[2] Much of this discussion carries the explicit or implicit message that economics should be so embarrassed by the ubiquity of procrastination, as well as of addiction, loss aversion, salience effects, and other "anomalies" of rational choice, that it should collapse into psychology. In this chapter, my modest aim is to survey recent work in the microeconomic modeling of procrastination so as to indicate resources available for dispelling such embarrassment.

Economic rationality implicates two aspects of agency: (1) consistency of choice from one consumption or investment opportunity to another and (2) use of full information in arriving at beliefs about the relative expected payoffs from possible choices ("rational expectations"). The case for the displacement of economics by psychology rests in part on the claim that people are systematically inconsistent in their choices and prone to act on scanty information even when more could be obtained with relatively little effort.

The economist trying to model procrastination can trade off these aspects of rational agency against one another. On the one hand, he or she can suppose that people procrastinate in full awareness that they are doing so but exhibit intertemporal preference inconsistency. That is, they choose courses of behavior that are rationalized by the payoff that would accrue to completion of various specific investments, then choose not to complete the investments in question, then subsequently reverse preferences a second time and suffer regret over their irresoluteness. Alternatively, procrastinators can be modeled as having intertemporally consistent utility functions but lacking accurate information about their probable future behavior when they choose schedules of activities. Since what is mainly of interest is *recurrent* procrastination, the poverty of sound

---

1. O'Donoghue and Rabin, "Procrastination in Preparing for Retirement."
2. E.g., Ariely, *Predictably Irrational*; Thaler and Sunstein, *Nudge*.

expectations here must be comparatively radical: the procrastinator fails to learn to predict future procrastination from his or her own history of past procrastination.

If effort is assumed to be aversive, then procrastination expresses at least temporary preference for smaller immediate rewards over later larger ones. This more general disposition has a range of other common manifestations, including addiction, impulsive spending, and impulsive risk taking. It can be argued that procrastination is the basic form of this family of behaviors.[3] For example, the addict who wants to discontinue use at some point, but not today, fails to quit because she continually procrastinates, and the difficulty of overcoming such procrastination is the main *problem* with addiction. Noneconomists are often suspicious of economists' standard assumption that effort is aversive; artists, athletes, craftspeople, and even businesspeople engrossed in their work tend to report when probed that such experiences of "flow" are highly rewarding. However, this simply makes the point that later rewards from avoidance of impulsive consumption, including impulsive consumption of leisure as in procrastination, *do* tend to be larger. Procrastination is, in fact, evidence for the aversiveness of effort.

The first extended account of procrastination in the economic literature was offered in a 1991 paper by George Akerlof.[4] He drops without apology the assumption that people are economically rational, emphasizing instead the extent to which they tend in nearly all of their decisions to overweight the inferential relevance of salient perceptions. A necessary condition for procrastination, according to Akerlof, is that people perceive immediately present costs of action more vividly than they perceive future benefits or (especially) than they perceive the marginal values of increments of benefits that accumulate gradually. Akerlof does not explicitly address the question of why experiences of regret do not teach chronic procrastinators to discount vividly perceived immediate costs (or, alternatively, to augment dimly perceived future or incremental benefits). However, he indicates the conceptual resources available for addressing this problem when he partly attributes procrastination to the fact that "individuals possess cognitive structures of which they are less than fully aware." He adds immediately that "The assumption that such structures influence behavior is unfamiliar in economics, but central to other social sciences."[5] Thus, Akerlof implicitly drops commitment to both aspects of economic rationality as relevant to explaining procrastination: procrastination is assumed to result from factors exogenous to rational choice.

In Akerlof's model of the procrastinator's revealed value function, costs of action made salient by temporal immediacy are multiplied by a parameter $\delta > 1$ that represents entrapment by a brute force of perceptual

---

3. As, in fact, George Ainslie argues in chapter 1 here.
4. Akerlof, "Procrastination and Obedience."
5. Akerlof, "Procrastination and Obedience," 10.

vividness. The parameter, which does all of the work in the model, amounts to a black box in which resides everything that personal psychology might identify as relevant to procrastination. The explicit model—the only part of Akerlof's otherwise verbal account that has the flavor of economic analysis—thus sheds no extra light on the phenomenon; it simply encodes the fact that some psychological forces, and not merely relationships between valuations and prices, drive patterns of intertemporal choice. Much of the "behavioral" literature in economics continues in this vein, while adding richer psychological detail. As we well see, however, this is not the only available option.

The next section of this chapter reviews a leading psychological approach to intertemporal self-control problems and regulation, including procrastination, the "picoeconomic" framework descended from Herrnstein and most extensively developed by Ainslie. The section after that identifies affinities between Ainslie's picoeconomic interpretation of effective self-control (or "willpower") and Michael Bacharach's model of team reasoning. Despite its name, picoeconomics does not provide a genuinely *economic* modeling framework. By an "economic" model, I mean a model that admits of solution by maximizing one or more utility functions (possibly interactively, using game theory) and that can be tested econometrically against behavioral or neural processing data. The following section considers ways in which the elements of the picoeconomic framework can be modeled economically. The final section concludes by arguing that economic analysis helps to clarify distinct modeling ideas within the picoeconomic framework that otherwise remain obscure.

## PICOECONOMICS

There is a straightforward general strategy for economically modeling inconsistent people. This is to drop the assumption that a person implements one economic agent over his whole biography. Instead, the person is broken up into interacting subagents on synchronic and/or diachronic dimensions.[6] An analogy can be drawn here between people and countries. It is obvious that countries often behave irrationally—erecting self-harming barriers to imports, for example, or alternately running down national savings and enforcing unpopular belt tightening—as a result of the interactions of rational citizens acting in pursuit of their parochial interests. Nevertheless, for many purposes, especially macroeconomic policy analysis, economists model countries as agents. It is quite natural to talk of countries procrastinating when their institutions repeatedly defer hard policy choices. In these cases, there is no mystery about what is going

---

6. Strotz, "Myopia and Inconsistency"; Schelling, "Economics," "Intimate Contest," and "Self-Command"; Ainslie, *Picoeconomics* and *Breakdown of Will*; Ross, *Economic Theory and Cognitive Science* and "Integrating the Dynamics."

on; we explain national procrastination by reference to strategic interactions of politicians, bureaucrats, and lobbyists with divergent preferences. This can be adapted as a model for the dissolution of puzzles about weakness of will in individual people.

If the person is divided into agents synchronically, he becomes a *community* of agents. If the person is divided diachronically, he becomes a *sequence* of agents. In either case, we can model the whole person using game theory: the person's "molar" behavior is treated as a dynamic equilibrium of bargaining games among synchronic or diachronic agents.

An early proponent of this approach to modeling procrastination and related phenomena was the economist Thomas Schelling.[7] However, it has been most extensively developed by a group of psychologists whose intellectual roots lie in the laboratory of the late Richard Herrnstein. The group's most notable contributors, aside from Herrnstein, are Drazen Prelec, George Ainslie, and Howard Rachlin.[8] Herrnstein's group from the beginning made central conceptual use of a basic *economic* concept, which Akerlof mentions but puts to no formal work—namely, discounting of future relative to present utility.

As Akerlof notes, early neoclassical economists such as Fisher considered the discounting of utility as a mere function of temporal delay to be irrational.[9] In the mid-twentieth century, however, such discounting became a fundamental element of welfare economics based on cost-benefit analysis. The case for the rationality of temporal discounting crucially rests on the idea that risk increases with delays to consumption and with the length of intervals between investments and returns. Risk factors arise with respect to two general issues: (1) accuracy in estimating magnitudes and signs of future returns and (2) questions about which agents will still be around to enjoy benefits. Assuming an intertemporally consistent utility function and rational expectations, an agent will discount delay to returns and consumption as a linear function of the passage of time. In the simple linear case, the discount formula is given by

$$v_i = A_i e^{-kD_i}$$

where $v_i$, $A_i$, and $D_i$ represent, respectively, the present value of a delayed reward, the amount of a delayed reward, and the delay of the reward; $e$ is the base of the natural logarithms; and the parameter $0 < k < 1$ is a constant that represents the influence of uncertainty and the agent's idiosyncratic attitude to risk.

Picoeconomic accounts of molar-scale intertemporal preference inconsistency model it around properties of the personal discount function.

---

7. See Schelling references in note 6.
8. Key highlights of this literature are collected in Herrnstein, *Matching Law*. See also Ainslie, "Specious Reward," *Picoeconomics*, and *Breakdown of Will*.
9. Akerlof, "Procrastination and Obedience," 6.

Based on experimental work, Herrnstein and Prelec[10] and Ainslie[11] argued that the default intertemporal discount function for animals, including people, is given not by the exponential function (1) but by a hyperbolic function as described by Mazur's formula (2):[12]

$$v_i = \frac{A_i}{1 + kD_i}$$

A second exponent parameter on the right-hand denominator typically produces closer fits for empirical discounting data in people, but I will henceforth ignore this technical complication.[13] Hyperbolic intertemporal discounting allows for (though it does not entail) intertemporal preference reversals when agents choose between smaller, sooner rewards (SSRs) and larger, later ones (LLRs). A pair of temporally spaced rewards $a$ (at $t_1$) and $b$ (at $t_2$) for which the person's utility function gives "$b$ preferred to $a$" at a point well out into the future from the current reference point where the slope of the discount function is relatively gentle may swivel into the relation "$a$ preferred to $b$" as the time of $a$'s possible consumption comes closer to the reference point, where discounting is steeper. Here, $b$ is an LLR (say, beginning a major home renovation) and $a$ is an SSR (such as spending the weekend at the cottage).

Figure 2-1 shows a standard diagram of the sort used by Ainslie to illustrate preference reversal. The short bar shows the value of an SSR, perhaps a bit of goofing off when there is work to be done. The long bar gives the value to be realized if procrastination is avoided. The crossing of the two hyperbolas illustrates preference reversal: at choice point $Y$, perception of relative values is such that the agent will choose to avoid procrastination; at choice point $X$, temptation looms large, and the agent postpones the task. At the point where the curves cross, we would expect a probe of the agent to find him wavering.

Among the earliest empirical findings of the Herrnstein group was that animals allocate responses to two choice alternatives proportionally to the relative frequencies of reinforcement received from them.[14] The relation $B_1/B_2 = R_1/R_2$, where the B's and R's refer to scalar measures of, respectively, responses allocated to and reinforcements received from the two alternatives, became known as the matching law because it claims that animals match relative behavioral allocation to relative reinforcement. Herrnstein later showed that a choice rule that directly compares the local rates of reinforcement of the two alternatives and selects the alternative with the higher local rate describes the process that produces matching, which he termed *melioration*.[15] Subsequent work

10. Herrnstein and Prelec, "Theory of Addiction."
11. Ainslie, *Picoeconomics*.
12. Mazur, "Adjusting Procedure."
13. Myerson and Green, "Discounting of Delayed Rewards."
14. Herrnstein, "Relative and Absolute Strength of Response."
15. Herrnstein, "Melioration."

**Economic Models of Procrastination** 33

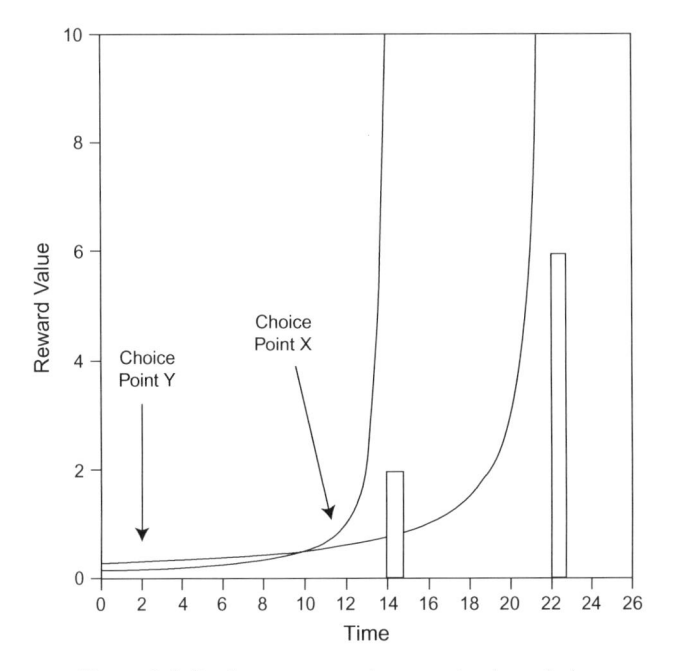

**Figure 2-1** Preference reversal as crossing hyperbolas.

building on these basic relations showed that we get accurate predictions of human and animal choice behavior if we model organisms as maximizing local rather than overall expected utility. The models that represent melioration specify that an animal will distribute its resources to a range of activities during a time interval in exact proportion to the value of the rewards it experiences for each activity *in that time interval*. The time intervals over which local rates of reinforcement are computed and compared may vary in response to exogenous influences both across and within individuals. If variation in the temporal interval over which rates are computed changes the estimate of those rates, this alters the valuation of the choice options and leads to a change in behavioral allocation. Thus, if the organism is modeled as a single agent, then the economist's assumption of intertemporal preference consistency as a criterion of rationality may be violated.

Ainslie's picoeconomic framework represents this situation as a bargaining game between two synchronous subpersonal interests, one of which (the "short-range interest") has a utility function such that SSR > LLR, while the other (the "long-range interest") has the opposite preference ordering over these alternatives. The short-range and long-range interests are motivated to bargain because the former controls behavior but typically depends on resources harvested by the latter. However, their bargaining game has the structure of a prisoner's dilemma (PD): if the long-range interest will allow the short-range interest to obtain a payoff at *some* point, then the short-range interest prefers to obtain its payoff now, but that amounts to defection in the PD; if the long-range interest will never indulge the short-range interest in future, then the short-range interest is also best off defecting at the first opportunity. Thus, defection on any bargain with the long-range interest is a dominant strategy for the short-range interest. This, in turn, implies that the long-range interest never maximizes by indulging the short-range one; it also defects. The fact that it will not be indulged if it is patient reinforces the rationality of defection by the short-range interest.

This analysis predicts, among other things, that everyone should *always* procrastinate. Ainslie must therefore explain how it is that people frequently get things done (including breaking free of addictions). He attributes this to coalitions of long-range and short-range interests that form around *personal rules*. A personal rule may take two forms: a ban on consumption of a particular kind of SSR (e.g., cigarettes) or restriction on the circumstances under which the SSR may be indulged (e.g., drinking is only permitted on social occasions). For most people, an attempt at complete prohibition of procrastination would not be credible; therefore, in focusing on this most general expression of hyperbolic discounting, we will be especially interested in personal rules that make concessions to indulgence.

Ainslie argues that governance by personal rules can be made consistent with hyperbolic discounting if the agent recognizes that present behavior *predicts* future behavior. In that case, the person can derive *present* satisfaction from evidence that the personal rule is in place, making it a currently valuable asset. If the rule is broken, then this asset is damaged or destroyed near the reference point for discounting, where its value might thus dominate the value of the competing SSR. Ainslie analyzes the hoary philosophical and popular idea of "the will" as a nominal "device" for generating personal rules.[16] He supposes that satisfactory explanation requires avoidance of the temptation to posit an *organ* to stand in for this device and believes he achieves this by showing that personal-rule production and maintenance—"willpower"—emerges endogenously as a virtual process from his picoeconomic bargaining dynamics.

## PICOECONOMICS AND TEAM REASONING

The short account of picoeconomics given above does not remotely do justice to the empirical richness of Ainslie's account, which is its most attractive and persuasive property. However, considering it from the perspective of economic analysis reveals some problems in need of solution.

---

16. Ainslie, *Breakdown of Will*.

Consider the kind of personal rule that I suggested is most relevant to procrastination, in which bargaining occurs among interests. In a one-shot PD, there is no room for such bargaining; mutual defection is the unique Nash equilibrium. In personal correspondence, Ainslie replies to this by suggesting that games between interests in SSRs and interests in LLRs have the structure of a *repeated* PD, in which equilibrium vectors include cooperative strategies. However, this raises two further problems. First, it conflicts with Ainslie's suggestion that interests, in having access to all of a person's cognitive and behavioral resources, coincide with complete time slices of a person. A present time slice of a person does not recur and so cannot play repeated games; interests can play such games only if they persist through time. Second, the repeated PD has an infinite set of Nash equilibria. Thus, limiting the analysis to identification of such games risks draining it of explanatory power.

A helpful idea for dealing with both of these problems is to combine the picoeconomic model with the "team reasoning" model of Michael Bacharach.[17] Consider a person who establishes a policy to watch sports on TV in the evening only after completing three hours of work and to watch until no later than midnight. Suppose, contrary to Ainslie's suggestion that interests coincide with personal time slices, that the interest in watching sports has some *standing* interest in a present expectation that it will get to go on watching sports *generally* (though it always prefers watching sports *now*, in part because it cares *only* about watching sports). Then this interest faces the problem that its standing expectation is threatened unless it allows long-range interests some scope to harvest resources. Given these assumptions, the person can emerge from the bargaining dynamics as a corporate institution with which the distinct short- and long-range interests partly identify. Formally, as Bacharach shows, this must amount (if it is to be coherent as noncooperative game theory) to the claim that where personal rules are effective, the bargaining game among the implicated interests has the structure of an assurance game instead of a PD.

Here is how this alchemy works. Begin with the familiar one-shot PD as in figure 2-2, and imagine it as played between a long-range interest, Player I, and a short-range interest, Player II. As usual, C denotes the strategy of "cooperating," and D denotes "defecting." The unique Nash equilibrium is (D, D). In equilibrium, to continue the example above, the short-range interest will watch sports all evening, no evening work will get done, revenue will dry up, and the TV will be repossessed, putting an end to all sports watching. If this, in turn, facilitates the resumption of work and the eventual recovery of financial well-being, the long-range interest, playing D in the game, will not support investment in another TV.

Bacharach argues that under many circumstances, people reframe games by reasoning as *teams*, that is, asking "What is best for *us*?" instead

17. Bacharach, *Beyond Individual Choice*.

| | | II | |
|---|---|---|---|
| | | C | D |
| I | C | 2, 2 | 0, 3 |
| | D | 3, 0 | 1, 1 |

**Figure 2-2** One-shot prisoner's dilemma, strategic form.

of "What is best for *me*?" More precisely, players view enhanced welfare—and, perhaps, solidarity—of the collective as an additional basis for utility ranking. Such reasoning does not produce cooperation in one-shot PDs, which violates the axioms of game theory. Rather, by increasing payoffs associated with circumstances in which the team coordinates, it has the effect of transforming the one-shot PD of figure 2-2 into the assurance game of figure 2-3. This has two Nash equilibria, (C, C) and (D, D), where the former is Pareto-efficient.

Bacharach supposes that teams—corporate entities with which individual players identify their utility—arise from natural psychological framing by people. Thus, if we try to appeal to Bacharach's model in the picoeconomic context, we must hypothesize that a person as a unified economic agent—a utility function that survives over multiple periods—arises

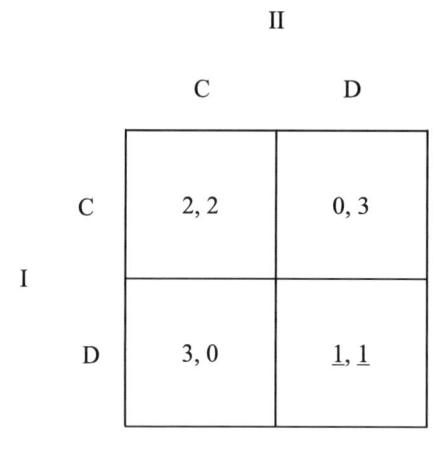

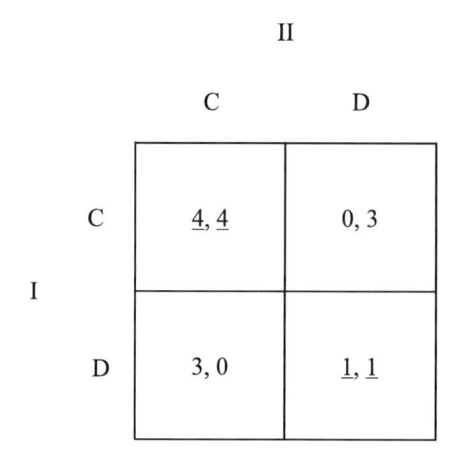

| | | II | |
|---|---|---|---|
| | | C | D |
| I | C | 4, 4 | 0, 3 |
| | D | 3, 0 | 1, 1 |

**Figure 2-3** One-shot assurance game, strategic form.

from psychological framing by subpersonal interests. Many readers are likely to find this proposal incredible. In fact, I read Ainslie (in *Breakdown of Will*) as suggesting some affinity for the idea. It is consistent with the philosophical thesis of Dennett, substantially elaborated on by Ross,[18] that people are narrated post-hoc rationalizations of sequences of behavior, where the rationalizations in question feed back to influence behavioral choice because personal consistency is valued and incentivized by other people for the sake of social coordination (including division of labor), and most of the projects of loosely associated subpersonal interests rely on degrees of interpersonal collaboration. The sense in which "interests" are the sorts of entities that could *frame* choices—that is to say, could make perceptual judgments—requires embedding in a certain kind of theory of consciousness, for which the reader is again referred to Dennett and Ross. This road evidently leads us well away from economic modeling considerations and deep into the foundations of psychology. Note, however, that it threatens no *collapse* of economics into psychology. The appeal to a theory of the relationship between consciousness and value is used to explain the genesis of basic, exogenous, utility functions. This reflects the traditional relationship of psychology to economics, in which tastes are treated by the economist as given. What is novel is that the utility functions in question are utility functions of subpersonal interests, with personal utility functions then emerging *endogenously* (i.e., within the *economic* model) through games among the interests.

Recourse to recursive processes is crucial if this style of modeling is to address the problem we started with. That problem has a chicken-and-egg logic: a bargaining game that does not yield procrastination in equilibrium must include as a player a short-term interest in the maintenance of a personal rule; but according to the modeling framework characterized above, the person for whose welfare these rules are generated is himself a product of the dynamics of self-control. The answer to the puzzle lies in the fact that optimization in ranges of games that humans play gives them standing long-range interests in consistency *and* short-range interests in not risking embarrassment *now*. These general interests beget more specific interests in specific circumstances—for instance, an interest in preserving the rule that requires evening work before indulgence.

How might this picture be captured in formalism suitable for specifying games? Suppose, to begin with, that we allowed a long-range interest facing a game with short-range ones to summon into being by fiat a new agent with a new utility function—namely, a short-range interest in maintenance of a personal rule. In that case, long-range interests would simply create whatever new short-range interests they needed as circumstances arose, and procrastination would never occur. (In Ainslie's terms, all personal rules would be complete bans on indulgence in consumption of

---

18. Dennett, *Consciousness Explained*; Ross, *Economic Theory*.

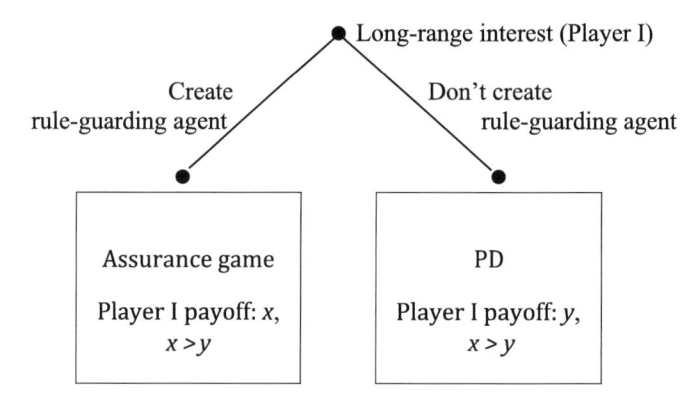

```
                    • Long-range interest (Player I)
         Create    /                    \  Don't create
    rule-guarding agent                    rule-guarding agent
         •                                        •
  ┌─────────────────┐              ┌─────────────────┐
  │ Assurance game  │              │      PD         │
  │                 │              │                 │
  │ Player I payoff:│              │ Player I payoff:│
  │      x,         │              │      y,         │
  │     x > y       │              │     x > y       │
  └─────────────────┘              └─────────────────┘
```

**Figure 2-4** Ainslie bargaining game.

SSRs.) The analyst would still construct and solve games that generated procrastination in equilibrium; but these would be counterfactual games[19] elaborated for the sake of inferring the actual assurance games, featuring personal-rule police, engineered by long-range interests to avoid internal PDs. More precisely, we would have the structure depicted in figure 2-4, with the long-range interest receiving a higher payoff in the left-hand assurance subgame than in the right-hand PD subgame. The long-range interest would always play "left" given subgame perfection, so procrastination would occur only off the equilibrium path and would not be observed. Let us call games with this generic structure "Ainslie bargaining games."

It is easy to get from this limiting case of the model to a more satisfactory one in which procrastination sometimes or often appears: simply introduce a production function for the long-range interest such that creating short-range interests has nonzero cost. Depending on the relationship of these costs to other costs and benefits in the game, we can then get instances where long-range interests play to the right-hand side of figure 2-4, and procrastination is observed.

## PICOECONOMICS AS ECONOMICS

We have now arrived at a model of self-control that we can compare with those that have recently become prominent in economic modeling of the problem. Let us begin with Fudenberg and Levine, who model the general family of impulse-control problems, with procrastination as the simplest instance, using what they call a "dual self" approach.[20] In this

---

19. That is, they would be subgames lying off the equilibrium paths of the larger games of which they formed parts.
20. Fudenberg and Levine, "A Dual Self Model."

model, long-run selves choose actions that influence the utility functions of short-run selves. Short-run selves then choose behaviors for the organism. Short-run selves are completely myopic and are therefore (in the first place) meliorators rather than expected utility maximizers. Costs to long-run selves of manipulating short-run selves are functions of the differences between what nonmanipulated and manipulated short-run selves would do and thus are endogenous. When decision problems concern only future options, short-run selves are indifferent, so long-run selves can determine their actions at minimal cost. Some manipulations of current short-run selves constrain options available to future short-run selves; these manipulations are sometimes efficient with respect to expected utility optimization. The solution concept imposed on the games is what the authors call "SR-perfection," which requires that short-run selves maximize in every subgame, and long-run selves anticipate that they do. (This is equivalent to what is elsewhere called "Markov Perfect Nash Equilibrium.") Since this is sufficient for unique equilibria in the games, there is no motivation for going all the way to imposing subgame perfection. Every SR-perfect Nash equilibrium profile is provably equivalent to a reduced-form optimization problem for the short-run self. Equilibria exist in which self-control costs are too high to be rationally paid; thus, the model predicts manifestations of procrastination and molar-scale preference reversal.

There are clear differences between the dual self model and picoeconomics (as I have reconstructed it). Ainslie supposes that long-range and short-range interests have different, often conflicting, preferences. By contrast, Fudenberg and Levine's selves differ only in the extent of their information about the future. But the second difference is sufficient to generate different strategic choices by them. Fudenberg and Levine's short-run selves are completely myopic. There is therefore no room in the dual control model for short-run selves that value personal rules, as in picoeconomics. Thus, short-run selves are not equivalent to short-range picoeconomic interests. These differences in the models are reflected in divergent possibilities for philosophical interpretation. Fudenberg and Levine say that "while we find the language of multiple 'selves' to be suggestive, the model can equally be interpreted as describing the behavior of a single 'self' whose overall behavior is determined by the interaction of two subsystems."[21] As will be discussed below, the dual self model thus allows for a reductionist (molecular) interpretation that the picoeconomic model does not.

Let us emphasize, for now, what the models have in common. Both explain the frequency and distribution of procrastination and related phenomena as a function of the *cost* of natural meliorative processes emulating expected utility maximization. Asked to explain why such emulation

---

21. Fudenberg and Levine, "A Dual Self Model," 3.

occurs, defenders of both models could appeal to the same evolutionary and institutional pressures operating on people. Both models, then, rely fundamentally on the idea that transcendence of matching is not free. Thus, they are compatible with the dominant hydraulic perspective in the clinically focused psychological literature on self-control, according to which future-directed prudence requires expenditure of an energy resource that renews itself at a fixed rate and may thus be depleted if consumed at a faster rate.[22] (Fudenberg and Levine build this link explicitly, extending their model to make cost of self-control sensitive to current cognitive load.) Neither the dual self nor the picoeconomic model requires basic units of action that are irrational in the sense of having cycling preferences or access to information that they willfully ignore or distort.

In constructing the Ainslie-bargaining game model, I suggested that short-range interests need to attach some present value to the future maintenance of their consumption patterns. Part of Ainslie's motivation for resisting this suggestion emerges when we see how it is in tension with a favorite example of his, an annoying interest in scratching an itch. This interest, Ainslie emphasizes, will fade entirely if even briefly ignored; unless the itch is caused by a foreign irritant, as most itches are not, the interest in scratching *is* the itch. Ainslie characterizes itches as very short-range addictions. Failing to stop scratching at the current instant involves the same sort of procrastination, at a more micro scale, as failure to stop smoking today. If short-range interests are purely *instantaneous* interests, then, as I argued in the general case of such interests, they cannot be bargained with, because there is no bribe they will be around to collect. Now, in the case of itches, it seems that bargaining indeed does *not* occur. An interest in scratching now is not bought off by an offer to scratch more at a less inconvenient time. Itches must be overcome by being ignored. One might, of course, say the same thing about many longer-range addictions; although allowing limited drinking works for some former alcoholics, others must suppress the behavior entirely. The dual self model handles this kind of case straightforwardly: the long-run self knows, but the short-run self does not, that scratching will give rise to further demand for scratching, and there is no self that now wants to scratch later. Scratching will thus occur when and only when the long-run self declines to pay to arrest it.

What this suggests is that Ainslie bargaining games are not the only scenarios Ainslie has in mind as models of self-control. In some instances, instead of choosing to play assurance games with a short-run interest $B_1$, a long-range interest recruits a purely rival short-range interest $B_2$ to play a game that is zero-sum with respect to $B_1$. Such recruitment cannot be costless on pain of vacuity. Thus, one kind of self-control model Ainslie

---

22. Baumeister, Heatherton, and Tice, *Losing Control*; Baumeister and Vohs, *Handbook of Self-Regulation*.

seems to have in mind, for application to some cases, is equivalent to the Markov games of Fudenberg and Levine; this point will emerge as important in later discussion.

Another problem that must be addressed if picoeconomics is to be rendered as economics is that utility functions based on Mazur's formula are not guaranteed to converge. Concern about this is not merely a matter of methodological dogma. In practical terms, it blocks use of standard econometric tests of specific models against data, which rely on asymptotic properties of functional forms: as we collect more preference data, fit to an estimated function must get no worse. It should not be intuitively surprising that this fails for hyperbolic discounting, since the slope of a function estimated from two indifference points will be sensitive to their relative positions in time and to the temporal reference point from which they are evaluated. This practical problem has a popular solution among economists who require workable functional forms for model testing but recognize the reality of the intertemporal preference inconsistency that procrastination implies. Laibson showed that the intertemporal preference reversals between SSRs and LLRs modeled by hyperbolic discount functions can be represented by an alternative form of discount function called "quasi-hyperbolic" or "β-δ," borrowed from Phelps and Pollack.[23] This class of functions is expressed by $v_i = A_i \beta \delta^D$, where $v_i$ represents the present value of a delayed reward, $A_i$ the amount of that reward, β a constant discount factor for all delayed rewards, δ a per-period exponential discount factor, and $D$ the delay of the reward. Where β = 1, the equation reduces to standard exponential discounting; where β < 1, discounting is initially steeper up to some inflection point, then flattens. β-δ discounting predicts that value drops precipitously from no delay to a one-period delay but then declines more gradually (and exponentially) over all periods thereafter.

One possible way of understanding β-δ discounting is as an approximation to "true" hyperbolic discounting, adopted simply to achieve convergence of functions that sum over flows of values. On this interpretation, the hyperbolic function is taken to give the correct molar-scale account of discounting, with β-δ discounting then treated simply as an approximation for the sake of making closed-form representation and conventional econometric testing analysis tractable. Phelps and Pollack developed the β-δ model in the first place to study intergenerational wealth transfers; procrastination can readily be modeled as such a problem for a person decomposed diachronically into subagents. The present agent, like the present generation, discounts the utility of future agents (generations) relative to its own at the β rate, while setting policy for later agents (generations) who discount one another's utility at the δ rate. Models of this

23. Laibson, "Golden Eggs"; Phelps and Pollack, "On Second-Best National Saving."

kind, applied to the more general class of myopic-choice phenomena, can be found in a number of influential papers.[24]

More recently, however, Laibson and colleagues have exploited β-δ discounting to interpret neuroimaging data in support of a molecular-scale account of intertemporal preference reversal. McClure et al. (including Laibson) obtained fMRI evidence which they interpret as suggesting that prefrontal brain areas discount more steeply than frontal areas.[25] They then propose that hyperbolic discounting at the molar scale be understood as an aggregation of the tug of war between neurally localized β-discounting prefrontal and δ-discounting frontal subagents. This idea can, in turn, be given either of two generic kinds of interpretation in economic modeling. On the first interpretation, one *reduces* the picoeconomic interests involved in self-control to the brain's rival discounting systems. This amounts to *eliminating* picoeconomic models in favor of neuroeconomic ones. It entails a commitment to seeking a neural site for the kind of personal agency involved in the formation of personal rules, since people quite evidently *do* formulate, express, and use such rules. Theoretical and neuroimaging study of working memory by psychologists has furnished some evidence that people can make conscious decisions that buttress their δ-discounting system's relative strength in internal conflicts.[26]

The reductionist interpretation of the McClure findings has recently encountered empirical difficulties. Glimcher, Kable, and Louie report fMRI data which they interpret as indicating that neurons in both midbrain and prefrontal areas in fact implement similar discount functions to the molar subject.[27] They find (as have others)[28] variability in activation levels in striatum between subjects, which correlates with variability in molar steepness of discounting. However, they find no areas in which activation levels are correlated with steeper or shallower discount functions than those inferred from molar behavior. Glimcher, Kable, and Louie interpret these findings as directly challenging the McClure hypothesis and indeed generalize this doubt: it undermines not only the idea of distinct δ- and β-discounting areas in the brain but also, they say, the very existence of "separable neural agents that could account for multiple selves that are used to explain hyperbolic-like discounting behavior."[29] Delaney et al. report neuroimaging evidence for activation of separate neural areas for discounting in different behavioral domains (health maintenance

---

24. Laibson, "Life-Cycle Consumption"; Laibson, Repetto, and Tobacman, "Self-Control and Saving"; O'Donoghue and Rabin, "Incentives for Procrastinators" and "Choice and Procrastination."
25. McClure et al., "Separate Neural Systems."
26. Engle, "What Is Working Memory Capacity?"
27. Glimcher, Kable, and Louie, "Neuroeconomic Studies."
28. Hariri et al., "Preference for Immediate over Delayed Rewards."
29. Glimcher, Kable, and Louie, "Neuroeconomic Studies," 143.

# Economic Models of Procrastination

and financial planning) but no evidence for separable processing across time horizons.[30]

An alternative interpretation of the McClure proposal, and one that is more interesting from the perspective of economics, associates it with a family of models that has recently come to dominate the economics of self-control problems. These treat prefrontal processing as outside the boundary of the economic agent: β discounting is understood as an *exogenous* challenge to personal utility maximization. Loewenstein (along with Read) points out that only certain sorts of goods are hyperbolically discounted at the molar scale—for example, desserts and hamburgers but not gasoline or computer paper.[31] The former sorts of reward are referred to as "visceral": they are hypothesized to be perceptible *as* rewards with minimal cognitive processing. The idea is, then, that people may procrastinate in their saving as a result of being lured by visceral consumption (which includes consumption of idleness). If personal utility is identified with valuation resulting from relatively cognitive or "cold" processing, then the siren call of visceral satisfactions can be treated as a form of *disutility* to the person, a threat to successful maximization lying in ambush in the "external" environment within the brain.

Several economic models unpack this general idea in different specific ways. Gul and Pesendorfer provide the most direct such approach.[32] Their model defines a "temptation" as a choice option with the property that its presence in the choice set makes an agent worse off, either because this results in the agent making a worse choice than he or she would have made in the option's absence or because to cope with the option, the agent must incur a cost of self-control. Thus, the agent is incentivized to take steps to avoid encountering temptations. These may include personal-rule formation, along with other generic devices itemized by Ainslie: precommitment, control of attention, and preparation of emotion.[33] Gul and Pesendorfer point out that despite predicting some of the same behavioral phenomena as they do, the picoeconomic model admits no role for self-control *in their sense*, that is, as resistance "at the point of choice" to a storm of visceral temptation. In the picoeconomic model, overcoming "weakness of will" is identified with reconfiguration of commodity spaces, with personal rules being added to possible consumption bundles. In Gul and Pesendorfer's model, by contrast, choice is distinct from the action or failure of willpower, which furthermore has nothing directly to do with discounting. Of all existing accounts, this is the only model of intertemporal vacillation that requires no revisions to standard consumer

---

30. Delaney et al., "Event-Related Potentials."
31. Loewenstein, "Out of Control" and "Visceral Account"; Read, "Is Time-Discounting Hyperbolic." On desserts and gasoline, see Hoch and Loewenstein, "Time-Inconsistent Preferences"; on hamburgers and computer paper, see Read, "Is Time-Discounting Hyperbolic."
32. Gul and Pesendorfer, "Temptation and Self-Control" and "Simple Theory."
33. Ainslie, *Picoeconomics*.

theory: the agent discounts exponentially and can use as much information as the modeler thinks the data warrant.

A second approach that implicitly makes prefrontal processing exogenous to the economic agent is promoted by Loewenstein and explains self-control problems as informational deficits.[34] According to this account, cognitive memory for visceral intensity is systematically unreliable. In consequence, people routinely underestimate the effect that past and future visceral states will have on future behavior, thus neglecting to incorporate their influence in making present choices. For example, an abstinent substance abuser may reinitiate consumption in part because he fails to remember the effect of past craving on drug use and thus underestimates how much future craving will make it difficult to quit. Applied to procrastination, someone might be unable to anticipate that she will feel a temptation to put off work tomorrow that will be every bit as strong as today's feeling of temptation. This psychological hypothesis admits readily of an economic interpretation based around *self-signaling*.[35] This can, in turn, be modeled in either a unified or a multiple agency setting. In the multiple (diachronic) agent context, present agents with some degree of special concern for their descendent agents choose prudently because prudent choice now *predicts* prudent choice later, and the *present* agent gets lightly discounted *present* utility from this reassurance. As in picoeconomics, this explains personal rules as presently valuable assets. However, the potential value of self-signaling depends neither on hyperbolic discounting nor on dividing the person into intertemporally multiple agents. As Bénabou and Tirole demonstrate rigorously, self-signaling can be justified by any imperfection in an agent's knowledge about his or her own capacity to cope with temptations.[36]

Although self-signaling models preserve full agent rationality in not requiring intertemporally inconsistent preferences, they must clearly involve a hypothesis of compromised inferential rationality. Suppose we grant Loewenstein's hypothesis that people are poor at remembering and imagining the qualitative intensity of states resulting from visceral consumption. It would nevertheless be puzzling if the procrastinator or the addict could not *infer* from his or her past failures at maximization that the visceral temptations must have been quite powerful. Indeed, some such inference seems crucial to motivate the anxiety that is alleviated by self-signaling. But in that case, one wonders why, for most or many people, the tendency to fall into procrastination is chronic and recurring.

As far as difficulties for economic modeling are concerned, there is an asymmetry between relaxing the two basic aspects of rationality. Allowing preference reversal without decomposing the agent blocks application of standard tools altogether; we lose assurance that we can formulate and

---

34. Loewenstein, "Visceral Account."
35. Prelec and Bodner, "Self-Signaling and Self-Control."
36. Bénabou and Tirole, "Willpower and Personal Rules."

solve an optimization problem. By contrast, the only objection to relaxing rational expectations is that in many circumstances, such as modeling financial markets, any *specific* such relaxation seems arbitrary and invites questions about why other agents have not learned to exploit the particular less-than-rational expectations that are hypothesized. But if psychological research independently shows that people tend to make certain systematic errors, then the worry about arbitrariness goes away. And although chronic procrastination can lead to unnecessarily high interest payments, it does not undermine itself in the way that less-than-rational expectations about future prices do; procrastination is not necessarily disadvantageous in markets in which asset prices are random walks, and in other kinds of markets, procrastinators and nonprocrastinators do not generally face zero-sum games in which nonprocrastinators must drive out procrastinators in equilibrium. Thus, economists have been much more attracted to models of self-control problems with exogenous temptations than they have been to models involving hyperbolic discounting by unified agents.

O'Donoghue and Rabin have produced a specific model of procrastination based on imperfect expectations about the strengths of future temptations.[37] They use a $\beta$-$\delta$-discounting framework and construct as their crucial variable the difference between $\beta$ and a person's perception of $\beta$, represented as $\hat{\beta}$. A person for whom $\hat{\beta} = 1$ is completely naive about her future behavior; although she procrastinates now, she never expects to procrastinate in the future. As noted above, this would be a peculiar sort of agent. The more interesting and realistic case is the person for whom $\hat{\beta} \in (\beta, 1)$. This person is *partially* naive; she expects to be tempted to delay but underestimates to some extent the force that the temptation will have on her. O'Donoghue and Rabin show that a partially naive person will delay doing a worthwhile task indefinitely whenever she believes that her future tolerance for delay will be at least one period less than her actual (including her current) tolerance for delay. This implies that any degree of partial naiveté is sufficient to produce procrastination in some circumstances.

O'Donoghue and Rabin also expand the scope of the model to address the phenomenon of procrastination in a richer context than has been treated by other economic literature. They introduce the new element as follows:

> [Previous] models of procrastination assume that a potential procrastinator has only one task under consideration, and hence the only concern is when the person completes the task. In most situations, however, a person must decide not only *when* to complete a task, but also *which* task to complete, or how much effort to apply to a chosen task. If a person must revise a paper

---

37. O'Donoghue and Rabin, "Incentives for Procrastinators" and "Choice and Procrastination."

for resubmission, she can either respond minimally to the editor's suggestions or expend more effort to respond thoroughly. If she is choosing how to invest some money, she can either thoughtlessly follow the advice of a friend, or thoroughly investigate investment strategies. If she is putting together a montage of Johnny Depp photos, she can either haphazardly throw together a few press clippings or work devoutly to construct the shrine that he deserves.[38]

O'Donoghue and Rabin's analysis of procrastination in the context of choice among tasks produces two interesting results in their model, which the reader can evaluate for empirical plausibility. First, they show that a partially naive agent who would complete a particular worthwhile task now might do nothing at all if offered a more attractive alternative action that had a higher cost relative to its immediate benefit. One possible sense of "more attractive" is "more *important*," in the sense of yielding higher long-run benefits. This leads to the second striking result in their extended model: higher importance can lead agents to choose costlier tasks, on which, if partially naive, they then procrastinate. For example, "the person may severely procrastinate [on investment choice] when her principal is $10,000, but not when her principal is only $1,000. [S]he plans and executes a quick-and-easy investment strategy for the $1,000, while she plans—but does *not* execute—a more ambitious investment strategy for the $10,000."[39] However, one should not infer from this that adding options tends *in general* to induce procrastination. In the model, a person with *many* tasks to be spread over several periods will tend to procrastinate *less*, because costs of delaying any task rise by threatening to crowd out other tasks.

Thus, it should be acknowledged that combining imperfect expectations with β-δ discounting has produced the richest existing economic model of procrastination, which offers distinctive empirical predictions. Note, however, that in this instance, β-δ discounting can be justified purely on grounds of analytical tractability; all of the model's insights would carry over if discounting were "really" hyperbolic. Indeed, no aspect of discounting per se merits being regarded as the cause of procrastination in O'Donoghue and Rabin's model; that honor goes to false beliefs about how future opportunity costs will be perceived.

From the perspective of picoeconomics, a straightforward criticism of the O'Donoghue and Rabin model can be given. This is that, like Fudenberg and Levine, they implicitly restrict attention to Markov Perfect Nash Equilibria in the choice games among the β-discounting and the various δ-discounting intervals of the person. That is, no choosing agent takes account of anything other than its utility function and whatever expectations it has about choices in future intervals; there is no room for any agent to learn the value of strategic self-commitment. But this is the core

---

38. O'Donoghue and Rabin, "Choice and Procrastination," 121–122.
39. O'Donoghue and Rabin, "Choice and Procrastination," 149.

of the picoeconomic account, at least insofar as it is expressed in analyses of the sort I reconstructed as Ainslie bargaining games. The criticism applies generally to models that rely on a β-δ-discounting framework.

Benhabib and Bisin relax this restriction.[40] Their highly general and elegant model relies on no explicit appeal to discounting at all. Once again, as in the general family of models we have been considering, the temptation of impulsive consumption (including impulsive consumption of leisure) is made exogenous to the agent. They assume that the agent can pay a cost to inhibit responses to temptations. Whether payment of this cost is justified in a given case is a function of the exponentially discounted relative values of the consumption plans with and without purchase of self-control measures. Conceptually, there is no gain here over the Gul and Pesendorfer model. However, the greater generality of Benhabib and Bisin's formulation allows them to reduce to variations in a single parameter $b$ the difference between their model and, respectively, (1) the model of a perfectly consistent optimizer of permanent income, with or without smoothing over the life cycle, and (2) the model of a β-δ discounter restricted to Markov Perfect Nash Equilibria. This allows them to generate and test relative empirical predictions of aggregate saving behavior for each of the three models. Of course, the agent who must pay a cost to avoid succumbing to temptation saves less than the agent who is not tempted in the first place. The more interesting result is that the agent who can buy self-control saves more than the agent whose successive selves play Markov games, even in circumstances where the latter never actually procrastinates. The reason is that the former agent, but not the latter, expects to be least likely to procrastinate when it matters most; therefore, the marginal expected value of present savings are higher for that agent.

Benhabib and Bisin compare these generic differences in prediction with three bodies of empirical evidence. First, they note a systematic tendency for people to indulge in extra consumption, relative to the plans implied by previous consumption, that is greater for small windfalls than for larger ones. This is predicted by the Benhabib and Bisin model and is opposite to the qualitative prediction of the O'Donoghue and Rabin model. Second, in the model restricted to Markov games, since β-δ discounters have no available mechanism for internal self-control, they can restrain their impulses only by buying illiquid assets. This implies that they should be willing to buy such assets even when they yield negative returns, up to the limit of the value of self-control. For agents who can adopt effective personal rules, illiquid assets are complementary self-control aids, so they should be purchased only when they yield positive or slightly negative returns. Benhabib and Bisin cite data that are on their side in this respect. Finally, they note that in their model, overstability of

---

40. Benhabib and Bisin, "Modeling Internal Commitment Mechanisms and Self-Control."

investment plans may be explained by a factor that is the opposite of procrastination: personal rules become more fragile as they become more complex, so agents who rely on them will tend to be inflexible and show overcommitment to prudent courses they have adopted. It is difficult to see how this last point can be genuinely said to favor the Benhabib and Bisin model, since it makes the same qualitative prediction as the rival model but by a different mechanism. However, it seems that we can say, at least, that the Benhabib and Bisin model of intertemporal resoluteness of choice fares just as well in the face of current evidence, both conventional economic and neuroeconomic, as the variants based on $\beta$-$\delta$ discounting.

## CONCLUSION

Comparison of the precise analysis of Benhabib and Bisin with those of Fudenberg and Levine and O'Donoghue and Rabin allows us to appreciate an implicit underlying structure in Ainslie's account that is otherwise obscure. In reconstructing picoeconomics game-theoretically, I argue that long-range interests might sometimes achieve self-control by inducing assurance games, in which short-range interests are bought off, and sometimes achieve self-control by inducing games in which one short-range interest is set into a zero-sum game with another. The latter mode of self-control is essentially the case analyzed by imposing Markov perfection as the solution concept, with the Fudenberg and Levine model as the general case and the O'Donoghue and Rabin model as an application that captures further special features of the control of procrastination and other impulsive choice *when it is suppressed instead of bribed*.

However, we do not yet find in the literature an economic model of Ainslie bargaining. Benhabib and Bisin, while sharing many of Ainslie's qualitative insights, do not imply any appeal to bargaining dynamics, since in their model, temptations are simple exogenous threats to optimization rather than strategic agents in their own right. Nor does their model suggest, as picoeconomics does, that procrastination and related phenomena are best explained by reference to properties of discounting.

I propose that one moral picoeconomists should take to heart from the attempt to provide an explicit economic account of their framework is that hyperbolic discounting *describes* procrastination but cannot *explain* it. Mazur's formula tolerably fits most human and animal time preference data—although models that allow for mixes of hyperbolic and exponential discounters in groups of people consistently give the best fit of all.[41] Drawing hyperbolas is a very handy way of illustrating dynamic inconsistency of choice in behavior. However, hyperbolic discounting, unlike exponential discounting, involves more than *discounting*. Hyperbolic

41. Andersen et al., "Eliciting Risk and Time Preferences."

curves do not have the shapes and slopes they do simply as a function of the contribution of the passage of time to estimates of relative risk. Their relationship mainly reflects contributions of psychological framing, which almost certainly is, in turn, influenced by properties of neural dynamics and by social learning. Because they summarize such a range of background influences, hyperbolic discount functions resemble Akerlof's δ parameter. To request an explanation of hyperbolic discounting and to request an explanation of procrastination is to ask for the same thing. And to explain how such discounting can be made approximately exponential is to explain how procrastination is avoided.

The point I am making can be put in a different way: the economist and the picoeconomist do not disagree about how to represent discounting, but, rather, they mean slightly different things by the concept. The economist aims to refer to the effect of delay on present value *as mediated by risk*. The picoeconomist refers indiscriminately to the entire set of influences of delay on predictions of future choice.

If we drop the idea that picoeconomic and economic models differ in empirically hypothesizing different styles of discounting, then it is possible to characterize the picoeconomic account using the elements of economic models that have been reviewed here. Suppose that, by fiat, we follow most recent economists in identifying the person with the current long-range utility function. I suggest that no meaningful empirical question is begged by doing so as long as we don't foreclose the idea that (1) the short-range interests have different utility functions of their own, and (2) the person is dynamically sculpted over time as a recursive output of bargaining among these interests. Then we can identify the picoeconomic account as a variant of the Benhabib and Bisin model, in which the cost of self-control at any given point is a function of bargaining games, instead of simply an exogenously given price to be taken or left.

Are bargaining and nonbargaining models of self-control exclusive alternatives? The O'Donoghue and Rabin model predicts that a tendency to procrastinate should get worse if a person who is not very busy formulates a plan with significantly higher long-run returns, but also higher short-run costs, than the standing alternative activities. The Benhabib and Bisin model predicts the opposite. Forcing Ainslie's account into a stricter game-theoretic perspective helps us to see that these may be not rival models of the same phenomenon but models of different forms of self-control that may occur on different occasions.

What experiments does the picoeconomic account suggest? Both Fudenberg and Levine and Benhabib and Bisin stress the significance of cognitive load as a major determinant of the cost of self-control. Both sets of authors recommend that neuroimaging studies be used to investigate this relationship. The relevant concept of cognitive load, however, is extremely vague. In typical experiments, it is proxied by asking subjects to do arithmetical puzzles or hold lists of items in memory. These are not really the kinds of psychic stress that beset people faced with ecologically natural decisions. Picoeconomics suggests an alternative method: Cue subjects with various short-range interests, some of which are in tension with long-range ones and some of which are complements. Does sheer complexity dominate in such cases, leading to impaired self-control, or is self-control capacity at least sometimes better predicted by the balance of forces? If the latter turned out to be the case, it would be natural to represent the contents of the "cognitive load" black box as games among interests.

At the theoretical level, we might try to use the insights to which picoeconomics has led us to produce a more general model of self-control than any we yet have. Suppose, as emphasized here, that self-control is sometimes implemented by suppressing short-range interests and sometimes by allowing them limited scope for expression. How might we try to construct a model that would allow us to analyze the determinants of the relative effectiveness, from case to case, of the two forms of self-control? We have already seen that Benhabib and Bisin's model can represent the Fudenberg and Levine model as a special case. An obvious way to try to formally unify the models is to nest Ainslie bargaining within Benhabib and Bisin as another special case. Suppose that long-range interests, when they make offers to short-range interests instead of trying to overcome them, change the population of interests in the game, as suggested earlier. We might then set out to adapt an overlapping generations model, a standard part of the economist's toolkit, to represent such dynamics.

I suggest that the prospects for such modeling, along with the accomplishments already in hand that have been reviewed here, make the case that economics complements partner sciences in shedding light on procrastination and related phenomena, without simply abandoning its distinctive restrictions and collapsing into psychology.

# 3

# Is Procrastination Weakness of Will?

## Sarah Stroud

Why ask whether procrastination is weakness of will? Here is one reason to pursue this question. It may seem obvious that procrastination is some sort of rational failing. (More on this shortly.) But it is not obvious what *kind* of rational failing it is. One way to approach that broader, more difficult question is to ask whether procrastination might be a species of weakness of will. For weakness of will is generally accepted as a rational failing—or, even more strongly, as a paradigm case of practical irrationality. So if we find that procrastination is a species of weakness of will, that supplies a neat diagnosis of what *kind* of irrationality procrastination involves: the same kind as weakness of will. If, on the other hand, we find that procrastination is not a species of weakness of will, then either the former constitutes some distinct type of rational failing, or perhaps it is not a rational failing at all. In either case, asking whether procrastination is a species of weakness of will ought to be a fruitful way to begin. Furthermore, the question seems worth pursuing because procrastination does present, at a minimum, some important affinities with weakness of will. These similarities suggest that procrastination may well be a subcategory of weakness of will—or, at least, that we can learn something about why and in what way procrastination constitutes a rational failing by examining the aspects it shares with weakness of will.

Before diving into the examination of whether procrastination is a species of weakness of will, however, I want to devote a few moments to the assumption that procrastination is a rational failing. I said it may seem obvious that this is so. For when we assess a person as procrastinating, this seems never to coexist with our finding that person's current exercise of her agency unimpeachable. Rather, when we make such a judgment, we seem invariably to consider her conduct to be defective in some way—and not in a moral way (or an aesthetic way, or a culinary way, or a sartorial way), but in some *rational* way. We seem to think that the person who procrastinates is open to rational criticism in virtue of doing so.

Now this sounds similar to something other theorists of procrastination have said. Maury Silver and John Sabini—and Chrisoula Andreou, who follows them in this respect—hold that procrastination is necessarily irrational.[1] I want to demur from this in two respects, however. First, "irrational" is a very strong term.[2] It seems safer to say that procrastination opens one to rational criticism, or to call procrastination a rational failing or defect or shortcoming, than to take on board at the outset the idea that procrastination is one of the most egregious kinds of rational failing and thus deserving of the especially extreme form of criticism delivered by the flat verdict "irrational."

Second, and more important, Silver and Sabini and Andreou draw an inference here that I would not want to join them in drawing. As I have said, I agree with them that procrastination seems to be a rational failing (or, as they put it, irrational). But they seem to think it follows from this that the very *definition* of procrastination must be couched in evaluative terms that bring out or make salient the irrationality of the agent's conduct. That is, they seem to think that irrationality constitutes one of the *criteria* for procrastination, that whether something is a case of procrastination turns directly on its normative status. This is implicitly to deny that there could be any purely descriptive or nonevaluative characterization of what constitutes procrastinating; procrastination, they seem to think, has no purely descriptive profile. Silver and Sabini motivate in the following way this appeal to normative status to demarcate the genuine cases of procrastination. They note that while procrastination appears to fall under the general category of "putting things off," not all puttings-off constitute procrastination. "Which [cases] would we call procrastination and which not? We shall show that rationality does the sorting," they write.[3] Procrastination is, specifically, *irrational* putting off: "a person is procrastinating if (s)he is irrationally putting off."[4] Andreou similarly says that procrastination involves "leav[ing] too late or put[ting] off indefinitely what one *should* . . . have done sooner."[5] Thus for her as well the criteria for procrastination are in part evaluative or normative: whether something constitutes procrastination depends in part on whether you should have done it sooner.[6]

I agree with these theorists that procrastination cannot be adequately characterized simply as putting something off, or even as putting it off until the last minute. But it does not follow, and I am not yet convinced,

---

1. Silver and Sabini, "Procrastinating"; Andreou, "Understanding Procrastination."
2. See Parfit, *Reasons and Persons*, 119; Scanlon, *What We Owe*, 25–30; McIntyre, "What Is Wrong," 285n. 1.
3. Silver and Sabini, "Procrastinating," 209.
4. Silver and Sabini, "Procrastinating," 218; there is a second condition not relevant here (but which we shall mention later; see note 14) whose presence means that they are not actually claiming that irrationally putting off is *sufficient* for procrastination.
5. Andreou, "Understanding Procrastination," 183 (emphasis added).
6. The words I omitted from the previous quotation ("relative to one's ends and information") soften the normativity involved but do not eliminate it, insofar as the *actual* advisability (in light of one's ends and information) of doing x can depart from one's *judgment* of its advisability (again, relative to one's ends and information).

that procrastination must be demarcated or characterized in explicitly normative or evaluative terms. Nor do I think it is necessary so to characterize it in order to validate the idea that someone who procrastinates thereby exposes himself or herself to rational criticism. Akrasia, for instance, can be characterized in purely descriptive, nonnormative terms, as we shall see later; but once we reflect on what descriptive state of affairs it involves, we can feel confident that it constitutes a rational defect. So while–as I said–I am on board with the idea that procrastination is a rational failing, I am not yet ready to make this part of the definition of what *constitutes* procrastinating. It seems to me entirely possible that there is an adequate purely descriptive characterization of what constitutes a case of procrastination.[7]

However, it seems clear—and important to underline—that Silver and Sabini are right that procrastination cannot be equated with putting something off, or even with putting something off until the last minute. (So if there is a purely descriptive characterization of what constitutes procrastination, it will have to be more complicated than these candidates.) For we put things off all the time; indeed, this is an ineliminable part of rational agency. As agents, we cannot do everything *now*. One of the central elements of rational agency is thus to order tasks and activities in time, which will necessarily involve putting some things later in the queue, that is, deliberately choosing to do them later rather than now. The mere fact of ordering activities in time—which entails that some activities will be "put off" or delayed until later—does not constitute procrastination. For example, I wager that every morning you delay putting on your shoes until you've got your socks on; this obviously does not constitute procrastination! Deliberate choice to do some things later rather than now—even when they *could* be done now—is an inescapable aspect of being a temporally extended rational agent, not a defect in such agency. So putting off, as such, is not objectionable and is not procrastination.[8]

What if we added a few more conditions? Perhaps procrastination is not merely putting off, but putting off until the last minute a task you are not looking forward to performing. But this, too, is too broad. It is half an hour before dinner, and I am ensconced in the comfy chair in the living room reading an article. It is my job to set the table before dinner each night. (Need I add that I could not be described as looking forward to this exciting activity?) I could, of course, interrupt my reading to get up and

---

7. Dylan Dodd similarly underlines the contrast between descriptive and normative characterizations of weakness of will in a recent article, arguing that "to say that an action is weak-willed is to make a *descriptive* rather than a normative claim" (Dodd, "Weakness of Will," 4).

8. The maxim "Never put off until tomorrow what you could do today" is not just terrible advice—I *could* pack my suitcases for my upcoming year abroad today, even though I don't leave for another month, but my clothes would get very wrinkled—it is actually a conceptually incoherent injunction when addressed to agents like us, as it asks us to abdicate one of the core tasks of being a temporally extended rational agent.

do it now—there is nothing stopping me. Nor is there a particular reason why I must wait (as there was with the shoes and socks). But in fact I generally only get up to set the table five minutes before dinner. I am highly confident of my ability to set the table perfectly adequately in five minutes or less, and I simply deem there to be no reason to interrupt my reading to do it sooner. Am I procrastinating? Not a bit of it. I have put off until the last minute a task I was not looking forward to, but I have not procrastinated. Such puttings-off fall within the purview of my rational prerogative to order activities in time, and I am fully satisfied with the way I have ordered them here. As examples like these show, a blanket rational prohibition on putting off activities until the last minute would be too strong.

So, to echo and endorse Silver and Sabini's point, procrastination cannot simply be equated with putting off but is at best a subclass of it. In fact, though, I'm not entirely sure that procrastination *is* a subclass of putting off. That is, I'm not sure that all instances of procrastination actually involve putting something off. This may sound surprising, so let me elaborate. What exactly is involved in a person's putting something off? That is, to speak more precisely, what must be the case in order for it to be true at a time $t$, or over a time interval $t_m$ to $t_n$, that a person $S$ has put off, or is putting off, doing $x$? One obvious necessary condition is that $S$ not be *doing x* at $t$ or over the interval $t_m$ to $t_n$. Anything I am now doing I do not count as now putting off. But this is just as obviously not sufficient. I am not now vacationing in Uzbekistan, nor have I been over the past several months. But it is not now true, nor has it been true over the past several months, that I am *putting off* a vacation in Uzbekistan. Vacationing in Uzbekistan is not even on my radar; it has not even risen to the level of being a *candidate* for putting off. Clearly something else beyond not doing it is required in order for someone to count as having put something off.

What is that further factor? Putting something off, I think, involves *choosing* or *deciding* to do that thing later rather than now. I never made any such choice or decision with respect to vacationing in Uzbekistan, which is why my simply "not getting to it" does not amount to having put it off. If this suggestion about the conceptual analysis of "putting off" is correct, then putting something off involves something like *making a decision* or *forming an intention* to do the thing later. Is this true in every case of procrastination? In every such case, was such a decision made, such an intention formed? I wish simply to keep this issue open for now; we will return to it later. But if the answer is "not necessarily," and if I am right about what "putting off" involves, then not all cases of procrastinating are even guaranteed to be cases in which it would be true to say the person *put off* the task in question.[9]

---

9. The psychologist Piers Steel makes a similar questionable assumption about the necessary conditions for procrastination when he says that "one procrastinates when one delays beginning or completing an *intended* course of action" (Steel, "Nature of Procrastination,"

## PROCRASTINATION AND AKRASIA

We are now ready to turn to our main question: whether procrastination is a species of weakness of will. It turns out that we will have to answer this question twice. I will first consider what the answer is if we assume the "classic" understanding of weakness of will as akrasia, which is the subject of most of the literature on weakness of will. Then I will consider what the answer might be on a recent, revisionist understanding of weakness of will proposed by Richard Holton and Alison McIntyre. In both cases we will have the benefit of working with a clear, precise demarcation of what constitutes weakness of will, against whose salient contours we can compare the range of cases we consider to constitute procrastination to see how close a match we find.

According to the "classic" understanding, weak-willed or akratic action is (free, intentional) action contrary to one's better judgment.[10] On this conception, what marks an action as weak-willed or akratic is its conflict with a certain evaluative judgment made or held by the agent at the time of acting. While philosophers differ in their precise formulation of that judgment, we can adequately convey the central idea by saying that an agent does $x$ akratically if she does $x$ even though she judges that she ought not. (Or, to follow Davidson, if she judges that it is better all things considered to do something else,[11] or that she has more reason to do something else.) In akratic action, there is a mismatch or discrepancy between what the agent does and what she deems it best that she do. Rather than the two—action and judgment—being in concert, there is a dissonance or lack of correspondence between the two that marks off the action as akratic.

We should underline some pertinent aspects of the "classic" understanding of weakness of will. First, akratic action must exhibit dissonance with an evaluative judgment *of the agent's*. *My* thinking that Sam should not do that does not make his doing it akratic—even if I am right that he should not. *He* has to think he should not do it in order for his action to be akratic. Second, in order for $S$'s doing $x$ at $t$ to count as akratic, the

---

66; emphasis added). The reason he gives for this restriction is that we need some way not to count a person as *putting off* all the myriad tasks he or she *could* now be performing (such as vacationing in Uzbekistan, presumably). I agree with this point but do not think it entails a restriction as specific and as demanding as that the procrastinator must *intend* to do later the task about which he or she is procrastinating. While I agree that the agent must stand in some special relation to that task in order for him or her to count as procrastinating, it is not clear (as I discuss below) that the agent's relation to that task has to be, specifically, that of intending to perform it. There are many cases intermediate between the relation in which I stand to vacationing in Uzbekistan and the relation in which $S$ stands to $x$ when $S$ intends to do $x$.

10. I'll just leave out the "free, intentional" from now on, assuming that we are always talking about free, intentional actions in this discussion. I take it that this will not prejudice any important questions about procrastination.

11. Davidson, "How Is Weakness of the Will Possible?"

object of the agent's unfavorable judgment must be his doing *x at t*. If the agent thinks that starting in 2010 he should no longer do *x*, his doing *x* in 2009 need not be contrary to his better judgment or akratic. The agent must make an unfavorable judgment about his doing what he is doing when he does it. This is also true in another sense. *S*'s doing *x* at *t* is akratic only if *S* judges *at t* that *S* ought not do *x* at *t*. *S*'s having *previously* deemed it best that he not do *x* at *t* does not make his current action akratic, since he may simply have changed his mind since then about whether it is best that he do *x* at *t*; and changing your mind is not akrasia. Only conflict with a *contemporaneous* "better judgment" can render an action akratic.

When all of these conditions are incorporated, it is easy to understand why akrasia has typically been viewed as constituting practical irrationality of an especially stark kind. In performing an action that is weak-willed in this sense, the agent seems to be doing what is contrary to reason by his own lights. After all, he has reached a determination of what it is best that he do or what he has most reason to do all things considered, and yet he has deliberately done the opposite. By his own lights, then, there is no sufficient reason to do this thing. There is at least one other course of action that (according to him) is both open to him and superior to this one, and yet he freely makes a choice that he himself considers ill advised, possibly disastrous. According to Davidson, the akratic agent must thus "recogniz[e], in his own intentional behaviour, something essentially surd."[12]

Is procrastination weakness of will in this sense? I think that in broad outline there are significant affinities between the two. If we think about the kinds of cases we would most confidently classify as procrastination, I believe they match the profile of someone who is not doing *x even though he in some sense judges that he ought to be*. Like weakness of will, I am suggesting, procrastination also involves a discrepancy between the agent's conduct with respect to *x* and his assessment of the advisability of his doing *x*. To the extent that this is true, procrastination and weakness of will are both marked by conflict or dissonance between an agent's intentional behavior and a certain kind of judgment or state of the agent's—something like his judgment of what he ought to be doing.[13]

---

12. Davidson, "How Is Weakness of the Will Possible?" 42.

13. My proposal is thus in some ways consonant with something Silver and Sabini put forward as a further feature of procrastination. The procrastinating agent's irrational putting off (which, for them, is constitutive of procrastination, as we discussed earlier) is, they say, parasitic on or caused by his "recognition of what he ought to do" ("Procrastinating," 210). "Thus," they continue, "only agents capable of recognizing what they ought to do are capable of procrastinating" (211). This last claim would also be supported by my proposal that procrastination involves a mismatch between the agent's conduct and his judgment of what he ought to be doing. Note the contrast with the condition Andreou proposes, which does not require the agent to make any such dissenting judgment (or, indeed, any judgment at all) in order to count as procrastinating. On her proposal, the issue is whether the agent should

Let me reinforce this claim by returning to an earlier discussion. We noted that procrastination with respect to *x* cannot be characterized simply as not doing *x* (over the specified interval), or as putting off or delaying doing *x*. Some further condition is required. Consider my not getting up to set the table until five minutes before dinner, which was not a case of procrastination (even though I certainly could get up and set it sooner). Why not? It seems relevant that I simply deem there to be no reason to interrupt my reading to do it sooner. I do not think I *ought* to get up and do this task sooner than five minutes before dinnertime; as I continue reading in my chair, I am fully satisfied with how I am ordering actions in time. My "putting off" getting up thus involves no dissonance among my attitudes, no conflict between my action and my assessment of my options, no dissatisfaction with how I am using my agency to accomplish tasks over time. These features seem to exclude the case from the domain of procrastination, even though the case involves my putting off—and, indeed, putting off until the last minute—a task I am not especially eager to perform.

You might object that what is doing the work in removing this case from the category of procrastination is not that I *judge* that there is no reason for me do this task sooner but that there *is* no reason for me to do it sooner. On this interpretation, procrastination involves a mismatch with what the agent really has most reason to do, not with what she thinks she has most reason to do. I would be inclined to resist this interpretation. But the present case does not help us decide between these two options, because it qualifies as procrastination on neither. In order to choose between these two views we would have to think about cases in which

(a) S ought, in fact, to be doing *x* now (or, anyway, sooner rather than later), but S doesn't think so, or
(b) S thinks she ought to be doing *x* now (or, anyway, sooner rather than later), but she is wrong about this.

On the view I am proposing, cases of type (b) are candidates for being instances of procrastination, whereas cases of type (a) are not. On the view that appeals to what S *really* ought to be doing as one of the criteria for procrastination, the reverse would be true.

With respect to cases of type (a), my intuitions match those concerning what it takes to make an action akratic.[14] We noted earlier that *my*

---

have done the thing sooner (relative to his ends and information), not whether he thinks he should have done it sooner. Consider then an agent who wrongly assesses what will best serve his ends given the information he has: he incorrectly deduces from the information he has that doing a certain task later will better serve his ends. This agent can count as procrastinating on Andreou's account even though his conduct is fully consonant with his own judgment. The next three paragraphs of the text pursue this issue further.

14. On cases of type (b), see the example offered by Silver and Sabini ("Procrastinating," 219n. 5), which they classify as a case of procrastination (in keeping with my view).

thinking that Sam ought not do $x$ does not make his doing $x$ akratic, even if my opinion on this point is absolutely correct. Similarly, it seems to me, if Sam is fully satisfied with how he is ordering $x$ in time, then while his delaying $x$ may, in fact, be the substantively incorrect choice, he is not thereby *procrastinating* in putting $x$ off. An example: people differ in how early they think one should leave for the airport. Susie, given her views on this, plans to leave for her flight at 4:00, and does. Now suppose that Susie's view of how early one should leave for the airport is not correct: in fact, one should leave more room for error than Susie does. Still, Susie does not count as *procrastinating* as she does other tasks between 3:30 and 4:00. Moreover, it seems to me that whether she is procrastinating as she does other tasks between 3:30 and 4:00 cannot turn, as the present view would have it, on which view about how early one should leave for the airport is the correct one.

I have suggested that in broad outline procrastination and weakness of will are similar. Both, I have argued, centrally involve a conflict between the agent's intentional behavior and some other pertinent evaluative state or judgment of the agent. This congruence between the two phenomena gives us some reason to think that procrastination is indeed a subclass of weakness of will. But if we look more closely at the precise way akrasia has been characterized in the literature, it seems less likely that it furnishes an appropriate model for procrastination. Two preliminary points of dissimilarity between the two concepts should raise questions; and there is, I think, a further, deeper reason why it seems ultimately unpromising to seek to subsume procrastination under akrasia.

We can collect two initial points of divergence by noting the characteristic logical forms of attributions of akrasia, on the one hand, and procrastination, on the other. Despite the existence of the noun forms "akrasia" and "weakness of will," the "classic" literature on weakness of will has focused on adjectival uses of these terms. In particular, it has focused on analyzing and assessing weak-willed or akratic *actions*. In the "classic" literature on weakness of will, then, being weak-willed or akratic is fundamentally a property of individual actions, and the "atomic sentences" ascribing these properties typically take the form "$S$'s action [of doing $x$] was akratic." But attributions of procrastination are not most naturally formulated as attributions of a property to a particular action. The most natural "atomic sentence" for attributing procrastination would have something like the following form: "$S$ is procrastinating with respect to doing $x$ over the period $t_m$ to $t_n$." Because such sentences appear to have a very different logical form from those ascribing akrasia, it is not immediately clear how procrastination could be a subclass of the latter.

Furthermore, the paradigm case of akrasia is an action that is undertaken despite being rejected by the agent's better judgment. In akratic action, the agent has another drink, or gets up to brush his teeth, or sleeps with someone, against his better judgment. The primordial mark of akrasia is thus *doing* something one deems ill advised. The primordial mark of procrastination, on the other hand, is *not* doing something:[15] procrastination necessarily involves a *failure* (over a certain interval) to do something. This difference should also make us wonder whether procrastination can aptly be classified as a type of akrasia.

There is also a deeper reason to be dissatisfied with subsuming procrastination under akrasia. It follows from what we have discussed that akrasia is an essentially *synchronic* phenomenon. It is constituted by conflict or lack of correspondence between two necessarily *contemporaneous* entities: the agent's action and her assessment of whether she ought to be performing that action. (Recall that if these two are held at different times, the action does not count as akratic. Whether you *used* to think you ought not to do $x$ at $t$, or whether you later come to think you should not have done $x$ at $t$, is irrelevant to whether your doing $x$ at $t$ was akratic. What *is* relevant is what you thought *at t* about doing $x$ at $t$.) This has an interesting consequence. An "instantaneous" agent—an agent who was destined to exist for only one moment, and who knew this—could, in that one moment, be akratic. If he viewed $y$ as his best option, yet in fact did $x$, he would have performed an akratic action. Akrasia seems perfectly possible, then, even when there is no issue about how to extend one's actions and agency out across time. Considerations of time are inessential to the possibility of akrasia.

Procrastination, by contrast, seems intimately bound up with issues of time and with an important challenge that faces us as rational agents, even if it would not face an instantaneous agent: that of ordering and performing actions over time. (Note that an instantaneous agent could not *put* something *off*, properly speaking.) Unlike the instantaneous agent, *we* are temporally extended agents, and this seems essential rather than ancillary to the possibility of procrastinating. Indeed, procrastination seems to be some kind of defect in precisely this function, that of placing activities in time. Because of its close conceptual connection to issues of time, we might go so far as to characterize procrastination as an essentially *diachronic* phenomenon. This would make it a poor fit with akrasia, which, as we have seen, is essentially synchronic and free of any temporal dimension. Shoehorning procrastination into akrasia would thus be liable to leave out, distort, or obscure something that is essential to procrastination and that is therefore worth highlighting rather than hiding.[16]

---

15. "The procrastinator," write Silver and Sabini, "is, we shall develop, someone who knows what (s)he wants to do, in some sense can do it, is trying to do it, and yet *doesn't do it*" ("Procrastinating," 207; emphasis added).

16. In suggesting that procrastination cannot be reduced to akrasia, I am in no way denying that cases of procrastination can involve akrasia. The following could certainly feature in an episode or period of procrastination: "I *must* start grading those papers I've been putting off looking at *now*," you think (where this is a sincere judgment on your part and where your "must" is all things considered), and yet your hand reaches for the remote control and you turn on the TV. But your procrastinating with respect to grading the papers over the period

## PROCRASTINATION AND WEAKNESS OF WILL

I've argued that procrastination is not simply akrasia. But could it still be weakness of will? Richard Holton and Alison McIntyre would argue that this question remains open, for they reject the traditional identification of weakness of will with akrasia.[17] Weakness of will, they argue, is not action contrary to your better judgment but something quite different: it is a species of irresoluteness, or failure to follow through on your intentions. It is a failure to do what you have decided you will do—a failure to stick to your plans. On their view, it does not matter what you judge to be best at the moment you abandon, or fail to act on, your previously formed intention. What matters—for purposes of charging you with weakness of will—is the abandonment itself.[18]

The "new" weakness of will is not entirely dissimilar to the old. Like the old, the new weakness of will involves a mismatch between the agent's conduct and certain of her states. But the specific criteria for weakness of will proposed by Holton and McIntyre depart significantly from those built into the traditional conception: they are in certain respects more demanding and in other respects more relaxed. One important difference between the two characterizations of weakness of will is the type of state which the weak-willed agent's conduct fails to match. On the "classic" conception of weakness of will as akrasia, the pertinent state is, as we saw, a certain evaluative judgment of the agent, such as his judgment about which course of action is best all things considered. On the new conception, however, the pertinent state is of a different type: it is an *intention*. Holton and McIntyre emphasize the special character of intention as a state that goes beyond a mere assessment of options or a judgment about what it is best to do all things considered.[19] In this respect, then—that is, with respect to the type of state that is demanded—the new criteria are

---

$t_m$ to $t_n$ does not seem to *consist wholly* in such episodes of akrasia. You are unlikely to have held it to be the case, at every moment between $t_m$ and $t_n$, that you ought to begin grading the papers *now*, and you would have been ineligible for akratic action (at least as far as grading the papers was concerned) at any moment at which you did not hold or judge this.

17. Holton, "Intention and Weakness of Will"; McIntyre, "What Is Wrong."

18. I do not mean to imply that for Holton and McIntyre any abandonment of a previously formed intention counts as weakness of will. As we shall see later, this is certainly not the case. At present I am simply underlining the broader category into which all cases of weakness of will (as they understand it) fall.

19. On this difference, see, for example, the amusing case offered by McIntyre ("What Is Wrong," 301). Of course, the mere possibility of akrasia already shows that these two (intention and judgment) are not the same thing, since the akratic agent judges it to be better all things considered to do $y$ and yet does not form an intention to do $y$, choosing to do $x$ instead. Note that the difference between the two remains even if, like Davidson, you think an intention is a special kind of evaluative judgment (see Davidson, "Intending"). For even then—as is crucial to Davidson's analysis of how weakness of will is possible—an intention is not the *same kind* of evaluative judgment as the one contrary to which the akratic agent acts.

stricter than the old. Since you can manifest "new" weakness of will only when you fail to carry out an intention you previously formed, you are "eligible" for weakness of will (so to speak) only when you previously formed such an intention. Having judged that $x$ is or would be the best thing to do is not enough; you must have formed an *intention* to do $x$, or *decided* to do $x$.

The new criteria are, however, in another respect less demanding than what is required for akrasia, for Holton and McIntyre drop the requirement of contemporaneity which was so central to the characterization of akratic action. A weak-willed action exhibits a lack of conformity with a state of the agent, but it is a prior state rather than a contemporaneous state. Thus the basic ingredients of weakness of will (on the new conception) constitute a sequence rather than a synchronous bundle. They are:[20]

(1) the formation at $t_m$ of an intention to do $x$ at $t_n$ (where $m < n$) and
(2) the failure to do $x$ at $t_n$.

Of course, these are not sufficient for weakness of will. (Setting aside the further conditions Holton and McIntyre propose, there is also the possibility that you have died prior to $t_n$.) But this skeleton is sufficient to show that the new weakness of will, unlike the old, is an essentially *diachronic* phenomenon. (Note the intriguing affinity with procrastination.)

What is the rational status of weakness of will so understood? New weakness of will does not involve the kind of synchronic incoherence among attitudes that characterizes akrasia. Because of this, the former does not seem to instantiate the especially stark kind of irrationality that the latter is usually held to embody. But new weakness of will may be a rational defect all the same. We can begin to see why abandoning your prior intentions could constitute a rational failing if we reflect on the nature and purpose of future-directed intentions in general. A further feature of the Holton-McIntyre account will then help us see more precisely how and why new weakness of will is a rational defect.

We should start by asking why we form future-directed intentions. What is the point of doing so? Suppose, for example, that I form today the intention to run five miles tomorrow. Why bother to do this? Surely (one might think), I could just leave the issue open until tomorrow and decide then whether to run five miles. If it is, indeed, best that I do so, then that is what I will decide then. Now it is true that we *could* exercise our practical thought only on the question of what to do *now*, and never on the issue of what to do in the future. But there are often significant advantages to settling now what one will do in the future. For example, as Michael Bratman has emphasized,[21] forming future-directed intentions can permit coordination of related activities and coordination with other agents.

---

20. I here adapt McIntyre, "What Is Wrong," 296.
21. Notably in Bratman, *Intention, Plans, and Practical Reason*.

There are, in short, significant benefits to planning, as opposed to making every decision only when the time comes. If we fail to act on our future-directed intentions, however, this defeats much of the point of forming intentions and plans: that is why the abandonment of prior intentions may be grounds for rational criticism. More generally, if planning is an important part of managing our agency over time and for that reason a central component of temporally extended rational agency, it makes sense that defects in our planning behavior should count as rational shortcomings, even if they do not involve the stark synchronous internal conflict that is characteristic of akrasia.

Holton and McIntyre exploit this idea, sharpening the point by building a further specification into their account of weakness of will. Weakness of will, they say, consists specifically in failing to act on a prior intention *because of a contrary inclination which you anticipated and expressly formed your intention in order to defeat*. This seems especially rationally criticizable because in such cases you give in to precisely the enemy against which you specifically aimed to fortify yourself.[22] One reason to form a plan now to run tomorrow evening is that if I simply leave it open until tomorrow evening whether I will run tomorrow evening, I know I may well end up not running. It is predictable that I will feel tired after a long day of work on my procrastination paper, and I may well at that time just prefer to relax with a glass of my favorite beverage. But if I now make a commitment to running tomorrow evening, by forming an intention or adopting a plan to do so, that plan may help get me into my running shoes when the time comes. So I may now form such an intention precisely in hopes of defeating the contrary inclinations I anticipate. (Holton and McIntyre call intentions that are formed for this kind of reason "resolutions.")

If, however, when tomorrow evening comes, I give in to precisely the feelings of lassitude that I predicted and that were the basis for my resolution, then my resolution has been defeated by exactly the contrary inclinations it was expressly designed to overcome. This, for Holton and McIntyre, is weakness of will. And such weakness of will constitutes "a practical defect" or "a failure of practical rationality" because, as McIntyre puts it, "a technique of self-management . . . that partly constitutes practical rationality for adult human agents" has been deployed but has failed.[23] Weakness of will, then, is a rational failing even if it does not involve synchronous conflicting attitudes. When I am weak-willed in this sense, I have at least partly failed at self-management over time, a task that is essential to practical agency for entities like us. This is sufficient grounds for rational criticism of my conduct.

Could procrastination be a subspecies of new weakness of will? Thinking of procrastination as new weakness of will would eliminate at least

---

22. This is emphasized especially by McIntyre, "What Is Wrong," 295–297.
23. McIntyre, "What Is Wrong," 296, 299.

two of the worries I raised about the prospects for subsuming procrastination under akrasia. Akratic action, I noted, is typically conceptualized as *doing* something you deem ill advised, whereas procrastination most saliently involves *not* doing something. But this is no longer a worry on the present account, since new weakness of will is also defined as a not doing of something, namely whatever was the content of your prior intention. More important, I had also objected that akrasia was a purely synchronic phenomenon, one that could be manifested even by an instantaneous agent, whereas procrastination seems essentially to involve a temporal dimension, removing it from the potential purview of such agents. But this worry, too, dissolves on the present picture, since, as we have just seen, new weakness of will is constituted by a sequence that is extended in time and that involves the attempt to project one's agency forward in time through the formation of future-directed intentions. An instantaneous agent, then, could not manifest weakness of will in this sense, just as he could not procrastinate. In this respect, we have a significant structural match between the two phenomena. The essentially diachronic temporal character of this kind of weakness of will mirrors one of the central aspects of procrastination.

Turning now to a more phenomenological analysis, I also think that in broad outline there is much to recognize in a picture of procrastination as a failure to implement one's plans. Canvassing my own extensive experience with procrastination, I find that it is very typical that I start by thinking, "Oh, I'll do that next week." Then next week rolls around, and, lo and behold, I don't do it. I move instead to a plan to do it the following week; but you can predict what happens the following week. Like a self-sustaining chemical reaction, the story continues in similar vein for a surprisingly long time. In this sequence, we seem to observe a repeated series of failures to live up to the intentions I formed in the past concerning $x$, a perfect match for the basic profile of new weakness of will (see again the "skeleton" offered above).

There is, then, considerable resonance between the profile of new weakness of will and that typical of procrastination. Furthermore, understanding procrastination along the lines of new weakness of will would yield a novel and interesting analysis of the type of rational failing which the former involves. New weakness of will is therefore a considerably more promising model or template for procrastination than akrasia; but can we subsume all cases of procrastination under this rubric? In order to answer this question, we should take a closer look at what is *excluded* from constituting weakness of will on this new picture. Every view takes its own hostages, and Holton and McIntyre choose to draw a bright line around the agent's intentions. If you never formed an intention to do $x$, you necessarily get off scot-free on the charge of weakness of will with respect to doing $x$. But is the same true of procrastination? This seems less clear; indeed, I incline toward the view that procrastination cuts across the demarcation line proposed by the Holton-McIntyre account.

We have discussed the idea that forming intentions is a way of planning. Continuing in this vein, we could say that for Holton and McIntyre, weakness of will is exclusively a defect in plan implementation: you make a plan, but then you don't implement it or carry it out. For Holton and McIntyre, weakness of will resides exclusively in what we might term the executive branch of our agency, the aspect of agency that consists in actually carrying out, or following through on, what we have so to speak legislated. Weakness of will can only be triggered by a mismatch between a certain legislative act and what the executive branch actually implements; any shortcomings within the legislative aspect of our agency cannot themselves amount to weakness of will. Defects in plan design and formation, in short, cannot open one to a charge of weakness of will in the Holton-McIntyre sense.

Earlier we motivated the idea that new weakness of will is indeed a rational failing by appealing to the centrality of planning activity to temporally extended agency. But the range of potential defects in our planning activity broadly construed is very wide, and certainly not limited to defects in plan implementation. By parallel reasoning, other kinds of flaws in our planning activity should also count as practical failings.[24] And if we turn our attention to all the ways in which we can plan badly, we find a rich variety of flora underfoot. For example, we plan badly when we adopt an instrumentally ineffective plan whose implementation will likely frustrate rather than achieve its aim. We plan badly when we adopt an overly demanding, unrealistic plan. And, in a case of special interest in the present context, we plan badly when we adopt only a vague or undemanding plan when a stronger, more specific plan is required. (We can, of course, also plan badly by failing to make a plan at all.)

These forms of bad planning are all flaws in plan drafting and plan adoption, not flaws in plan implementation; so they are all debarred from counting as new weakness of will. Could procrastination ever consist in any of these? It seems to me that it could. Consider, for example, the following case offered by McIntyre:

> Suppose I carry some student essays around with me planning to do some essay grading at some point in the next few days. If the essays should be returned *soon*, then I have formed only a temporally indeterminate intention when a resolution that is quite specific about the time to act is needed to get the job done.[25]

Such familiar conduct (at least to me) could not constitute weakness of will in Holton and McIntyre's sense. The flaw this agent exhibits is not at

---

24. McIntyre ("What Is Wrong") agrees, emphasizing the variety of possible planning defects that could also be considered shortcomings in our practical rationality. (Indeed, I have taken most of the ones I mention here from her.) But she takes pains to *distinguish* these other defects from weakness of will.

25. McIntyre, "What Is Wrong," 298.

the level of intention implementation—she very well may implement her anemic intention to do "some" essay grading in the next "few" days—but rather at the level of intention *formation*, which, as we have seen, is excluded from the purview of new weakness of will. As McIntyre says, such a case instances "a distinctive kind of practical failure: a failure to form a sufficiently demanding resolution when one is necessary in order to realize one's practical goals."[26]

So this is not weakness of will—but could it be procrastination? I have the strong intuition that it could, that one way to procrastinate with respect to doing $x$ is precisely to form an insufficiently specific intention with respect to doing $x$. Indeed, reading this case, I recognized some of my actual bouts of procrastination as having taken exactly this form. In such cases, it is as if one's avoidance behavior with respect to doing $x$ extended even to the level of the intentions one forms concerning $x$, making the latter vague or weak. The very fact that one forms only an anemic, temporally unspecific intention concerning $x$ may itself constitute procrastinating with respect to $x$.

Indeed, one might extend this thought and wonder whether procrastinating concerning $x$ sometimes involves never actually *deciding* to do $x$, never actually forming an intention to do $x$, at all. As mentioned earlier, there is an entire continuum of possible attitudinal relations between an agent $S$ and a task or activity $x$. Could any such relation falling short of, specifically, intention be compatible with procrastination concerning $x$? Holton and McIntyre emphasize that intention is a particular type of mental state, one that goes beyond simply making a judgment that one ought to do $x$. We ought to be able to exploit this distinction to describe a case in which an agent arguably procrastinates with respect to $x$ without ever rising to the level of forming an intention to do $x$ or deciding to do $x$.

Consider the following example. Grant application season has rolled around once again. Amanda, who has in the past regularly failed to submit applications for research grants that many of her colleagues successfully obtain, feels that she really should apply for a grant this year. She prints out the information about what she would need to assemble and notes the main elements thereof (description of research program, CV, and so on) and—of course—the deadline for submission. She puts all of these materials in a freshly labeled file folder and places it at the top of the pile on her desk. But whenever she actually contemplates getting down to work on preparing the application—which she continues to think she should submit—her old anxieties about the adequacy of her research program and productivity flare up again, and she always finds some reason to reject the idea of starting work on the grant submission process now (without adopting an alternative plan about when she will start). In the end the deadline passes without her having prepared the application, and once again Amanda has missed the chance to put in for a grant.

26. McIntyre, "What Is Wrong," 298.

Did Amanda ever decide to apply for a grant this year? Did she ever form or adopt an intention to do so? It seems to me that she did not. She certainly judged that she should prepare and submit an application, but, as Holton and McIntyre emphasize, this falls short of actually deciding to do it. On the other hand, it seems plausible to describe Amanda as procrastinating, over the period described, with respect to getting down to work on putting together a grant application. To the extent that these two attributions are plausible, we have a case of procrastination without intention: procrastination eligibility for which was generated merely by judging that one should do $x$, rather than by forming a definite intention to do $x$. That is why I am skeptical of building into the definition of procrastination either that one must intend to perform the activity one is procrastinating about or that one must put that activity off by making a choice or decision to do it later rather than now. Amanda's case suggests that these characterizations require too much and that procrastination is compatible with failing to form the specific kinds of mental attitudes toward doing $x$ that Holton and McIntyre would require.

If procrastination can take either of the two forms we have been discussing—insufficiently robust intention or no intention at all—then we must once again return a negative verdict on whether procrastination is weakness of will. While I do think procrastination often follows the basic pattern outlined by Holton and McIntyre, on which there is a (usually repeated) failure to implement one's plans and intentions, procrastination cannot be fully subsumed under weakness of will in their sense, since it seems that procrastination can infect the design-and-planning phase of our agency as well as the execution phase. From the point of view of Holton and McIntyre, this would make procrastination a hybrid rational defect, since it cuts across what they count as distinct categories of practical failure.

## CONCLUSION

I have argued that procrastination can be descriptively characterized and that, like weakness of will, it involves a mismatch between the agent's conduct and some pertinent state or judgment of the agent. However, when we looked at existing accounts of weakness of will to see how they characterize the state or judgment in question, we found that neither the classic nor the revisionist understanding of weakness of will could capture the full range of cases of procrastination. The second, because of its essentially diachronic structure, offers a much more satisfactory model for procrastination. But its insistence on the violation of an intention as the mark of weakness of will seems to exclude some genuine varieties of procrastination. What fundamentally unifies all of those varieties is, rather, that when we procrastinate we are doing a bad job at something essential to temporally extended agency: placing activities in time.

## ACKNOWLEDGMENTS

I wish to express my gratitude to the Centre for the Study of Mind in Nature and to the editors: this chapter benefited from fruitful discussion at the CSMN workshop and from further written comments from the editors.

# 4

# Intransitive Preferences, Vagueness, and the Structure of Procrastination

*Duncan MacIntosh*

Procrastinating is irrationally failing to do something in good time. According to Chrisoula Andreou, agents are sometimes induced to procrastinate by having intransitive preferences, possibly in combination with vagueness in the circumstances of choice.[1] I argue that her model cannot explain procrastination and that its true explanation is in things already familiar from the literature on weakness of will.

## PROCRASTINATION AS IMPRUDENT DELAY

One is guilty of procrastination when one has a self-acknowledged best reason in favor of doing something today but instead does it tomorrow (or never). This should not be confused with excused delay, where, for instance, one physically could not do the thing until tomorrow, nonculpably did not realize that it would be better done today,[2] had not figured out how to do it today, had ambivalence about whether one really wanted it done, or was prevented from doing it by some irresistible urge outside one's desire structure, that is, by something that prevented one from being fully an agent. Another species of excused delay is where one ceased to have a best reason to do the thing in question because one underwent a rationally faultless change in what one desired; for good reasons, perhaps from further experience, new second-hand factual knowledge, reflection on or deduction from one's information, or changed circumstances, one changed one's mind about one's goals or had a rationally permissible

---

1. Andreou's theory has unfolded over a series of papers: "Instrumentally Rational Myopic Planning," "Going from Bad (or Not So Bad) to Worse," "Environmental Damage and the Puzzle of the Self-Torturer," "Temptation and Deliberation," "Understanding Procrastination," "Environmental Preservation and Second-Order Procrastination," and "Making a Clean Break: Addiction and Ulysses Contracts."

2. By nonculpability, I mean that one was not guilty of self-deception, took suitable care in investigating the facts, and so on.

change of heart and so no longer had a practical duty to take the best means to the end at which one had been aiming.

Nor should procrastination be confused with prudent delay, where one puts off doing until tomorrow what one could have done today because it would be better done tomorrow (e.g., one would be able to do a better job of it) or because one had other ends that one ranked cumulatively at least as highly and that could best be attained by putting off the attaining of the end in question. (In fact, delay resulting from a rationally permissible change of heart about one's goals might better be classed as prudent delay rather than excused delay.) Procrastination proper is imprudent delay, where one puts off until tomorrow what one admits would, everything considered, be better done today. If one's reasons are grounded in one's desires and beliefs, then one acknowledges that, given these, doing this thing today is the best means toward servicing one's overall attitudinal structure. This is the only genuine form of procrastination: procrastination is necessarily irrational.

It is natural to class procrastination in with weakness of will, something that, since Donald Davidson, is often analyzed as acting to bring about an end one desires less than one's ostensibly most strongly desired end.[3] And it is commonly thought to be caused by such things as fear, nervousness or loss of nerve, boredom, aversion to the means needed to attain the end, wishful or unclear thinking, culpable ignorance or failure of foresight, failure to trace the logical consequences of one's beliefs, distraction or forgetfulness, lack of gumption, exhaustion, laziness, depression, and accidie or loss of affect. Some of these phenomena may need recategorization, depending on their analysis. For example, failure to do something to bring about a self-ascribed end because of aversion to the means may entail that one's overall preference ranking does not make the end whose attainment one is nominally procrastinating against, one's highest end (for, really, one's highest end was to not engage in that means), and so one is really engaging in prudent delay, not procrastination or any other form of weakness of will. Or maybe here we can speak only of procrastination relative to a nominal goal taken in isolation, not irrational delay relative to one's all-in ranking. Something similar might be said when someone fails to take the required means to her supposed ends from laziness: she may really prefer lying around. Meanwhile, failure to act in a timely way because of exhaustion may really be excused delay, as when exhaustion makes action impossible. And ostensible procrastination resulting from cognitive failures, such as forgetfulness, distraction, or not seeing the logical consequences of one's beliefs, may at least sometimes count as excused delay (one did not know there was something it would on balance advantage one to be doing) or as prudent delay (given how the facts seemed, delaying was rational).

---

3. For a survey of accounts of weakness of will, see Stroud, "Weakness of Will." As Jon Elster points out, this behavior, in turn, requires explanation; see Elster, "Weakness of Will."

## ANDREOU'S THEORY: PROCRASTINATION AS INDUCED BY INTRANSITIVE PREFERENCES

Let us turn now to Andreou's work on procrastination. Note first that an agent's preferences are transitive just in cases where if she prefers $x$ to $y$ and $y$ to $z$, then she also prefers $x$ to $z$; otherwise, her preferences are intransitive. Andreou thinks that some cases of procrastination result from the agent's having intransitive preferences. Suppose you have some large goal, such as quitting smoking, losing weight, saving the environment, or writing a book. But suppose also that you find pleasant each individual act of smoking, eating, polluting, or lazing around not writing, and you believe that no individual such act will put your larger goals out of reach. Then, for each occasion on which you could indulge in smoking, for instance, you may prefer indulging then to beginning to quit smoking, even though, given the choice, you would prefer never indulging to always indulging, since always indulging would doom your larger goals—call this latter preference your *global preference*. You will then be led by pair-wise choices to having always indulged, with disastrous results—cancer, obesity, an unlivable environment, no book—results you will regret and yet be unable to reverse. You will be led to this even though, given the choice, you would take back all of the indulgences, because you prefer having never indulged to having always indulged (hence the intransitivity in your preferences). Your choices are then arguably irrational, because they result in your getting the opposite of what you globally prefer. Indeed, you may foresee this, even though, in each choice between indulging and working toward your larger goals, you take yourself to have justification for delaying the cessation of indulgences—for procrastinating.

Andreou takes her theory to be nicely illustrated by, and indeed based on, Warren Quinn's puzzle of the self-torturer.[4] In Quinn's story, you are connected to a machine that delivers electric shocks. It has 1,000 settings from lower to higher shock levels, with the levels becoming unbearable at some point in the progression of settings. Each week, you get to experiment with the shock levels, finding out which ones are intolerable. Then you have the option of either staying at the shock level you are presently at or moving up one level; you are never allowed to go back down. Each time you move up, you will get $10,000. Adjacent shock settings are stipulated to be indistinguishable in pain level to you, though settings far enough apart are distinguishable.

Arguably, each week, you will reason, "The next setting will not feel any more painful than the current one, and I will get another ten grand," so each week, you move up. But you will eventually wind up at level 1,000, which will be unbearable, even given the compensation of the money you will have; and you will desperately wish to go back to level 0,

---

4. Quinn, "Puzzle of the Self-Torturer," 198.

but you will not be allowed to do so. Supposedly here, your preferences are intransitive, because you prefer each higher setting to the one below but also the lowest to the highest. Procrastination here is supposedly your delaying the stopping of the raising of the settings.

Procrastination with regard to quitting smoking, losing weight, and so forth, is the repeated delaying of acting on these larger goals one more time, on the rationale that one more time will not make a significant difference to their attainability but is itself desired. In the self-torturer case, your global preference, your preference for never raising the shock level rather than always raising it, is never expressed in action; only your pairwise preferences, your local preferences, your preferences to raise, are expressed. One appeal of Andreou's model is that it supposedly shows how the agent is seemingly rationally tempted into making certain choices and yet will regret them, culminating in a net irrationality.

I now begin a series of criticisms of Andreou's position. The first few speak to the intelligibility of the self-torturer scenario and whether there is any irrationality in having, or in acting upon, intransitive preferences, an irrationality that is necessary if the preferences are to explain procrastination conceived as necessarily irrational. I will argue that we can see delaying behavior of the sort Andreou has in mind as irrational only if we presume that the agent's preferences are transitive rather than intransitive. Later, I will critique another element of Andreou's view: the idea that procrastination can be explained by an inherent vagueness in what would count as an appropriate point to stop indulging and start fulfilling the more ambitious goals that figure in one's global preferences.

## THE INCOHERENCE OF THE SELF-TORTURER SCENARIO: INDISCERNIBILITY, THRESHOLDS FOR SUBJECTIVE STATES, AND TRANSITIVITY

Andreou's model is ingenious and, on the face of it, plausible. But I think there are several fatal difficulties with it. First, it is doubtful whether the self-torturer scenario as usually described is coherent; and so it is doubtful that it can be used to make the points Andreou wishes to make. It is stipulated of the scenario that setting 1,000 is intolerable; furthermore, it is implied that what it means for a setting to be considered intolerable by an agent is that it is painful enough to not be worth the money he would earn from it. This implies that the agent prefers more money to less money, less pain to more pain, and that his aversion curve to increasing pain is steeper than his affinity curve for increasing amounts of money. It is also stipulated that adjacent settings are indistinguishable in terms of pain, but settings far enough apart are distinguishable, that some lower settings are tolerable, and that the number of settings is finite.

But now there is a problem. Suppose that when the agent is experimenting with the settings, he sets the level to 1,000, finds this is intolerable, and backs down the settings. It follows from everything we have said that if he backs the settings down far enough, he finds a tolerable setting. But this, in addition to there being only a finite number of settings, entails that, compared with setting 1,000, in backing down, he will find a first tolerable setting.[5] Suppose this is setting 995; then setting 996 will be intolerable. But then settings 995 and 996 are distinguishable in comparison with setting 1,000; 996 is intolerable, 995 tolerable. But then at least one pair of adjacent settings, 996 and 995, are distinguishable, contrary to the stipulation that adjacent settings are indistinguishable.

But the scenario remains of interest if we relax that stipulation, so we will; let us regard adjacent settings as distinguishable at the threshold of intolerability. There are now two possibilities: either the agent would stop raising settings each week at 995, or he would raise the setting to 996. If he stops and is rational in stopping, then his preferences are transitive: he prefers 995 to all other settings because it is the setting that best balances pain and financial reward. Higher settings are dispreferred because they are too painful, and lower settings are dispreferred because they involve less money. On the other hand, if he increases to 996, either he is rational in doing so, or he is not. If he is not, then, barring an excusing condition, he has procrastinated, irrationally delaying the ceasing of the raising of the settings. But then, contrary to what Andreou says, we would have no explanation for this in the intransitivity of his preferences, since we have just decided that his preferences are transitive; and we would have no explanation in the form of the vagueness of the intolerability of the settings, since we have already established that this cannot be vague. So, the agent has just made some mistake; perhaps he has been weak-willed in some standard sense.

Now, let us consider the other possibility: the agent increases to 996, keeps going up to 1,000, and then wishes he could go back to setting 0, having been moved in all of this by his preferences. It follows, as Andreou induces from his behavior, that his preferences are intransitive: he prefers each higher setting to the one just beneath it and at the same time prefers the lowest setting to the highest setting, and this preference intransitivity explains his behavior. But if his preferences really are intransitive, then, since his choices express his preferences, it is not clear that his choices are irrational, as they would have to be in order for his proceeding to setting 1,000 to count as procrastination, which is necessarily irrational. Whether he is being irrational depends on whether having, or choosing from, intransitive preferences is irrational.

## WHERE IS THE IRRATIONALITY IN HAVING AND CHOOSING FROM INTRANSITIVE PREFERENCES?

If, as Andreou thinks, it is the intransitivity of the agent's preferences that explains his delaying something, and if this delay is to be seen as irrational—as

---

5. Thanks to Darren Abramson for discussion on this point.

it must be in order to count as procrastination—then there must be something irrational about having intransitive preferences or about the choices they would induce their holder to make. I will consider later whether there is anything irrational about having intransitive preferences. But now I will argue that even if an agent's preferences are intransitive, there will be no obvious irrationality in the choices they will induce the agent to make; and if, as Andreou allows, to be rational is to best advance one's preferences, the agent's making these choice would seem indeed to be rational.

Consider an agent whose preferences look like this: A > B > C > A (where > signifies "is preferred to"). Imagine that he is never asked to choose among A, B, and C all at once (all-wise) but only two at a time (pair-wise). Then each choice justified by his intransitive preference structure seems perfectly rational, for each choice always improves his position relative to his current position. True, each choice also always leads him to an outcome he disprefers in comparison with the possible outcome of a further choice, and so he would always make yet another choice given the chance, and so on. If he has A, he would rather trade it for C; if he has C, he would rather trade it for B; if he has B, he would rather trade it for A; and if he has A, he would rather trade it for C; and so on. But this is not in itself even prima facie irrational.

If the self-torturer really has intransitive preferences, he, too, would be irrational to refuse to make the next advance. (Ironically, here, it would only be his refusing to advance that would count as procrastinating, that is, as his delaying a choice that would advance his preferences. And, contrary to what Andreou says, we would need recourse to something other than his preferences to explain his refusal—perhaps one of the standard explanations of weakness of will.) He would be irrational in refusing to raise his level because, at each setting, he prefers not stopping. So, he rationally should proceed to the maximum level. But of course, since his preferences are intransitive, he also prefers the minimum level to the maximum; and since he is not allowed to go back, he is stuck at the maximum level that he disprefers to the minimum. Has he not, then, been irrational?

No, there is no irrationality in his having gotten himself into a situation where he faces an obstacle to further choice, for there is nothing irrational about his wanting something he cannot have (or if there is, this is not the basis of Andreou's argument). Imagine that our agent's preferences are of the form A > B > C > A and that when offered a choice between C and B, he chooses B, and then when offered a choice between B and A, he chooses A. But then he is prevented from choosing between A and C, where, given the option, he would choose C. His preferences, plus his circumstances, have left him stuck with A when he would rather have C. But there is no evident irrationality in his finding himself in this predicament.

However, it might be argued that he finds some options acceptable and others unacceptable and that he ends up with an option in the latter category, though it was in his power to end up with one in the former. Surely, he is being irrational?[6] Again, no; for no matter what state he winds up in, he will find it unacceptable relative to another possible state. That is, no matter what state he is in, he would rather be in a different state. So, no state for him is such that it was acceptable while other options to which he moved were unacceptable. Therefore, no state is such that his failing to preserve it amounts to his being irrational for failing to preserve an acceptable state.

Nor does any of this change if, in order to respect the idea that the agent in Andreou's case is supposed to have been irrational for pushing on to a state he globally disprefers, we define one of the states in the intransitive preference cycle as the state of not having indulged at all and each of the others as being cumulative indulgences, so that the agent's preferences look like this (where < signifies "is less preferred than"):

$$(C) < (B \& C) < (A \& B \& C) < -(A \& B \& C) < (C)$$

Suppose this is the smoking case. The agent prefers having smoked a second cigarette, (B & C), to stopping smoking after the first cigarette, (C); he prefers having smoked a third cigarette, (A & B & C), to stopping after the second, (B & C); he prefers having smoked none of the cigarettes, −(A & B & C), to having smoked all of them, (A & B & C); and he prefers having smoked one cigarette, (C), to having smoked none, −(A & B & C); and so on.

He will always prefer each possible next indulgence to stopping; call these preference pairs his local preferences. And he will always prefer abstaining altogether to engaging in all of the indulgences; this is his global preference. Finally, he will always prefer an indulgence to refraining from all indulgences. Note that the mere fact that some of these preferences are global, since they involve all of the states over which his other preferences range, does not make their objects automatically highest-ranked states—in an intransitive ranking, there is no highest-ranked state. Anyway, there is nothing obviously irrational about this ranking or about making the pair-wise choices the agent would make were he presented with the options two at a time.

Meanwhile, if we introduce an obstacle at the point where the agent would elect to retract all of his indulgences, he cannot get what he wants; and since this is his global preference, he cannot get it satisfied. But again, there is no irrationality in that, for there is nothing here that privileges the global pair-wise preference over any of the other pair-wise preferences, the local ones in particular. Indeed, the agent would also have been unhappy had he been forced to stop after the first cigarette.

This means that there is, again, a reply to the worry that the agent finds some options acceptable and yet voluntarily moves from them into an

---

6. Thanks to Andreou for this objection.

unacceptable option.[7] Again, no matter what state he winds up in, he will find it unacceptable relative to another state he could have had. So, again, no state is such that his failing to preserve it amounts to his being irrational for failing to preserve an acceptable state.

An agent's not getting his global preference satisfied is no worse for him than his not getting any of the others satisfied; it is not as if he had a transitive preference hierarchy with the object of this global preference ranked as the most-preferred object. There is no special irrationality here and no irrational delay; there is no failure of the agent to stop putting off decisions to preserve himself from some state he most disprefers. There is only, at worst, what we might call relative procrastination: he fails to take steps in time to prevent his arriving at a state he globally disprefers. But this is not irrational, and since procrastination is necessarily irrational, it is not genuine procrastination.

There may be a reply to this. Suppose that for each possible stopping point, the smoker with intransitive preferences weakly prefers having another cigarette to stopping but strongly prefers having smoked no cigarettes to having smoked all of them. Arguably, we can then say that there are things he prefers more strongly and things he prefers less strongly, and perhaps he should stop smoking before he gets to the state he disprefers most strongly. Perhaps then, upon surveying his intransitive preferences, he is rationally obliged to ensure that as they guide his pair-wise choices, they do not guide him to a forced stopping point that is the most strongly dispreferred of his options. He should choose as if he had transitive preferences, with that item as the least-preferred item.

But even if he has these varying strengths of preference, it is not clear that it is rational for him voluntarily to stop at any given point; for there would always be the argument that he would, however weakly, prefer not stopping until the next point, and so on. A rational person guided by his intransitive preferences would not, in fact, voluntarily stop. Indeed, this is precisely what distinguishes choosing on the basis of intransitive preferences from choosing on the basis of transitive preferences.

We have been trying to find something inherently irrational either in an agent's having intransitive preferences or in the choices that they would induce him to make. One familiar such argument is that having intransitive preferences is irrational because an agent with them can be money-pumped: regardless of which state he is currently in, he would trade some of his money to move to a different state he prefers to it, and since he always prefers another state to the one he is in, he would keep doing this until he had no more money. Surely, this makes him irrational, for there is the air of being self-defeating about him.

---

7. Thanks to Andreou for this objection.

However, the money-pump argument does not by itself prove the irrationality of having or choosing by intransitive preferences. At the very least, we would have to assume that the agent has, in addition to intransitive preferences over various outcomes, a preference to keep his money. Let us assume that this is so: he will only trade his money for something he values as much or more. Suppose, further, that he prefers A > B > C > A. Suppose that he is now in state C, which we define as him having, say, a brooch and three dollars. Given a choice, he would rather spend a dollar and trade the brooch for, say, a watch; that is, he would rather be in the state of having a watch and only two dollars, which is state B. And maybe he would trade that to have, say, a pen and only one dollar, which is state A; and he would trade that to be in the state of having a brooch and three dollars, which is state C again. (Maybe someone will accept the trade, maybe not.)

Where is the irrationality? The traditional answer: in the agent's voluntarily moving to a situation that is worse (relative to his preferences) than the situation he started off in.[8] (He started with a brooch and three dollars, and now he wishes he could get back to that state.) But in fact, each position he could have been in is such that if he does not move to a different position, he is pair-wise worse off. So, he would have been irrational to stay where he was. In moving, he has not made himself any worse off than he was before. (After all, even if he made it back to the original state, he would still want to renounce it for another state, and so on.)

## INTRANSITIVE PREFERENCES IN OVERVIEW AND THE IMPOSSIBILITY OF ALL-WISE CHOICES

But maybe we have not been sufficiently charitable to the idea animating Andreou's model. Perhaps the idea is this: the agent has pair-wise preferences between indulging and abstaining that always require him to indulge. But looked at from an overview, he also has global preferences according to which he would rather eschew all indulgences than engage in all indulgences. And it is this latter preference that gets frustrated by his sequence of pair-wise choices, resulting in a net irrationality. If only the agent were to take the global view, he would not engage in the indulgences but would instead act to satisfy his global preference. (One might think he would be induced to do this simply by having had occasion to take the global view, or maybe he would need to make changes to his circumstances of choice in order to prevent himself from returning to choosing by his pair-wise local preferences.

---

8. Thanks to Andreou for this suggestion.

# Intransitive Preferences, Vagueness, and the Structure of Procrastination

Andreou seems to think agents would have to take the latter strategy.) And if he does not take this view, he will have been irrationally myopic.

Let us see if we can represent this using a case where your preference structure incorporates global preferences, ones regarding totalities of indulgences:

$$(C) < (B \& C) < (A \& B \& C) < -(A \& B \& C) < (C)$$

Again, each letter stands for a cigarette smoked. You have the global preference for having smoked no cigarettes, –(A & B & C), rather than having smoked all of the cigarettes, (A & B & C). But now, suppose that you are asked to choose among all of the options at once, not pair-wise. Looked at from the vantage of an overview and trying to make not a pair-wise choice but an all-wise choice, you should be paralyzed, unable to make any choice, let alone one that involves satisfying your global preference. You are trying to figure out how many cigarettes to smoke, but for any number, your preferences give you reason not to pick it. You cannot pick smoking just one cigarette, because you prefer smoking two to smoking just one; you cannot pick two, because you prefer three to two; nor can you pick three, because you prefer smoking none to smoking three; nor can you pick none, because you prefer smoking one to smoking none; and so on. So, it would not be true that rationally, ideally, you should be induced by your preferences not to delay quitting smoking. For it would not be true that some number of cigarettes is the number after smoking which you should quit smoking; nor would it be true that you should stop before violating your global preference to have smoked none rather than three. And so, again, even though when offered choices only pair-wise, you will choose to violate your global preferences, there is no vantage from which this is irrational. Furthermore, since procrastination is necessarily irrational, but there is no behavior of yours that your intransitive preferences could succeed in inducing here that can count as irrational, it cannot be intransitive preferences that explain any so-called procrastination.

Note further that the paralysis you would experience in trying to make an all-wise choice from your intransitive preferences is not obviously irrational, either. For there is nothing such that, because you all-in prefer it, you are failing to advance your preferences by failing to make a choice. You are just not equipped for making choices in this situation (apart from the choice of making no choice). True, the fact that an agent's intransitive preferences allow him to make pair-wise choices but not all-wise choices has been used to argue that we cannot understand a wholly well-ordered preference ranking as just a construct of pair-wise rankings; we must add that the pair-wise rankings must be transitive. But all this means is that unless your preferences are transitive, there will be some situations in which your preferences cannot justify you in choosing one among several options. There is no further obligation of rationality to be such that your preferences would always enable you to make such choices.[9]

## PROCRASTINATION, TRANSITIVE PREFERENCES, AND EVER-BETTER PROBLEMS

We now know that to have irrational delay from an agent in the advancing of his global preferences in the way Andreou sees it, the agent's preference structure must be transitive. There must be something he ranks highest, something he globally prefers, his ambitious goal, as well as other things he ranks beneath it, his indulgent goals, and somehow he must be led by temptation and his preference structure to put off his global goal until it is too late. In fact, we need something even more complicated: that what the agent wants most is some big, important, globally preferred thing, plus a bunch of smaller things, ones the getting of which makes him better off than just the big thing alone, but where his getting too many of the smaller things ruins the big thing. Plausibly, then, what the agent wants is as many indulgences as possible compatible with still reaching his global goal.

Let us reimagine the self-torturer puzzle to make it capture these features. If you are in the new version of the puzzle, your preferences look like this:

> maximal tolerable indulgences > maximal-1 tolerable indulgences > maximal-2 tolerable indulgences > maximal-$n$ tolerable indulgences > 0 indulgences > intolerably many indulgences

But if you can tell intolerable levels—something that, as we saw, has to be true for self-torturer-like cases to be intelligible—then you can tell where to stop, namely, just before the first setting that is intolerable compared with the zero setting. But this means that there would be limits on pairwise temptations to move up; and so you would not, if guided by your preferences, fail to attain your ambition, what you globally prefer. Normally, then, there would be no procrastination, no irrational delaying of stopping before it is too late. But suppose you do not then stop. What could explain this? Not your overall preferences but only the usual explanations of weakness of will, such as distraction, confusion, and the others mentioned above.

We have been exploring problems with Andreou's view on the assumption that procrastination is modeled well by the case of the self-torturer.

9. There is, however, an obligation under certain conditions not to move from having transitive preferences to having intransitive preferences. For argument to this effect, together with a general discussion of well-orderedness in preferences, see MacIntosh, "Prudence and the Reasons of Rational Persons," especially 350.

And it has proved problematic as a model, because its intelligibility depends on there being a threshold of disaster. It relies on subjective intolerability, and, given other stipulations about the model, without a threshold of intolerability, there can be no subjective intolerability in the model, no disaster, and so no rational objection to the agent's indulging indefinitely; therefore, his behavior could not count as procrastination. But Andreou also sees as part of the problem that when we are induced by our preferences to procrastinate, this is because there is no obviously appropriate place to stop indulging. I now turn to a family of structures with this feature. I begin with cases in which there are infinitely many prima facie acceptable stopping points, with an incentive at each point not to stop before the next, where not stopping sooner or later would result in disaster but where no given stopping point is the one proceeding beyond which is itself disastrous. I will explore whether this should present a problem for agents. I then turn to cases where, however many possible stopping points there are, they exist on a vague continuum. I shall argue that the infinite case has a solution and that the solution can be applied to the vague cases. I then explore what it would mean if I am wrong about this, suggesting that even then, such structures cannot explain procrastination.

So, suppose that Andreou had in mind "ever-better" problems, problems whose structure is nicely illustrated by the following question: On what day should you drink a bottle of wine that improves every day? Each day, there is an argument for delaying another day, for the wine will then be better; but some day must be chosen, or else one never gets the benefit of drinking. Likewise, maybe before the intolerable point in the self-torturer case, there are infinitely many acceptable stopping points, each one such that there is an incentive not to take it. Your preferences look like this:

> maximal tolerable indulgences, where the last indulgence must be chosen from pair-wise incentivized options among which there is no optimum > maximal-1 tolerable indulgences > maximal-2 tolerable indulgences > maximal-$n$ tolerable indulgences > 0 indulgences > intolerably many indulgences

Let us add some structure to the self-torturer case in order to have a concrete example of this sort of ranking. Suppose that you are given the usual options of moving up a setting, and suppose also that you can determine the highest tolerable level. So, you advance to there, and now you want to stop. But you will only be allowed to stop if, in the next ten minutes, you pick a number between one and infinity. If you do not pick a number, you will be forced to the first intolerable level. Let us make the case more vivid: if you do not pick a number, you will be shot dead. You are also told, however, that whatever number you pick, you will be given its value in dollars. Can you rationally pick a number?

For each number, there is an argument for not picking it, because it would be better to pick a higher number, since that will get you more money; and there is no highest number; so there is no uniquely rationally choice-worthy number. Thus, we can imagine an agent in this situation nominating a number, rejecting it for a higher number, and then rejecting that number for an even higher number, and so on, the net effect being the procrastination of picking a number. We would then have a case of procrastination explained much as Andreou saw it: each option available to the agent is preference-dominated by a later (in this case, higher) option, and the effect of delaying stopping the consideration of options results in a globally dispreferred outcome (in this case, death).

On the other hand, since not settling on a number is disastrous, the agent should settle on a number. But how? He could use a symmetry-breaking technique: each number is such that choosing a higher number than it is incentivized, but each number is also such that settling on it is less disastrous than not settling on any number. That is, from the point of view of averting disaster, each number is equally serviceable. And since it is more important, given the agent's values, that he pick some number than that he not pick a number (in comparison with which a higher number would get him more money), more important because he thinks it better to be alive with some money than dead with a little more, it is the latter reasoning that should control him. And this deliberative style allows him to treat all of the numbers as equally good, period, rather than just equally good in a crucial respect, for it allows him to discount the respects in which they are not equally good—if he does not discount those respects in this way, he cannot get what he most wants, namely, to keep his life.

At this point, the problem has the same logic as the one Buridan's ass faces in choosing between two equally good options. And paralysis of choice is not rational in the Buridan case. Instead, an agent in such a case should break the tie using a symmetry-breaking technique whereby a randomizing process arbitrarily nominates one of the options, thereby making it salient and therefore choice-worthy. (The arbitrariness lies in the fact that there is nothing inherent in any of the options that makes it choice-worthy; rather, the eventual choice-worthiness of one of the options derives from the fact that a process, designed arbitrarily to pick some option or other, picked it, a process whose use is justified independently of the properties of the objects among which it picks.) In a tie between two equally good options, one might flip a coin; in a tie between infinitely many equally good options, one might use a random-number generator. Perhaps one has such a generator in one's head, which one activates simply by thinking, "I shall now pick the first number that pops into my head." At any rate, we should be able rationally to do something like this if we can generally use symmetry-breaking techniques to choose among things we are tied about, which we can.[10]

Is this satisficing?[11] No; satisficing is forgoing an available optimum in favor of something suboptimal that is good enough. But in our case, there is no optimum to forgo. So, we have an agent who has found it maximizing to take the vantage of avoiding the worst; and looked at from that vantage, the case presents him with many equally good options, choosing among which must be done with a symmetry-breaking technique such as random choosing.[12]

Of course, it is possible that the agent's choice in this and similar cases should not be purely random. Often, there are constraints from our other goals that should affect the choice of stopping point in a given continuum.[13] For example, there are many opportunities for me to quit smoking, but they are not all equally good. Quitting just before a conference, for instance, would make it impossible for me to perform at the conference, so I should quit only after. And if I were in our new version of the self-torturer scenario, maybe I would have a rough idea of how much money would meet my foreseeable needs and would believe that getting very much more money would cause me other problems—attract criminality, ruin my personal relationships, deflate the value of the currency, and so on. So, I should randomly choose only among items in the remaining range. Of course, if there is a highest number in this range, I should pick that.

But perhaps what counts as in that range is vague. And Andreou is interested in scenarios that feature vagueness, so let us proceed to these.

## CHOOSING WHERE TO STOP IN VAGUE CONTINUA

One problem agents face in Andreou's scenarios is that it is not clear what counts as too many indulgences when trying to maximize the number of

---

10. Things are more complicated if you and I must coordinate by agreeing on one of some many options among which each of us is indifferent (or slightly dissimilarly incentivized), each of us using our own symmetry-breaking technique in proposing to the other agent which option to settle on. I argue in MacIntosh, "Buridan and the Circumstances of Justice," that since there is no guarantee that our several symmetry-breaking techniques will nominate the same option, and since an infinite regress may begin in trying to use symmetry-breaking techniques to solve *that* problem, there is no guarantee of a rational solution to this coordination problem. I thus endorse Andreou's invoking coordination problems to explain why people procrastinate—or at least delay, for it is not clear that there is irrationality here—in dealing with issues such as pollution, where agents would have to coordinate to solve the problem; see Andreou, "Environmental Preservation." In fact, I raise her worry (in the poker sense of "raise") and claim that there may be no rational solution to these *n*-party coordination problems, barring certain lucky events that themselves cannot be rationally coordinated for by agents seeking to coordinate.

11. Thanks to Elijah Millgram for the question.
12. Sorenson, "Originless Sin," and its associated literature may be relevant here.
13. Thanks to Sue Sherwin for pointing this out.

them compatible with avoiding disaster for one's global preferences. Having one more cigarette will not be the difference between getting cancer and not, although having many more will likely make the difference (or at least some significant difference), even though there is no definite number (or at least no known one) that will do it. This is likewise true for one more act of pollution and catastrophic global warming or one more night of watching TV rather than working on your book. If we think of the indulgences as arrayed in a sequence on a continuum, these cases have the following structure: At the start of the sequence is a vaguely bounded range of indulgences that you could engage in with no significant risk to your larger ambition. This vaguely transitions into a range where the more you indulge, the less likely it is that you will be able to attain your ambition, but it is in decreasing degree likely that were you to stop indulging, you could still attain it. And this, in turn, vaguely transitions into a range where it is very likely too late to attain your ambition, so that further indulgences do not significantly worsen your chances at it, and there is little point to stopping.

For these situations, there are several possibilities. First, perhaps you can assign utility values to attaining your ambition and to each indulgence, and for each incremental indulgence, you can determine the degree to which it reduces the probability of your being able to attain your ambition. We then have a straightforward problem in expected utility theory: you must maximize your individual expected utility, and there will be some indulgence that is the last one that increases rather than decreases it, a point at which the increasing utility from further indulgence is canceled by the decreasing likelihood of attaining your ambition, an ambition with a high and known utility.

A second possibility is that you do not know precisely the utilities of the indulgences and the ambition and/or the probabilities of attaining the ambition given each further indulgence. But you know the odds of each thing having any possible utility it could have for you and the odds of each indulgence having any possible effect on attaining your ambition that it could have. So, again, you can do an expected utility calculation by first multiplying your estimates of the utilities and probabilities by your estimates of the likelihood of the correctness of your estimates, giving you a probability-weighted value for the utilities and probabilities, which you then multiply together for each choice of indulgence, stopping indulging after the last indulgence that increases your expected utility.

A third set of possibilities is that either the probabilities or the utilities or both are such that each can be specified only within a certain limited range of accuracy. Perhaps you know that the utility of attaining your ambitious goal is somewhere between 100 and 120 happiness units or that the probability of the next cigarette's reducing by 1 percent the chance of attaining that goal is between 2 and 4 percent. Again, expected utility calculations come to the rescue: you should compute the expected utilities of each choice on each assumption of the utilities and probabilities in your accuracy range, average them together, and then keep indulging to the point of highest average expected utility. (Admittedly, these calculations are becoming pretty daunting in practical terms for ordinary agents, who lack actuarial acumen, but the calculations afford—in principle—a solution to the problem.)

In all three cases, procrastination would consist in indulging beyond the stopping point dictated by the varyingly complicated expected utility calculations. But to explain why you would so indulge, we would need the usual explanations from the weakness-of-will literature—it would have nothing to do with intransitivity in your preferences or even with vagueness.

A fourth possibility is that while there is a utility-maximizing choice, you do not know it, and you are aware of this; you know only that the longer you indulge, the more money you get, but the less likely you are to attain your larger goal, and that this goal is more important to you than any amount of money. Here, you should take no chances and should stop indulging immediately; you should take the step certain to avoid disaster. And were you to fail to do this, the explanation could have nothing to do with intransitivity in your preferences or with vagueness.

A fifth possibility is that you face inherent vagueness, itself at best only crudely specifiable. Imagine a variant of the self-torturer case where you must satisfy an administrator before you are allowed to stop raising the shock levels. For example, suppose that in order to exit the self-torturer scenario, you must watch the administrator dropping grains of sand onto a table, and you must tell him to stop before he has made a heap, but you will also be given a dollar for each grain you let him drop.

Here, the difference between something's not being a heap and being a heap will not be one grain of sand. Nevertheless, there will be some clear cases of a nonheap and some clear cases of a heap. Your job is to allow grains of sand to be dropped but only to the point beyond which it would be strongly arguable that there was a heap. Unfortunately, there is no precise such point for heaps, but there is a range of points within which all of the points are such that there is no argument whatsoever for thinking that there is yet a heap—call this the safe range. Of course, the safe range itself has vague boundaries, and likewise for the continuum of any vague concept.

Must an agent having to choose here be pulled into procrastination? No, because he should be able to think this way: no criteria internal to the concept of the vague thing in question can guide the fine-tuning of where to draw the line. Suppose that you are our self-torturer and that the administrator is playing fair; he will be as reasonable as you in drawing lines, and he must accept that, provided you do not misdraw a line by labeling a case that is clearly one thing as clearly another, you have chosen permissibly, and you will be allowed to stop raising the shock levels. It is rational for you randomly to choose a point within the vaguely bounded safe region, a point toward its later extreme in order to get more money. The same applies to deciding how many more cigarettes to smoke. Doctors think that smoking for 20 years strongly increases cancer risks, smoking between one day and five years not so much. So, it is within that range, roughly, that one should make a random choice of when to quit (see the concerns I discussed earlier about when exactly to quit). The same goes for how many more days you can delay enacting pollution legislation or how many more evenings you can laze around failing to work on your book.

An agent rationally should not be pulled into procrastination by vagueness. Of course, I concede to Andreou that if the agent deals with vagueness irrationally, and so procrastinates, her procrastination will have been caused in part by vagueness. But since both the rational and the irrational person are contending with vagueness, it must be something other than vagueness that explains the difference between them—that explains the irrationality of the irrational person.

## IMPLICATIONS FOR THE POSSIBILITY OF PROCRASTINATION AND ITS EXPLANATION

We have considered many forms of choice problems, posed to agents with either transitive or intransitive preferences. But for each problem, there are only (coincidentally) five possible implications for the possibility of procrastination and its explanation.

First, there may be a rational solution to the problem of where to stop indulging, a solution dictated by the agent's preferences and beliefs about the circumstances (including his mastery of the concepts in play in the event of vagueness), and the agent knows it and would therefore take it, in which case we will not have procrastination. If he does not take it, then his behavior is not properly under the control of his preferences, in which case, in opposition to Andreou, his preferences are not the problem.

Second, perhaps there is a rational solution, but the agent does not know it and therefore will not take it. But then there is still no procrastination, which is defined as irrational behavior; as long as the agent has the excuse of ignorance about which solution is rational, he cannot be called irrational for failing to take it, at least not unless he is culpable for not knowing. But if he is so culpable, as a result of wishful thinking or whatever, then the procrastinating is being caused by one of the usual suspects in the explanation of weakness of will, and, in opposition to Andreou, we have no special explanation for procrastination in preference intransitivity or vagueness.

Third, perhaps there is no rational solution. (For example, maybe some of the proposals I made above about what would be rational solutions to some of these problems fail, and maybe no proposals could succeed.) But if there is no rational solution, then neither is there such a thing as culpably failing to take it. So, again, the agent is guilty of no irrationality and is not guilty of the form of it which is procrastination.

Fourth, it could be that what counts as a rational solution is inherently vague. But then it is, at worst, vague whether the agent is irrational, at least if his choice fell in the vague area of arguably rational but also arguably irrational solutions. If it fell in the clearly irrational range, again, we would have to invoke one of the usual suspects cited in the explanation of weakness of will—nothing special about procrastination.

Fifth, maybe some of these problems, such as those we considered earlier for agents with intransitive preferences, have prudent delay as their solution. (For example, if one has intransitive preferences over the number of cigarettes to smoke, one should keep smoking more cigarettes, which is to say that one should delay quitting smoking.) But then, again, an agent taking this solution will not be guilty of procrastination, for she will not be guilty of any form of irrationality.

It appears, then, that, in spite of the plausibility and elegance of Andreou's conjectures, neither intransitivity in an agent's preferences nor vagueness in what counts as an appropriate point to stop indulging in favor of attaining larger goals in the course of advancing transitive preferences can explain procrastination conceived as irrational delay. Andreou correctly sees that an agent with intransitive preferences, for example, concerning how many cigarettes to smoke, will delay quitting smoking, resulting in his not satisfying his global preference to have smoked no cigarettes rather than many.

But since his preferences are intransitive and since there appears to be nothing irrational about having such preferences or about making local-preference-advancing pair-wise choices from these preferences—choices to keep smoking one more cigarette—Andreou cannot represent the agent's failing to satisfy his global preference as irrational. She can explain his delay in failing to stop smoking in time to satisfy his global preference but not the supposed irrationality of the delay. Andreou is also right to see that vagueness, namely, in what counts as an appropriate place to stop indulging in pleasant activities that delay the attainment of more important goals, can pose difficult choice problems for agents with transitive preferences. But if, as I have suggested, these problems can be rationally overcome with symmetry-breaking techniques, then, if an agent fails to overcome the problems in this way, the explanation must lie elsewhere than in the vagueness regarding when it is best to stop indulging. We must appeal to things such as weakness of will to explain the agent's failing rationally to solve his problem. Meanwhile, if I am wrong about there being a rational solution to the vagueness problem, then an agent who fails to solve it cannot be accused of any irrationality, for there would be no rational course that he has failed to take. And so his failure could not amount to procrastinating, for it could not count as irrational delay.

## ACKNOWLEDGMENTS

For useful conversation, my thanks to Steven Burns, Sue Campbell, Richmond Campbell, Carl Matheson, Chris Olsen, Susan Sherwin, Heidi

Tiedke, Michael Watkins, Sheldon Wein, and a colloquium audience at Dalhousie University. For written comments, my thanks to Darren Abramson, Chrisoula Andreou, Bob Martin, Mark White, and Greg Scherkoske. Thanks also to the participants in the workshop held for this volume, particularly George Ainslie, Olav Gjelsvik, Elijah Millgram, Sergio Tenenbaum, and Frank Wieber. Finally, thanks to Gjelsvik and to Jennifer Hornsby for their sponsorship of and their work in putting together the workshop and to Andreou and White for their organizational and editorial efforts.

# 5

# Bad Timing

*Jon Elster*

Actions may be taken too early or too late. Although most of this chapter will be devoted to excessively delayed actions, I believe the contrast with premature actions can provide a useful perspective. What looks like procrastination may, on closer inspection, be a form of wise restraint. Although it is sometimes true that "he who hesitates is lost," it may also be the case that "haste makes waste." Whereas Cicero asserted that "slowness and procrastination is hateful,"[1] Seneca claimed that "reason seeks to postpone action, even its own, in order that it may gain time to sift out the truth; but anger is precipitate."[2]

We may want to distinguish between procrastination with regard to *actions* and with regard to *tasks*. Whereas actions (such as proposing marriage) are punctual, tasks (such as writing a term paper) extend over time. Filling in a tax form is somewhere in between. Yet since task initiation and task completion are actions, it is possible to assess their timing as well. A person might procrastinate in task initiation and yet complete the task on time, and vice versa. To avoid procrastinating, she would have to start at the right time and finish at the right time.

I shall only consider cases in which the timing of action—whether premature or delayed—is *irrational*. To the extent that rational-choice theory tells us what to do and when to do it, it provides a criterion for distinguishing between the excessive delay denounced by Cicero and the prudential approach advocated by Seneca. Although the definition of procrastination in terms of the subjective notion of rationality rather than by an objective criterion such as success or fitness has some counterintuitive consequences, I suspect that would be true of objective criteria, too. The preanalytical idea of procrastination may be too amorphous to be captured accurately by any criterion.

The conception of rational choice on which I shall draw is set out in figure 5-1.[3] In the figure, arrows stand simultaneously for optimality

---

1. *Philippics* VI.7.
2. "On Anger," I.18.
3. See Elster, *Explaining Social Behavior*, chap. 10, for a fuller discussion.

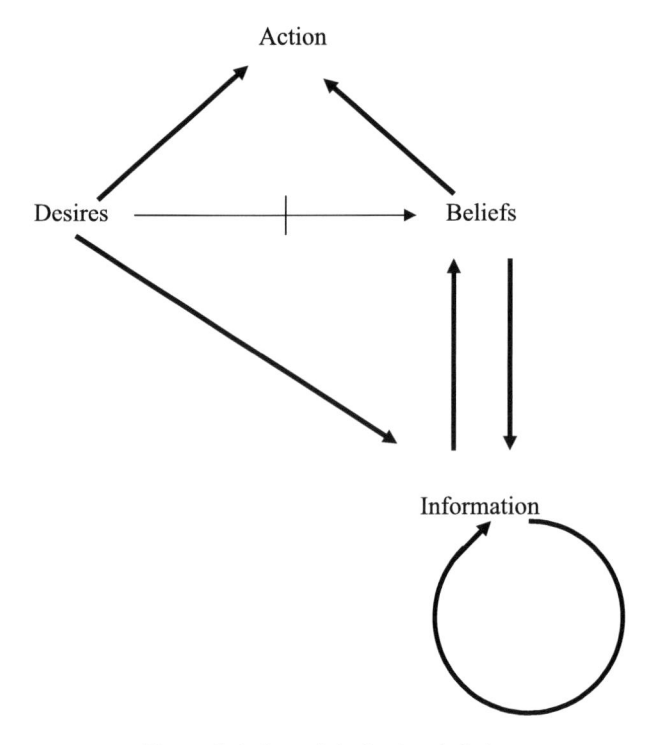

**Figure 5-1** A model of rational choice.

relations and causality relations. The blocked arrow from desires to beliefs is intended to exclude wishful thinking as a rational mode of belief formation. Note that an *indirect* influence of desires on beliefs, mediated by the acquisition of information, need not be irrational. It makes sense to gather more information about decisions we care strongly about than about more trivial issues. Also, a rational agent who cares little about the future will not spend much time and other resources to determine the long-term consequences of present behavior. Yet if our desires make us spend a less-than-optimal or more-than-optimal time gathering information, the ensuing action will be irrational.

In the first section of this chapter, I use this conceptual machinery to discuss three mechanisms that can lead to premature action: hyperbolic time discounting, urgency, and the need for cognitive closure. In the second section, I consider a number of mechanisms that can generate procrastinating behavior: hyperbolic discounting, emotion, lack of emotion, loss aversion, perfectionism, wishful thinking, self-deception, and "cold" cognitive biases. The final section offers a brief conclusion.

The chapter is more a catalogue raisonné of causes of irrational delay than an in-depth exploration of one particular mechanism. Yet the focus on rationality provides a unifying framework that may be useful. I believe, moreover, that the dual focus on excessively early and excessively delayed decisions provides an approach to a more general explanandum than what has been found in earlier studies.

A few comments about the literature on procrastination may be in order. The work by economists provides a crisp and clear model of how hyperbolic time discounting can induce procrastination.[4] Their theoretical framework—hyperbolic discounting—derives from the work of Strotz and Ainslie.[5] The psychological studies on procrastination that refer to Ainslie's work tend, however, to blur the distinction between hyperbolic discounting and other forms of discounting.[6] If people discount the future consistently (e.g., exponentially), they may *rationally* choose to put off aversive tasks. (This fact is one of the counterintuitive implications of my definition referred to earlier.) Irrational procrastination occurs when an agent intends, at time 1, to carry out the aversive task at time 2 but, when time 2 arrives, postpones execution to time 3.

For a nonspecialist, the psychological literature on procrastination is often opaque and disappointing.[7] Many studies take the form of displaying correlations between scorings on procrastination scales and scorings on other character traits, such as perfectionism, neuroticism, self-efficacy, and so on. Given the fragility of constructs based on self-reports and the many pitfalls of statistical analysis, it is difficult (for me, at least) to have much confidence in the findings. Only a minority of the studies use behavioral data.[8] With a few exceptions, there is little emphasis on the search for simple and robust causal mechanisms. These remarks are, to repeat, those of an outsider to the field.

For obvious reasons, much of the empirical literature on procrastination deals with the tendency of students to postpone work on exams, term papers, and theses. When the deadline is flexible, as in the last two cases, one may observe procrastination both in task initiation and in task completion. With an exam, which occurs on a fixed date, only task initiation (beginning to study for the exam) lends itself to procrastination. Yet according to one study, students who study less and later than others do just as well on an exam, suggesting a self-selection bias.[9] Independently of the flexible/rigid distinction, tasks can be either one-shot (thesis writing) or repeated (exams and term papers). For the second category of tasks,

---

4. See, for instance, Akerlof, "Procrastination and Obedience," and O'Donoghue and Rabin, "Doing It Now or Later."
5. Strotz, "Myopia and Inconsistency," and Ainslie, "Specious Reward" and *Picoeconomics*. (See also Ainslie's chapter 1 in the present volume.)
6. See, for instance, Pychyl, Morin, and Salmon, "Procrastination and the Planning Fallacy," 249; Ferrari, Johnson, and McCowen, *Procrastination and Task Avoidance*, 32; Schouwenburg, "Academic Procrastination," 82.
7. See, for instance, Ferrari, Johnson, and McCowen, *Procrastination and Task Avoidance*; Ferrari and Pychyl, *Procrastination*; Steel, "Nature of Procrastination."
8. For example, Tice and Baumeister, "Longitudinal Study" Conti, "Competing Demands."
9. Pychyl, Morin, and Salmon, "Procrastination and the Planning Fallacy."

one might expect learning over time to induce less procrastination in the later years of college than in the first. It is not clear, however, that this expectation is confirmed.[10]

## SOURCES OF PREMATURE ACTION

Consider first hyperbolic discounting, and suppose (without loss of generality) that the present value of one unit of utility at time t in the future is $1/(1 + t)$. The agent has bought a bottle of wine and knows that it will appreciate with time. If she drinks it this year, she derives a pleasure of 2.75; next year, it will be 5.00; and the year after 9.00. From today's perspective, the present values are, respectively, 2.75, $5.00/(1 + 1) = 2.50$ and $9.00/(1 + 2) = 3.00$. She therefore plans to drink the wine in the third year. From the perspective of the second year, however, the values of drinking the wine in the second and third year are, respectively, 5.00 and $9.00/(1 + 1) = 4.50$. She will therefore change her mind and open the bottle, prematurely, in the second year. Actually, if she is sophisticated and knows that she discounts the future hyperbolically, she will anticipate in the first year that if she waits until the second year, she will drink the wine then and not wait until the third year. Given that knowledge, she will prefer to drink the wine right away, in the first year.[11] In this scenario, what induces the premature consumption is merely the passage of time or, with a sophisticated agent, the anticipation of the effects of the passage of time.

In the case just described, no emotions or irrational beliefs are involved. A mechanism involving both of these is *urgency*, defined as a preference for early action over later action (not to be confused with a preference for early reward over later reward).[12] As illustrated by the proverb "Marry in haste, repent at leisure" and by many everyday situations, strong emotions can induce an urge to act immediately, with, as a consequence, little investment in information gathering. In situations of acute danger, where the opportunity costs of gathering more information exceed the benefits, such behavior can be rational. An agent who sees a shape on the path that may be either a stick or a snake is well advised to run away without trying to find out whether it is the one or the other.[13] To dawdle would be irrational procrastination. I consider the causes of such dawdling in the next section. Here I only want to emphasize that when the opportunity cost of waiting to find out more is negligible, as in a proposal of marriage, the urge to act immediately is irrational.

In an agent in the grip of a strong emotion, inaction can generate an intolerable tension. There is a felt need for what one might call *decisional*

---

10. Buehler, Griffin, and Ross, "Exploring the Planning Fallacy."
11. O'Donoghue and Rabin, "Doing It Now or Later."
12. Elster, "Urgency."
13. LeDoux, *Emotional Brain*.

*closure*, which leads the agent to act immediately and, as a consequence, to form low-quality beliefs based on poor information. A related but distinct mechanism arises from the need for *cognitive closure*.[14] Because the mind abhors a vacuum, the state of not having an opinion on a given subject may be felt as aversive. As a consequence, people may rush to form a belief—some belief or other—without gathering the amount of information that would be optimal from a rational-choice perspective. Actions taken on the basis of such will be irrationally premature.

## SOURCES OF PROCRASTINATING BEHAVIOR

Again, we begin with hyperbolic discounting. Suppose, as before, that the present value of one unit of utility at time t is $1/(1 + t)$. The agent has an ache and expects that the treatment by the doctor will be more painful the longer he delays the visit. If he goes today, he will suffer a pain of −2.75; tomorrow, it will be −5.00, and the day after −9.00. From today's perspective, the present values are, respectively −2.75, −5.00/(1 + 1) = −2.50, and −9.00/(1 + 2) = −3.00. The optimal choice is to postpone the visit until tomorrow. However, if the agent waits until the next day, the present values of seeing the doctor on that day and the next day will be, respectively, −5.00 and −9.00/(1 + 1) = −4.50. The agent will therefore change his mind and postpone the visit until the third day. As mentioned earlier, it is not the deferral of the visit from the first to the second day that qualifies the agent as irrational but his inability to stick to that deferral. If we assume that the agent is sophisticated, however, he will anticipate on the first day that he will wait until the third day. Since from the perspective of the first day, visiting the doctor that day is preferred to waiting until the third day, he will go immediately. In this case, unlike in the wine-drinking case, being inconsistent *and knowing it* improves the situation.

As shown by Ainslie, a sophisticated agent can also overcome her tendency to procrastination by *bundling* or bunching her choices, assuming that she faces the same choice between a small, early reward and a large, delayed reward on many successive occasions.[15] If she takes account of a sufficiently large number of occasions,[16] the sum of the present values (hyperbolically discounted) of all of the large rewards will exceed the sum of the present values of all of the small rewards. If she can persuade herself, by some kind of magical thinking, that choice of the small reward today predicts the same choice on all future occasions, she has an incentive to choose the large reward today. One kind of irrationality (procrastination induced by hyperbolic discounting) is overcome by another (magical thinking).

14. Kruglanski and Webster, "Motivated Closing of the Mind."
15. Ainslie, "Specious Reward" and *Picoeconomics*.
16. Skog, "Hyperbolic Discounting."

Consider next emotion and the lack of emotion as causes of procrastination. Lay claims that whereas procrastination often causes anxiety, "affect, per se, plays a minor role in producing dilatory behavior."[17] It is easy, however, to think of exceptions. To use Lay's own example,[18] a student who delays calling her parents at home might (1) feel a vague guilt about not having done so and (2) anticipate the acute guilt she will feel when her parents ask, "Why haven't you called before?" If the desire to avoid the second emotion is stronger than the desire to alleviate the first, she will defer calling. If the deferral has a larger impact on the second guilt than on the first, she may delay indefinitely (unless she needs to call her parents for money). Introspection suggests that this kind of thing happens frequently. Along somewhat similar lines, Fee and Tangney argue that individuals who suffer from perfectionism (more specifically, the belief that others expect them to be perfect) and also are prone to shame tend to procrastinate: "Shame-prone individuals, who are especially fearful of negative evaluations and the consequent feelings of shame, may be especially motivated to put off the 'moment of abysmal truth'—delaying, avoiding, and procrastinating."[19] While procrastinating, they will presumably also feel uncomfortable yet prefer that milder discomfort to anticipated shame.

Assuming that these behaviors occur, are they irrational? To the extent that they rest on hyperbolic discounting, they are. I may form the intention to call my parents this evening, but at the last minute, I am deterred by the imminent confrontation. These behaviors are also irrational to the extent that the emotions induce faulty cognitive processing. Fear and other emotions often cause objects to loom larger than they really are.

Consider next *lack* of emotion as a cause of procrastination. Antonio Damasio argues that in certain brain-damaged patients, the incapacity to experience emotion causes needless dawdling over trivial matters. Although I have questioned this causal link elsewhere,[20] I shall take it for granted here.

The patients in question spend inordinate amounts of time on trivial tasks. Damasio says about one of his patients that "the particular task . . . was actually being carried out *too* well, and at the expense of the overall purpose."[21] About another of his patients, he tells two strongly contrasting stories. On one day, his lack of "gut reactions" was highly advantageous when driving on an icy road, where most people tend to hit the brakes when they skid rather than gently pulling away from the tailspin. On the next day, Damasio says,

---

17. Lay, "Trait Procrastination," 111–112.
18. Lay, "Trait Procrastination," 98.
19. Fee and Tangney, "Procrastination," 181.
20. Elster, *Alchemies of the Mind*, 291–298.
21. Damasio, *Descartes' Error*, 37.

I was discussing with the same patient when his next visit to the laboratory should take place. I suggested two alternative dates, both in the coming month and just a few days apart from each other. The patient pulled out his appointment book and began consulting the calendar.... For the better part of a half-hour, the patient enumerated reasons for and against each of the two dates: previous engagements, proximity to other engagements, possible meteorological conditions, virtually anything that one could reasonably think about concerning a simple date. Just as calmly as he had driven over the ice, and recounted that episode, he was now walking us through a tiresome cost-benefit analysis, an endless outlining and fruitless comparison of options and possible consequences. [We] finally did tell him, quietly, that he should come on the second of the alternative dates. His response was equally calm and prompt. He simply said: "That's fine."[22]

Regardless of the causal origin of this behavior in the missing emotional dispositions, it is clear that the patient had a deficient understanding of the opportunity costs of decision making. (Maybe he would also have dawdled if he had seen a snakelike shape on the path.) Neglect of opportunity costs among non-brain-damaged subjects is also quite widespread, for two distinct reasons.

On the one hand, prospect theory has established that people are lossaverse, causing them irrationally to attach more importance (about twice as much) to out-of-pocket expenses than to opportunity costs.[23] A person engaged in comparison shopping might walk all around the city searching for the best deal, not realizing that the value to her of the time spent looking is greater than the economies she can expect to make. This amounts to irrational procrastination.

On the other hand, people often want to *act for a sufficient reason* rather than, say, simply tossing a coin among the available options.[24] Many people are so averse to ambiguity that they prefer to waste resources to determine and implement the decision that would have been optimal had the decision-making process itself been costless. The mechanism is reinforced by the one described in the previous paragraph but independent of it. To illustrate, let us consider an experiment reported by Shafir, Simonson, and Tversky.[25]

Some subjects received the following problem:

Imagine that you face the choice between two otherwise similar apartments with the following characteristics:
($x$) $290 a month, 25 minutes from campus
($y$) $350 a month, 7 minutes from campus
You can choose now between the two apartments or continue searching, in which case there is a risk of losing one or both of the apartments you have found.

22. Damasio, *Descartes' Error*, 193–194.
23. Kahneman and Tversky, "Prospect Theory."
24. Neurath, "Die Verirrten des Cartesius."
25. Shafir, Simonson, and Tversky, "Reason-Based Choice."

Other subjects received a similar problem, except that option *y* was replaced by option *x'*: $330 a month, 25 minutes from campus. Whereas the comparison between *x* and *y* involved a (presumably aversive) need to make a tradeoff, the comparison between *x* and *x'* is simple, since the former weakly dominates the latter, being better on one dimension of choice and equally good on the other. On average, subjects requested an additional alternative 40 percent of the time in the dominance condition and 64 percent in the tradeoff condition. These findings are inconsistent with rationality, according to which subjects should search for additional alternatives if and only if the expected value of searching exceeds that of the best alternative currently available. Because the best alternative offered in the dominance condition is also available in the tradeoff condition, rationality implies that the percentage of subjects who seek an additional alternative cannot be greater in the tradeoff condition, contrary to the observed data. Hence the subjects in that condition were engaging in irrational procrastination.

I suggest that the desire to act on sufficient reasons is an aspect of *perfectionism* and the concomitant indecisiveness, which are frequently cited causes of procrastination.[26] Samuel Johnson was highly aware of this tendency, as shown by the following observation from Boswell's *Life*: "We talked of the education of children; and I asked him what he thought was best to teach them first. JOHNSON. 'Sir, it is no matter what you teach them first, any more than what leg you shall put into your breeches first. Sir, you may stand disputing which is best to put in first, but in the mean time your breech is bare. Sir, while you are considering which of two things you should teach your child first, another boy has learnt them both.'" Johnson, being a Shakespeare scholar, may have had in mind the King's remark in *Hamlet* (3.3): "like a man to double business bound I stand in pause where I shall first begin, and both neglect."

Elsewhere I have argued that the rule in contested child-custody cases of determining which parent is more fit for custody undermines the very principle—promoting the best interest of the child—it is supposed to implement.[27] Assuming (probably contrary to fact) that courts, with the help of expert witnesses, are reliably able to identify the parent who is better fit for custody, the time-consuming and acrimonious legal process of doing so is likely to impose more harm on the child than allocating custody by the toss of a coin. In such cases, rationality is replaced by hyperrationality or pseudorationality.[28]

I conclude by considering "hot" and "cold" *cognitive biases* as a source of irrational procrastination. A frequently cited cold (nonmotivated) bias is the "planning fallacy," according to which people rely on inadequate heuristics when estimating how long it will take them to complete a given

---

26. Knaus, "Procrastination, Blame, and Change," 156.
27. Elster, *Solomonic Judgements*, chap. III.
28. Neurath, "Die Verirrten des Cartesius."

task.[29] They tend to underestimate the time partly because they fail to take account of how long it has taken them to complete similar projects in the past (the base-rate fallacy) and partly because they rely on smooth scenarios in which accidents or unforeseen problems never occur. The primary upshot is not that completion of the project takes longer than it should have, on rational-choice grounds, but rather that it takes more time than was anticipated. A secondary upshot, however, is that the longer completion time tends to induce further delays that could have been avoided had the planning fallacy not been committed in the first place. In some cases, moreover, the projects would not have been initiated at all if the planners had had more realistic ideas about the time needed. Finally, intuition suggests that committing the planning fallacy may cause agents to commit the sunk-cost fallacy.[30]

Concerning motivated or hot cognitive biases, we may distinguish between wishful thinking and motivated ignorance (a nonparadoxical form of self-deception). Not surprisingly, wishful thinking tends to induce underestimation of the time it will take to complete a given aversive task.[31] Motivated ignorance might be linked to the phenomenon of self-handicapping, which is often cited as an important cause of procrastination. If a person is uncertain about her true ability and afraid to find out what her true ability is, she might refrain from doing the work that might reveal her as having low ability. If she nevertheless does well, she can congratulate herself on her exceptional ability; if she does badly, she can blame it on lack of effort rather than on lack of competence. Because there is no prior belief that has to be suppressed, the paradoxes of self-deception do not arise.

## CONCLUSION

I said at the outset that rational-choice theory may provide a useful criterion for what counts as procrastination to the extent that it tells us what to do and when to do it. In other words, the theory has to include an *optimal stopping rule*: when to stop searching and pass to action. In many cases, however, this rule is subject to considerable indeterminacy. Sidney Winter observed that the idea of maximizing may create an infinite regress, since "the choice of a profit-maximizing information structure itself requires information, and it is not apparent how the aspiring profit maximizer acquires this information or what guarantees that he does not pay an excessive price for it."[32] Along the same lines, Leif Johansen

---

29. Kahneman and Tversky, "Prospect Theory" Buehler, Griffin, and Ross, "Exploring the Planning Fallacy."
30. Arkes and Blumer, "Psychology of Sunk Costs."
31. Sigall, Kruglanski, and Fyock, "Wishful Thinking."
32. Winter, "Economic 'Natural Selection,'" 252.

characterized the search process as "like going into a big forest to pick mushrooms. One may explore the possibilities in a certain limited region, but at some point one must stop the explorations and start picking because further explorations as to the possibility of finding more and better mushrooms by walking a little bit further would defeat the purpose of the hike. One must decide to stop the explorations on an intuitive basis, i.e. without actually investigating whether further exploration would have yielded better results."[33]

In such cases, rational-choice theory can at most set a lower and an upper limit to the time to be spent searching. When picking mushrooms, one should obviously look around a bit first, unless one is lucky enough to hit on a rich spot right away (this corresponds to the loop in figure 5-1). At the same time, on a day trip, it would be a self-defeating form of procrastination to wait until nightfall. Yet there is room between these extremes for choice among several *nonirrational* strategies. To the extent that we see procrastination as a violation of rationality, the indeterminacy of the latter notion implies some indeterminacy of the former.

---

33. Leif Johansen, *Lectures*, 144.

# Part II

# 6

# Prudence, Procrastination, and Rationality

*Olav Gjelsvik*

This chapter defends an aspect of the standard view that procrastination is doing things later in time than you should.[1] In particular, I defend the idea that procrastination involves violating some "should" and then discuss the nature of the "should" in question. My topic is therefore normative aspects of time discounting and preference reversals as a result of the passage of time. There might be many more ways of getting the timing of actions wrong than those I consider, but I shall not get into that here. Simply accounting for the wrongness of the preference reversals on which I will focus is a major task involving fundamental issues about rationality and consistency. It raises some delicate questions about reasons, such as whether the reasons in question can or must be external reasons.

## DEFINITIONS AND EXAMPLES OF PROCRASTINATION

Let me start by reviewing some definitions of procrastination.[2] The 1996 *Oxford English Dictionary* (*OED*) defines *procrastinate* as "to defer action, especially without good reason," while the *Cambridge International Dictionary of English* defines it as "to keep delaying something that must be done, often because it is unpleasant or boring." Academic scholars have also offered their own definitions: Solomon and Rothblum claim that "procrastination is delay in conjunction with subjective discomfort";[3] Silver and Sabini maintain that "procrastination is the illogical delay of

---

1. This phenomenon can, of course, also have positive consequences in particular cases, but that is a different issue.
2. Many others can be inspected at http://www.procrastinus.com, run by psychologist Piers Steel, from which the following two dictionary definitions are taken.
3. Solomon and Rothblum, "Academic Procrastination," 503.

behavior";[4] and Piers Steel writes that to procrastinate is "to voluntarily delay an intended course of action despite expecting to be worse off for the delay."[5] We can contrast Steel's definition with this one from economist Geir Asheim: "People procrastinate when faced with a task with immediate costs and future benefits, if they end up doing the task later than they thought they would and later than they wish they would."[6]

These different definitions all shed some light on procrastination. The last two are particularly useful, as well as usefully different. Let us consider the economist's definition first and provide some examples. Example 1 is as follows: I am on my way to the university to study (which has immediate costs and future benefits). I come across someone who has had a bad fall and is in need of help, with no one else around. I help the person, call for an ambulance, and so forth, and wait a long time for better help to arrive. I get to my task at the university much later than I thought I would. I wish that the person had not suffered the fall, that I had not been delayed in getting to the university, and that I had started studying earlier this day. According to Asheim's definition, I procrastinated in this case—but surely I did not. His definition therefore fails (in this case, at least).

This example can be modified to arrive at example 2, in which we assume that I was paid by the hour for my studying. The rest of the example is as before. I still did what I did, but now I lost two hours' pay. Then I would, *in a certain sense*, be worse off for the delay. I still did what I did, expecting to be worse off in this sense. So, it seems, I might have satisfied the conditions of Steel's definition, as long as being worse off is taken in this way. But it does not seem that I procrastinated in the modified example, either.

For example 3, let us forget about being paid by the hour and suppose instead that I had some subjective discomfort in doing what I did because I knew I was already behind in my studying. Yet I still did what I did, thinking it my duty to help the injured person, and this would seem to satisfy Solomon and Rothblum's definition. But in that case also, I would not say I procrastinated.

Consider, then, the *Cambridge* definition, which looks better than the others. There is, however, doubt about whether the act or goal that we delay when we procrastinate is always something we *must* do and, thus, doubt about whether the *must* condition in the *Cambridge* definition must always be satisfied. Furthermore, this definition also says that in cases of procrastination, what we delay is often unpleasant. "Often" is too vague for positive use here, and the unpleasant or boring nature of what

---

4. This is Steel's way of summing up Silver and Sabini's view (cited from www.procrastnus.com); Silver and Sabini ("Procrastinating," 208) use "irrational" rather than "illogical." (I shall not go into their view here.)
5. Steel, "Nature of Procrastination," 66.
6. Asheim, "Procrastination," 2.

is delayed might be important for the psychological understanding of a range of cases of procrastination, but it is not clear how this fact matters for a general definition, leaving its utility in question.

Note that in all three versions of the example above, in which I did not procrastinate, I did what I did for a good reason. Then, according to the *OED*, I did not procrastinate, implying that the *OED* seems to be closer to being right than the other definitions quoted. The point about the boring or unpleasant nature of what is delayed seems to be a way of identifying a reason for delaying that does not stand up as a good reason. So the *OED* definition can include all cases covered by the *Cambridge* definition but is clearly more general.

We must turn our attention to what a "good reason" here means, which is left too vague by the *OED*. Of course, this is a normative question and brings with it issues about how to understand reasons. In the central cases of procrastination, it is clear that we are speaking about prudential reasons, and it seems as if we are committing ourselves to particular normative views on prudential reasons by thinking of an act as an example of procrastination. If that is so, normative issues are essential for understanding the phenomenon we are out to understand.

## AKERLOF'S CASE

George Akerlof's famous case of procrastination involved sending a box of clothes belonging to his departed colleague Joseph Stiglitz.[7] The task was a bit complex, and it would take some hours, perhaps an entire workday, to complete. On each day, the story goes, Akerlof thought it best that he send the box the next day. But when the next day arrived, more immediate tasks loomed large. Then it seemed best that he do those immediate tasks that day and send the box the day after. This happened every day, and toward the end of the year, there was no point in sending the box. He could bring it with the rest of his own things at the end of the year, and the benefit to Stiglitz of sending it before his own things became smaller and finally insignificant.

This seems to be a case of preference reversal and dynamic inconsistency, the sort of case that is wonderfully captured by George Ainslie's theory of hyperbolic discounting.[8] Of course, it can also be accounted for by different mechanisms, such as O'Donoghue and Rabin's approach in their economic models of procrastination.[9] Let me leave that aside and focus on some of the essentials of the case, remaining neutral regarding the choice between Ainslie's and O'Donoghue and Rabin's explanatory

---

7. Akerlof, "Procrastination and Obedience."
8. Ainslie, *Picoeconomics*; see also his chapter 1 in this volume.
9. O'Donoghue and Rabin, "Choice and Procrastination," for instance.

mechanism underlying preference reversal as a result of the passage of time.

The preference reversal in both cases is connected with the "looming large" of the present day's tasks, the salience they exemplify in virtue of their temporal nearness. This, we think, plays a role in the explanation of the reversal: on every new day, what is close looms large in a special way. This is plainly a substantial assumption about a case that can be understood in different ways, but for now, I shall make the assumption that temporal salience is the crucial factor. The question is, of course, whether delaying the task of sending the box happened *for a good reason*. As I have described the case, Akerlof did himself see his actions as done for good reasons every day during their performance, which is not to be disputed. Our question becomes whether he changed his mind for no good reason from one day to the next, not whether he saw himself as acting for good reasons when acting each day. It is the question of whether his dynamic inconsistency is subject to criticism, and if so, why. If it is irrational, why is it irrational?

It might be useful to remember the example of heading to the university and finding the injured person who had fallen. Something unforeseen by me came up and provided a good reason for changing my mind; I realized I had better reasons for helping the man and delaying my task than for not delaying my task. That is how we think of this case, precisely because I had such a good reason for changing my mind about when to study; therefore, we do not regard it as a case of procrastination. If the change of mind, the preference reversal from day 1 to day 2 in Akerlof's case, is a response to the fact that something provides a good reason for changing one's mind, then the case is not a case of procrastination by the OED definition.

The only possibly relevant thing that has happened during the night in the Akerlof case is, by assumption, that time has passed. As a result, he thinks it better to do the immediate tasks at hand on day 2. He then finds himself thinking those things more worthwhile, as I found it more worthwhile to help the injured person. That is what explains why he did what he did and what explains the curious fact that the box was never sent.

Let me now introduce a fourth version of our example. In this version, I cycle slowly toward the university. On the way, I meet someone who asks me to help him in a quite pointless task. He wants to see whether he is able, with the help of another normal person, to lift a stone that lies there. It seems pretty clear that lifting the stone serves no further purpose; he is basically doing this to pass the time. I do not like exercise much, yet I find myself spending a lot of time trying to find out whether the two of us can lift this stone. I may even think of myself as acting for good reasons. Still, I claim, we are prone to think, "I am just doing all this stone lifting because I do not want to study." So, I am inclined to say, "I am procrastinating, since there is no *good* reason for delaying my studying."

There might be further questions about whether this is a case of procrastination: the case might point to different mechanisms in procrastination and may touch upon the *Cambridge* definition. In this case, I seem to indulge myself with a pointless task, and in so doing, I effectively delay an important task. If that is how we should understand the case, it satisfies the *OED* definition of being delay for no good reason. The question before us is whether we should think of the Akerlof case as one where the delay is for no good reason. That, it seems to me, is a substantial normative question, and there is also a question of whether the change of mind is bad because it is irrational or on alternative grounds. There are views that are committed to seeing the change of mind as a result of hyperbolic discounting as simply a change of preference outside the scope of normative considerations. That seems to be a natural way of understanding Ainslie's view, given certain further assumptions.[10] Part of our *problématique* concerns what is subject to normative considerations and in what way. There are, in fact, at least two normative issues here, one about time discounting in general and another about dynamic inconsistency, and in both cases, we face the question of whether the failures are rational failures or just bad in some other way. Furthermore, in either case, there are issues about the conception of reasons. I shall approach both cases by looking at a view that differs from my view on at least one of these normative issues.

## ELSTER: A CONTRASTING VIEW

"In my view," Jon Elster writes in his recent book *Explaining Social Behavior*, "pure time discounting, by itself, is not irrational." He also holds that "rationality is subjective through and through."[11] This statement is part of an argument in which he establishes that it *could not* be rational to take a pill that changes your discount rate. This is so because you see the world through your "discount lenses," and that is the only perspective on value that you have available. There is no reason available, no reason you can perceive, to change the way things look to you, Elster argues. The plausibility of this argument depends on the plausibility of an internalist view of reasons, and it also exhibits the limitations of such a view. We might also say that Elster's view at this point ties in with an explicitly explanatory view of rationality: excepting the cases of irrational beliefs, explaining

---

10. Of course, Ainslie tries to explain how one can nevertheless achieve dynamic consistency in a range of cases. I am now simply assuming that this is not one of them. We can hold that when all rational means are employed to combat dynamic inconsistency, and we are as rational as we can be, then there are no further reasons that can account for the badness of the dynamic inconsistency. As we then see things on an internalist conception of reasons, the remaining inconsistency is not bad as long as "ought" implies "can." In that case, this delay is not against reason. See Bratman, "Planning and Temptation," for a very good discussion of rationality issues around hyperbolic discounting.

11. Elster, *Explaining Social Behavior*, 116, 209–213.

action delineates the use we make of rationality here.[12] My exponential discount rate is a given in this type of explanation; since that is so, the discount rate is not, in itself, irrational.

Assume that you also exhibit a pattern of preference reversal. Why should this pattern be irrational? Let us assume that the shape of your discount function explains why your preferences reverse (this is so according to Ainslie and O'Donoghue and Rabin). If any actual discounting is not irrational as long is the discounting is exponential, why should consequences of the shape of the discount function—that is, reversals—be irrational in the hyperbolic case? Elster writes, indeed, that dynamic inconsistency is standardly taken as a hallmark of irrationality, and in chapter 5 of this volume, he explicitly endorses that view himself. What are his reasons for holding this view? His more general views concerning discounting seem to suggest that dynamic inconsistency is *not* irrational. It is natural to think that an actual preference reversal cannot be irrational if it is just a causal result of something that is not, as such, subject to rationality requirements; and an actual discount rate is not subject to rationality requirements on Elster's view.

Suppose that you are a hyperbolic discounter and have done everything in your power to prevent a preference reversal. You have accepted all of the rational arguments an internalist about reasons can recognize about the issues. Suppose also that "ought" implies "can," and you cannot prevent the reversal. Then why should the reversal be irrational? There is not even a good reason against the reversal if no "ought" against it can be established. Note also that if hyperbolic discounting is not irrational, then there may be nothing irrational in the Akerlof case (if there is nothing he fails to do that could have prevented the reversal). In that case, Akerlof never changed his mind without good reason. He actually *had* a good reason for his new preference on day 2, and there was no reason against changing his mind *if he could not do otherwise*. Therefore, either Akerlof did not procrastinate, or our working definition of procrastination is wrong.

There are some aspects of Elster's general view on rationality that pull in a different direction, and these aspects come up in the general discussion of consistency of preferences. Elster accepts the transitivity of preferences as a requirement of rationality.[13] Inconsistency arises out of the failure of transitivity, for example, "by offering the agent a move from a less preferred to a more preferred option in return for a sum of money. Since intransitive preferences cycle, this operation can be repeated indefinitely, bringing about the person's ruin by a series of stepwise

---

12. It is interesting to note that Bernard Williams's conception of internal reason cannot really add anything to this explanatory conception of reasons in this particular case of discounting. You cannot simply reason your way out of discounting if you are a discounter and all of the facts are in. This is Elster's point as well, and it seems correct.
13. Elster, *Explaining Social Behavior*, 193.

improvements."[14] Elster thus accepts a money-pump argument against the possibility of intransitive preferences being rational, a type of reasoning that goes back decades. Reasons provided by money pumps are pragmatic in the sense that they essentially account for irrationality by appealing to the (bad) consequences of having intransitive preferences: you lose money. That is an external fact, and this is a different type of appeal from what Elster perhaps ought to accept; as he himself stresses, consequences by themselves do not explain anything.

Elster rejects a very similar type of reasoning in favor of seeing excessive discounting as irrational: "one might, to be sure, take the word 'rational' in an objective sense, implying that a rational agent is one who makes decisions that make his life go better as judged by objective criteria such as health, longevity or income."[15] Elster is thus perfectly clear that your life may go worse because you discount, but your life may go worse for any number of reasons: you are selfish, too keen on lifting stones, or whatever. Life may go badly if you spend much time lifting stones, but it is not irrational to spend your time lifting stones instead of getting an education or not caring much about other human beings. It might be a failing of sorts, but it is not a rational failing. Failing transitivity is, however, a rational failing. On this latter point, we agree, but we seem to reason differently. I do not hold that intransitivity is bad because of its bad consequences but because of the wrongness of the intransitivity, independently of its consequences.

I thus find a difference and a possible tension between how Elster reasons about synchronic consistency and how he reasons about discounting. He allows appealing to bad consequences in the first case but not in the second. I find this tension interesting; I shall argue that there is pressure from the general considerations in favor of the view that intransitive preferences are wrong that can be brought to bear on the case of dynamic inconsistency and possibly on discounting. I want to bring this out by looking in much more detail at issues around preference and consistency. I aim to argue that the problems about transitivity themselves point us toward seeing rationality as not, as such, constrained or delineated by explanatory notions—that is, the notion of explanation of action. The normative aspects of deliberation transcend the explanatory perspective, and external reasons provide the ground we have for thinking of actual cases of intransitive preferences as irrational.

To sum up before proceeding: If the Akerlof case is to be made to fit into the *OED* definition of procrastination—which seems a very good start—then we must see preference reversals as a result of hyperbolic discounting as bad. Furthermore, we must at least see such changes as changes that there is reason against, and the way to do this, it seems, is to see them as irrational. There is, admittedly, a question about whether the badness in question is irrationality and what conception of rationality can

---

14. Elster, *Explaining Social Behavior*, 193–194.
15. Elster, *Explaining Social Behavior*, 209.

uphold that view of the badness. To explore this question, I will look at transitivity of preferences in general.[16]

## PREFERENCES AND TRANSITIVITY

There is wide agreement about transitivity being a requirement upon rational preferences, but there are quite different approaches and arguments in support of the view. My strategy here will be to look at reasons in favor of seeing synchronic transitivity as rational and to ask whether these reasons have implications for how to think about the dynamic case. Since many (or even most) writers endorse money-pump arguments to support transitivity in the synchronic case, I shall look at what that stance presupposes.

I mentioned above the pragmatic arguments in favor of transitivity. We know quite well what transitivity is and what it means. If A, B, and C stand for the sort of thing we have preferences between and > stands for "is preferred to," then the requirement upon a rational person is that if A > B and B > C, then A > C. We see immediately that if this requirement is to amount to anything that makes a practical difference in real life, it needs to be combined with an ability to keep track of options, remember them, and so forth. If the subject does not keep track of the fact that A stands for the same option throughout, it is easy to explain what looks like intransitivity. Subjectively speaking, it would then not be an instance of intransitivity. We would then perhaps take intransitivity as decisive evidence that the person thinks of the options differently from how we do. If there were no objective requirement about identifying and keeping track of options in the background, then there is a possibility that transitivity of preferences could collapse to a formal requirement upon interpretation. If it did, then no money-pump argument and no pragmatic argument of a similar sort would get a hold. A possible conjecture is this: If the explanatory perspective had full priority when it came to rationality, and rationality is subjective through and through, then we should probably reject pragmatic money-pump arguments. Such arguments are acceptable on the view that real-world consequences determine what is rational; if there are no questions about the rationality of ends beyond the actual ends that determine what the agent does, then one cannot appeal to money pumps to settle issues about rationality.

To rely on real-world consequences, we need both to say something about the identities of the things between which we have preferences and to impose transitivity as a requirement upon the preferences we have between such things (thus individuated). Then it is possible to employ a money-pump argument. It does not follow that it is a generally valid

---

16. We are here discussing discounting the value of well-being, not the value of commodities; a modest discounting of commodities is quite acceptable in a productive economy.

argument, and the validity would, among other things, depend on the identity conditions of the things between which we have preferences.

I believe there are two natural ways to think of these things and two notions of preference. The first is what we may call standing preference or ordinary preference, a general attitude toward two types of things. For instance, I may prefer walking to running or prefer that I am walking to that I am running. This does not determine what I will do in a particular choice situation. In the same way, it does not mean that there are no situations in which I prefer to run. This is simply because actual options between which I choose have very many properties, and I have to weigh many standing preferences against each other.

I will discuss options and preferences between options, but first I will point out one important aspect of standing preferences. In order for me to have this standing preference between walking and running, it is clear that I need to know or have reasonable beliefs about what the activities of walking and running are and thus be able to hold on in thought to the sort of thing I prefer to another thing. Of course, the types of things in question can be refined in very many ways, but what remains is that this type of preference is an attitude toward an activity type.

The other type of preference is between options or events, the sorts of things we sometimes have to make choices between and that we can intend to do. Again, there is a requirement on us to know or have reasonable beliefs about the properties of these options, which may be numerous. We might be mistaken about what properties they have, of course, as we may be mistaken about the properties of walking and running. But without the ability to have thoughts about these options, keep track of them, and grasp the conditions that would make it true that something is the same option again, it does not make much sense to require transitivity.

Assume that we allow an entirely subjective way of individuating options, so that the identity of an option depends essentially on what other options are presented when we are asked for a preference. Assume that we are always asked for a preference between two options and that the identity of the options depends on the other options presented. Then there is no way for options to keep their identity from question to question in the sequence of questions that could reveal cyclic preferences, and we would not be able to detect failings of transitivity. For transitivity to have any bite, we need to keep track of options and be able to know what it would take to be the same option again, even if presented in a different way. If we fail at these things, then transitivity is an empty requirement; a money-pump argument presupposes that we keep track of options.

## PREFERENCES AND JUDGMENTS

What, then, makes something a preference? How can we reason with preferences? Here I rely to some extent, but not wholly, on John Broome's work. I will, however, flag a disagreement with Broome that matters here. Broome holds that we can always move from a judgment about what is best to do to an intention to do it by reasoning only. I disagree. The failure to form the intention need not be a reasoning failure. Let us note that for now and move on.

One issue from Broome is whether we should think of the transitivity of preference as derivative of the transitivity of the "better than" relation. Preference transitivity can be explained in that case by the transitivity of the notion of thinking or judging something better than something else. Broome argues in favor of seeing preference and judgment as amounting to the same thing, especially for the case of an ordinary or standing preference, such as that between walking and running.[17] Looking at the case of standing preference, it may be somewhat difficult to make a case for a real difference between a judgment to the effect that walking is better than running and a preference for walking rather than running, perhaps because there are no direct consequences for action from preferences of this type. But logically speaking, there is always the possibility of a mismatch between judgment and the corresponding motivational state (preference), which Broome seems to fail to acknowledge properly.[18]

If we turn to the other type of preference, that between options, we see that one type of irrationality consists in failing to respond motivationally to one's judgments about which option is best. The motivational response could be in the form of an (irrational) intention, which is common enough. It exhibits the general structure of weak will and requires us to see judgments about which option is better or best as a normal judgment employing the "better than" relation and also to see failing to be motivated in accordance with such judgment as a rational failure. Whether this rational failure is a failure of reasoning is a further question, and this is where Broome and I go in different ways; I hold that it is a rational failure but not necessarily a failure of reasoning. (I will not here go into the possibility of incomplete reasoning.)

Let us look at the strategy of starting with the "better than" relation. Note that when it comes to preferences of the first type, standing preferences, the "better than" relation says that something that is a walking is better than something that is a running as far as the exemplification of these two properties are concerned. In the second case, however, we compare options, each one with many potential properties and dimensions of comparison, and we judge that A is better than B. We then presuppose that all that matters for value and comparison is provided by the identities

---

17. See Broome, "Reasoning with Preferences?" 206–207.

18. Of course, some writers are hesitant about the contents of judgments to the effect that something is better, and some will explain the contents of such judgments *starting from* the notion of preference. I am discussing such views in relation to preference reversals that result from time passing, arguing that the views in question will have great difficulty in accounting for the badness of many such preference reversals.

of the options A and B. All issues about value must depend on the constitutive properties of the options. If they did not, there would be no truth of the matter about whether A is better than B, all things and all dimensions considered.

Looking at things this way, we can see the transitivity requirement on preferences as stemming from the transitivity of the "better than" relation, and we can see preferences as actual motivational states that ought to reflect the value relations we commit ourselves to in correct judgments about which action type or which option is better.

## FIRST ROUND OF CONSEQUENCES: RATIONALITY AND EXPLANATION OF ACTION

If we see things this way, there is always the possibility that we fail when we respond motivationally to our value judgments, and in such cases, we are irrational. One possible such failure is the failure of transitivity; in that case, the preferences we have do not match the transitivity of the "better than" relation that we must rationally judge to hold if confronted with the issue.

It is good that we can account for the possibility of this particular type of irrationality. Another benefit of adopting a substantive view of rationality is the perspective it brings to the pragmatic arguments in favor of transitivity, which often point to the fact that being exposed to money pumps might ruin us if our preferences are not transitive. This is true but fails to distinguish between crucially different cases, namely, cases where we value some other aspect of the choice more than we value money and cases where no such complication exists. Consider this example, discussed by Philip Pettit: I prefer a large apple to an orange and an orange to a small apple, yet I still prefer a small apple to a large apple. The explanation is that we are speaking of particular options, and the situation is such that it would be impolite to choose the larger of the two apples, but the issue of politeness does not arise in the other comparisons involving either apple and an orange.[19] In cases where it does arise, it might be right and rational to lose money through repeated choice for the sake of politeness. Losing money is your correct and reasoned choice. On the other hand, if money is the only concern we have in some repeated choice situation, which is normally assumed by the money-pump examples, then the present account provides a perfectly good explanation of why we could not lose money in a repeated choice by responding rationally in our motivations to

---

19. Pettit, "Preferences." With this example in hand, we can also see the plausibility of a case where we judge that politeness considerations do not stand in the way of preferring the larger of two apples in the present situations—we know these people so well, for instance—but where we still fail to respond motivationally to that insight. We need to be able to capture this irrationality as well.

correct judgments about which option is better. This can therefore account for the general correctness of the money-pump argument, properly understood.

If we look at an approach that makes explanation the concern that delineates rationality and ask whether that perspective can account for the general validity of the money-pump argument in favor of transitivity, it seems that the answer is no. Accepting money pumps means rejecting the view that rationality is subjective through and through. If some money pump is ruining us, there is probably some explanation of that fact in how the options are seen and valued. If the explanatory demands determine what is rational, then it seems that we will not necessarily be in a position to say that it is irrational to be subjected to a money pump, at least not if it is entirely up to the subject how options are individuated and given value. To be able to explain the irrationality of a money pump, we need to impose requirements on how to individuate and conceive of options, and the burden we then take on seems to be as heavy as the objectivist and cognitivist way of thinking about rational value judgments employed above. This seems to follow if we are out to account for the correctness of a money-pump argument.

Can we just use a money-pump argument and abstain from accounting in a deeper way for its correctness? Certainly, in some sense we can, but that position has severe shortcomings. It seems to be mute on how to account for the difference between the case where it is rational to lose money and the case where it is not. A money-pump argument approach to rationality that cannot account for that difference seems too weak. It cannot, in general, account for the difference between rationally losing money and irrationally losing money, and that is a difference we cannot afford to lose.

## SECOND ROUND OF CONSEQUENCES: PREFERENCE REVERSALS AND NORMATIVITY

What is the importance of all of this to the synchronic notion of transitivity of preference? We seem to have established the plausibility of a general type of approach that accounts for the requirement of transitivity of preference by invoking the transitivity of a betterness relation, an external relation that we track in normative judgment. We achieve the position by making it a rationality requirement that we respond motivationally in accordance with the correct judgment about what is better. This approach can see an actual objective failure of transitivity (possibly inviting a money pump) as a failure to respond motivationally as we should to transitivities we hold on to in thought or as a failure to recognize or track transitive relations in our judgments. These failures are distinct, and both failures are possible.

With these distinctions in hand, we see how the explanatory issues and the normative issues may come apart and also how certain types of rational failure can be explained without this having any normative significance. Taken together with a recognition of the general difficulties that face an explanatory approach to rationality when accounting for the correctness of a money-pump argument, we can finally raise the question of whether the dynamic inconsistencies of preference should be treated differently from the synchronic inconsistencies of preference when it comes to normative issues. And I cannot see why they should be treated differently at all.

Of course, I recognize that there are very nice explanatory approaches in the dynamic case, particularly Ainslie's approach; also, we may be better placed to get hold of good explanations in the dynamic case than in the synchronic case. When things are stretched out in time, there might be much clearer patterns to study, and we might be able to study the mechanisms governing these patterns better and understand them better. The normative facts are also much harder to grasp in these cases of decision making than, for instance, in logical and statistical reasoning. In those cases, the correctness of the logical or statistical facts has a robust independent standing, and we are not in doubt that tendencies in our actual reasoning, when failing these correctness standards by employing heuristics, shortcuts, and snap judgments with evolutionary benefits, are without relevance for the correctness issue.

Thinking about the relationship between explanation and rationality in the synchronic case of intransitive preferences, we tend to think in ways quite parallel to the cases of heuristics in logic and statistics. The actual deviations from the norm of transitivity have no normative significance in the synchronic case. The way I see things, the preference reversal through time is a candidate for being seen in exactly the same way, as it represents a change on the motivational side with no clear relevance for the question of how we ought to be motivated, in a normative sense of "ought." This is further boosted by the natural view that the evaluational judgment about what choice brings the most well-being need not change through time; it is the motivational response to that judgment that changes in significant patterns while the judgment remains correct. If so, a preference reversal is just a very vivid type of example of a general phenomenon, a failure to respond in motivation to what we think right. Of course, with stretching out in time, it is much easier to allow one's thoughts be flavored by one's actual motivation and in that way make it easier to live with the motivations one has than it is in a synchronic case. Manipulation of oneself also requires time.

The situation, then, is that we have established the shortcomings of an explanatory approach to rationality by arguing that it cannot account properly for the correctness of the money-pump argument. In the dynamic case, we can also see the motivations resulting from hyperbolic discounting as inviting a money pump; people are all the time worse off than they would have been without such discounting. This real-world money pump works by exploiting preference reversals and irrational motivations. The only difference compared with the other money pump is, again, the way things are stretched out in time; for that reason, you cannot get ruined on the spot but only get much poorer in the long run than you might have been otherwise. The more you discount, the poorer you get.

A very basic fact when considering the normative matter is that, normatively speaking, we are beings with a rational requirement for something we can think of as motivational unity, which is exemplified by transitivity. We are also beings whose existence is stretched out in time and whose motivational unity ought to be similarly stretched not to be subjected to money pumps. Of course, we know that our motivational unity is not stretched out in time the way it ought to be, but for the present, we are focusing on the normative point. Doing so, we see first that the point about the way we ought to be motivated, or the way it would be right to be motivated, can easily be seen as an issue about prudential values and prudential motivation. We might think that it is a prudential value that we have this motivational unity and a failure of prudential motivation if we do not have it. But is it a rational failure? That depends essentially on how substantial a notion of rationality we ought to work with.

I do not want to commit myself to very detailed views here, since that would involve large and complex issues about whether there are reasons to be rational.[20] My point is simply that as long as we have left the purely explanatory notion of rationality behind—and we have to do that to be able to make proper sense of the money-pump arguments about rationality—then there is no good reason not to treat the "ought" questions about motivational unity in the dynamic or diachronic case as we treat them in the case of synchronic transitivity. There is no consideration against doing this apart from, possibly, points about explanation. We must also note that synchronic transitivity must be understood as a response to an external normative fact, the transitivity of the betterness relation. The notion of rationality is therefore fully tainted by external normative facts as soon as you accept money-pump arguments, and there is no general motivation against that. Recognizing that we are already externalists, the synchronic and dynamic cases look alike. If they look alike, the rationality issues and the normative issues are also the same; we have no ground for differentiating between them. Motivational unity is a rational requirement in both cases.

With this point, I conclude my normative discussion. The issue I have addressed is whether preference reversal merely as a result of time's passing can be considered rational, and I have answered that it cannot. My argument exploits the parallel to the fact that transitivity of preference is a requirement of rationality. Preference reversal is a central case for understanding procrastination, and I have provided a ground not just

---

20. See Broome, "Does Rationality Consist," and Gjelsvik, "Are There Reasons."

for saying that it is bad but also for saying that its badness is that it is irrational.

The general issue of time discounting as such may, however, be relevant for assessing this conclusion. There are at least three positions on the nature of time discounting. Discounting the future might be just a taste, and as such it is beyond being rational or irrational.[21] On the other hand, if it is more than a subjective taste, then either there are procedures by which we can reach some intersubjective verdict starting from exemplary motivations, or there is an objective and external fact about correctness in discounting. In the last case, we might go wrong both in our judgments about what discounting is correct and in our motivational responses. One might hold that we are irrational only when the discounting revealed by our motivations fails to match the judgments we make about correct discounting. The latter position needs to explain why the case of discounting here is different from the case of intransitive preferences: in the case of intransitivity, the preferences are irrational as soon as they fail to match the objective value relations. I will not pursue the point, but perhaps the cases that can be supported directly by an appeal to motivational unity only are special, because in those cases, we are clearly dealing with a rationality requirement. The case of discounting in general (including exponential discounting) is different; perhaps we are dealing with a prudential requirement in that case, however much you discount.

## CONCLUSION (RETURN TO AKERLOF'S CASE)

I interpreted Akerlof's example of procrastination as a case of dynamic inconsistency with repeated preference reversal. It seems to fit into the view of procrastination as delaying for no good reason, since the preference reversal is something that happens for no good reason. The preference reversal is, in fact, irrational.

Now, it also seems clear that the case is not at all specific about what sort of insight the subject has into his own situation or whether the person expects to be worse off because of the delay. A sophisticated agent would have insight into the mechanisms of discounting and understand what is going on. The Akerlof case is, however, described such that the agent's insight into his own self-control problems is not necessarily present. I would think that in real life, such insight is often partially present, sometimes fully present, and sometimes not present at all. We tend to think of all of those cases as procrastination. If that is right, procrastination does not necessarily mean acting against your better judgment. You may procrastinate without perceiving what you do as exemplifying a self-control problem, even if you sometimes are aware of the self-control

21. My understanding of discounting in general owes much to Broome's discussion in *Ethics out of Economics*, chap. 4.

problem when you procrastinate. Since this is so, it seems that there are cases of procrastination that are not cases of weak will (understood as acting against your own better judgment).[22]

The relationship between weak will and procrastination is therefore complex. There is an interesting difference between the Akerlof case and the example of meeting the person who wants you to take part in lifting the stone. The difference is that there is a new element you have to take a stand on in the latter case; the stand you take might reflect poor judgment, and in that case, you delay your action for no good reason. Is it then procrastination? Or is it just poor judgment about the value of lifting the stone? Does it matter for the issue of whether this is a case of procrastination whether your poor judgment in the case is driven by a desire to delay, such as that caused by aversion to today's task? Is this a case of procrastination only if such a desire to delay succeeds in boosting your judgment of the value of lifting the stone? I would suggest that either the preference reversal that causes the delay in action is irrational in itself, or the delay is caused by an irrational desire for delay. In both cases, we delay for no good reason, and there are prudential reasons for not delaying, whether recognized or not. But there is no requirement on procrastination that we recognize these good reasons for not delaying, as there would be in a case of weak will.

I confirm the view that procrastination is delaying an action for no good reason. My view is also close to that of Steel, according to which procrastination involves delaying while expecting to be worse off for the delay. Central cases of procrastination seem to fit that pattern, but the borderline issues are very delicate, as is the notion of expecting to be worse off. Akerlof saw himself as having good reason to delay on each day. In one sense, he did not expect to be worse off, as he did not see past what was happening day after day. Still, it seems to me, he procrastinated. Expecting to be worse off is therefore not the only way of making true that the delay is for no good reason. I have established a sense of "good reason" in which Akerlof had no good reason for delay, even if he saw himself as having good reasons for what he did each day, by establishing the irrationality of dynamic inconsistency. This irrationality rests on external reasons and can exist even if it goes unrecognized. Procrastination can thus exhibit recognized or unrecognized irrationalities, and the notion of good reason employed to capture the concept is externalist.

---

22. I am therefore in broad agreement with Sarah Stroud's chapter 3 in this volume.

# 7

# Procrastination and Personal Identity

## Christine Tappolet

As Ilia Ilitch Oblomov was perfectly aware when he woke up, there were a great many things that he had to do.[1] For one thing, he had to reply to an alarming letter from his estate manager. So, as soon as he woke up, he formed the intention to get out of bed, have his tea, and do some serious thinking in order to decide which measures had to be taken to save his estate. But after half an hour spent worrying about the intention he had formed, Oblomov judged that he could just as well have his tea while in bed as he usually did; nothing, he thought, would prevent him from thinking while being stretched out. And as the morning proceeded, he just kept postponing doing any thinking, taking any action, and even getting out of bed. Indeed, Oblomov spent his entire life putting off the things he had to do, so that in the end, he died in poverty and loneliness.

Oblomov's procrastination clearly had a very high cost, something of which he must have been aware. What, one wonders, does such apparent lack of concern for one's future entail with respect to our conception of personal identity? It would seem that Oblomov failed to consider his future as truly his own. If so, procrastination would point in the opposite direction of phenomena such as promising, which have been used to argue against reductionist accounts of personal identity that place psychological continuity at the heart of personal identity.[2] My aim in this chapter is to examine what procrastination entails with respect to personal identity theories.

In the first section, I explain why the kind of concern we seem to have for what have been called our "future selves" has been thought to be problematic for psychological continuity theories of personal identity. An important assumption in these debates is that we normally have what is often referred to as a "special concern" for our future selves. I think this assumption is far from warranted, something that becomes particularly clear when one considers procrastination. In the second section, I turn to procrastination with the aim of getting a better understanding of its nature.

1. See Goncharov, *Oblomov*.
2. See Williams, "Persons," 7.

In the third section, I consider how procrastination involves harming one's future selves. I argue that in most cases of imprudent procrastination, the procrastinator imposes an uncompensated burden on her future self, something that is best explained by a lack of concern for her future self. In the fourth section, I conclude with some remarks on the lessons that follow for personal identity theories. I suggest that the objections to psychological continuity accounts based on the idea of a special concern we have, or have reason to have, for our future selves are in serious trouble.

## "SPECIAL CONCERN" AND PERSONAL IDENTITY THEORIES

We usually take it for granted that whatever kind of beings we happen to be, we are beings who persist over time. When we project into the future, such as when we plan for a holiday, sign a contract, or make a promise, we, and the people around us, assume that *we now* are the same, numerically speaking, as *we in the past* and *we in the future*. In particular, each of us appears to have a special concern for what he or she considers his or her own future. We seem to care in a very special way for how our so-called future selves will fare. As John Perry noted, when I am told that someone will be run over by a truck tomorrow, I might be saddened, feel pity, and think reflectively about the frailty of life. But if my informer adds that I am the person who will be run over, "a whole new set of emotions rise in [my] heart":[3] fear or even panic will overcome me. The thought that death awaits *me* and not some other person seems to make an important difference with respect to the kind of emotion I feel. In the same way, the thought that good things will happen to *me* rather than to someone else seems to make a difference. The hostage who is told that someone else from the group will be liberated might feel happy for that person, but she might also feel envy. If she is told that she is the one to be liberated, her attitude is likely to change to hope or joy.

The concern in question, then, seems to involve being disposed to undergo a range of emotions, depending on how our future selves fare: fear if we think that things will go badly for them, happiness if we think that they will go well, hope if we think that there is a fair chance that they will improve, and so on.[4] It is a kind of caring. We normally care for a number of different persons. What is supposed to be special about the concern we have for our future selves is simply the intensity of the emotions involved.[5]

---

   3. Perry, "Importance," 66.
   4. For that notion, see Shoemaker, "Caring."
   5. See Jennifer Whiting, "Friends and Future Selves," 557, for the claim that other types of relations can come with and seem to justify the same kind of concern as the one we have for ourselves. When a mother is told that it is her own child who is going to be run over, she is likely to be overcome not by some vague sadness and pity, but by fear and panic.

We usually care more for our future selves than we care for the future of other persons.

It has been suggested that the special concern we have for our own future is a natural feature, one we share with other living things and which is the result of natural selection. As Derek Parfit puts it, "animals without such concern would be more likely to die before passing on their genes."[6] (In fact, this is not as obvious as Parfit suggests. A being that readily sacrifices itself for its offspring might, in fact, be much more successful in spreading its genes.)

Whether natural and fitness-enhancing or not, the putative fact that we have a special concern for beings we consider to be our future selves has long been thought to make for an important objection to reductionist conceptions of personal identity. In particular, it has been argued that psychological continuity accounts sit poorly with the alleged fact that we have this special sort of concern.

According to the best-known version of such accounts, namely Parfit's, X at $t_1$ is the same person as Y at $t_2$ if and only if X is uniquely psychologically continuous with Y, where psychological continuity consists in overlapping chains of strong psychological connectedness, itself consisting in significant numbers of direct psychological connections.[7] So, what is needed is the holding of particular psychological connections, such as when I remember having climbed the Gran Paradiso or when I now act on a New Year's resolution to play the clarinet more often. Since I might now have forgotten things I could remember 10 years ago, what is required is that there are overlapping chains of such connections. The strength of the psychological connectedness is a matter of quantity. What is required is that X and Y have a significant number of psychological connections, not just that Y has one or two memories related to X's experiences, for instance. It has to be noted that Parfit's psychological criterion also requires that there is no "branching." That means that cases in which X has continuous psychologies with two or more putative future selves are excluded by definition; this is why Y has to be *uniquely* continuous with X.

In brief, the "special concern" argument against psychological continuity accounts starts with the claim that such accounts fail to explain this concern.[8] It could be explained only if one postulated some entity, such as a soul or a Cartesian ego, to which the past, present, and future experiences would belong. But if it is true that our future selves are only psychological descendents of our present selves (or at least, if it is true that we *believe* them to be psychological descendants), it should not be expected that we have such a special concern for our future selves. Rather, we

---

6. Parfit, *Reasons and Persons*, 308. For the naturalness claim, see McDowell, "Reductionism," 246; and Johnston, "Human Concerns," 158–159.
7. Parfit, *Reasons and Persons*, 207; see also Shoemaker, "Personal Identity and Ethics."
8. This argument goes back to objections to the Lockean theory of personal identity; see Butler, "Of Personal Identity"; and Sidgwick, *Methods of Ethics*, 419.

would expect that our feelings toward these selves would be more like the feelings we have with respect to the future of other people. However, since we have this special concern, there must be something wrong in the assumption that one's identity is a matter of psychological continuity.

Furthermore—and this, in fact, makes for a different argument—it would seem that if one's identity with future selves is only a matter of psychological continuity, no special concern of the kind envisaged would be justified or rationally required. The problem, it is claimed, is that it is natural to think that we have reason to have such a concern for our futures selves. Prudence might indeed be thought to involve the claim that we are rationally required to have such a concern for our future selves or, maybe even more stringently, that we are rationally required to have an *equal concern* for our present and futures selves. This, in any case, is what Sidgwick thought: "my feelings a year hence should be just as important to me as my feelings next minute, if only I could make an equally sure forecast of them. Indeed this equal and impartial concern for all parts of one's conscious life is perhaps the most prominent element in the common notion of the *rational*—as opposed to the merely *impulsive*—pursuits of pleasure."[9] Thus, an important objection to psychological continuity accounts, which goes back to Parfit's "extreme claim,"[10] is that on such accounts, a present self has no reason to be concerned about her future selves or, in any case, that she has no more reason to be concerned about her future selves than she has to be concerned about the future of other people.[11]

The question of whether or not this second objection is convincing has been extensively discussed. Some, such as Perry, have argued that psychological continuity accounts can make room for reasons to have a special concern for one's future selves even if we don't assume that we are numerically identical with our future selves. After all, our futures selves are the most likely to carry out the projects for which we care.[12] Others, such as Parfit himself, claim that we ought to bite the bullet; no such special concern would be rationally required. This does not mean that it is right to act against the interest of one's future selves, for, as Parfit suggests, we might want to extend our moral theory and claim that acting against one's interest in one's old age is, or at least can be, morally wrong.[13]

More drastically, the existence of a relation between theories of personal identity and issues regarding our attitudes toward our future selves

---

9. Sidgwick, *Methods of Ethics*, 124n. 1, quoted in Perry, "Importance," 88. Also see Whiting, "Friends and Future Selves," and Shoemaker, "Personal Identity and Practical Concerns," 362.
10. Parfit, *Reasons and Persons*, 307–312.
11. See Whiting, "Friends and Future Selves," for the distinction between different versions of the extreme claim.
12. Perry, "Importance."
13. Parfit, *Reasons and Persons*, 318–320.

has been questioned. Susan Wolf has argued that these two issues are independent.[14] We can happily adopt a reductionist account of personal identity while justifying the special concern we have for ourselves, for such a justification depends on completely different considerations, such as the good that follows from a concern for persons and, more particularly, for the person we are ourselves. Whether persons are constituted by temporal slices or not would have nothing to do with the kind of concern we have and are justified in having.

One important assumption in these debates is that we normally have a special concern for what we consider to be our future selves. Perry starts "The Importance of Being Identical" with the following claim: "most of us have a special and intense interest in what will happen to us."[15] The question in which I am interested is to what extent it is true that we have such a special and intense interest or concern for our future selves.

It would seem clearly wrong to claim that we *necessarily* have such a special concern for our future selves. There is thus a contrast with the concern we have for our present selves. It is certainly plausible to claim that because it seems inconceivable that we should be indifferent to our present pains and pleasures, a special concern for our present selves is necessary.[16] But there seems to be no conceptual impossibility involved in the claim that we can lack any concern whatsoever for our future selves—that is, that we should be quite indifferent to their pains and pleasures, not to mention their more general interests and projects.

But maybe it is true that human beings normally have such a special concern. To fail to have this concern would be pathological. As Fabio Sani reminds us, a "lack, or seriously weakened sense, of self continuity is considered one of the most typical disorders of the self. . . . Some people suffering from schizophrenia, organic states, or neuroses and depression may experience this condition."[17] Sani mentions the cases of the psychotic patient who considered his past self as a little dwarf inside himself.[18] It does not take much effort to make up a forward-looking syndrome of the same kind. One can easily imagine the case of a Kafka reader who believes his future self is some monstrous cockroach whose future schemes have to be counteracted. Thus, one might be tempted to claim that it is only in some abnormal and pathological cases that there is a lack of emotional identification with one's past or future self. If so, maybe one could put aside such cases when discussing the nature of personal identity.

---

14. Wolf, "Self-Interest."
15. Perry, "Importance," 66.
16. See Shoemaker, "Comments," 121; Kind, "Metaphysics," 547. Note, however, that certain drugs and some forms of leukotomy can lead patients to insist that they still *have* the pain but no longer *mind* it (see Dennett, "Why You Can't Make a Computer"). The question is whether the patients are right when they claim they feel pain.
17. Sani, "Introduction," 3.
18. See Jaspers, *General Psychopathology*, reported in Sani, "Introduction."

This would be a mistake. As I will argue, the lack of concern for one's future self need not be pathological; it is at least as common as procrastination. Before we address that, however, we must ask, what exactly is procrastination?

## KINDS OF PROCRASTINATION

Procrastination involves putting things off, deciding to do something later.[19] But of course, not any putting off will amount to procrastination.[20] A first point is that the putting off has to be free. If it were under threat, with a gun pointed at him, that Oblomov reluctantly decided to stay in bed a bit longer, his putting off getting out of bed hardly would count as procrastination. Correlatively, Oblomov has to be free, or at least to believe himself to be free, to perform, be it now or later, the action that he puts off. And he has to either be able to perform it or at least believe that he is able to perform it. If he did not believe he was free and able to perform that action later, he could hardly decide to put it off.[21] But freely putting off an action that one believes one is free and able to perform is not yet procrastination. If Oblomov decided to have his tea a bit later because he wanted to first finish writing his letter, this certainly would not constitute procrastination. There must be something *wrong* in the putting off for it to be procrastination.

Maury Silver and John Sabini argue that the kind of wrongness that must be involved is irrationality, and the irrationality they have in mind seems to be of the same kind as that usually attributed to akratic actions, actions that are freely and intentionally performed in spite of the agent's better judgment.[22] The irrationality in question thus comes from the conflict between what one does and what one knows or believes one ought to be doing. In Silver and Sabini's terms, "putting offs are procrastination only when they are irrational, and the irrationality is caused by recognizing (or fancying) what one ought to be doing."[23] So, according to them, Oblomov would need to know (recognize) or believe (fancy) that he ought to take his tea before writing his letter in order for his putting off to amount to procrastination. There are certainly cases in which this is

---

19. As the Latin etymology of the term indicates, *pro* means "for" or "toward," and *crastinus* means "of tomorrow," from *cras*, which means "tomorrow."

20. See Stroud's chapter 3 in this volume for more on procrastination as an instance of "putting off."

21. It often happens that by putting off doing something, one ends up being unable to do it. But if someone puts off with the intention of ensuring that he will be unable to perform the action, this would not count as procrastination; in fact, it would hardly count as genuine putting off. (Thanks to David Shoemaker for raising this issue.)

22. See Stroud and Tappolet, "Introduction."

23. Silver and Sabini, "Procrastinating," 211; see also Andreou, "Understanding Procrastination," for the assumption that procrastination has to be irrational putting off.

what happens. In analogy with "clear-eyed akrasia," we might call such cases "clear-eyed procrastination".

However, there are also cases in which the agent changes his mind when the time of action comes. Before going to bed, Oblomov might judge that he has to get up at 8:00 the next morning to write his letter, and he might even form the corresponding resolution, but when the time comes, the warmth and comfort of his bed make him change his mind, something he is likely to regret. In such cases, there might be a preference shift. On the day before, his preference was to get up at 8:00, while when the time comes to get out of bed, his preference is to stay in bed longer. In fact, there might be cases in which there is no such previous judgment, resolution, or preference, but it is simply true that one has more reason to do an action by a given time, something one could have easily realized had one done proper thinking; but when the time comes, one nonetheless decides to do the action later.[24] Indeed, it would seem that what is likely to cause the failure to see one's reason clearly is the aversion to performing the action that one ultimately postpones.

Thus, what is wrong with putting off that constitutes procrastination cannot only come from the conflict between judgment and action. While in clear-eyed cases, there is a conflict between the agent's judgment and her motivation, there are cases in which the practical judgment aligns itself with the motivation to put off. The definition Andreou gives leaves open the possibility of such cases, which could be called "blind procrastination". According to her, procrastination consists in putting off, sometimes indefinitely, what one should, relative to one's ends and information, have done sooner.[25] As long as the agent fails to make the judgment that, given her ends and her information, she should do a given action at a given time instead of later, that kind of procrastination is not clear-eyed.

The problem with this definition is that it does not allow for cases in which the agent's ends and information or, put differently, her reasons, militate in favor of putting off, but the agent fails to realize this and erroneously judges that the action ought to be performed at or by a certain time rather than later.[26] Oblomov might on balance have more reason not to get up that morning. Let us suppose that, in fact, he needs more sleep and would not be able to write the letter. Though aware of this, he judges that he ought to get up. His failing to get up will thus constitute a case of procrastination. But given that his reasons are on balance in favor of putting

---

24. The reasons at stake are internal, which the agent could easily access if he did some thinking. Putting off an action for which the agent has external reasons, or even reasons that are not easily accessed, clearly fails to count as procrastination. On the distinction between internal and external reasons, see Williams, "Internal and External Reasons."

25. Andreou, "Understanding Procrastination," 183.

26. See McIntyre, "Is Akratic Action Always Irrational?"; Audi, "Weakness of Will"; and Arpaly, "On Acting Rationally."

off, the procrastination can be considered reasonable. This does not mean that there is nothing wrong or irrational involved in the putting off. For one thing, the judgment is irrational, for it fails to properly represent the agent's reasons. Moreover, what is also irrational about such cases is the conflict between the practical judgment and the decision. However, just as in the cases of akratic actions, in which the agent's reason and her practical judgment come apart, procrastinating can be less unreasonable or irrational than not putting off an action.

In order to take into account the different kinds of cases I have discussed, we need a broader definition. I propose:

> S procrastinates with respect to action A if and only if
>
> (a) S is or believes he or she is free and able to do A at $t$ and at $t + n$, and
> (b) S's reasons require, or are believed by S to require, doing A at the latest at $t$, but
> (c) when $t$ comes, S freely decides to do A at $t + n$.[27]

A final point to stress is that, depending on the kind of action involved, two cases can be distinguished. In some cases, the action that is postponed is just a one-off action, such as writing a letter or getting married. But procrastination often concerns extended action, such as exercising, dieting, or smoking. For a smoker, smoking a cigarette is just one among the many elements that constitute the extended action of smoking. So, to stop smoking altogether requires not smoking this and all of the other cigarettes one might have smoked. Typically, what will happen is that once someone has decided to stop smoking altogether, she postpones putting an end to her habit by smoking yet another cigarette, so that she might never end her habit.

Now, in all of these cases, there is something irrational with procrastination. The question is whether procrastination involves dissociation from one's future self.

## AN ASSAULT ON THE SELF

In a telling passage, Silver and Sabini describe procrastination as involving "an assault on the self, one the actor appreciates."[28] What kind of assault on the self does procrastination involve? And does this assault involve a lack of concern for one's future selves? The voluntary infliction of pain or

---

27. As Olav Gjelsvik pointed out to me, the agent could decide to put off the action but nonetheless perform that action at the right time. So, maybe we should require that the decision to postpone the action is successful. However, given her decision to put off the action, I would be inclined to count such cases as procrastination even if the agent happened to perform the action at the right time.

28. Silver and Sabini, "Procrastinating," 208.

of a burden to oneself need not involve dissociation from one's present self, let alone from one's future selves. But, as will become clear, procrastination often involves harming one's future selves in a way that clearly seems to manifests a lack of concern for them.[29]

Let me first put aside cases of immoral procrastination, that is, cases in which procrastination produces harm, but the harm is inflicted on some other people. To avoid any ambiguity, we can assume that the agent has no psychological ties to the person on which she imposes a burden. For example, someone might procrastinate sending a letter in which she confesses to some terrible crime and would thereby clear a wrongly accused person. In such cases, her *will* may fail to be properly extended. She may suffer from a radical preference shift when the time to act approaches. Her initial preference to confess may yield to the preference to stay put. She might also be internally divided. This will be so if it is a case of cleareyed procrastination, in which the agent judges that she ought to perform the act now but nonetheless puts it off. But such cases certainly do not suggest that there is a lack of identification with one's future selves. Quite on the contrary, intense self-concern is likely to be at the root of immoral procrastination; it is because you care *too* much for yourself that you fail to do what you had correctly seen to be the morally right action.

Thus, procrastination need not involve a lack of concern for one's future self. However, there is a wide range of cases in which it does. This is so in the vast majority of imprudent procrastination cases, which involve postponing something that is necessary or believed to be necessary by the agent for the well-being of her future selves.

The first cases of imprudent procrastination that will come to mind are likely to involve extended actions. You have the familiar examples of the smokers who put off quitting and instead have one more cigarette; the obese who put off the diet and have another piece of cake; the intellectuals who put off exercising; and so on. As Andreou points out in chapter 12 of this volume, such cases can be considered to involve an intertemporal free-rider problem.[30] The present self fails to contribute her share to maintain or produce a "collective" good—that is, the good, such as health or fitness, which the present agent and all her future selves hope to share.

According to Andreou, such cases need not involve a lack of emotional identification with one's future selves. The reason, according to her, is that the cost of putting off might well be minimal. The cost of smoking yet

---

29. Note that not all conflicts between time slices of selves involve a lack of concern. Consider Ainslie's example of Ulysses' current plotting against his future self (*Breakdown of the Will*, 40); clearly, it is because he cares for his future self and wants to protect him against the Sirens that he arranges that his future self gets attached to the mast of the ship.

30. Note that since the future selves cannot be expected to do anything in the present, the analogy with intrapersonal free riding is imperfect. (Thanks to Sarah Stroud for pointing this out.)

another cigarette or having yet another piece of cake, say, may be so small that it is reasonable to see it as insignificant. In such cases, it seems correct to say that "she can face this intertemporal free-rider problem even if she cares about and identifies with . . . her future self. . . . For she may correctly see her current decision as to whether or not to stay on task as negligible relative to her long-term goal and to her future well-being."[31]

Is this so? It has to be stressed that these cases usually involve reiteration. Given this, the imposed burden is in general very substantial; by repeatedly discounting even negligible costs, the agent ends up seriously harming herself.[32] The question is whether this involves a lack of emotional identification with the agent's future selves. Given that the repetition itself is not intentional—it is not the case that the agent decides to repeatedly put off ending her smoking habit—it might be argued that such cases do not involve any lack of concern at any given moment. However, the simple fact that the agent repeatedly procrastinates and thereby harms her future selves is in itself a good reason to attribute to her a lack of concern for her future selves. Clearly, if she were really worried about the well-being of her future selves, she would not do something that puts their health at risk.

Moreover, there are cases in which even putting off that concerns parts of extended actions can involve a nonnegligible burden to one's future selves. Imagine that cigarettes are a bit different from the ones we know: suppose that each cigarette you smoke significantly increases the chance of painful illness. So, when you postpone putting an end to your smoking habit, your procrastination with respect to each cigarette imposes an important burden on your future selves. Harming your future self in that way surely amounts to a lack of concern for your future selves.

We have seen that procrastination can also involve one-off actions. In such cases, the harm that is inflicted on one's future self can be quite small, but it can, of course, also be considerable. Consider again Oblomov and his putting off any decision until it is too late. By doing so, he imposes a considerable burden on his future self. And as Oblomov could not but agree, this burden is clearly not compensated for by the present pleasures in which he indulges. Here, too, we seem to have a patent lack of concern for one's future selves.

Finally, I want to consider cases in which the lack of concern is even more obvious. In these cases, the result of procrastination is not that undesirable things will happen but that the agent brings it about that her future self has to perform the task that she puts off. For instance, you procrastinate about washing the dishes, though you are quite aware that the dishes have to be washed at some point—nobody will do it for you, and you lack the money to buy a new set—and you are aware that by the

31. See Andreou's chapter 12 in this volume.
32. Thanks to Sarah Stroud for pointing this out.

time you do it, you will have a huge pile of dirt-encrusted dishes to wash, something you consider much worse than washing the dishes right now. When we can afford to do so, we are often tempted to get someone else to do what we loathe doing, such as washing the dishes. We are trying to pass the buck on to others. It seems to me that this buck-passing model applies to the procrastination cases I just considered. When you fail to wash the dishes now, though you think that washing the dishes now is clearly preferable to doing it later, it seems that you end up consciously burdening your future self, the one who will have to do the chore. In such buck-passing cases, it seems particularly clear that you have a lack of concern for your future selves and that you fail to consider your later selves as fully identical with your present self.

Depending on the burden you impose on your future self, cases of imprudent procrastination can be compared to what Parfit calls "deliberate and great imprudence": "For the sake of small pleasures in my youth, I cause it to be true that I shall suffer greatly in my old age. I might, for instance, start smoking when I am a boy. I know that I am likely to impose on myself a premature and painful death. I know that I am doing what is likely to be much worse for me."[33] In such cases, the agent clearly fails to be equally concerned about her future selves as she is about her present self. She fails what Parfit considers to be central to the Self-interest Theory or Classical Prudence,[34] that is, the "Equal Concern Claim," according to which a "rational person should be equally concerned about all parts of his future."[35] Indeed, not only is she not equally concerned with the fate of her future self, but she also seems to fail to be really concerned at all.

What explains imprudent procrastination in which a nonnegligible burden is imposed on one's future selves seems to be a lack of concern for one's future selves. Future selves are considered to be strangers, to whom one can pass the buck and impose a sometimes heavy and uncompensated burden.[36] Were the agent to fully grasp that it is on herself that she imposes the cost of slowly dying in terrible pain, say, she would react in the same way as someone who is told that she is about to die in terrible pain.

The lack of concern for one's future self is particularly obvious in cases of clear-eyed procrastination, in which the agent realizes or at least believes

---

33. Parfit, *Reasons and Persons*, 317.
34. Parfit calls this "Classical Prudence" in his 1982 paper, "Personal Identity," and in "Self-Interest Theory" in *Reasons and Persons*.
35. Parfit, "Personal Identity," 231. Parfit argues against this requirement.
36. What compensates for the burden is not necessarily some advantage for the person. If you volunteer for the soup kitchen next Saturday night, your future self is going to have to give up his or her Saturday night to fulfill this commitment. But insofar as you rightly judge this sacrifice of yours to be justified, the burden can be considered to be compensated. (Thanks to David Shoemaker for raising this issue and also for the example.)

that her reasons require not putting off the action. But even in cases of what I called blind procrastination, it would seem that the failure to act is best explained by a lack of concern. Suppose that doing something now is what your reasons require, though you fail to make the corresponding practical judgment. It would seem that had you really been concerned about your future self, you would have been more careful to figure out the reasons you have.

It might be objected that the fact that the clear-eyed procrastinator judges that she ought to perform the action at a certain time shows that she fully identifies with her later selves. Surely, it is because she believes that her present self is identical with her later selves that she thinks she ought to do this action now. Let us assume that this is correct. It will nonetheless be true that when she decides to put off the action, not only does this belief fail to influence her action, but her decision also manifests a clear lack of concern for her future selves. So, despite the supposed belief in her identity over time, which is likely to come with the belief that she ought to be concerned about her future, the procrastinator fails to manifest this concern. This is like judging that one ought to feel an emotion, such as love for mankind, but one fails to experience the given emotion. That kind of intellectual identification with your futures selves need not come with a concern for your future selves.

Another worry is that there might be alternative explanations for the procrastinator's behavior. Instead of lacking concern for her future self, she might have a concern for them that is overridden by some other concern, such as a stronger concern for her present self.[37] This is certainly not impossible. In the same way, someone might have an overriding self-concern while also caring to a certain extent for others. The question is whether regularly inflicting (often heavy) burdens on someone is compatible with a genuine concern for that person. Thus, if future selves regularly lose to the present self, the conclusion to draw, it would seem, is that real concern for the future selves is lacking.

The vast majority of imprudent procrastination cases seem to involve a lack of concern for one's future selves. In such cases, the agent imposes an uncompensated burden on her future selves. Given this, such procrastinators appear to lack the *special concern* philosophers seem happy to believe to be almost universal. Imprudent procrastination is recognized to be a pervasive syndrome. In fact, it seems more common than the cases of "great and deliberate" imprudence that Parfit considers. Thus, given the pervasiveness of procrastination, it can be inferred that the absence of a special concern for one's future selves is, in fact, quite common. It is thus a mistake to think that we usually have a special concern for our future selves.

37. Thanks to Sergio Tenenbaum for raising this question.

## BACK TO PERSONAL IDENTITY THEORIES

We have seen that there are two arguments against psychological continuity accounts that use the idea of a special concern. The first one is grounded on the *descriptive* claim that we have a special concern for our future selves, while the second one starts from the *normative* claim that we have reason to have or are justified in having such a special concern.

Although recent debates often start with the descriptive claim, it is the normative argument that is, in fact, discussed. This gives the impression that the two arguments are not clearly distinguished. In a more charitable reading, the descriptive claim is just meant to be a warm-up for what is considered to be the real argument, which is the normative argument. However, I think it is useful to distinguish the two lines of thought. For one thing, this allows for a better understanding of how they relate to each other. As I will suggest, the two arguments are intimately related.

The first argument is quite clearly threatened by the claim that we often fail to have a special concern for our future selves. The descriptive argument starts from the observation that we have a special concern for our future selves and concludes that this results in a problem for psychological continuity theories. This could be so because, from the fact that we have a special concern for our future selves, it can be concluded that we *believe* that more than psychological continuity is at stake. Theories that suggest the contrary would lack intuitive plausibility. Or this could be so because, from the fact that we have such a concern, it can be inferred that it is likely that some ego persists over time to ensure numerical identity. If this were not the case, we surely would not have the erroneous belief that there is such an ego, and we surely would lack the special concern. More modestly, one could at least argue that an explanation of why we have such an erroneous belief is required. These might be less than watertight conclusions, but an argument along those lines would nonetheless have some force. It would, in any case, shift the burden of proof in favor of those who oppose psychological continuity accounts. But of course, if I am right to claim that we often fail to have such a special concern for our future selves, no version of this argument can even take off.

The normative argument, however, seems unthreatened by the present considerations. It argues from the premise that we have reason to have a special concern for our future selves to the conclusion that we should reject theories that question the belief that a persisting ego ensures numerical identity with our future selves. This is because such theories could not explain why we have reason to have a special concern. It could, of course, be true that we have reason to have such a special concern even if, in fact, we happened to lack any concern for our future selves. At most, the requirement entails that we *can* have such a concern, something nobody doubts.

It seems, however, that the supposed fact that we normally have such a concern nonetheless plays a role in the argument. The reason is that the normative argument seems threatened by a petition of principles that can be avoided only if the normative claim is grounded on the descriptive claim. Suppose you entirely lack any concern whatsoever for your future selves, and some benevolent philosopher (or economist) tries to convince you that you ought to have such a concern. What would she tell you? Quite naturally, she would try to convince you that your present self is identical with your future selves, so that the pain that will result from some inconsiderate present action of yours will be one that hurts yourself—you will feel this pain in your own bones. This argument might work with you, but it certainly will not work with someone who has doubts about her permanent existence. In particular, that consideration can hardly be used in an argument against theories that are accused of severing the link between present and future selves.

Now, compare this case with that of trying to convince someone who presently has a special concern for her future self that she has a reason for having such a concern. This does not seem to require much argument. The reason, it seems, is that someone who has the concern in question is likely to believe that she is identical with her future self, and she will take this fact to be a reason for having the concern in question. Given this, the descriptive claim appears to have more than a rhetorical role to play in the argument. The opponent of psychological continuity accounts has to add it to his premises to try to get his opponent to adopt the normative claim. But then the normative argument is not in better shape than the descriptive argument. In particular, the doubts that can be raised with respect to the claim that we normally have a special concern for our future selves undermine both the descriptive and the normative argument against psychological continuity accounts.

## CONCLUSION

By way of conclusion, I would like to suggest what seems to be a neglected strategy against procrastination.[38] The picture of procrastination I have sketched suggests that our relation to our future selves is not significantly different from the relation to our fellow human beings. Given this, it is plausible to claim that what one has to do to cope with procrastination is the same as what one has to do to get rid of a lack of concern for one's fellow human beings. In both cases, one has to increase one's concern. In the moral case, it is agreed that a good strategy for this is to imaginatively identify with the other.[39] One has either to imagine being in the shoes of

---

38. It is mentioned neither in Andreou, chapter 12, nor in Heath and Anderson, chapter 14, in this volume.

39. This is sometimes called empathizing or perspective taking, though, as cases of psychopathy show, the technique is not infallible. See Nichols, *Sentimental Rules*, chap. 2, and Maxwell, *Professional Ethics Education*, esp. pp. 62–67.

this other person or else to imagine feeling what she feels from her own point of view, given her psychological makeup. This will help because such an empathic engagement with others tends to come with an increased concern for others. Thus, the coping strategy I propose to the procrastinator consists in the imaginative identification with the fate of her future selves. Had Oblomov attempted to imaginatively identify with his future selves, he might well have accomplished what was needed to avoid his sad fate.

## ACKNOWLEDGMENTS

An earlier version of this chapter was presented at the New York CSMN procrastination workshop organized by Chrisoula Andreou and Mark White, whom I wish to thank. For helpful input, I would like to thank George Ainslie, Jennifer Baker, Christopher Cowley, Olav Gjelsvik, Joe Heath, Jennifer Hornsby, David Hunter, Daniel Laurier, Duncan MacIntosh, Bruce Maxwell, Elijah Milgram, Frédéric Nef, David Owens, Sergio Tenenbaum, Manuel Utset, Mark White, and especially Chrisoula Andreou, David Shoemaker, and Sarah Stroud. My work was supported by the Canada Research Chair program, which I gratefully acknowledge.

# 8

# The Vice of Procrastination

*Sergio Tenenbaum*

My aim in this chapter is to understand more precisely what kind of irrationality is involved in procrastination. I will argue that procrastination is one of the corresponding vices of an overlooked virtue, which I will call "practical judgment." In the first section, I provide the background model I will employ in my account of procrastination, the Policy as Action Model (PAM). Relying on this model, in the second section, I characterize a form of procrastination that will play a central role in my account of "long-term procrastination." The third section defines the instrumental virtue of practical judgment; I argue there that procrastination is the vice of deficiency that corresponds to this virtue. The fourth section extends this account of procrastination to cases that do not fall under the heading of long-term procrastination. Finally, the fifth section argues for an important consequence of this view: procrastination so understood is a failure of instrumental rationality that can be so characterized without assuming the correctness of any further substantive norms of rationality. If this argument succeeds, it constitutes an important objection to Christine Korsgaard's claim that a purely instrumental conception of rationality is incoherent.

## BACKGROUND

I outline below the main features of the theory of long-term actions, plans, and policies—the "Policy as Action Model," or PAM—that will inform the rest of the chapter. I do not want to claim that different views of long-term activity could not accommodate the account of procrastination I present here; however, the exposition of the account is made much simpler by assuming PAM.[1]

---

1. I do argue elsewhere, however, that the two central features of PAM discussed below are incompatible with the central motivation of Bratman's influential "two-tier model" (see Bratman, *Intention, Plans, and Practical Reason*) and that for this very reason, PAM provides a better account of the rationality of actions in light of plans, policies, and intentions (see Tenenbaum, "Intention and Commitment"). If I am right about that, and if the account of the irrationality of procrastination presented here is persuasive, this would be further evidence in favor of PAM.

According to PAM, plans, policies, and long-term projects are simply ordinary actions, or, at least, they should be viewed as ordinary actions as long as we're considering solely the issue of rational evaluation of these plans, policies, and long-term projects (for short, I will call all of these "long-term activities").[2] At first, PAM might seem implausible: actions are continuous through time, while long-term activities such as policies involve multiple steps at different points in time. If I am swimming, I am engaged in one continuous act of swimming, while if I have the long-term project of writing a novel, I will write a few sentences today, make some revisions tomorrow, send a chapter to my publisher next month, and so forth. However, actions often, if not always, have stages, and for most, if not all, ordinary actions, it is possible that the stages do not succeed each other continuously or without interruptions. If I am baking a cake, I will need to measure the flour and break some eggs, but these actions need not follow each other immediately. Between measuring the flour and breaking the eggs, I might step outside to check if the mail has arrived. This interruption makes my action of baking a cake no less unified than if I had moved from measuring the flour to breaking the eggs without even catching my breath.[3] In other words, measuring flour and breaking eggs are parts of the same action of baking a cake whether or not they are separated by other actions that are not themselves parts of the action of baking a cake. So, the central idea behind PAM is that instances of long-term activities stand in the same relation to the more general long-term activity as parts of an action stand to an ordinary action. My typing a few sentences is part of my action of writing a novel, just as my measuring the flour is part of my action of baking a cake; similarly, my exercising today is part of my policy of exercising every week in the same way as my pulling my hand out of the water is part of my action of swimming.

The chart in figure 8-1 represents our ordinary action of baking a cake. We can think of this kind of chart as representing the higher actions (in this case, "baking the cake") as controlling the smaller actions and actions to the left as preceding actions to the right at the same level. The meaning of "controlling," when we look at the relation between baking the cake and measuring the flour, is quite clear: measuring the flour is undertaken as a means to baking the cake. It is less clear how to understand the relation between baking the cake and listening the radio as one in which the former controls the latter. Obviously, I do not listen to the radio as a means to baking the cake. But we can say that the larger actions control the whole pattern of action, including actions that are better seen as interruptions in the following sense: insofar as I am rational, which smaller actions are performed (such as checking the cat) are performed only insofar as they do not conflict with the ends of the larger action (that

---

   2. It is widely agreed that adopting a policy, for instance, is an action. However, the claim here is that *having* a policy is an action.
   3. Michael Thompson makes similar points in part II of *Life and Action*.

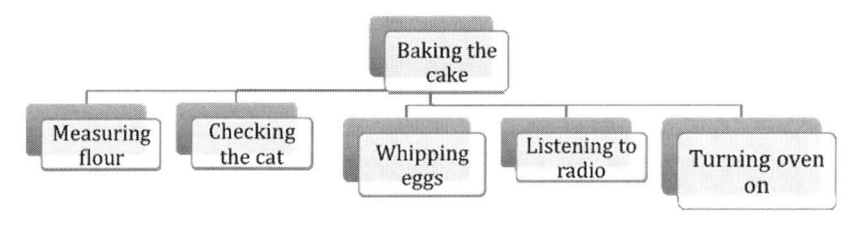

```
                    ┌─────────────┐
                    │ Baking the  │
                    │    cake     │
                    └─────────────┘
   ┌──────────┬──────────┼──────────┬──────────┐
┌────────┐ ┌────────┐ ┌────────┐ ┌────────┐ ┌────────────┐
│Measuring│ │Checking│ │Whipping│ │Listening│ │Turning oven│
│  flour  │ │the cat │ │  eggs  │ │to radio │ │     on     │
└────────┘ └────────┘ └────────┘ └────────┘ └────────────┘
```

**Figure 8-1**

is, baking the cake). In other words, other things being equal and insofar as I am rational, I would not have performed this action if it were not for the fact that I judged that it could be part of a set of actions that would lead me to the successful realization of my aim of baking the cake. We can say that, according to PAM, policies control the actions I engage in within the life of the policy in the same way that ordinary actions control smaller actions. In fact, we could draw a parallel chart for my exercising policy (figure 8-2).

Needless to say, instances of a policy might be separated by much larger temporal gaps than parts of an ordinary action. For instance, suppose I have a policy that I keep walking in the same direction if I am lost. Since I am almost never lost, I am rarely doing anything that instantiates the policy (at least, if we do not count vacuous instantiations). However, even while years elapse without my ever getting lost, it is still true that I have the policy. But once we allow that ordinary actions allow for temporal gaps between their parts, it is unclear why the size of the gap would disqualify something from being an action. In fact, there seems to be a seamless continuum between baking a cake and long-term activities such as exercising regularly in terms of "gappiness" that includes, for instance, sightseeing, taking care of the children for a day, studying for an exam, and so forth. Someone who thinks that temporal gaps of a certain size disqualify something from being a continuous action needs to provide a principled reason to draw at least a rough line somewhere in this continuum.

I do not want to dwell on this model, but I do want to point out two related consequences of PAM.[4] First, notice that as long as I exercise regularly and my exercising regularly is produced in a normal way, my pattern of activity exhibits no irrationality with respect to this policy. Leaving aside the cases in which I execute my policy as a result of sheer luck (which would be rather bizarre cases in our example of exercising

---

4. I do not want to claim that these consequences are unique to this model or that these consequences are not compatible with other views about the nature of long-term activities but only that PAM provides a clear formulation of, and a straightforward route to, these consequences.

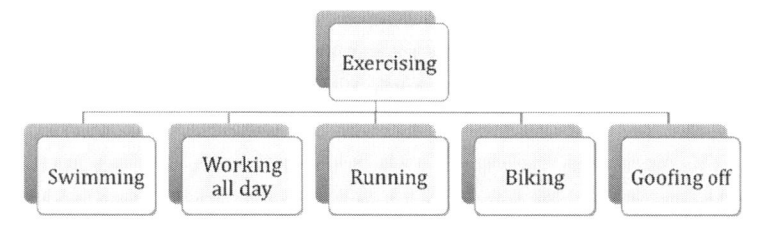

```
                    ┌──────────┐
                    │ Exercising│
                    └─────┬────┘
    ┌──────────┬─────────┼─────────┬──────────┐
┌────────┐ ┌────────┐ ┌───────┐ ┌──────┐ ┌──────────┐
│Swimming│ │Working │ │Running│ │Biking│ │Goofing off│
│        │ │all day │ │       │ │      │ │          │
└────────┘ └────────┘ └───────┘ └──────┘ └──────────┘
```

**Figure 8-2**

regularly), I can display irrational behavior with respect to this policy only if I fail to execute it. This is not true for any account of long-term activities. According to some accounts, there might be requirements about when I am allowed to reconsider a policy or consider an exception for it or requirements that determine that I have to undertake particular actions in light of a certain project.

Suppose, for instance, that I have a long-term project of eating healthily. Of course, this project does not necessarily require that I *never* eat any kind of food that is nutritionally subpar. Suppose now that I choose to eat a large brownie. Under which conditions would my eating a large brownie be irrational? One possible answer would be to hold the view that "exceptions require rules," or ERR. According to ERR, I should eat a large brownie only if my reason to eat the brownie right now could be generalized without undermining my long-term project. Two possible reasons for eating a brownie right now would be "I feel like it" or "I have been really good for a whole month." The second reason would obviously generalize; if I allow myself to eat brownies only if I have not eaten anything nutritionally dubious for at least a month, I am certainly acting in accordance with my long-term project of eating healthily. However, according to ERR, if I eat brownies on the basis of the first reason, I am most likely being irrational, since I probably know that if I were to eat everything that I felt like eating, I would not succeed in my long-term project of eating healthily.[5] So, if I go ahead and eat the brownie for this reason, I would be acting irrationally on this occasion, irrespective of whether I end up succeeding or failing to have an overall healthy diet. According to PAM, however, as long as I succeed at carrying out my long-term project of eating healthily nonaccidentally, there could be no failure of rationality with respect to this long-term project.[6]

---

5. See Gauthier, "Resolute Choice," and Bratman, "Temptation Revisited," for similar constraints on exceptions. I argue in more detail that their views are committed to this consequence as well as to the impossibility of top-down independence (see below) in Tenenbaum, "Intention and Commitment."

6. Needless to say, there are many other ways in which I could be irrational in carrying out the policy: I could be doing things that conflict with other ends of mine, or I could be doing things that I have other reasons not to do. But in these cases, the irrationality does not reside solely in the relation of my action, or set of actions, to a particular long-term activity.

This leads to the second consequence: PAM is committed to the possibility of long-term activities that are what I call "top-down independent." We can define this notion roughly as follows:

> The rationality of a long-term activity A is top-down independent if and only if the following obtains: If an agent engages (or ought to engage) in A, there is a set of possible choices S for the agent such that:
>
> (1) No particular choice in S would be irrational.
> (2) If the agent were to make all of the choices in S, she would be for that very reason irrational.

For instance, my failing to execute a policy of exercising regularly could be irrational, without any particular action being irrational. It is possible that the only failure that we can identify in the pattern of my activity is that it failed to instantiate a pattern of exercising regularly; each particular action considered in isolation might not manifest any kind of irrationality. Since, for instance, a policy of exercising regularly might not demand that I exercise on any particular occasion, I might fail to exercise regularly while being rationally justified in each action in which I fail to exercise. My view is not only that the existence of long-term activities that are top-down independent is a conceptual possibility but, rather, that most policies, plans, and projects are like that. Moreover, I will argue that there are particular virtues and corresponding vices of rationality that relate to an agent's capacity to execute top-down independent policies; my claim is that procrastination is one of these vices.

## THE CENTRAL CASE

I will start with a central case of procrastination that can be described as "long-term procrastination";[7] I will generalize this account later. Although I don't claim that the account ultimately covers everything that we might want to call procrastination, I do argue that it covers a large and interesting part of the phenomena that fall under this rubric. But at first, I will be concerned with cases with the following structure. There is a certain end (E) that an agent wants to bring about, and E can be brought about only by repeatedly engaging in a characteristic activity (A). Moreover, the following are true of E and A:

1. Opportunities for engaging in instances of A stretch potentially indefinitely through time or through an indefinite time period (at least, as far as the agent is aware).

---

7. But, as will be clear later, the sense in which I use "long-term procrastination" does not exactly match what O'Donoghue and Rabin discuss in their paper "Procrastination on Long-Term Projects."

2. At certain points in time, one can assess whether E has been properly brought about or not.
3. If the agent engages in A at every opportunity, E will be brought about (or at least, the agent expects that E will be brought about).
4. The agent's momentary preferences, those that the agent has regarding the objects of his (nearly) instantaneous choices,[8] are such that:
    a. At various times, when the agent has an opportunity to engage in an instance of A, the agent prefers to engage in some other activity.
    b. Were the agent always to choose according to these momentary preferences, he would not bring about E.
    c. At every time, the agent prefers always to choose to engage in A when there is an opportunity to engage in A over not bringing about E.[9]
    d. At every time, there are *some* sets of choices over time such that:
        i. The agent does not engage in A at every opportunity, and E is brought about; and,
        ii. The agent prefers any of these sets to the set of choices in which the agent engages in A at every opportunity.
    e. There is no precise weak ordering known to the agent of all sets of choices in which the agent has an opportunity to engage in A; that is, there is no ordering of the agent's preferences that satisfies the axioms of decision theory and that the agent would recognize as the single correct ordering of his preferences. The agent can at most identify certain acceptable and unacceptable sets of choices.[10]

It might be worth looking at an example that has all of these features. Suppose I want to write a novel that is about as good as I can write (for short, I will just refer to the project as "writing a decent novel"). That is, I do not want to end up not writing a novel or writing a novel that is significantly worse than the novel I would have written had I spent significantly more time on it. There will be a loosely classified characteristic activity in which I engage in order to achieve this end—namely, the actions constitutive of writing a novel, such as typing, reading over the manuscript, and so on. As long as I am in close proximity to a computer, I can invest time in writing the novel. Leaving aside the possibility of knowing the time of my death, I know of no specific point in time by which the writing of a

---

8. David Gauthier contrasts the momentary preferences of an agent with what he calls her "vanishing point" preferences (see Gauthier, "Resolute Choice"). As will be made clear below, I am using "momentary preference" in a slightly different sense.
9. A weaker version of this condition will do just as well, but the stronger version makes for ease of presentation.
10. I will say more on the notions of acceptable and unacceptable sets below.

novel must be finished in order for me to have achieved the end of having written a decent novel.[11] And leaving aside also the possibility of my untimely death and some bizarre circumstances, if I take every opportunity that I am near my computer to engage in writing a novel, at some point, I will have written a decent novel (it might not be a great novel, but it will be as good a novel as I can write).

It is also plausible to suppose that my momentary preferences will be such that, even though I would in some rare moments choose to engage in writing a novel independently of my concern with achieving my end of having written a decent novel, I would almost always much prefer engaging in some other activity, as long as engaging in such activities would not prevent me from writing a decent novel. And given that in all such cases, it might be true that engaging in some other activity just this once does not undermine the general project, if I choose to write a novel only when my momentary preferences dictate writing a novel, I will never achieve my end of writing a novel.

However, the worst-case scenario for me is not to write a decent novel, and I would rather always be engaged in writing a novel till the end is brought about than to end up not writing the novel.[12] But, finally, this is obviously not my most preferred long-term policy from any point of view in time; I would rather have a more balanced life in which I write enough to complete a novel in a reasonable amount of time while still pursuing other interests. Although not many of us engage in writing a novel, many important projects in our lives have this structure, such as saving for retirement, investing time in a career, spending enough time with the children, and staying fit.

A couple of things will be important for our discussion later. First, the temptation to procrastinate is intrinsic to the nature of this kind of project. Not only does the agent have momentary preferences that, if jointly satisfied, would conflict with her long-term preferences, but her long-term preferences also favor the satisfaction of the momentary preference, as long as we hold fixed all of the other choices the agent makes.[13] In fact, "momentary preference" is a bit of a misnomer here, since it is not essential that the agent shifts her preference over time in any way to generate the problem. It would be more precise perhaps to call these preferences "preferences for momentary actions," but since this is a mouthful, I will leave the terminology intact.

---

11. I might have a deadline to write a novel, but this could be understood as a further end that I have. And even if I incorporate the deadline to my end, if the deadline is not specific enough, it will still satisfy condition (1).

12. This might make me more fanatical about writing than the typical novelist, but it does simplify the example.

13. Chrisoula Andreou has identified a similar structure in a number of choice situations, including procrastination-prone situations; see Andreou, "Environmental Preservation" and "Understanding Procrastination."

Second, the temptation to procrastinate is generated, at least in part, by the vagueness of the ideal outcome. The vagueness is, in fact, multilayered, and its elements include the following: there is no precise time by which the novel must get written (or no precise amount of time that constitutes spending enough time with my children, investing in my career, and so forth); there is no precise number of occasions in which I need to engage in the characteristic activity in order to achieve the end; there is no precise start time to engage in the characteristic activity; and there is no precise characterization of the end (of what counts as "as good a novel as I can write"). Based on the vagueness of these various aspects of my choice situation, we can understand better what will count as "acceptable" and "unacceptable" sets of choices in condition 4(e). Given the structure of the choice situation that I face, there are many sets of choices through time that are clearly unacceptable, sets of choices that the agent thinks are significantly worse than other options available to her. I would find, for instance, any set of choices in which I do not end up writing a decent novel unacceptable.

More controversially, I will assume also that there are many sets of choices that are clearly acceptable. To briefly explain why this is a controversial assumption, let us take a candidate for being an acceptable set of choices S, in which I write a decent novel, and I have spent $x$ amount of time engaging in activities that my momentary preferences favor over writing a novel. Assuming that there is no precise amount of time that is the minimum amount that I will need to write a decent novel, I could have achieved the same result by having spent $x + \varepsilon$ amount of time engaging in other activities. Let us call S' the set of choices in which I spend $x + \varepsilon$ amount of time engaging in other activities. Now, by hypothesis, S' is preferred over S, so it seems that we should conclude that S is not acceptable. Since this is perfectly general, and given that by stretching enough the time that I spend in other activities, I will end up never writing a book, it seems that, there is no acceptable set of choices. In other words, given that the sources of vagueness identified above seem to generate an intransitive ordering, there will be no acceptable set of choices.

I do not want to delve into the issue of whether we should characterize the agent as having, in fact, an intransitive preference ordering. I simply want to point out that even if the agent in this case does have an intransitive preference ordering, we can think of a weaker notion of acceptability, such that it does not follow from the fact that S is an acceptable set of choices that there is not an S' that the agent strictly prefers to S. Since the precise contours of the notion of acceptability are not important for my purposes, I will just use a very loose idea to capture the notion of acceptability.

Suppose, for instance, that I choose S and end up writing a decent novel. Let us now look at how I might evaluate the choice once the novel is written. I might remember a Sunday morning when I was reading the newspaper and decided to stop and work on writing my novel. I realize that I probably would have written just as good a novel if I had spent five more minutes reading the newspaper. However, I am unlikely to regret having picked the choice set I actually did on the basis of such a consideration alone. After all, I realize that given the vagueness and uncertainty in my situation, I needed to strike a reasonable compromise, and stopping when I did might seem to me (and might also in fact be) a reasonable enough compromise. I will assume thus that for any situation in which all of the above conditions (1 through 4) obtain, there are a number of sets of choices such that no rational agent who chose one of these sets would regret having made this choice; these sets of choices are clearly acceptable. Similarly, a set of choices that any rational agent would have regretted picking would be clearly unacceptable.

I will also assume that there are sets of choices that are neither acceptable nor unacceptable, sets of choices that some, but not all, rational beings would regret even when we hold everything else equal. The fact that there are such sets of choices is exactly what allows agents to procrastinate; we procrastinate when we move imperceptibly from a clearly acceptable set of choices to a neither acceptable nor unacceptable set and then to an unacceptable one. And, as we will see, this generates various problems for limited rational agents faced with these kinds of temptations to procrastinate.

## PRACTICAL JUDGMENT AND CORRESPONDING VICES

Suppose that an agent engages in the project of writing a novel and makes choices through time as illustrated in figure 8-3. As explained above, according to PAM, the action of writing a novel controls not only the necessary steps in writing a novel but also the actions such as "playing soccer" and "having lunch" which I perform while writing the novel. Also according to PAM, as long as the ordered set (typing on computer, playing soccer, typing on computer, having lunch) is an acceptable set of choices, the agent acted rationally. However, in executing the project of writing a novel, the agent might also have engaged in intermediate activities, activities that stand between the "top" action of writing a novel and the

Figure 8-3

"bottom" actions of typing on computer, revising the manuscript, and so on. For instance, the agent might have settled on a policy of writing at least a page a day. Of course, the agent might also have had no need of any such intermediate policies in order to successfully write a novel. In fact, we can think that the ideal rational agent will not need any intermediate steps; an ideal agent just makes sure that the chosen set is an acceptable set.

We can use our central case to characterize the basic form of irrationality involved in procrastination. Any time the agent's choices form a pattern such that she starts engaging in a long-term activity but does not properly complete the long-term activity without ever changing her mind about choosing to engage in it and without ever encountering unexpected obstacles, the agent exhibits a basic form of irrationality. In such cases, the agent chooses the end but fails to take the necessary (instrumental or constitutive) means to bring it about. Procrastination will be exactly a case of this kind of instrumental irrationality.[14] In our example, we would have a case of this kind if the agent were to write a few sentences or a general plan for the novel but then seldom took any further steps to complete the novel despite the fact that no unexpected circumstance prevented her from working on her novel (such as breaking her typing hand, for example).

Notice that the project of writing a novel can be top-down independent irrational, and our characterization of procrastination so far is exactly a case of top-down independent irrationality. Since for any pattern of activity in which I fail to write a decent novel there is no momentary action that prevented me from writing the novel on its own, when I procrastinate, none of my momentary choices is irrational (at least, in respect to this project) when considered in isolation.[15] This, of course, generalizes to any long-term activity that satisfies constraints (1) through (4). However, this characterization of the irrationality of long-term procrastination does not take into account the possibility of adopting intermediate policies and how this possibility might affect our assessment of the rationality of an agent in a situation in which she is prone to procrastinate.

I will examine the significance of intermediate policies by looking at how they could be introduced as we revise our strategies in trying to carry out a long-term activity. If we look back at our example of the ordinary

---

14. A couple of caveats. First, this is just a first approximation; I add to this account of the vice of procrastination below. Second, we could characterize the irrationality more generally as cases in which the agent *forms the intention* of engaging in a long-term activity rather than actually *starting* to engage in the activity. I have nothing against this kind of emendation. However, I am skeptical that we can attribute to the agent the intention to engage in a long-term activity if the agent does nothing that counts as an instance of engaging in this activity.

15. Of course, I could engage in momentary actions that will immediately prevent me from writing a decent novel; I could, for instance, shoot myself in the head. However, the failure of rationality in this case would obviously not be a case of procrastination.

action of baking a cake, we can imagine that as I am baking the cake, some things turn out badly. As I beat the eggs, I notice that they are not getting the texture I expected. I might then check the egg beater, see if there's anything stuck in it, or change my plans for how to move my hands. Part of being a rational agent involves, of course, that we check the progress of our actions and revise the actions undertaken as means to other actions or ends in light of what we learn in the course of acting. And the same thing will go for projects and policies, and the complications and difficulties introduced by the vagueness of what counts as an acceptable set will spill over to complications about how a rational agent revises the actions undertaken as means to more general projects and policies.

Suppose that I decide to write a decent novel, and after a while, I look back at my actions and see the pattern I have exemplified, as shown in figure 8-4. I might have two distinct attitudes in relation to these actions. I might think that this is an overall slow start, but it is to be expected given that the Euro Cup was on, people were sending me scamming e-mails when I was a bit drunk, and so forth. Since there are many acceptable sets that include those initial choices, I might think that I am engaging in the appropriate actions toward my goal of having written a decent novel. But it is unlikely that this kind of judgment is warranted. More likely, I should realize that I cannot write a novel without further planning; I will not write a novel unless I adopt intermediate policies such as "write at least two pages a day," "do not go online before writing at least one page," and so on. Cases in which I recognize the need for further planning seem to allow us to locate failures of rationality more precisely than just in the general pattern of activity; if I can't expect to write a novel without an intermediate policy, the failure to adopt the intermediate policy is itself a failure of rationality. However, I want to argue that even in those cases, the irrationality is top-down independent; even in those cases, the ultimate source of irrationality resides entirely in

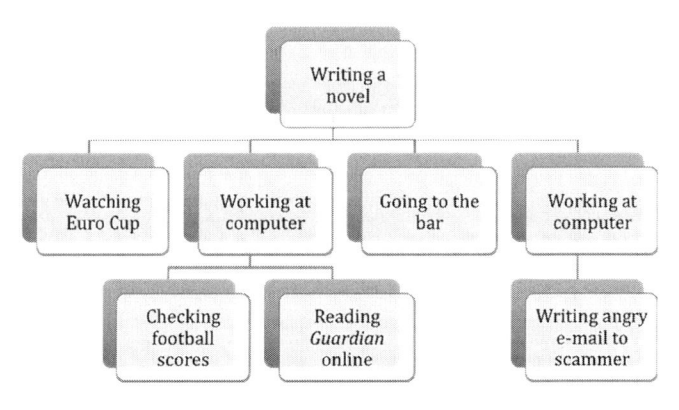

**Figure 8-4**

# The Vice of Procrastination                                                                 141

the fact that I failed to write a novel. And even in those cases, it is possible that none of my momentary actions was irrational. In order to make this argument, we need to examine more closely the process of revising intermediate policies.

Suppose that I recognize the need to have an intermediate policy. This conclusion must lead me to revise my view of what the feasible sets of choices are and, consequently, of the acceptable sets of choices. Given that our menu of options has shrunk, we might find acceptable now what we previously thought should be ruled out, just as someone who has weight-control problems might end up reluctantly adding a life without chocolate desserts to the list of acceptable sets of choices. Let us start by thinking that I take a very conservative strategy and choose to have a very rigid schedule, which I would not at first have thought to be an acceptable choice. I decide to, say, work continuously from 9:00 A.M. to 7:00 P.M. on my novel; in other words, I adopt what I will call a 9-to-7 policy. To simplify matters, I will look first into the unlikely possibility that this is an absolutely strict policy. Figure 8-5 shows how my writing a novel leads me to act so far.

As I engage in this new intermediate policy, I do make good strides toward finishing my novel. However, the policy is obviously too strict; it does not allow me to eat, to have coffee breaks, or to go to my best friend's wedding. There are at least two ways I can react to this. I can just allow certain exceptions from time to time and transform my 9-to-7 policy into a loose and vague policy. In the case of a loose and vague policy, I expect to be writing my novel most of the time between 9:00 and 7:00, but I allow that from time to time, I take a break to do other things. Or I can form a different strict policy that is essentially like my 9-to-7 policy, but I also now incorporate into the policy precisely specified conditions under which breaks are acceptable.

Note that the vague intermediate policy leaves us with a problem much like the original project of writing a novel. I might be quite good at managing a few exceptions here and there, but it is also perfectly possible

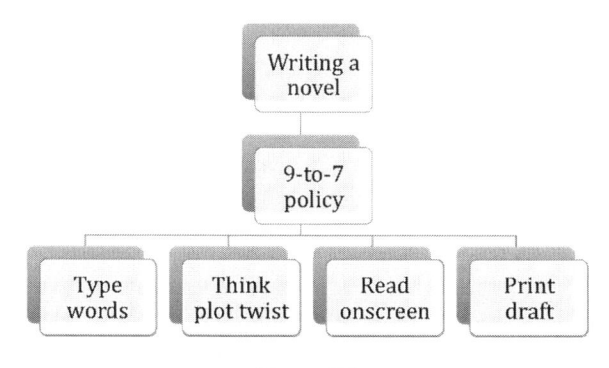

**Figure 8-5**

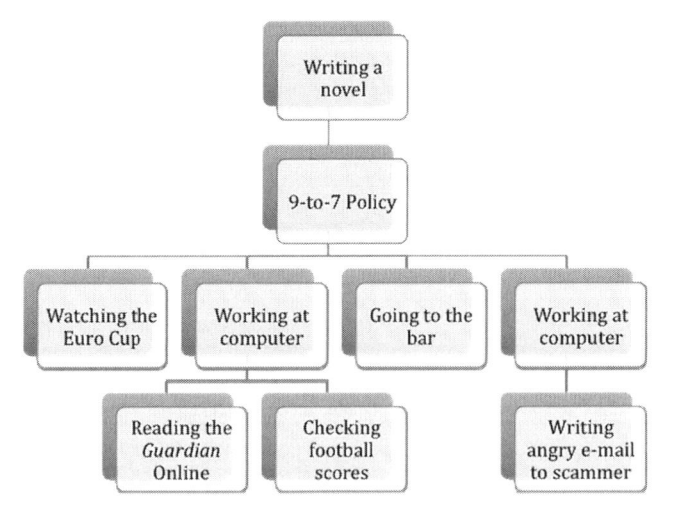

```
                    Writing a
                     novel
                        │
                   9-to-7 Policy
     ┌──────────┬──────┴──────┬──────────┐
 Watching the  Working at  Going to the  Working at
  Euro Cup     computer      bar         computer
                   │                         │
              ┌────┴────┐                    │
          Reading the  Checking          Writing
           Guardian    football         angry e-mail
            Online      scores          to scammer
```

**Figure 8-6**

that my actions controlled by my loose policy are identical to the ones that were directly controlled by the project of writing a book (see figure 8-6). But notice that, again, none of these momentary choices on its own is instrumentally irrational; after all, each exception on its own is compatible with my 9-to-7 policy. Just as in the case in which the agent does not adopt an intermediate policy, the irrationality of the agent consists solely in the fact that these choices do not constitute an acceptable set. So far, adding intermediate policies to the picture does not change in any significant way our understanding of the irrationality of procrastination.

In the second strategy, rather than allowing for exceptions, I choose a less strict but still precise policy. I could cut down on the hours I expect myself to be writing a novel or incorporate clearly laid-out exceptions to my plan. And here one might think that I move from a vague policy that allows unspecified exceptions to a precise but less strict policy for the same reason that an intermediate policy was adopted in the first place; that is, the agent suspects that the vague policy is not a feasible one. But even a less strict but still precise policy will probably not be ideal. Not all exceptions can be thought out in advance, and even habits and dispositions must be flexible enough to allow some wiggle room in unexpected circumstances. A policy whose system of exceptions is part of the policy itself or is limited only by preexisting rules and regularities is almost always a second best; the flexibility of leaving open when and how many exceptions are permitted is likely to be advantageous to the agent, as long as this is a feasible option for the agent. In fact, most of our strict policies are either policies that we think are intrinsically choiceworthy or rather desperate reactions to powerful temptations. Avoiding extramarital affairs and not betraying friends fall under the first category, while quitting smoking completely and becoming a teetotaler fall under the latter.[16]

At any rate, as I find out that the direct implementation of a vague policy proves difficult to me, I might tweak it either by revising how to carry out my policy one level up or by implementing it with further policy one level down, which could be more or less precise. Of course, excessive tweaking or fine-tuning might be itself a failure of the will. But here, too, it seems correct to say that whether all of this tweaking and fine-tuning resulted in any case of irrationality (and whether some aspects of my fine-tuning should count as procrastination) depends solely on the result. If I ended up with an acceptable set of choices, then there is no room for any accusation of irrationality; every sin is forgiven. Given that I nonaccidentally ended up in a desirable outcome guided by my end, then my behavior is rationally unimpeachable, at least insofar as we are concerned solely with instrumental rationality. Similarly, it is worth noting that if I do now adopt and carry out a successful policy, there is no reason to think that I engaged in any kind of irrational activity, and, perhaps more controversially, there might also be no reason to think that I had not already engaged in writing a novel before adopting the intermediate policy. My initial engagement might have not contributed much to the final product, but it is part of the overall pattern of activity, much as my missteps in baking a cake are part of the process of baking a cake. If my adopting of an intermediate policy delivers a decent book after a certain time, I ended up hitting on an acceptable set of choices, one that happens to include these seemingly procrastinating actions in my first days at the job of writing a novel. In fact, if anything, the set that includes those early misdeeds can only be better than one that replaces some of these early misdeeds with more instances of A; it is certainly not worse. Since the outcome was good, and it was nonaccidentally brought about by my acting with the goal of writing a novel, there is no room for any accusation of (instrumental) irrationality to stick.

We are now in a better position to gain a more precise understanding of the nature of the rational failing involved in procrastination. This structure reveals an important executive virtue. There has been much debate in the philosophical literature about the importance of resolution for carrying out our plans.[17] Resolution can be roughly described as the executive virtue that ensures that we will carry out our plan in the face of temptation and shifting preferences. One can show resoluteness or lack thereof in a momentary action; if I give in to the temptation to have a cigarette despite my intention to quit, I fail to exhibit this virtue. Procrastination is not typically thought of as the same as irresolution, since

---

16. See George Ainslie's discussion of the need for bright lines in trying to overcome addictions in Ainslie, *Breakdown of Will*, chap. 6.
17. See, for instance, McClennen, *Rationality and Dynamic Choices*, and Gauthier, "Resolute Choice."

procrastination does not seem to involve (at least, not necessarily) any change of mind or rejection of a previously accepted plan. Resolution, insofar as it is a virtue, can be classified as one of the executive virtues—the virtues we need in order to bring about our ends. If we are too fickle with regard to our plans, many long-term projects that require commitment will be beyond our reach. However, if my view is correct, we must conclude that in order to carry out vague policies and projects, one needs more than resolution; one also needs the executive virtue that I will call practical judgment.

Practical judgment is a dual-aspect virtue, involving both the capacity to carry out vague plans and projects (and long-term actions in general) in the absence of an intermediate policy and the capacity to adopt and revise intermediate policies that are effective but not overly inflexible. Ideally, rational agents would exhibit only the first aspect of the virtue; not needing any intermediate policies or plans, they would simply engage in the long-term activity by choosing an acceptable set. But a lesser than perfect degree of virtue will require both that one can execute well fairly vague policies and that one can choose well among intermediate policies when direct execution of long-term activity is not feasible.

If the structure of one of our plans bottoms out in a vague policy, we will need the virtue of practical judgment in order to act well. In a classical Aristotelian fashion, I want to argue that there are two correlative vices to this virtue. The vice of inflexibility is the vice of performing the characteristic actions of a project too often or in the wrong times. For instance, if I hear that my friend has been suddenly hospitalized, but I do not visit him or call his family because my schedule requires that at this moment I should be writing a novel, I certainly exhibit the vice of inflexibility. And it should come as no surprise that the opposite vice is, in my view, the vice of procrastination. We procrastinate when our attempt to execute a vague plan fails because we engage in the characteristic activity on too few occasions or we engage in noncharacteristic activities on the wrong occasions. This account also explains an intuitive feature of procrastination: it seems to be a vice of inaction, in that we succumb to temptation when we do something that we have conclusive reason not to do, but we procrastinate when we fail to do something we have conclusive reason to do. But in many accounts of value and reason, this distinction is spurious; values are comparative, and decisive reasons are all-things-considered reasons. So, by failing to do something that I had decisive reason to do (or by choosing the option of greater value), I thereby did something that I had no decisive reason to do (or I thereby chose the option of lesser value). But if my account is correct, we can understand the sense in which procrastination is indeed a vice of inaction; procrastination must be primarily characterized as a failure to have chosen the characteristic action on enough occasions (or at the right times). Given that the irrationality of procrastination does not apply to any momentary action, there is no particular action in which we can say that the agent "fell into temptation" and chose the lesser option. We can only say, for instance, that I acted irrationally given that I *did not* write a decent novel; my procrastination consists not in any of the actions that I undertook when I could have been writing but in not having written a novel.

## GENERALIZING THE ACCOUNT

Obviously, procrastination is not restricted to cases that satisfy conditions (1) through (4). In fact, it is not even clear that one cannot procrastinate with respect to a strict policy. Even if I have a strict policy to start writing my novel at 9:00 A.M., I might put off getting out of bed until 9:30, and this does seem to be a case of procrastination. So, it is worth starting by trying to extend the account to strict policies. We must notice first that even a strict policy needs to be implemented through various steps. So my 9-to-7 policy might need a first step such as "Begin writing at 9:00 A.M." But this first step has the same structure as a vague policy; it does not determine a precise moment in which my finger needs to hit the keyboard, but it can be executed by a number of different choices (idle finger drumming from 9:00:01 to 9:00:05, finger hits keyboard at 9:00:07, and so on). And here, too, we will need the virtue of practical judgment to avoid frittering away time until, without my noticing, my choices clearly are not within an acceptable set (i.e., it is already 9:01, and my fingers are still drumming). This also allows us to generalize this account to short-term procrastination. Suppose that I want to bake a cake for my wife, and I want it to be a nice cake, not put together at the last moment. However, as the day goes by, I check the Internet, I go out to buy coffee and bagels, and so forth. By the end of the day, I only have time to bake a cake from a boxed mix, an outcome that surely was not one that I considered acceptable.

Ordinarily, we would think that I begin to engage in the action of baking a cake when I take the first ingredient out of the cupboard. But if we consider the plan to bake a cake also an action, then we can stretch ordinary language and call "baking a cake" the long-term action that begins with the planning of the cake and ends (or, at least, aims to end) with a cake coming out of the oven. And now we can see that the same structure applies to the action of baking a cake as applies to my writing a novel. In particular, we can think of the plan to bake a cake as a vague plan that I try to implement without the help of any intermediate plans. It is vague, since, again, there are clearly acceptable sets of choices (such as the set of choices in which I got coffee and bagels and still managed to bake my spectacular Black Forest cake), clearly unacceptable ones (such as the one that describe my actual choices in our example), and some that are borderline cases (some cases in which my cake fell somewhere between the boxed mix and my spectacular Black Forest cake). In order to end up in an acceptable set of choices, I must be capable of making momentary choices that will strike the right balance between baking the cake and doing other things that might also be important. Here, too, insofar as I failed to end up at an acceptable set of choices, I failed to exhibit the virtue of practical judgment, just in the same way that I failed to exercise the virtue when I did not end up writing a decent novel.

It is important to notice that this account of procrastination does not depend on any kind of discounting or preference reversal for greater rewards in the present.[18] This might be considered a disadvantage of the view, but I think not. Suppose that I actually enjoy writing more than performing household chores. However, every time before I begin to write, I decide to engage in the household chores so I will not forget to do them, or I just think that it is better to do the things I do not enjoy before I engage in something I do enjoy.[19] If I keep thinking, "I will just get this one more thing out of the way, and then I will start writing," I do exhibit procrastination. After all, I put off a valuable project, and as a result of putting it off in this way, I fail to achieve an important end. Of course, this is not to say that often what causes procrastination, what prevents me from displaying the virtue of practical judgment, is exactly the kind of hyperbolic discounting described by Ainslie (and others).[20] However, procrastination on its own does not require preference shifts, let alone hyperbolic discounting; one can procrastinate even if one is a perfect Sidgwickean agent who counts every good the same way irrespective of its temporal location.

Notice also that on this account, one can be very strong-willed (capable of resisting temptation) and yet be a serious procrastinator. Of course, at some point, one will expect that if one is strong-willed enough to move to a precise enough policy, one will not have trouble in executing the policy without the help of further policies or habits or dispositions. But there is at least the theoretical possibility that this is not the case; it might be possible that without a more specific policy that makes my starting time more precise, I cannot execute an intention to start working at 9:00 A.M. As the milliseconds pass by, I can see no reason to start working *right now* rather than at the very next moment; I can continue on this path of inaction until I realize that it is already 9:01 without at any time having succumbed to any specific temptation.

One might argue that certain cases we ordinarily describe as procrastination will not be covered by this account. Suppose, for instance, that I need to get my grading done by the end of the week. I keep putting it off, but I do finish it on time, even though I waited till the last minute to do it. Does this count as procrastination? Ordinarily, we would think that

---

18. Andreou makes a similar point in "Understanding Procrastination."
19. One might think that this shows a preference for household chores. But suppose that my coauthor were to offer this: "I can either do your household chores or write the book for you." I would always ask him or her to do the household chores.
20. See Ainslie, *Breakdown of Will* (as well as his chapter 1 in this volume).

someone who leaves things to the last minute is a paradigmatic procrastinator, but it seems that my account would not count such action as procrastination. After all, it seems that it follows from the fact that the grading was completed that I did nothing irrational,[21] and it follows from the fact that I did nothing irrational that I did not manifest any kind of vice of irrationality.

However, this account classifies at least some cases of putting off a task to the last moment as irrational. Suppose, for instance, that during the week I chose to forgo various activities in the hope that I would finish my grading. Suppose, for instance, that on Wednesday, I turned down an invitation to go for dinner at my favorite restaurant, thinking that I should do my grading instead. However, rather than doing my grading, I spent the evening aimlessly browsing the Internet, deleting old files from my computer, nibbling, or in any set of activities that I find much inferior to fine dining. Suppose that Thursday goes by more or less the same way. We might think that on Saturday, as I look back at my week and what I did accomplish (a slightly less cluttered desktop, all of the comments on a cantankerous political blog having been read, and, of course, the grading), I might think that nothing other than my own pattern of choice was responsible for my ending up with an outcome that I find unacceptable. This will be a case of procrastination under our account.[22]

I do not mean to deny that I might put off my grading in such a way that I can look back at my week as pleasant and stress-free up to the fated Friday evening of grading. Absent any further relevant circumstances, no plausible view would classify this behavior as irrational; in this case, the account I present here would certainly return the verdict that I had not procrastinated. I must confess that I do not have settled intuitions about whether this is something that in ordinary parlance we would call "procrastination." But even if such cases are ordinarily classified as procrastination, these are cases in which procrastination is not a vice. So, I am happy to restrict my ambition: I hope to have provided an account of the vice of procrastination or of procrastination insofar as it is a vice.

## PROCRASTINATION AND INSTRUMENTALISM

There is a further important implication of this understanding of procrastination. In "The Normativity of Instrumental Reason," Christine Korsgaard argues for the incoherence of a view according to which the only principle of practical reason is the principle of instrumental rationality.[23]

---

21. Again, this is assuming that my ends are rational and I know them to be so.
22. I am also assuming that there are no unexpected irrelevant circumstances. If the fact that I had enough time to finish my grade turned out to be sheer luck (say, there were a number of exams that were just blank), my procrastination would still have been irrational.
23. Korsgaard, "Normativity," esp. 229–230.

I do not count myself among such instrumentalists, so it saddens me to say that I bring good tidings for those who do. Korsgaard's argument against the instrumentalist is complex, and I do not claim to address it here in its entirety (and I certainly do not claim that I am about to refute it). However, one aspect of her argument loses some of its force in view of our account of procrastination. Korsgaard argues that an instrumentalist will ultimately be unable to account for the possibility of violating the principle of instrumental reason. Let us take a seemingly typical case of violating instrumental rationality: an agent refuses to undergo a lifesaving operation out of fear. However, as we explain why the agent violated the principle of instrumental rationality, we at the same time identify an end of the agent that *is* furthered by such an action—namely, the end of avoiding pain (or avoiding certain procedures). But if this is the case, why shouldn't one say that the agent did *not* violate the instrumental principle; she efficiently pursued a different end. It seems that the instrumentalist faces a dilemma: either she will have to identify certain things as the "real ends" of the agent (and claim that violations of the instrumental principle are failures to pursue the agent's real ends), or she will have to treat any apparent violation of the instrumental principle as adoption of a different end that is, in fact, furthered by the agent's actions. In either case, instrumentalism turns out to be false; in neither case is it true that the principle of instrumental reason is the sole principle of practical rationality. The first strategy amounts to accepting implicitly a second principle of instrumental rationality, that one ought to pursue one's real ends. The second amounts to rejecting the normativity of the instrumental principle: if no action, or combination of actions, could count as a violation of the principle of instrumental rationality, then the principle does not prescribe anything.

When we look at momentary actions, this argument seems persuasive.[24] Suppose that I spend the bonus I earned on Monday on a nice watch, instead of saving it to procure nourishment on Sunday as I had planned to do before I cashed my bonus check. When the instrumentalist looks at my action on Monday, it seems that she has only two options. She could say that given that I chose the watch, my end (or my most preferred option) on Monday was to buy the watch rather than to have a proper meal on Sunday; in other words, I must have changed my mind when I cashed the check. But if the instrumentalist always reads off my ends from my actions in this manner, no violation of the instrumental principle seems possible. On the other hand, the instrumentalist might not want to say that all cases in which I choose to buy the watch are cases in which my end (or my most preferred option) is to buy the watch. The instrumentalist might insist that at least in some such cases, for the purposes of assessing my

---

24. I do, however, have some doubts that it is ultimately persuasive even in this case; see Tenenbaum, "Speculative Mistakes."

rationality, my real end on Monday is to eat properly on Sunday. But then the instrumentalist must distinguish between the end I actually pursue (buying the watch) and the real end (eating properly on Sunday) and claim that I ought to pursue the latter rather than the former. But in this case, the instrumentalist has smuggled a new principle of rationality, the principle that prescribes the pursuit of those ends that the instrumentalist identifies as my real ends.

However, this problem for the instrumentalist disappears when we look at cases of procrastination. It is worth focusing again on the case of my writing a decent novel. Suppose that I procrastinate and never finish writing the novel. Here we seem to have a simple case of adopting an end without taking the necessary means that were available (and known to be available) to me. In order to understand this failure of instrumental rationality, we need not ascribe to the agent a real end hidden behind the ends he actually pursues. My end of writing a novel is revealed precisely by my pursuit; despite the fact that I fail to achieve my end of writing a novel, I do engage in its pursuit. Notice that, unlike the case of my buying a watch, saying that I changed my mind at a certain point in time will not make the charge of irrationality go away.

This point is easier to see if we think I have a deadline to write a novel. I might need to have it sent to the publishers by a certain date (say, one year from today). Given the vagueness of acceptable plans, it is likely that I will still be trying to write a novel when it is no longer feasible to finish it in time. But now let us look at two points in time in which one can say that I changed my mind: before I stopped writing and after (or exactly at the point that) I stopped writing. If one chooses to locate the change of mind before I stopped writing the novel, if I no longer had the end of writing a novel when I stopped, then I was instrumentally irrational by engaging in the characteristic activities of writing a novel without having any end that was furthered by this activity. If, more plausibly, one locates the change of mind after (or exactly at the point that) I stopped writing, then at the moment before I changed my mind, I would have been instrumentally irrational. It was true then that I had the end of writing a novel but had taken insufficient means to bring it about.

Of course, one could claim that the instrumentalist must attribute to me in this case a certain gerrymandered end rather than the end of writing a novel. Perhaps one can argue that the instrumentalist is for some reason committed to saying that I did not (ever?) have the end of writing a novel but only had ends such as typing the words "It was a dark and stormy night" on the paper or engaging a number of times in the characteristic activities of writing a novel. But since these ends would not be capable of explaining my actions as well as the simpler end of writing a novel, there is no reason to think that the instrumentalist must stop short of attributing to me the end of writing a novel. And obviously, what I say about the case of my writing a novel extends to many, if not all, cases of procrastination. According to the account presented here, procrastination is a failure of instrumental rationality, and we can attribute this failure to an agent without presupposing any further norms of rationality.

## FINAL WORDS

By saying that procrastination is a vice in virtue of being a specific failure of instrumental rationality, I do not mean to imply that every such failure is vicious. If I procrastinate in my plans to assassinate my neighbor, my procrastination might be neither vicious nor irrational. If my account is correct, practical judgment is an instrumental virtue, and whether such virtues still count as virtues when manifested in the pursuit of bad ends and whether their corresponding vices are still vices (or instances of irrationality) when manifested in the pursuit of bad ends is something on which the account presented here remains neutral. My aim here was simply to understand how procrastination could count as an instrumental vice. The more precise demarcation of which instances of procrastination are, in fact, vicious or irrational will depend on a more general understanding of the role of instrumental virtues in assessing the practical rationality of an agent.

## ACKNOWLEDGMENTS

I would like to thank all of the participants in the CSMN procrastination workshop for very helpful feedback and stimulating discussion. I would also like to thank in particular Chrisoula Andreou, Phil Clark, Joe Heath, Jennifer Nagel, Ulrike Heuer, and Mark White for excellent comments on drafts of this chapter.

# 9

# Virtue for Procrastinators

*Elijah Millgram*

In one prominent recent tradition, acting virtuously is conceived in terms of the responses of an ideal role model: the virtuous thing to do is what that role model would do.[1] That tradition has repeatedly come in for criticism, on the grounds that ideal role models are not necessarily the best guides for people who fall too far short of that ideal, and I think there is an insufficiently discussed question to which the complaint should direct our attention, one that is constructive rather than merely critical: What can virtue theory recommend to such people?

To show that the question pays back the asking, I want to discuss an aspect of virtue for procrastinators.[2] There are various ways to address procrastination from a virtue-theoretic point of view, because, like the common cold, procrastination is a symptom produced by various—and structurally quite different—underlying conditions. Here I am going to confine myself to just one of those many sorts of procrastination, one that springs from a deep but perhaps insufficiently appreciated fact about some important human goods: that their value is in a quite distinctive way not simply the sum of momentary goods. I will consider one of the strategies we resort to in coping with the problems that arise from this fact and draw conclusions from that discussion for the current debate about the centrality of instrumental rationality.

---

    1. Well-known examples of the view include McDowell, *Mind, Value, and Reality*, chap. 3, and Hursthouse, *On Virtue Ethics*. The general drift of this tradition is that virtue is something that we are to aim at for ourselves, which means that I am leaving to one side theorizing about virtue directed toward the management and supervision of the unimprovably base. However, many of the points I want to make can be adapted to such alternative approaches.

    2. By way of explaining my choice of case study: I have elsewhere proposed that it is theoretically fruitful to pick out virtues as preconditions for effective practical reasoning (Millgram, *Ethics Done Right*, chap. 4). There are many conflicting theories of what counts as practical reasoning, correctly executed. But doing what you have decided to do, when you have decided to do it, will turn out to be such a precondition, on almost anyone's theory of practical reasoning. And procrastination looks to most people to be a vice, even when they have not signed on to my proposal. So the suggestion that procrastination is a vice ought to serve as neutral ground for exploring fallback virtues.

I hope to persuade you that we should be thinking about virtue for procrastinators and, by extension, the fallback virtues of those who are less than perfect in other respects. One reason to do so is perhaps to give them better moral advice than they have been getting. But if I am right, there is a further payoff: work on such virtues may speak to other and more theoretical philosophical problems—in this case, the merits of the widespread view that instrumental or means-end reasoning is all there is to figuring out what to do (or, in a more nuanced version I will consider, all there *has* to be to figuring out what to do).

## VIRTUE AND THE CONDITIONAL FALLACY

The complaint with which we began the discussion takes the form, nowadays, of an observation that what Robert Shope dubbed the *conditional fallacy* can be applied to certain Aristotelian accounts of virtue, those that define the virtuous thing to do as what the fully virtuous person would do in one's own circumstances.[3]

Shope's treatment was a recipe for disqualifying definitions that took the form of the one at which we have just gestured. It consisted of picking a test case, one that the proposed definition ought to count in, for which the antecedent of the counterfactual conditional used by the definition comes out invariably false. Here, the proposed definition of "$x$ is the virtuous thing to do" is, roughly, "if a fully virtuous agent were in your circumstances, he would do $x$." So the sort of test case recommended by Shope's formula would involve circumstances a virtuous person would never allow himself to get into, or, alternatively, a case in which one of the circumstances is, precisely, one's not being virtuous.

Bernard Williams provided the following example, in an argument directed against John McDowell.[4] Faced with the question of whether to keep alcohol around the house, the fully virtuous person maintains a well-stocked liquor cabinet—first and foremost, we may imagine, under the heading of hospitality, itself one of the virtues. An alcoholic is admittedly not virtuous, but there are nonetheless better and worse ways for him to proceed: keeping something to drink around the house is definitely one of the worst, and getting rid of the liquor cabinet is evidently the prudent and upstanding thing to do. If the virtue theorist maintains that the alcoholic's choice should imitate that of the ideally virtuous person, he is giving what is clearly the wrong answer. The right answer is not generated by the proposed definition. And if the theorist insists that people

---

3. The conditional fallacy is introduced in Shope, "Conditional Fallacy"; more recent discussion of the general phenomenon is sometimes conducted under the heading of "finkish dispositions."
4. See Williams, "Replies."

who are not in a position to imitate the ideally virtuous are thereby not virtuous, but rather *base*, and that is where his ethical advice stops, he is narrowing the scope of application of his theory to the point of making it ethically irrelevant. Human beings are, almost all of them, only human.[5]

As a refutation of a certain sort of first pass over a certain sort of ethical theory, the conditional fallacy is clean and compelling. But the refutation does not amount to useful advice, and in any case, the thought driving virtue theory—that what matters, ethically, is what kind of person you are—has application even to the people whom the objection adduces. *Given* that one is an alcoholic (or afraid of heights, or stingy, or gossipy, or shy. . .), surely there are both more and less admirable ways to comport oneself in the face of such a fact. The alcoholic who is aware of and compensates for his dispositions is a *better person* than one who passively lets himself be overwhelmed by them. An account of what virtue is ought to reflect that fact.

---

5. Robert Johnson's "Virtue and Right" is a lengthier application of Shope's technique to virtue ethics. (He suggests that the reach of his argument extends somewhat further than the conditional fallacy; 818n. 20.) Johnson is focused on self-improvement but seems to think of it as, in the first place, making oneself more virtuous; probably for this reason, although he does at one point consider prosthetic devices that might serve the unimprovable, for the most part, character change in the direction of full-fledged virtue is his target. Millgram, *Ethics Done Right*, section 5.2, discusses related difficulties with ideal advisor theories, to which virtue theorists of the type we have been considering tend to retreat under pressure. It is worth noting that not all philosophical definitions that deploy counterfactual conditionals succumb to the conditional fallacy—or anyway, it is not obvious that they do. For instance, Millgram, "Williams' Argument," explains how it was that Williams thought his definition of a reason for action to be immune to it.

The neo-Aristotelian approach to ethics is, in part, a response to criticism by G. E. M. Anscombe, "Modern Moral Philosophy," and Bernard Williams, *Ethics and the Limits of Philosophy*, to the effect that secular philosophers had better not deploy theoretical constructs that could only be anchored theologically. In the neo-Aristotelian's self-conscious attempt to return to ancient Greek roots, the species form is taken as the replacement anchor; this is why such views appeal to the ideally virtuous *human being*. But suppose you are unconvinced that there is anything prescriptively special about species membership, and suppose you are willing for a moment to entertain theological-sounding contrasts: then it becomes obvious that *all* virtue is fallback virtue. God doesn't get into fights, and so He doesn't need courage; God doesn't spend money, and so He doesn't need the virtue of generosity; for that matter, God doesn't have to figure things out, and so He doesn't need our epistemic virtues, either. Our virtues are virtues for *us*, and only because we ourselves are less than ideal beings. With a bit of perspective, the turn I am going to be recommending—I mean, redirecting our attention to fallback virtues—should not be thought of as deeply different from the theoretical enterprise in which we were already engaged. (I'm especially grateful to Tom Pink for this point.)

This means that there is no call fastidiously to insist that if it falls short of full-fledged virtue, it is not virtue at all, and then to turn to the task of, say, providing rules to govern the behavior of the uncultivated (instead of urging them to be as virtuous as they can be). After all, the only excellences that are not—in the really big scheme of things—fallbacks are not intelligible as *virtues* at all.

## JAM YESTERDAY, JAM TOMORROW

Procrastination is the vice of putting off what one means to do, until later than one meant to do it. (And if I am right about "procrastination" being a classification on a par with "colds," we can leave it at that for now; there's a reason we don't put a lot of work into a precise definition of the common cold.) Now, like alcoholics locking up the liquor cabinet and throwing away the key, procrastinators can avail themselves of a familiar range of countermeasures that will make them better behaved. Some are more or less generic antidotes, such as side bets: when you promise to pay someone a stiff penalty if you have not done such and such by tomorrow at 6:00, you are externalizing and amplifying your incentive structure, which may well forestall or overcome the tendency to let things slide. But since procrastination is a symptom that may be produced by many different etiologies, not all of it is to be treated with the same medicine. Some of the more effective remedies are tailored to the particular underlying problem, and so to explain how one form of procrastination appears in human lives, I want now to take up a puzzling feature of many central human goods.

At one point in Lewis Carroll's *Through the Looking Glass*,[6] the White Queen offers its hero a position as a domestic servant. And when Alice asks about her compensation package, she is surprised to find that, in addition to a weekly salary, it consists of jam tomorrow and jam yesterday, but never jam today. Alice objects that it *must* sometimes come to jam today and declares herself confused to hear that it does not. Call this the *jam-yesterday-jam-tomorrow* structure of a good; Alice is not alone in being confused by it.

The really confusing surprise is that many acknowledged goods possess the jam-yesterday-jam-tomorrow structure, and a couple of examples should suffice to remind us of that fact. Children are often thought, and not merely by those who do not have them, to be one of the things that make life worth living. But when you look at just about any given point in time, over the period in which you raise your child, you find yourself changing diapers, or trying to herd the children out the door, or correcting their manners, or breaking up a sibling squabble, and so forth. Each of these moments is frustrating, or tiresome, or at best mildly rewarding, and so the good that is able to make life worth living cannot be located at any of those moments, or even in all of them taken together.[7]

---

6. Chapter 5.
7. Of course, just as Alice had her salary in addition to her jam ration, there is the distinguishable good of merely *having* a child, to which 1950s American breadwinners, off in the workplace for almost all their progeny's waking hours, largely confined themselves. And there *are* the rewarding moments also: your infant's first word and the like. Although inspection shows that these will not sum up into the good of childrearing, they are typical in this respect: most jam-yesterday-jam-tomorrow goods are impure, and involve or are tied to occasional goods of more straightforward kinds.

I love my job, enough so that it is hard to imagine being willing to trade it in for almost any other. But when you look at any particular moment of it, you are likely to find me desperately trying to figure out what I am going to say to tomorrow's class, or sitting in an airport waiting for my plane, or grading student work, or writing yet another letter of recommendation, or fretfully pacing up and down my living room as I try to make sense of some philosophical point. Once again, the good that can be located in each of these moments does not add up to the explanation of the great value that academic work has for me. And I think that these examples can do duty for a great many more. When you look at important human goods, the good in them is jam yesterday, jam tomorrow—but, very rarely indeed, jam today.

Procrastination arises in such circumstances because human motivation is relatively tightly tied to goods that are concretely visible in the moment (or moments). Not necessarily *this* moment: we are often (not always!) pretty good at deferring satisfaction when we can see a clear path to the later satisfaction, and when we can see that satisfaction, clothed in its apparent goodness or value, present at that later time. When the later or overall good, however, can only be seen (as it were) at the edges of one's peripheral vision—in the ways that jam-yesterday-jam-tomorrow goods typically are seen—motivation turns out to be relatively loosely tied to it. It is easier to take steps toward a good that is temporally locatable.

The existence of this feature of human psychology is corroborated by plentiful anecdote. I love my job, but I do not particularly feel like writing another academic assessment, even though that, and many other things like it, are a large part of my job. Someone may love her children, and love raising them, without feeling like getting out of bed to prepare breakfast, dress them, and get them off to school—even though raising children *is* mostly chores like that one. If the good of the job, or of childraising, were visible in the moment, one would not have nearly the problems that so many people do in getting oneself to do the task of the moment. But the good is not visible in the moment, and so one puts off writing the assessment, or getting out of bed, or whatever else it is: a certain kind of procrastination is a perfectly understandable response to the structure of many important human goods.

I claimed earlier that not all procrastination is produced in the same way, and this is a good occasion to provide some support in passing for that point. Sometimes procrastination itself functions as an extremely powerful motivation. The sort of procrastination we are now considering is not that at all, but rather a persistent failure to sustain one's grip on a consideration that should be motivating, but which somehow can't be seen straight on: an inability to get going, rather than energetic evasion. Here the different explanations exhibit themselves in differences in the phenomenology; we really are considering only one of the presumably many forms that procrastination can take. And for this reason, we should not expect people to be consistent procrastinators. Someone who puts off work-related chores may also turn up compulsively early to dinner parties, when each sort of behavior is produced by a different psychological mechanism.

Philosophers often find modality—the subject demarcation that covers *woulds*, *coulds*, and *musts*—to exhibit structural analogies with temporal phenomena, and so we should not be surprised that there is a modal analogue of jam-yesterday-jam-tomorrow goods. The good of a life full of possibility and promise is not accounted for by examining the concrete outcomes that might materialize out of that possibility and promise. Perhaps the vice analogous to procrastination is that of being insufficiently motivated to protect and promote such goods as liberty, but right now I want only to remark on the vice on the other flank of the relevant Aristotelian mean. Someone might overvalue the goods of possibility and, in the name of keeping his options open, sacrifice far too much in the way of the actual goods for which he could cash his options in. Keeping his options open means postponing the conversion of possibilities into actual goods. And so that modally oriented vice has the effect of reinforcing the tendency to procrastinate.

## AN EXCURSION INTO TRIADOLOGY

Triadology was a stylistic lapse common in epistemology of a decade ago, that of starting off one's paper with the pronouncement: "The following propositions form an inconsistent triad." The jam-yesterday-jam-tomorrow goods we are considering look like they could well launch papers of this sort. To take a good that philosophers have worried over since ethics got going, it is very hard to believe that a life is happy if a preponderance of the moments in it are not happy—that is, you would have to tell a very special story to make a claim that such a life *was* happy convincing. (Notice that the sense in which a *life* is happy is of course different from but importantly related to the sense in which its *moments* can be happy.) Many people live happy lives. But most moments in those lives are not, when you live through them, noticeably happy moments. How can all of these be true together? The apparent pattern crops up too frequently to ignore. A marriage is loving pretty much only if most of the moments in it are loving, and people have loving marriages; they look fondly backward and forward to the past and future moments that bear the characterization. But at any particular present moment in such a marriage, the spouses are just, as it may be, brushing their teeth, and not being loving at all. I want to dispel the air of paradox around jam-yesterday-jam-tomorrow goods; if the reader is distracted by the thought that they just are not possible, it will be hard to keep the focus of the discussion where I want it, and so I'm about to take time out to propose an explanation for them. (However, I should state up front that I am much more confident in the pervasiveness of the phenomenon than I am in any explanation I am ready to offer for it.)

The primary direction of explanation, I speculate, is not from the worth of moment-bound components to the overall worth of the temporally extended good, but rather the other way around: jam-yesterday-jam-tomorrow goods leave a footprint in their momentary constituents. We are used to the idea of the semantic footprints left by a speaker's surroundings on the meanings of his thoughts and utterances, and the evaluative characterizations of the moment-bound elements of a jam-yesterday-jam-tomorrow good are a related phenomenon.[8] So far, so straightforward: someone's first reading of a particular book may have been a turning point in his philosophical development, but the characterization of it as a *turning point* is only available in retrospect, and with the trajectory of his philosophical development mostly in view. At the time of reading, it was perhaps only precious, implausible, and exasperating.

Allow a notion of experience on which evaluative assessments can be part of it, such as when the book was experienced as precious, etc. Although to some extent experience is shaped by expectation, to a surprising degree, it is able to override one's theory-driven view as to what *must* be going on just now; that is what makes observation, observation.[9] One's assessment of the present moment is determined primarily by experience, which overrides the evaluative footprint of the jam-yesterday-jam-tomorrow good to which it contributes. Because experience is only of the here-and-now, one's assessment of *other* moments is determined for the most part by awareness of the evaluative footprint of the temporally extended good. ("For the most part," because for all sorts of reasons, the derivative and moment-bound evaluative characterization may fail to find its foothold.) But now, here are two surprising features of the most prominent jam-yesterday-jam-tomorrow goods we have had under consideration. First, one's assessment of the moment-bound good is partly constitutive of the relevant evaluative characterization's holding of that good. And second, we apprehend the content of the assessment as *experiential*. For instance, the happy moments of the happy life are understood to *feel* happy. How they actually *do* feel is determined largely by one's encounter with the moment. But how they are evaluated with respect to their happiness in prospect or in hindsight (and so, how they are remembered and anticipated as feeling—that being the content of the assessment) is largely determined by the evaluative footprint of the life (or, since, as Aristotle noted, you cannot really evaluate a life until sometime after it is over, as much of it as one can see).

---

8. For semantic context-dependence of this sort, see Putnam, "Meaning of 'Meaning'," and Burge, "Individualism and the Mental."

9. For argument that we have to construe many of our evaluative responses as observation in the most literal sense, see Millgram, *Practical Induction*, esp. chap. 6, and *Ethics Done Right*, chap. 1.

Other authors have noticed that the value of a larger good is often not the sum of the values of its parts. G. E. Moore made the formal point in his well-known discussion of "organic wholes," and David Velleman has noted with respect to whole human lives in particular that we do not assess how well they are going by summing up the momentary goods in them: we think that someone who is born in a dumpster, and ends up a success, is doing better than someone who is born with a silver spoon in his mouth and ends up dying in a dumpster—even if the area under the curve of utility as a function of time is the same in both cases.[10] However, we can now see that, whether the explanation I have just advanced is satisfactory or not, these observations do not yet capture the central and most puzzling aspects of the jam-yesterday-jam-tomorrow structure.

## A VOLITIONAL PROSTHESIS

We have already mentioned a fact about the moral psychology of some human beings, that they can be fairly good at progressing, step by step, toward an end that is located in some particular moment. That fact underwrites a device widely used to cope with jam-yesterday-jam-tomorrow procrastination.

Hiking in the outdoors is another jam-yesterday-jam-tomorrow activity: done right, it is as a whole an immensely satisfying exercise in Applied

---

10. Moore, *Principia Ethica*, 27–36; Velleman, *Possibility of Practical Reason*, chap. 3. For some other objections to the "totting-up model," see Griffin, *Well-Being*, 34–36, 104, 180. The phenomenon is, of course, not confined to lives or personal well-being; for instance, the much-ridiculed 1980s fad of "quality time" was a misapplication of the totting-up model. The idea behind the fad was that by making some short periods of time spent with one's family of higher quality, one could spend less time together without impairing the family relationships or shortchanging one's children. The strategy makes sense on the assumption that the overall value of time spent with one's family is the sum of the values of the shorter periods of time into which the overall time is divided.

Two hedges: First, while it is tempting to characterize jam-yesterday-jam-tomorrow goods as a complicated special case of Moorean organic unities, if my speculations about how these goods work are on target, they are not covered by Moore's use of that term. He was reappropriating the notion from his British Hegelian predecessors, and in the interest of suppressing their rampant constitutivism, he insisted on the independence of the values of the parts themselves from the whole and their relation to it. The Putnam-Burge approach to semantics, as well as the evaluative relative of it that I was suggesting, would have been rejected by the logical atomists.

Second, Velleman joins many others when he tries to account for the phenomenon he is discussing by gesturing at the narrative structure of human life. I have never met anyone able to give me a satisfactory explanation of what is meant by "narrative," and would in any case want to avoid this way of talking myself. But whatever narrative is, and whatever it may tell us about other "organic unities," I don't see how it is able to handle jam-yesterday-jam-tomorrow goods (and evils). Adventure, G. K. Chesterton told us, is an inconvenience rightly considered. When it is adventurous in the past, adventurous in prospect, and at each particular moment not adventurous, but rather inconvenient or even terrifying, that is not accounted for by the narrative structure of adventure.

Romanticism, even though at any particular moment of any particular hike, you are likely to be slogging up the side of a hill through rain and mud, or sweaty and exhausted, or nursing a blister, or wondering where you are and how to get back down to the trailhead before dark. If, like me, you are committed to a weekly hiking quota, the decision to turn around and end the hike early becomes a form of procrastination. It is once again likely to be produced by the inability to see the good of hiking in the several bits of the hike.

Now, if you open a trail guide, you will notice that the hikes are frequently described as bringing you to an objective, typically a landscape feature or a view. (Objectives must be named, which has the odd side effect of generating names for such features, as for instance the "Three Gossips," a rock formation which terminates a walk in Arches National Park.) All the participants understand that seeing the view from that hilltop, or admiring the named rock formation, is not really the point of the hike; they went to spend the day immersed in nature, or catching up with their friends, or getting some exercise, and they do not think of the time on the trail as a sacrifice made for the sake of the final view: if they did, they would have driven to the trailhead closest to that view. Nonetheless, these hikes go better when there is a designated goal that can serve as the turnaround point. It is easier to maintain the motivation required for a satisfying full day's hike ("the Lake Catherine overlook is only two more miles!") when there is a temporally localized end.

A second example: any reasonably thoughtful student is aware that the elaborate graduation ceremonies organized by so many colleges are not why he or she is in school. But education is another good with that jam-yesterday-jam-tomorrow structure. I mean schooling just now, but the point is equally true of education in an earlier and more general sense, where the word serves as a translation for *Bildung*. *The Education of Henry Adams* is a well-known autobiography whose author presents his life as such an education; it has almost as a refrain the observation that his education seems not to have taken place in *this* stretch of his life.

Returning to education more narrowly conceived: On any given occasion, a student is likely to be plowing through a hard-to-read book, or writing a difficult paper, or trying not to doze off in lecture. . . . The education *is* all of these things, and is correctly understood to be a great (and an intrinsic) good; but it is hard to stay focused on its value just because one does not see it, moment to moment. If students had to make their own moment-to-moment decisions as to whether to read the book, or write the paper, or stay in the lecture, on the basis of its intangible contribution to their education, they would be all too likely to put off the unpleasant tasks to some other time. Often students succumb to the illusion that the rewards of education must be distributed among many or most of the moments of it, tacitly concluding that if the rewards are not found in this moment, they must be present in others. I am in college, they tell themselves, to be intellectually engaged; this particular class is not lively and stimulating; so I will save my energy for another class that is, and which does not involve tedious and uninteresting tasks. In the end, such students, acting on such illusions, get scarcely any education at all.

Consequently, administrators provide a dummy goal, the academic equivalent of the designated objective of a hike, and deck it out in colors and music and ritual to make it visible from afar. Then they designate what seem to them to be appropriate ingredients of an education as necessary means to the dummy goal: in order to graduate, you must satisfy so-and-so major and distribution requirements. Those requirements, typically courses one must complete, are in turn structured in much the same way: in order to get a grade, you must satisfy a further list of requirements designated by the instructor.[11]

The strategy, then, is to exploit an already present disposition to take steps toward temporally locatable ends, by overlaying a jam-yesterday-jam-tomorrow good with means-end structure, structure through which an agent may progress to an artificial and often only trivially valuable goal. Let me acknowledge that such devices are not magic bullets; giving the hike an objective does not, for instance, do much to prevent one from postponing the entire outing to some later occasion. And an agent who was a *principled* procrastinator—following recent philosophical literature, we could call him a Tortoise of Procrastination—would be unimproved by a regimen of dummy goals: such an agent would systematically procrastinate when it came to taking steps toward the prosthetic end.[12] Nonetheless, that a device is not an infallible solution to all of one's problems is not a reason to throw it out; what device is?

You would not want the device to be so powerful that the means-end structure hijacked the activity. The person whose job is *just* a long path to retirement ("Only 7,896 more days!") is not going to reap the jam-yesterday-jam-tomorrow rewards of his job; the student who is *just* trying to graduate will not get much of an education; and, as we remarked, the hiker who arranges his hike to reach the view most efficiently will not see much of the mountain. Of course, that is not just true of dummy goals: someone for whom the point was to be finished with raising his children probably would not get much out of raising them. Even if being able to look back and say that one has done it is genuinely rewarding, most of the real rewards happen along the way—but, apparently, at no particular time.

---

11. In the past generation or so, *graduating* and *graduation* have come apart; it is now almost always possible, in American universities, to obtain one's degree without "walking." (I'm grateful to Eric Hutton for pointing this out to me.) Perhaps the somewhat distinct dummy goals differentially serve different classes of agents: the prospect of the degree keeps the student on track, whereas the prospect of ceremony keeps the parents digging into their pocketbooks. While we have the example on hand, let us observe that many such deliberative prosthetics have other functions; for instance, graduation ceremonies help to loyalize a university's alumni.

12. For the Practical Tortoise (a would-be agent exhibiting a principled refusal to take the means to his ends), see Dreier, "Humean Doubts."

Because we are probably all prone to be insufficiently motivated by jam-yesterday-jam-tomorrow goods, we are probably all procrastinators. A perfectly virtuous role model would not need to rely on devices of the sort we have been describing, but would take his outdoor walks and his education straight, without the pretense of instrumentally organized progress to a goal. But if we are going to be as virtuous as *we* can be, we should not be trying to imitate *that* sort of role model.[13] Virtue for *us* consists, among other things, in adopting dummy goals of this sort, and in suppressing the thought that the view at the end of the trail is not any more important than the equally wonderful views we are seeing along the way. If we are virtuous (as virtuous as *we* can be), we will work at identifying jam-yesterday-jam-tomorrow goods, and at developing instrumental structure of this sort to impose on them.

Self-deception is generally understood, by moral philosophers, to be vicious. Surprisingly, then, it is not just that the strategy that is right for us would not be needed by a fully virtuous agent. Part of virtue for procrastinators amounts to engaging in something with a family resemblance to self-deception, that is, in something that looks like a vice.[14]

Aristotle points out that the virtuous are distinguished not only by what they do, but by how they do it. Someone who forestalls procrastination by this sort of self-manipulation may get things done when he means to, but he is doing it very differently from the person to whom acting in a timely way on his intentions comes naturally. However, some readers, at this point, may want to reconsider the labeling. If we are *all* prone to this sort of procrastination, and if it must always be overcome by self-manipulation, then doing so successfully is virtue plain and simple, and

---

13. If my speculative account of jam-yesterday-jam-tomorrow goods is correct, full-fledged virtue in this respect has its own pitfalls. It turns out to involve the ability to override the apparent deliverances of experience and observation, and to proceed confidently on the basis of one's theory of the contribution of the moment to a larger good. But, for many reasons, the disposition to depart from one's theory on the basis of what one can see (and, in particular, to lose confidence in one's theory when one does not see it borne out in one's ongoing experience) is a very good thing indeed. For instance, agents who lack this disposition often turn out to be fanatics.

More generally, volitional prosthetics that accommodate the evaluative perceptions of agents are normally better than entirely rigid ones. Ryan Spellecy, in "Reviving Ulysses Contracts," notices that Ulysses contracts are to the volitionally handicapped what wheelchairs are to the mobility-impaired. (A Ulysses contract may specify, say, that one is to be committed to psychiatric care if one's symptoms recur, even if, at the time, one thinks one does not need it.) However, where Ulysses had himself unconditionally bound to his mast, Spellecy sees the need to make room for reconsideration in his version of Ulysses contracts.

14. A related observation: the Paradox of Hedonism—that you cannot be happy by trying to be—can seem unsolvable. Wouldn't any steps taken to solve it amount to trying to be happy? But our evident ability to address the problem of procrastination by adopting dummy goals suggests that the same technique must be available to the hedonist. If you are unable to obtain pleasure directly, you can still obtain it by pursuing the dummy goal of winning the squash game, a goal you adopted in order to have fun.

not just a fallback virtue. So notice that the points I am arguing for stick even when we allow the relabeling.

## DEFUSING AN ARGUMENT FOR INSTRUMENTALISM

Recent work in the emerging Anscombian tradition in moral philosophy takes the view that instrumental—that is, means-end or "calculative"— reasons are, if not the *only* form that reasons for action can take, then at any rate the central, distinctive, and most important sort of practical reasons.[15] Instrumentalism, the notion that all practical reasoning is means-end reasoning, has been the default position in philosophy for a good while now, but it has also been remarkable for its lack of supporting argumentation. Where earlier instrumentalists seemed to think that their view was too obvious to need to be argued for, Anscombians have, laudably, tried to supply the missing arguments, and, in doing so, to account for their predecessors' sense that the correctness of instrumentalism *is* obvious.

Their arguments turn on and express roughly this thought: calculatively structured activity (that is, sequences of actions that exhibit step-by-step progress toward a termination point or stopping place: the sequence's "end") is pervasive in human life; therefore, means-end reasons must have a special status in human rationality. Anscombians sometimes advance a more muted expression of this thought than instrumentalism proper: it is not that all practical reasons are means-end reasons, but rather that means-end reasons are the only sort of reason you cannot do without, and still be practically rational. (All other sorts of reason for action are *optional*.)[16] In my own view, the Anscombians are correct about the pervasiveness of calculatively structured activity: when you look around, you can see it just about everywhere. But I want to suggest, drawing on our discussion of virtue for procrastinators, that the conclusions which Anscombians have been recommending do not follow as directly as that.

An instrumental reason is one that adduces the end to be attained: the point of taking the step the reason recommends is, precisely, to get you the end. So, in instrumental or calculative reasoning, the end is what both the reasoning and the activity are *for*. If all calculatively structured activities *were* being performed for the sake of their respective ends, perhaps it

---

15. Anscombe, *Intention*; Vogler, *Reasonably Vicious*, and "Anscombe"; Thompson, *Life and Action*, Part II (but see also pp. 3f). In Vogler's writing, "instrumentalism" and related expressions are reserved for psychologistic forms of the view (e.g., that all reasons for action serve the satisfaction of a desire, i.e., a psychological state), and "calculative," for her preferred and nonpsychologistic version. Here I will use the terms indifferently.

16. However, Vogler seems to me to be ambivalent about the concession, due to roughly the following train of thought. Reasons are, as it tends to be put in the local philosophical tradition, "normative"; normativity implies the possibility of correction; noninstrumental reasons are optional, which means that you can always shrug off corrections; therefore, putative noninstrumental reasons are not *really* reasons after all.

would be hard to avoid being impressed by the importance of ends, and thus of instrumental reasoning. But we have just seen that at least some calculatively structured activities are *not* performed for the sake of their ends: they exhibit stepwise progress toward an end, to be sure, but that end is a dummy goal, installed as a way of managing procrastination in the face of jam-yesterday-jam-tomorrow goods. Reaching the objective with the view is not the point of the hike, and graduating is not the point of going to college.

So we should not be so quick to read the importance of instrumental reasons off the pervasiveness of instrumentally or calculatively structured activity. It is hard to know how to give a quantitative answer to the question of how much calculatively structured activity is not really directed toward attaining an end, and thus not really driven by instrumental reasons. However, it does not seem unfair to estimate it as, in any event, a great deal. We have already seen that calculative structure is used as a volitional prosthesis in matters great and small. And we should bear in mind the possibility that coping with procrastination is not the only occasion for engaging in what looks like means-end reasoning, but whose point is not actually to bring about its ostensible end.[17]

An Anscombian might reply that it is my own conclusion that is being too quickly drawn. If in fact we can rely in these sorts of ways on a widespread proclivity to follow means-end sequences, even when we are aware that they are little more than stage sets which we use to coax ourselves into acting, surely that in itself demonstrates that instrumental rationality has some sort of special status, one that does need to be accommodated by an adequate theory of practical reasons. Just as people who abuse promises bear witness to the power of promising, people who bypass motivational obstacles by producing an illusion or imitation of compelling instrumental reasons thereby exhibit the grip that reasons of that sort have on us. And so I should not conclude, from the fact that we make use of such illusions and imitations, that they do not have a special sort of grip.

My assessment of the state of play is that this procrastinators' virtue makes clear the need for arguments tying the Anscombians' observation about the pervasiveness of calculatively structured activity more tightly to the conclusions they draw from it—or, alternatively, that demonstrate that the connection is too loose to support those conclusions. That in turn suggests how thinking about virtues of this general kind can be philosophically valuable, and advance debates in regions of philosophy outside of virtue theory proper.

---

17. Under this heading, Margaret Bowman's dissertation (in progress) argues that we often make long-range plans that we know we are unlikely to execute, and that the point of doing so has to do with orientation in the here and now. Someone who says "till death do us part" during the marriage ceremony need not be unaware of the divorce statistics; vows that reflected those statistics, however, would be the start of a very different, and presumably less satisfactory, sort of marriage.

## VIRTUE FOR LOSERS

Too much contemporary philosophical writing about the traditional virtues is thin and stereotyped, and it is easy to suspect that the problem has to do with who the authors are. We see battlefield courage being discussed by sheltered academics who have never held a gun; self-control praised by the staid and scholarly, bookish people who have never let themselves go and would not know how; largesse, discussed by middle-class wage earners and mortgage holders. (By this last, I mean *megaloprepeia*, the Aristotelian virtue of those who endow libraries and concert halls.) And so we naturally put down any complaints we have about how the virtues are rendered to the inexperience of the professorial class.

But if the line of argument we were pursuing rang true, perhaps the right explanation need not after all be a harsh indictment of the life-experience qualifications of the virtue theorists. Portraits of the full-fledged traditional virtues *are* unlikely to have been drawn from life. But that is not just because it was professors who were drawing them: almost all the virtue that anyone encounters, anywhere, is fallback virtue—that is, virtue in the general category to which the virtue that we have been considering belongs. And if that is correct, then we have a further reason to think about, well, virtue for losers. It is not just that, as I have been suggesting, doing so may add to the stock of advice, and not just that we are likely to find ourselves in the vicinity of contributions to philosophical debates about, say, practical rationality. Our renderings of these virtues are much likelier to be convincing and, because convincing, honestly instructive.

## ACKNOWLEDGMENTS

I would like to thank Chrisoula Andreou, Carla Bagnoli, Jerry Cohen, Roger Crisp, Avner Offer, and Tom Pink for conversation on these topics, and Eric Hutton for comments on an earlier draft. The chapter was improved by audience feedback at the CSMN workshop. I am grateful as well to All Souls College for lodging.

# 10

# Procrastination as Vice

*Jennifer A. Baker*

Philosophers often give procrastination an anemic description—a preference, a conflict, a case of irrationality. Presumably, this is done in order to make it susceptible to analysis. But if one makes use of ethical theory, particularly one with an accompanying account of moral psychology, no arid depiction of procrastination is necessary. An ethical theory that is robust enough—such as traditional virtue ethics—can meet procrastination head on, unhindered by its complex emotionality and opaque intentionality. It can then place it alongside similarly complex behavior, comparing and contrasting until we have some account of the darker alleyways of our nature and the limits of our self-control.

That the term *vice* is out of favor gives us no reason to deny that procrastination is a moral phenomenon. In this chapter, I want to demonstrate that the determinations a completed ethical theory must offer—what humans are capable of, likely to do, and ought to do—are the metrics necessary for any attempt to assess procrastination in a manner that answers the questions we have. Its measure taken, we will see that procrastination can, so to speak, return the favor to ethical theory by drawing out its resources and letting us consider how helpful ethical theory can be if applied.

As normal an event as procrastination is, we do not seem to understand it. Writers on the topic frequently offer earnest and ad hoc accounts of their own, as if there are no resources available but their hunches. For instance, I have read elaborately couched conclusions according to which writer's block is caused by a blank page being terrifying.[1] Ethical theory is

---

1. As an example of description standing in for explanation, the procrastination researcher Piers Steel describes the intractable procrastination of popular author Douglas Adams, who needed editors to lock him in a room and wait outside in order for him to finish writing. As Steel writes (in "Case Studies"), "The major reason for Adams' chronic delaying appears to be task aversiveness. Though he was an able writer and extremely creative, he found putting pen to paper unpleasant. He put it off as long as possible, and then produced in a frantic rush when eventually necessary. With his wealth from the earlier bestsellers, it became increasingly less necessary and these delays stretched into years."

put in a good light when it helps us to clarify what we find confusing in our very own behavior. And though we hardly ever think we need an ethical theory to tell us that something is wrong, in the case of procrastination, some ethical theories guide us to gentler judgments. Procrastination might not be, technically speaking, a vice, showing that ethical theorizing need not always increase moralism.

After all, ethical theory is not just a list of judgments or merely an additional force with which to condemn behavior. Ethical theories give a means for clarifying our views on behaviors by considering them systematically and in relation to particular takes on our psychology. For example, in this chapter, I consider three different ethical theories on procrastination, each with its own account of what has gone wrong when we find ourselves putting off a task. Each of these theories makes use of *vice* in a theoretical way, and I hope the example of this gives us a new appreciation for the ability of the term *vice* to refer to more than the charmingly roguish habits we associate it with outside of ethical theory (habits that typically fail to optimize decorum or health by the same degree to which they curtail hypocrisy).

But we have two challenges before us: pinning down vice and pinning down procrastination. Although the proper relationship between psychological research and philosophical analysis is a vexed one, and, to my mind, we easily get the priority wrong, in the case of procrastination, it seems to me that the psychologists ought to set the agenda for philosophers to follow.

## WHAT IS PROCRASTINATION? THE ROLE OF PSYCHOLOGICAL DATA

Philosophers inherit established problems—often fascinating ones, such as the nature of rationality or will—and aspects of procrastination can be relevant to these. But emphasizing only an element of procrastination with a squeaky-clean definition ("putting unavoidable things off") can fail to illuminate the costs and experience of procrastination. It is not always a paper turned in a day late. The rates of medical noncompliance, astonishingly high, have been connected to procrastination.[2] Furthermore, it is not as if the costs of procrastination are clear in the short term. One study suggests that most damage done by chronic procrastination comes only in midcareer, by which time procrastinators have developed a dispirited detachment to their chosen professions.[3] The impulsivity, mindlessness, and pessimism psychologists find associated with regular procrastinators suggest a relationship between more established and studied behavior disorders

---

2. Levy, "Failure to Refill Prescriptions."
3. Dweck, "Motivational Processes."

(such as impulsive eating). The procrastinator is also in bad company, as narcissists and sociopaths procrastinate frequently.[4] These features of procrastination do not readily occur to us unaided.

Procrastination is a rather opaque phenomenon, and philosophers' intuitions are likely unreliable. Joseph Ferrari has gathered data on how confusing procrastination can be to both the subject and the observer.[5] Procrastinators often report that they do not know what it is they are avoiding. And even longtime researchers such as Ferrari have found their results surprising and have had their studied assumptions upset.[6] It is an incredibly productive time for psychologists investigating procrastination.

I despair of the productivity of empirical researchers working on happiness and ethics when we do not even have agreement on what these phenomena are. But in the case of procrastination, the cart is not before the horse, because there is little dispute over what is under study. Daniel Boice's extensive research into procrastination (making great use of academics as subjects) found that observed subjects readily demonstrate procrastination, and both subject and observer agree that it has happened.[7] Unlike in the study of happiness or ethics, the standards for operationalization can be met, and Gopal Sreenivasan has generated a helpful list of these. According to Sreenivasan, there are three minimum characteristics a behavioral measure would have to include in order to properly operationalize a given trait: "each behavioral measure must specify a response that represents a central or paradigm case of what that trait requires; the concrete situation each specifies must not have any features that defeat the reason on account of which that trait requires the response in question; and the subject and the observer must agree on these characterizations of the specified responses and situations."[8]

Procrastination researchers seem to have some consensus about the paradigm case of the trait. Everyone can be said to procrastinate about some things, but regular procrastinators can be distinguished from the rest of us by displaying the following patterns during everyday work activities:

1. Busyness and impulsive rushing.
2. A product orientation (an articulated focus on the number of papers published or pages done), as opposed to a process orientation.

---

4. Boice, *Procrastination and Blocking*.
5. Ferrari and Patel, "Social Comparisons."
6. As one example, Ferrari's work (with Johnson and McCowen) in 1995, *Procrastination and Task Avoidance*, was more optimistic about potential benefits of procrastination than his work is now. Root explanations of cause are still at stake. Ferrari used to be sympathetic to the idea that procrastination is exacerbated by modern trends, but his own research contradicts that assumption. In other words, we are in need of data before we can pin down this subject.
7. Boice, *Procrastination and Blocking*.
8. Sreenivasan, "Errors about Errors," 61–62.

3. Discernible anxiety (fidgeting, tense facial expressions, ease of distraction).
4. Unrealistic beliefs stated spontaneously about how high-priority work will get done.
5. Hostile attitudes toward pressures for orderliness and timeliness.
6. Suboptimal outcomes.[9]

Since I have no intention of reducing the phenomenon to something else, any omissions or oversimplifications are not intentional. I am not aiming to tinker with the results of empirical research on procrastination. They ought to come first and then set the philosophers' agenda.

Studies on procrastination at work have led psychologists to conclude that it is a matter of poor work habits exacerbated by underlying, unrealistic attitudes toward work. Misleading self-conceptions are also involved, and these include perfectionistic expectations. These habits and attitudes are not resistant to changes in situations, and there are many external ways to discourage procrastination. On the other hand, the procrastinator can reinforce her own behavior by procrastinating. A cruel cycle exists: procrastinators are inefficient in doing their work, they make unrealistic plans in regard to work, and they are so cowed by perfectionist pressures that they become incapable of incorporating advice or feedback into their future behavior.[10] Procrastinators experience an "aftermath of disappointment, lowered self-confidence, depression and uncertainty about their abilities."[11]

One further interesting finding is that procrastination and "blocking" (as in writer's block) are too intimately connected to clearly distinguish from each other. Blocking is a "nervous slowing of activity, self-conscious narrowing of scope, and even immobilization."[12] This becomes significant because, if we are considering the impact of procrastination on efficiency, it means we have to recognize that it might keep us from accomplishing things altogether. (We may not just write papers in a rush, but neither will we get to rehab.) If "procrastination" can keep us from accomplishing things altogether, we may put less stock in the observation that procrastinators do "suboptimal" work (less work than average, work rendered

---

9. Boice, *Procrastination and Blocking*, 60. Boice makes it clear that we should not accept the things procrastinators say—the best work coming when under pressure, creative genius coming from frenzy. In a long-term study (six years) of the productivity of 104 new professors, some identified as regular procrastinators (by the measures listed above) and others identified as "efficient" nonprocrastinators, the procrastinators being engaged in what Boice termed "binge writing." They produced less and less successful work (it was not published as often) as "regular writers" (whom he termed "efficient" nonprocrastinators). He concludes that even those who profess to work best under pressure actually do not. The results are marked by the impulsive rushing (resulting in typos) that, along with such rationalization, is part of the phenomenon of procrastination.
10. Dweck, "Motivational Processes."
11. Boice, *Procrastination and Blocking*, 131.
12. Boice, *Procrastination and Blocking*, xii.

sloppy by rushing, and so forth). The determination that some work is "suboptimal" seems dependent on the possibility that better work could have been done. But what about the possibility that it was going to be suboptimal work or nothing at all? We will consider the possibility that procrastination hinders outcomes, but we have further reasons for rejecting the idea that this should be the locus of a moral evaluation.

Finally, though I do not mean to suggest that data I am not mentioning are irrelevant, I would like to highlight that Ferrari has found that there are different types of procrastinators and that they procrastinate for different types of reasons. These include "arousal types," who experience a "euphoric rush" by putting off their work until it is too late; "avoiders," who seem to have issues of self-esteem that they are confirming by putting off needed tasks and who also are very concerned with the opinions of others (they promote the idea that they did not have time rather than that they were not up to a task); and "decisional procrastinators," who procrastinate because they cannot make up their minds. This is said to be related to being kept from responsibility for any outcome.[13]

At this point, what contribution a philosopher can make might be in question. I would like to suggest that the question of whether procrastination is immoral is one that even nontheorists have. Furthermore, addressing this question will situate the phenomenon in ways that psychological research cannot (because ethics is not yet operationalizable), giving us a tentative, revisable, but comprehensive account of the role procrastination plays in our lives. Because of the promise of this, I suggest a two-step approach to a descriptive account of procrastination by first reading off psychological research and then categorizing these findings according to the moral psychology of ethical theory.

## VICE

If you search for "Is procrastination a sin?" online, you find the question asked earnestly on religious discussion boards. One woman carefully describes her habit of leaving packing until the last minute, discusses her husband's growing disdain for her habit, and asks, "Is what I am doing a sin?" She ends ruefully, "Whether it is or not, it feels terrible." The question seems very sincere, and one reason for this may be that religious teachings do not send the message we get from our culture about putting things off; as I will explain, there is a clash between Ben Franklin's aphorisms and biblical parables. Procrastination is also difficult to assess for ourselves, because it involves not meeting our own expectations, so the issue is whether our own standards are the right ones. We are typically not very self-aware of standards we have already internalized.

---

13. Ferrari and Dovidio, "Examining Behavioral Processes."

Let us get several ways of determining vice—namely, feeling regret, guilt, or anxiety about behavior—off the table of well-justified approaches. Regret is, of course, the most immediate and most common means of generating the label of vice (or whatever its modern verbal equivalent). Is procrastination something its practitioners find regrettable? Clearly, it is, but to call it vice for this reason is far too costly. If any behavior we regret made it vice, we have failed to distinguish between the behaviors that are actually immoral and those that are not. Regret is not tied to only moral concerns, nor do many of us think our moral compasses are such that they are always true. Listen to friends' confessions of their misdeeds, and you will realize how unduly hard we can be on ourselves. This is why the intense guilt and anxiety involved in procrastination is also not proper evidence for it being a vice.[14] And therein lies the role of ethical theory, which is, ideally, a repository for reflective and consistent assessments of behavior such as procrastination. But ethical theories can be wrong, too—particularly so, I suggest below, if they attempt to tie virtue to worldly achievement. I want to show, rather, that ethical theories that claim that morality is a matter of efficiency or worldly achievement are unsound. Procrastination cannot be a vice merely because it keeps us from getting things done.

## Vice and Outcomes

Let us consider what I will call the Poor Richard theory of virtue, which has been an influential touchstone for our shared ethics, even if—as some recent researchers suggest—Ben Franklin did his moralizing mostly in jest.[15] The Poor Richard account of virtue readily condemns procrastination, perhaps in more straightforward a manner than any other. The aphorisms we have memorized about prioritizing work are likely his. In his *Autobiography*, Franklin lists 13 virtues, and among them is industry, which requires that you "lose no time, be always employed in something useful; cut off all unnecessary action."[16] He also mentions a prayer he used to recite for inspiration, which includes the line "The precept of Order requiring that *every part of my business should have its allotted time,*" alongside the less specific exhortations to goodness. And, of course, Franklin notoriously reports that as a young man, he devised a scheme by which he would chart his progress toward his virtue "for the twenty-four hours of a natural day."[17]

---

14. Even though she emphasizes the crucial role of emotion in moral judgment, Martha Nussbaum, in *Hiding from Humanity*, has careful arguments regarding how emotions must be vetted before constituting the justification of a moral wrong.
15. Weinberger, *Ben Franklin Unmasked*.
16. Franklin, *Autobiography*, 38.
17. Franklin, *Autobiography*, 39.

Max Weber, of course, looked to Franklin's passages when he was writing about the Protestant work ethic, because he could not find a clear commitment to this value system in Presbyterian sermons.[18] Sloth is certainly not promoted, of course. But the significant task you can put off is not a workaday one; procrastination, as discussed by Christian theologians, including Jonathon Edwards in his famous sermon on the topic, concerns putting off redemption. The temptations that must be resisted can be the very duties Franklin's aphorisms take as the most serious. Edwards describes putting too much stock in the importance of "tomorrow" as taking too much pleasure and pride, "boasting" in a worldly existence.[19] The takes are nearly opposite. (Of course, this is why Weber deserves so much credit for engineering his elaborate thesis.[20])

Poor Richard's virtue ethic assumes that the good guy is the one who succeeds in life, and the bad guy is kept down. It also assumes, without any commitment to doing one's worldly work with a focus on godly duty, that this work is ethically salubrious. Is that where we get the idea that long hours of work will straighten out teenagers? Again, no religious view is this simplistic. Bad people do plenty well in life. You cannot keep the vicious from worldly success. No philosophical theory can take mere worldly accomplishments to be some sort of evidence of virtue or vice.

Maybe a second example will also help. Ayn Rand shares with Franklin's ethic the idea that success in life is tied to moral ability: the more virtuous you are, the wealthier you will become in the market.[21] But she is more consistent than Poor Richard; she writes that hers is a radical dismissal of conventional morality. She does not advocate for kindness or sharing, not even honesty, in the way that Poor Richard does. Of course, even though she acknowledges the costs of tying virtue to worldly success—for one, you have to uproot assumptions about conventional virtue—neither can she maintain the connection she wants. What destroys

---

18. It cannot be found in the Bible, either—it is almost amusing to note how scant are the passages that pro-industry Christians find to promote their more Franklinesque recommendations. Most of the examples from the Bible decry the person who avoids the "dinner party invitation" in order to do his workaday duties (Luke 14:15–24). Support for the idea that one should be efficient must be found in rather unexciting recommendations such as this one, from Proverbs 10:5: "He that gathereth in the summer is a wise son: but he that sleepeth in harvest, is a son that causeth shame."

19. From Edwards "Procrastination": "So, on the other hand, if we were certain that we should not live another day, some things would be our duty today, which now are not so. As for instance, it would be proper for us to spend our time in giving our dying counsels, and in setting our houses in order. If it were revealed to us, that we should die before tomorrow morning, we ought to look upon it as a call of God to us, to spend the short remainder of our lives in those things which immediately concern our departure, more than otherwise it would be our duty to do."

20. Weber, *The Protestant Ethic and the Spirit of Capitalism*.

21. Rand, "What Is Capitalism?"

her proposal is the fact that dedicated followers of her view do not become wealthy, and those who do become wealthy, in ways she admires, espouse contrary views to her own.

Through this brief discussion, I hope to have demonstrated that standards of worldly success do not coincide with standards of internal or psychological success. There is no regularly occurring, reliable connection between these. For this reason, attributing vice to people because they do not achieve something in the external world is a mistake. We have far more sound accounts of vice and virtue available; they are more unified because they emphasize internal standards.

But is there no way to incorporate a person's inefficiency into a moral evaluation of a person's character in a way that avoids the above mistakes? Surely, there are ways to blame people for being less productive, less practically efficacious, than they themselves might be otherwise. I think there are currently two ways in which this is being done. I want to cast them aside as well and make sure to distinguish them from what traditional virtue ethicists do.

I will be brief, because I simply want to express deep skepticism about the following. One of these is the attempt (usually not intentional) to equate an account of objective rationality with morality. If the reader has even a brief acquaintance with traditional virtue ethics, she will recall the equation of prudence with virtue. But this is a very loaded, fully normative account of prudence—an ethicists' account for ethical purposes—that is offered. It is based on a stated and rejectable standard, which itself depends on the accuracy of an account of moral psychology. Virtue ethicists' accounts of prudence are not, despite all-too-frequent claims to the contrary, what we take rationality to be today. (We should perhaps call it moral prudence to make the distinction clear.) And just because, say, we determine in some case that underproductivity is irrational, this does not translate into a moral judgment about a person. Our moral heroes were, in some arenas, incredibly unproductive. You would have to uproot thousands of years of consistent takes on moral goodness to claim that good people are also successful by worldly standards. I think the many examples of virtuous people who give up their lives or livelihoods for a beloved cause capture my point succinctly and completely.

Yet we slip into equating forms of rational behavior (not overeating) with moral behavior all the time. The first examples given by students in my ethics classes when I ask about bad behavior involve eating junk food, not being physically active, not doing their homework well enough. I do not, of course, mean to limit our evaluations, but I want to make a case for having distinctly moral evaluations available. Virtue is not an all-encompassing standard. It cannot, if it is presented meaningfully, encompass all possibly worthy goals. The traditional accounts of virtue are limited in all sorts of ways—they are not very good at promoting charity, for example. But limits on what the accounts prescribe can be a good thing. We might realize this if we reflect on how wrong it is to assume that overweight people are immoral. We might recommend both, but everyday prudence and morality do not simply overlap.

A second tactic is engaged in more consciously and can be found in many contemporary attempts to develop a virtue ethic (environmental virtue ethicists can be recognized by this assumption): certain types of behavior bring about less meaning, ergo they are vices. Or, perhaps, meaning comes from value, vice negates value, and virtue promotes it, ergo virtue is justified. This takes a shortcut that a virtue ethic should not take. My inelegant response to this type of move, one that would simply assert that procrastination is unseemly in a life, is to demand proof that procrastination, or any other possible vice, takes the meaning in question away. If you want to tell me that virtue has more value than vice, fine—prove it. We are certainly repulsed by all sorts of behaviors; Susan Wolf includes a list of the ones that repulse her in her work on the meaning of life.[22] Couch potatoes, for example, have less meaningful lives, she says: "for me, the idea of a meaningless life is most clearly and effectively embodied in the image of a person who spends day after day, or night after night, in front of a television set, drinking beer and watching situation comedies."[23] (In my class, we always respond to this by imagining Wolf trying to get the poor example's mother to agree that her son's life was of diminished value.) Meaning is a bizarre and untenable metric; we cannot simply assert, because of our attitudes toward it, that procrastination is immoral.

I hope the accounts of virtue ethics that I am going to present provide a further reason not to take the above approaches and that their explanations of vice seem far more justified. If they do, it will be because each relies on a stated moral psychology. This is not just something they provide in support of their ethical takes; rather, it is the source of their ethical takes. Consider Aristotle on vice: categorizing procrastination according to Aristotelian standards is, in the sense I explained at the start, extremely useful in clarifying Aristotle's ethical account itself. How many oblique and uselessly general accounts of Aristotelian virtue are available? And what do they help settle? There are fine-grained distinctions available to the virtue ethicist, and classifying modern behavior is the means to getting at these. The ancient categorization is too often taken as proclamation. (Wit comes in a mean!) If virtue ethics is presented as no more than a series of positions Aristotle took, it will never be capable of serving as a viable option among today's ethical theories.

## Aristotelian Vice and Procrastination

The depiction of procrastination beginning to emerge from empirical studies has these features that traditional virtue ethics is capable of handling:

---

22. Wolf, "Meanings of Lives," 62–73.
23. Wolf, "Meanings of Lives," 65.

- The behavior has costs, perhaps in terms of productivity (though, again, we can quibble with the measures) and anxiety.
- We do not have direct control over our procrastination.
- It involves false beliefs. (In one Boice study[24] false beliefs were discovered regarding work and work habits; when it comes to other areas of life, the false beliefs might be about impacts on our health and the like.)
- These false beliefs are always accompanied by emotion (for example, anger at those thought to be imposing the work being avoided).
- Procrastinators have different reasons for procrastinating (à la Ferrari).

I want to argue that, because of the above features of procrastination, particularly the role of emotion and our lack of direct control, Aristotle would not consider procrastination to be a vice. He would, I suggest, classify procrastination as akratic—which can be thought of as weakness of will, but, following Aristotle's lead, we would do better to leave will out of this. The difference between laziness, an Aristotelian vice, and procrastination is that laziness is not akratic. The way to distinguish the two, according to Aristotle, is that the vicious person has committed consciously to holding something like laziness as a goal; a vice is done in accordance with choice. But a procrastinator has not made this type of conscious choice. No one wants to be a procrastinator. It does not matter that we can be said to want to procrastinate; choice requires a process, which we will get to in a moment. Although no one wants to be a procrastinator, people sometimes do attest to the good of being lazy. It is not by accident that a vicious person lazes about; it is not that the person is acting at odds with his stated goals or intentions.[25]

The vicious, according to Aristotle, have consciously adopted the wrong norms. For a person with the vice of laziness, it might be "Why should I have to work? Others should, but I should not have to work." The vicious pursue bodily pleasure because they have judged it to be more important than other goals (especially altruistic ones). Thus, they choose pleasure as a good; indeed, their own satisfaction might be their most important good. This is not to suggest that they achieve the pleasure they are after, of course. Virtue ethics explains that this is one of the cruel ironies involved in going after pleasure directly. The akratic also aim for pleasure, bodily pleasure in particular, but they do so contrary to their conception of the good. To envision the contrast, picture the vice-ridden "procrastinator" consciously scheming to take credit for participating in a work assignment he avoids. The akratic procrastinator will feel very bad about having spent three evenings watching television while putting off her assigned share. She will feel very bad about not having done her fair share well (and if she

24. Boice, "Quick Starters."
25. Rocochnick, "Aristotle's Account."

is a typical procrastinator, she might, in fact, feel very bad about not doing more than her fair share very well).

## TRADITIONAL VIRTUE

According to the Aristotelian and Stoic accounts of virtue ethics, our pleasures change as we match norms that we endorse (culled from society or what have you) with sufficient motivation, and this is a good thing, because the pleasures we begin with—those, say, of a seven- or a seventeen-year-old—eventually result in unhappiness. This process, once I sketch it, will also explain why procrastination cannot be directly controlled, even according to virtue-ethics accounts of moral psychology that are not Aristotelian. At the level of generality with which I am presenting this account (in particular, I am leaving out the various takes on criteria for belief and the process of belief formation), it applies to the Aristotelian, Stoic, and (for the most part) Epicurean accounts of virtue ethics.

Let us begin by depicting someone who has not yet taken on the project of developing virtue. This person might do much to help others while being rather unaware that her behavior falls under this category. And certainly, this person has deep commitments to particular people, as well as to helping these people. This person has also, certainly, heard a host of ideas about helping behavior, such as "good people help others." But she might notice that people who help a lot get taken advantage of, have ulterior motives, and so on. She might, of course, at the same time have helpful people held up as heroes. Perhaps she has had opportunities to see such heroes in action and has been duly affected by the experience. Our typical situation, says a traditional virtue ethic, is one where we are engaged in projects and have commitments we have not analyzed and where we can also articulate a lot of unsorted, and perhaps even contradictory, norms about behavior. This is the material we work with. It is not a wholesale transformation that we can effect at once. Virtue does not require that we do more than this piecemeal work.

Traditional virtue ethics *recommends*, though, that we do this piecemeal work; we would do well to take the time to analyze both what we are doing and whether what we are doing matches norms to which we ought to be committed. This is a time-consuming project, to say the least. One would have to be acutely conscious of taking it on; think of the effort involved in properly assessing whether one is, in fact, a good friend (let alone a generally helpful person).

Data concerning our psychological tendencies would certainly be useful (such as whether our behavior is surprisingly susceptible to changes in situations). It is also a process we would benefit from conducting along with others, and they would hardly need to be experts in morality. If they merely point out our shortcomings or laugh at our phony self-assertions, this might still prove to be invaluable help. Also, the process depends on a great deal of trial and error. We might experiment with helping others more or less. We might try to identify with different notions of a helpful person. Norms will be assessed against our behavior ("I tried not helping others, and it didn't work out") and our behavior assessed against our norms ("I help my kids with homework on occasion, but I guess I could do more; a good parent would"). The process of attempting to find a match among these will result, says a traditional virtue ethic, in some revision of our behaviors and the norms to which we are consciously committed.

So, this is what happens when we decide to help others by volunteering as a tutor. We have matched the norm "help others in need" with some behavior that fits it. A mismatch would have nagged at us ("I really think people in general should help others, by tutoring children, for example, but I don't think I should have to do this"). A match, if made, suggests that we are not feeling confused about what we are doing. When there is no match, we feel the pull of contraries. Sometimes, these are two recognized norms that are in conflict ("My mother-in-law is awful! Awful people do not deserve my time!" and "People who cannot get along with their families have the wrong priorities"). And at other times, it is that you are not feeling motivated to do what you think you ought ("I know I should donate more of my time").

Another way to make this description familiar is to think of times when we do the right thing without a thought. Suppose that you run after a person who has dropped his wallet, and without a thought, you grab it and return it. A traditional virtue ethic predicts that this behavior was supported by norms so well endorsed by you as to be identifiable, easy to speak about, and easy to explain. ("Why did you return my wallet?" "Well, it was yours. You need it.") And this is everyday evidence for the boldest suggestion in a traditional virtue ethic: doing the right thing can become second nature.

As the story goes, if we analyze and revise our beliefs and behavior, we can have an impact on our psychology. (We can see this on a small scale if, for instance, we shoplifted as teenagers yet could not possibly do so as adults.) To the degree that the result of engaging in this process is a new psychological state, this state—realized or not—is part of the justification and completion of a theory, one that recommends that we go about analyzing our behavior as just described.

## PROCRASTINATION ACCORDING TO VIRTUE ETHICS

### Aristotle and Procrastination

Again, psychologists have determined that we do not have direct control over procrastination and that procrastination involves emotion, aspects that Aristotle's account can explain. These are the very features of behavior that, according to Aristotle, cannot be said to be "chosen." This is also the type of behavior that can never become fully automated. Procrastination will never become a person's "second nature" (a very apt phrase for describing Aristotle's view), for it is too upsetting an experience.

What about the idea that procrastinating behavior has costs, perhaps in terms of productivity and anxiety? Can Aristotle account for this? He does explain how an agent comes to accept costs like these; he blames confusion about value. And, as just mentioned, his account also predicts that procrastination will be both opaque and emotional. An advantage to Aristotle's approach over descriptions of procrastination as preference reversal or some form of discounting is that Aristotle predicts the emotional turmoil and the reinforcing cycle that damage a person's self-image.

What about the feature of procrastination by which it involves false beliefs? Psychologists have pinpointed the types of beliefs procrastinators have in far more detail than I have suggested here, but this is an element of the psychological account of procrastination that Aristotle has some success in accounting for, as long as the beliefs are those about work habits. For procrastination to remain a less-than-immoral aspect of character, it cannot involve false beliefs about expectations for yourself. Procrastination, less resilient than vice, if it is a case of akrasia, has to be a matter of being confused about means, not ends. So, the false beliefs, in his interpretation, are about means. He can account for the beliefs that encourage the "poor work habits," the "magical thinking" that encourages students to believe they can write a final paper (and do it well) in one night.

Finally, can an Aristotelian account handle Ferrari's suggestion that procrastinators fall into three different types? It can; Aristotle is particularly clear on how the "arousal" procrastinator would be exempt from moral blame because of the force of pleasurable temptations. But he would have something to say in the other two cases of the "avoiders" and the "decisional procrastinators." The avoiders are gratifying the part of themselves that enjoys the approval of others, which is bound to mislead a person. And those who cannot make up their minds are tapping into the arational part of themselves to too great a degree. Aristotle, however, might not handle the issue of self-image that arises in the three types of reasons for procrastination as well as the Stoics and the Epicureans would.

## Stoics and Epicureans

The Stoics and the Epicureans give us other examples of a traditional virtue ethic, each of which regards procrastination differently. Together, they give us one further example of how procrastination can be elucidated through its treatment as a moral phenomenon by an ethical theory with an accompanying moral psychology. Procrastination, for the Stoics and the Epicureans, meets the standards of vice. For them, the false beliefs involved in procrastination are about the relative importance of the ends causing the anxiety. Recall the biblical take: procrastination only counts as such if it is a way of delaying what is of the most value—redemption or putting off God. This, in one sense, is certainly a contrast to eudaemonism, which does not see God's grace as being delivered in a moment and clarifying the darkness in your soul. The Stoics and the Epicureans, like Aristotle, do not see procrastination as something we have some immediate remedy to, as Edwards thinks. But they do think procrastination is a sign that a person does not have a secure valuation of proper ends at hand. If you are up all night, worried sick once again about a presentation you have not sufficiently rehearsed, the Stoic or Epicurean voice in your head would be the one saying, "The presentation does not matter; the presentation is not worth this."

The Stoics and the Epicureans abandon the idea that there are parts, or discrete aspects, of a soul or human personality.[26] Therefore, they lose some of the explanations offered by Aristotle—namely, of how the right intentions can be defeated by something, a part of ourselves, that is not under our direct control. Presumably, without divisions in the soul, all of the parts should be under our cognitive control. So, why procrastination is not under our direct control could be harder to explain with the Stoic and Epicurean accounts if we had not explained the process required to determine which beliefs (and ends) are true (consistent) or not. Again, for the Stoics and the Epicureans, the false beliefs involved in procrastination will be about ends (perhaps as well as means, but they are relatively unimportant). But, as we have explained, these ends are the ones we might not recognize that we hold; this is a trope of Stoic and Epicurean thought. The ends we mistakenly take to be justified and final are difficult to access and difficult to change. This lack of consciousness of what we are aiming at is what causes emotional discord.

The perfectionism involved in procrastination is a good example of an end we hold inconsistent with other ends and only semiconsciously. If we know we hold perfectionist aims for ourselves, we might not realize how stultifying they are. And in either case, we are unlikely to realize how much of our perfectionism is a desire to please or impress others. The Stoics and the Epicureans are clear on how a focus on others' expectations is a disaster for us, morally speaking. Perfectionism in our physical achievements is a mistake to hold up as a value. It is part of an inaccurate self-conception; it is false. Your accomplishments through work are not what define you.

To put this in the form of an example, take someone's statement, offhanded but revealing nonetheless, that he "lives for his job." This person might agree with any of these simultaneously: my value is as a good performer at work; I am valuable despite failing at work; devotion to work

---

26. See Annas, *Morality of Happiness*.

does not completely satisfy me. These are the sorts of norms we have internalized that come into conflict, according to the Stoics and the Epicureans. (I hesitate to call them beliefs, as they might not have been formulated as such yet.) According to each take, the prime source of all of our immorality is to take limited pursuits—success at work, a good reputation—and give them the wrong sort of priority. Put in the right context, these things do not matter compared with virtue, and they are not satisfying without virtue.

The Stoics will argue that some things, the results of a process, are not "up to us." As Epictetus puts it in the *Enchiridion*, "What upsets people is not things themselves but their judgments about the things."[27] Events themselves are not under our control, so they are not things for which we should be morally responsible. If we falsely assume that we are, we are being irrational (admittedly, by their lights and given their standard of a good psychological condition). The result of this can amount to vice. The emotionality of procrastination demonstrates that it is intensive enough an irrational mistake to amount to vice. The Stoics want us to value process over outcomes—they call life a stochastic end, a goal that is valuable but not because of its products, a game with no scores or winners. They would not have you give up on the projects that cause you such anxiety, as the Epicureans would. There would be no reason to, as the moral strengthening that comes from performing a duty properly is so valuable to the rest of one's life. There is no need to switch out the duty. One must just get one's priorities right.

Although the Epicureans disagree with Aristotle and the Stoics over whether pleasures transform with coming to understand value properly, they do maintain that we are, from childhood on, tempted to distract ourselves from the actual value of things. We attribute false value to all sorts of ambitious endeavors—when these things do not bring us happiness. Stay home and wear a warm hat, they advised. Use "sober reasoning" to "work out" the cause of "every choice and avoidance," and "drive out the beliefs from which comes the greatest turmoil that grips the soul."[28]

You see how contrary this is to the Poor Richard view that life is bettered by doing more. The Epicureans used as their standard of virtuous behavior a calm and steady emotional life. They would want you to get rid of the projects that produce anxiety. This is where you have control, in addition to placing less (or the correct, instrumental kind of) value on them. Both approaches would suggest that you are dealing with a vice until you rid yourself of the guilt; it is just that you may not need to conquer procrastination to do this. Rather, you may simply need to apply "sober reasoning" to the cause of your procrastination. Most of the time, you will have false beliefs, particularly about your value and the task's

---

27. Epictetus, *Handbook*, 13.
28. Epicurus, "Letter to Menoeceus," 121–135.

value. And far more than Aristotle, the Epicureans would often suggest that the task at hand is not worthy of the importance you have associated it with. If you are a writer who never makes a deadline, the Epicureans would certainly not encourage you to strengthen your will; rather, they would question your choice of occupation. What could you do that would not cause this level of anxiety? No matter what you are procrastinating about, beyond the provision of basic needs, the Epicureans could say that the task itself is not necessary to a good life.

The Stoics might not encourage any student who procrastinated before tests to give up on his studies in the breezy way an Epicurean might, but they also would not put the onus on strengthening one's will when faced with issues of time management. They would recommend comfort with the consequences of procrastination instead. Take the bad grade. Lose the account. Be frank with your editor about how late you started your revision. Accept that you procrastinate, do not attempt to lie about or hide this, and move on to focus on what really matters.

The Stoics and the Epicureans give some unusual and perhaps untested advice to procrastinators. Do their accounts help us to understand procrastination as a phenomenon at all? Each of these virtue theories seems to do a fairly good job of predicting the close association between blocking and procrastination in a way Aristotle's does not. The unacknowledged causes of procrastination explain our many omissions of good behavior. For the Stoics and the Epicureans, a procrastinator has blind spots that would impede her ability to recognize all sorts of behavior that the proper valuation of morality would make clear. You are supposed to just identify with striving to be a good person. Anything short of this gets you to aim for nonmoralized ends. For example, suppose that a person has determined that her identity is, in part, as an efficient and responsible worker, one who would never need to request extra time to get something reasonable done. This seems harmless, but the Epicureans and the Stoics would predict trouble. They would envision a project, at some point, overtaxing this person's abilities. What happens then? The stress of having one's self-identity at stake over some worldly objective is what typically causes immoral behavior. For example, they predict that someone under this type of pressure will self-deceive and perhaps lie to others about how difficult it is for her to get the project done. If she had not associated her identity with something like work performance, which is not in all ways under her control, she would have been on safer ground. All vice is, in this way, connected to false appreciation of the independent value of ends. The Stoic and Epicurean accounts would argue that the procrastinator is fundamentally confused about value in a way Aristotle does not recognize as necessary.

Which approach is more practical? Aristotle would recommend the indirect route to curing procrastination: associate tedious work with something you enjoy, and then slowly build on successes. The Stoic and Epicurean approach would, instead, ask a person to directly reevaluate the tasks affected by procrastination. Research in psychology will have to determine whether changes in self-conception have an impact on procrastination rates. There are studies that look into whether procrastination can be forestalled by the inculcation of good work habits through external prompts.[29] If such measures are successful, Aristotle's account will seem more accurate. It will also then seem as if the cycle that involves the beliefs about one's self begins with poor work habits and attitudes. Self-image will be the chicken, not the egg. Aristotle would also be better situated if people with very clear Stoic or Epicurean self-conceptions still procrastinated.

As promised, it comes down to which account has more accurately described the levers and alleyways of our nature. Is procrastination a fundamental element in our nature, because humans are akratic? Should we normalize procrastination, because, as Aristotle writes of akrasia, it is "more pardonable to follow natural desires, since it is also more pardonable to follow those natural appetites that are common to everyone and to the extent they are common"?[30] Or does procrastination signal the need for personal change? The matter is simply unsettled, and we have to await arguments put forward for each side. Research will not settle this issue.

## CONCLUSION

So, why talk about vice? Why classify behavior in this manner? I hope to have shown that the normativity we need in order to make sense of procrastination is part of an account of our nature that a complete ethical theory can offer. The questions about our nature are not futile, as unsettled as the answers may be. And attempting to answer them, as we do when we make use of ethical theory, can elucidate both our behavior and our description of ourselves. The dance between psychology and philosophy, ideally, has the philosophers, when they lead, come up with ideas we would not otherwise test. And when they follow, they do so best by forcing us to put our discoveries about behavior in their fullest context: our description and expectations for human nature get put to the test. When someone asks, "Is procrastination a sin?" what we want in response is some explanation, or set of explanations, for how the behavior befits a human being, given the nature we have. We want to be able to explain what can we expect of ourselves and why.

---

29. Hall and Hursch, "Evaluation of the Effects."
30. Aristotle, *Nicomachean Ethics*, 1149b5–7.

# Part III

# 11

# Overcoming Procrastination through Planning

*Frank Wieber & Peter M. Gollwitzer*

Have you ever purposefully delayed or postponed a goal-directed action (for example, writing an essay or filling out tax forms) despite strong intentions to achieve the goal and sufficient opportunities to pursue it? If so, then you are in good company: so has a large percentage of the general (15 to 20 percent)[1] and the academic (80 to 85 percent of American college students) population.[2] In addition to academic examples, procrastination has been studied in the areas of personal health (dieting, exercising), social relationships (contacting friends), work (job-seeking behavior), and financial management (retirement savings).[3] Procrastination is a widespread phenomenon with potentially severe consequences, such as dropping out of school, compromised health, divorce, and job loss.

Intuitively, it would seem relatively easy to classify certain behaviors as procrastination. For example, the fact that a student put off reading a book chapter might at first glance be sufficient to label his or her behavior as procrastination. But after a closer look at the phenomenon, additional criteria that cannot be objectively judged from an outside perspective emerge. Building on the numerous definitions of the commonly used term *procrastination* that can be found in the scientific literature,[4] we suggest four criteria that must be fulfilled in order to classify a behavior or a lack of behavior as procrastination. A person has to (1) commit to the goal in question, (2) have the opportunity to act on the goal, (3) expect to be worse off later in the case of a delay, and (4) voluntarily decide to put off the intended action or inaction until a later point. For example, not

---

1. Harriott and Ferrari, "Prevalence of Chronic Procrastination."
2. Ellis and Knaus, *Overcoming Procrastination*, 143–149.
3. Akerlof, "Procrastination and Obedience."
4. Van Eerde, "Procrastination"; Ferrari, "Procrastination as Self-Regulation Failure"; Lay and Silverman, "Trait Procrastination."

reading the chapter would qualify as procrastination by our definition when the student intended to read it, had access to the book and an adequate amount of time to read it, knew that not reading the chapter would endanger the course credit (and ultimately degree fulfillment), and voluntarily decided to read the chapter later. To draw a parallel to the definition set out by Piers Steel,[5] procrastination is the voluntary postponement of an intended course of action despite having the opportunity to act and expecting to be worse off as a result of the delay.

In light of the high prevalence of procrastination and building on these four criteria, we now address the question of why people procrastinate from the perspective of the psychology of goals. We will analyze the relationship between procrastination and potential problems people may encounter during both goal setting and goal striving. Subsequently, we will suggest a strategy to overcome procrastination: the formation of *implementation intentions*, which are specific plans detailing when, where, and how one intends to initiate an action that one is prone to put off.[6] After explaining how implementation-intention effects come about and examining several moderators that might limit their effectiveness, we will discuss research on implementation intentions relevant to the problem of procrastination. We will examine whether implementation intentions help people to overcome procrastination in terms of getting started, staying on track, calling a halt to an unsuccessful action, and avoiding overextension. In addition, we will discuss research on the effectiveness of implementation intentions in critical populations (chronic procrastinators and subjects who are known to have problems with self-control), as well as in contexts that do not seem to be amenable to self-regulation, such as when bad habits must be overcome. Finally, we will suggest additional measures to improve motivation as a way of enhancing the effectiveness of implementation intentions.

## PROCRASTINATION, GOAL SETTING, AND GOAL STRIVING

Two sequential tasks have been differentiated by the psychology of goals during goal pursuit: goal setting and goal striving.[7] Traditionally, research on goals has focused on goal setting, aiming to illuminate the factors that determine the formation of strong goal intentions (goal-setting theories),[8] as strong goal intentions were regarded as the proximal determinants of goal achievement. Low perceived desirability and/or feasibility of a

---

5. Steel, "Nature of Procrastination," 66.
6. Gollwitzer, "Implementation Intentions."
7. Oettingen and Gollwitzer, "Goal Setting and Goal Striving."
8. Ajzen, "Theory of Planned Behavior."

potential goal as well as suboptimal framing (e.g., unspecific, distal) may lead to the formation of weak intentions to realize the goal and to subsequent procrastination. One might therefore be tempted to infer that procrastination primarily results from suboptimal goal setting; however, at least two arguments weaken this explanation.

First, numerous research findings demonstrate that even strong goal intentions are not sufficient to guarantee goal achievement (the so-called intention-behavior gap).[9] Second, procrastinators do not seem to differ from nonprocrastinators in their intention to pursue a goal.[10] For example, in studies on academic work and job-seeking intentions, procrastination has been found to be unrelated to the strength of goal intentions.[11] Still, the gap between intentions and goal-directed behavior was found to be greater in procrastinators than in nonprocrastinators.[12] On the other hand, it was observed that in some cases, goal-setting interventions, such as training sessions or tests, managed to decrease procrastination.[13] All things considered, strong goal intentions seem to represent an important factor for successful goal achievement. But given the residual intention-behavior gap, the lack of qualitative and quantitative differences between procrastinators' and nonprocrastinators' intentions, and the unreliable effects of goal-setting interventions on procrastination, there must be a more complete explanation for procrastinating behavior beyond merely weak goal intentions.

Goal-setting theories aim to explain the formation of goal intentions but do not address problems that arise when a person tries to realize a set goal. These problems are the focus of self-regulation theories of goal striving, which are concerned with the processes that mediate the effects of intentions on behavior.[14] In the following section, we will concentrate on four major problems that must be overcome during goal striving:[15] initiation of action on a goal, staying on track (warding off distractions), disengaging from failing courses of action, and avoiding overextension (ego depletion).[16] We will elaborate on how each of these problems can contribute to procrastination.

The most prominent challenge of successful goal striving is *getting started* with goal-directed actions; this issue is implicated in the definition of procrastination,[17] as it is assumed that a procrastinating person is committed to

---

9. Sheeran, "Intention-Behavior Relations."
10. Steel, "Nature of Procrastination," 79.
11. Lay and Brokenshire, "Conscientiousness."
12. E.g., Steel, Brothen, and Wambach, "Procrastination and Personality."
13. For an overview, see Schouwenburg et al., "Counseling the Procrastinator."
14. E.g., Bandura, *Self-Efficacy*; Carver and Scheier, "Principles of Self-Regulation"; Gollwitzer, "Implementation Intentions"; Kuhl, "Functional-Design Approach."
15. E.g., Gollwitzer and Sheeran, "Implementation Intentions."
16. Baumeister et al., "Ego Depletion."
17. Van Eerde, "Procrastination," 374.

a goal and has the opportunity to act on the goal but avoids the implementation of the intention. The differentiation of two kinds of intention-action discrepancies that has been proposed by research on goals[18] can also be applied to procrastination. A person may intend to act but does not (an *inclined abstainer*), or he or she may intend not to act but does so (a *disinclined actor*). Procrastination in terms of not getting started can refer to not starting to enact a desired goal-directed behavior (e.g., not starting to exercise despite the goal to be physically fit) as well as to the failure to cease an undesired goal-contradictory behavior (e.g., not quitting to smoke despite the goal to stay healthy).

What are reasons for not getting started? Three main explanations have been suggested by research on goal striving:[19] one fails to remember the intention to act, one does not recognize good opportunities to act, or one does not overcome an initial reluctance to act. Forgetting to act on the intended goal represents a common reason for failure to act (e.g., not remembering to regularly take prescription medication). But although this problem qualifies as a problem of getting started with goal striving, it does not qualify as procrastination, as it fails to meet the criterion of purposefully postponing or delaying an action. Similarly, not recognizing a good opportunity to act on the goal meets the criteria of a problem of goal striving but not of procrastination. However, the third reason, that a person has to overcome an initial reluctance, corresponds with findings on the strong relationship between task aversiveness and procrastination.[20] Initial reluctance is thought to result from a trade-off between attractive long-term consequences and less attractive short-term consequences. For example, a person might strongly intend to eat a low-calorie diet in order to stay healthy in the future, but in the moment of decision, he or she chooses to eat fatty French fries, which are more attractive in the short run than a healthy but less tasty low-fat salad.[21] In addition to health goals, such trade-off structures can be found in many areas of day-to-day life, such as environmental goals, consumer goals, safer-sex goals, and academic goals.

The second challenge of successful goal striving is *avoiding unnecessary disruptions*. Most definitions of procrastination refer solely to delaying the start of a goal-directed action.[22] However, deciding to put off an intended course of action (despite sufficient opportunities to act and expecting to be worse off for the delay) when in the midst of trying to realize a goal also fulfills the above-mentioned criteria of procrastination. For example,

18. E.g., Sheeran, "Intention-Behavior Relations."
19. E.g., Gollwitzer, Gawrilow, and Oettingen, "Power of Planning."
20. For reviews, see Van Eerde, "Meta-Analytically Derived Nomological Network"; Steel, "Nature of Procrastination," 75.
21. See Ainslie, "Specious Reward" and *Breakdown of Will*, as well as the chapters by Ainslie (chapter 1) and Ross (chapter 2) in this volume.
22. For an overview, see Steel, "Nature of Procrastination," 66.

a student might start writing an outline of his or her thesis but then become distracted and put off continuing this activity by checking e-mail or surfing the Web. What are the reasons for this kind of procrastination? Research on goal striving suggests that insufficient goal shielding plays an important role in suboptimal regulation of goal-directed responses.[23] Here, goal shielding refers to the protection of valued goals against other competing influences. When goal striving extends over a long time period, the goal has to be shielded from potentially disruptive stimuli, both internal (e.g., feeling anxious, tired, or overburdened) and external (distractions and temptations).

The third challenge, *disengaging on time* from faulty courses of action, also relates to procrastination. An example would be a person who voluntarily postpones necessary updates to his or her investment portfolio, despite having the opportunity to do so and the expectation of reduced gains or increased losses as a result of the delay. Reasons that have been suggested for not disengaging from failing courses of action include the application of a "don't waste" heuristic[24] (a compulsion to bring an investment to completion) and the motive of self-justification. As the "don't waste" heuristic suggests that no voluntary decision takes place and people may continue to expect positive results in the end, it does not qualify as procrastination. However, the self-justification explanation allows for the possibility that people know that they will most likely be worse off in the long term, yet still voluntarily decide to put off an intended action until a later point, as this allows them to postpone the short-term psychological costs of accepting that their prior resource allocation to the chosen course of action was mistaken.[25] As a consequence, people may end up throwing good money after bad (the *sunk-cost* phenomenon).

A final challenge to successful goal striving is *avoiding overextending oneself*. But how does overextension relate to procrastination? Following the resource model of self-regulation,[26] the capacity to effortfully regulate one's thoughts, feelings, and actions is limited. When this resource is taxed by excessive use, a state of *ego depletion* emerges that impairs subsequent self-regulation. For example, after forcing themselves to eat radishes instead of delicious cookies, participants put less effort into solving unsolvable puzzles (decreased persistence). Because counteracting the reasons for procrastination listed above (i.e., overcoming initial reluctance, goal shielding, and overcoming self-justification motives) requires self-control, ego-depleted people ought to be more likely to procrastinate. After depleting one's self-regulatory resources by acting on a goal (for

---

23. E.g., Achtziger, Gollwitzer, and Sheeran, "Implementation Intentions"; Shah, Friedman, and Kruglanski, "Forgetting All Else."
24. Arkes and Blumer, "Psychology of Sunk Cost."
25. Brockner, "Escalation of Commitment."
26. Baumeister et al., "Ego Depletion."

example, via thought or emotion suppression), an increased likelihood of procrastination with respect to other goals is to be expected.

In summary, procrastination is not restricted to the postponement of the start of a goal-directed action but can also affect other stages of goal striving, such as the shielding of ongoing goal striving from disruptive internal and external stimuli and the decision to halt a failing course of action. In addition, overextending oneself during goal striving can contribute to procrastination.

## ACTION CONTROL BY IMPLEMENTATION INTENTIONS

What can a person do to overcome procrastination? Several strategies have been suggested, including interventions strengthening the expectation of one's ability to enact the necessary goal-directed actions (self-efficacy);[27] changing the value of the task (e.g., piggybacking distant goals onto more immediate goals);[28] and reducing sensitivity to distractions through stimulus control (removing temptation cues in one's environment) or automation (habitualizing action control).[29] In the rest of this chapter, we will propose implementation intentions as an easily applicable planning strategy that can help to overcome procrastination by automating action control.

Implementation intentions support goal intentions. Whereas goal intentions in the format "I intend to achieve outcome X/to perform behavior X" describe desired end states and represent the result of the process of goal setting, implementation intentions additionally spell out in advance when, where, and how these goals should be realized. Implementation intentions have been demonstrated to be especially effective when they are formed in an *if-then* format ("If situation Y arises, then I will perform action Z"). In the *if* component of an implementation intention, a concrete situation is specified that is anticipated as a good opportunity to act. In the *then* component, a proper goal-directed response is included. For example, one could support the goal to finish an essay with the implementation intention "If I turn on my computer, then I will first work 20 minutes on the essay." As a consequence of this predecision, the control over the initiation of the writing behavior is delegated to the specified situation. Starting the computer should automatically activate the linked behavior to work on the essay first without requiring a second conscious decision. The effectiveness of implementation intentions has been demonstrated for all four challenges of goal striving described above (getting

---

27. Bandura, *Self-Efficacy*.
28. Ainslie, *Picoeconomics*.
29. Bargh and Barndollar, "Automaticity in Action."

started, staying on track, calling a halt, and not overextending oneself). A meta-analysis including 94 studies and more than 8,000 participants[30] revealed a medium-to-large effect size of implementation intentions on goal achievement over and above the effect of the respective goal intentions alone.[31] Implementation intentions are an easy strategy to apply, and they have remarkable effects on goal attainment and thus offer an effective countermeasure against procrastination.

## How Do Implementation Intentions Improve Goal Attainment?

Two processes have been proposed to explain how implementation intentions improve goal achievement. First, through the *if* component, they heighten the activation of the critical situation. Second, they automate the initiation of the action specified in the *then* component in response to the critical situation.

*The Specified Situation.* Heightened activation of the mental representation of the critical situation helps people to retrieve the specified situation from memory (superior recall) and to detect it even when concealed (perceptual readiness). Similarly, implementation intentions prepare people to attend to critical cues.[32] In fact, the effects of implementation intentions on attention are so strong that they even disrupt focal attention.[33] In two studies, the disruption of focal attention through implementation intentions has been tested by presenting stimuli that were part of an implementation intention for an unrelated task as task-irrelevant distractors. In the first study, participants either formed specific implementation intentions in an *if-then* format or just formed goal intentions. The intentions were directed at the goal of performing well in a subsequent categorization task. Next, participants worked on an ostensibly unrelated task in which they had to make word-versus-nonword decisions while neutral as well as critical stimuli (intention situations) were presented as task-irrelevant distractors. Participants' response times to the word-versus-nonword decisions served to measure the disruption of focal attention, such that slower responses indicated more attention disruption by the task-irrelevant distractors. The results revealed that the presence of critical stimuli as distractors slowed down participants' responses compared with the presence of neutral distractor stimuli—but only when participants had formed implementation intentions, not when they had formed goal intentions. In the second study, these findings were replicated using a

---

30. Gollwitzer and Sheeran, "Implementation Intentions."
31. Webb and Sheeran, "Does Changing Behavioral Intentions."
32. Aarts, Dijksterhuis, and Midden, "To Plan."
33. Wieber and Sassenberg, "I Can't."

task with vowel-versus-consonant classifications. Moreover, in this study, implementation intentions not only focused attention on critical cues during the unrelated classification task, but they also still improved the detection of the critical cues in the subsequent relevant task. Together, these findings imply that critical cues will not escape a person's attention, given that the relevant goal is activated and that the cues have been included in an implementation intention.

*The Goal-Directed Behavior.* As a second process, implementation intentions automate the initiation of the action specified in the *then* component as soon as the critical situation presents itself. To call a behavior automatic, it has to have at least one of several relevant features.[34] It has been demonstrated that implementation intentions lead to an immediate response to critical stimuli[35] and to a response without conscious intent,[36] both characteristic of automatic behaviors. Furthermore, they enable people to efficiently respond to critical stimuli. To test the efficiency of action initiation through implementation intentions, paradigms were used that required working on two tasks simultaneously (dual-task paradigms). As a person's resources to process information simultaneously are limited, greater efficiency in one subtask in a dual-task paradigm allows the performance of the second subtask to remain constant even as performance of the first improves. In a dual-task study by Brandstätter et al.,[37] participants worked on a primary task in which they had to keep a mouse-directed square on top of a moving circle. The secondary task consisted of a *go/no go* task that required a key press in response to numbers but not to letters appearing at random time intervals in the midst of the moving circle. Prior to working on the dual task, participants either formed an implementation intention to respond as quickly as possible to the number 3 or simply familiarized themselves with the number 3 by writing it down several times. Results indicated that participants who formed an implementation intention responded faster to the critical number 3 than those who only familiarized themselves with this number, and that this was done without impairing the performance in the tracking task. Apparently, implementation intentions forge a strong mental link between the critical cue specified in the *if* component and the response specified in the *then* component so that action initiation in the presence of the critical cue becomes automated. It is this automation of the initiation of goal-directed action that should make forming implementation intentions beneficial to overcoming procrastination.

 34. E.g., Bargh, "Conditional Automaticity."
 35. Gollwitzer and Brandstätter, "Implementation Intentions."
 36. Bayer et al., "Responding to Subliminal Cues."
 37. Brandstätter, Lengfelder, and Gollwitzer, "Implementation Intentions," studies 3 and 4.

## Moderators of Implementation-Intention Effects

In addition to the research on processes underlying implementation-intention effects, several studies have investigated the potential limits of the effectiveness of implementation intentions in terms of commitment to their respective goal intentions, commitment to the implementation intention, self-efficacy, and overlap with the personality factors of socially prescribed perfectionism and conscientiousness.

*Commitment to the Goal Intention.* In accordance with the theory of intentional action control,[38] empirical research indicates that people need to be strongly committed to their goal intentions in order for implementation-intention effects to occur.[39] In addition, the activation of the goal intention must be ensured. For example, in a study by Sheeran, Webb, and Gollwitzer,[40] speed-directed implementation intentions in an *if-then* format improved participants' response times and thereby their performance only when the goal to respond quickly was activated. Implementation intentions thus produce a kind of goal-dependent automaticity.[41] But while goal-dependent automaticity typically originates from the frequent and consistent pairing of situations and behaviors (see also *proceduralization*),[42] the goal-dependent automaticity of implementation intentions is established by just one conscious act of will. Functionally, the goal-dependent automaticity produced by implementation intentions helps prevent rigid action initiation, as it prevents executing implementation intentions in situations in which the goal is not in place. As procrastinators do strongly intend to pursue their goals,[43] the requirement of a sufficient commitment of the respective goal intention for implementation-intention effects to occur should always be fulfilled.

*Commitment to the Implementation Intention.* Additionally, the commitment to enacting the implementation intention needs to be strong. For example, in a study by Achtziger, Bayer, and Gollwitzer,[44] telling participants that they had the type of personality that benefits from staying flexible (low plan commitment) led to weaker implementation-intention effects in comparison to participants told that they had the type of personality that benefits from sticking to plans (high plan commitment). The necessity of commitment to the *if-then* plan also supports the effectiveness of implementation intentions, by ensuring that incidental or superficial

---

38. E.g., Gollwitzer and Schaal, "Metacognition in Action."
39. E.g., Verplanken and Faes, "Good Intentions."
40. Sheeran, Webb, and Gollwitzer, "Interplay," study 2.
41. Bargh, "Conditional Automaticity"; Gollwitzer and Schaal, "Metacognition in Action."
42. Anderson, *Architecture of Cognition*.
43. E.g., Steel, "Nature of Procrastination," 79.
44. Achtziger, Bayer, and Gollwitzer, "Committting Oneself," study 2.

*if-then* plans do not impair flexibility for goal attainment.[45] Although procrastinators might differ in regard to their planning behavior, it seems plausible that once they form an implementation intention, they commit themselves as strongly to the formed plan as nonprocrastinators do. Indirect support for this notion is provided by research that demonstrates the effectiveness of implementation intentions in procrastinators.[46] Therefore, the precondition of a strong commitment to the implementation intention should not represent a limitation for implementation-intention effects in procrastinators.

*Self-Efficacy.* A person must be confident that he or she has the ability to perform the actions instrumental to producing the desired outcomes (i.e., he or she must have a high level of *self-efficacy*)[47] in order for implementation-intention effects to occur. In an experimental study, we tested the moderation of implementation-intention effects by self-efficacy.[48] Participants' self-efficacy with respect to taking an abstract reasoning test (Raven matrices) was manipulated before they worked on a set of task trials. To establish low self-efficacy, participants worked on difficult training task trials that mostly led to experiences of failure; to establish high self-efficacy, participants worked on easy training trials that mostly led to mastery experiences. While all participants learned that double-checking their results for each trial was an effective strategy to improve their performance, only in the implementation-intention condition did they formulate this strategy into an *if-then* plan ("If I find an initial solution, then I will double-check it"). A positive effect of implementation intentions was only found in the high-self-efficacy condition; implementation-intention participants in the high-self-efficacy condition took significantly more time to work on the difficult matrices and indeed solved more of them correctly than participants with high self-efficacy who did not include the double-checking strategy in an implementation intention. For participants with low self-efficacy, implementation intentions neither increased time spent on the difficult matrices nor improved their performance. Low self-efficacy thus limits the effectiveness of implementation intentions. The formation of implementation intentions, on the other hand, cannot be expected to increase self-efficacy.[49] As low self-efficacy is also a strong predictor of procrastination,[50] it is especially important to ensure that people set realistic goals (not too easy or too hard), so that high self-efficacy to perform the necessary goal-directed actions is probable. Otherwise, forming implementation intentions will not help with overcoming procrastination.

45. E.g., Gollwitzer et al., "Flexible Tenacity."
46. E.g., Owens, Bowman, and Dill, "Overcoming Procrastination."
47. Bandura, *Self-Efficacy*.
48. Wieber, Odenthal, and Gollwitzer, "Self-Efficacy Feelings."
49. Webb and Sheeran, "Mechanisms."
50. Steel, "Nature of Procrastination," 77.

*Personal Attributes.* Personal attributes have been examined as moderators of implementation-intention effects in two lines of research. *Socially prescribed perfectionism* moderated the effectiveness of implementation intentions,[51] resulting in worse goal achievement among socially prescribed perfectionists. As with self-oriented perfectionism, socially prescribed perfectionism entails setting high personal standards and evaluating oneself stringently. But whereas the standards for self-oriented perfectionists are set by the individuals themselves, socially prescribed perfectionists try to conform to standards and expectations that are prescribed by others. A high level of socially prescribed perfectionism is related to depression, anxiety disorders, and obsessive-compulsive symptoms.[52]

In one study, participants who scored high on the socially prescribed perfectionism subscale of the Multidimensional Perfectionist Scale (MPS) rated their progress on their New Year's resolutions (three personal goals) after two and four weeks lower when they had formed implementation intentions than when they had received control instructions. In a similar second study, participants with high scores on socially prescribed perfectionism who formed implementation intentions not only rated their goal progress lower but also were less satisfied with their personal goal progress and thought that others were less satisfied with their progress (as compared with participants who formed implementation intentions but scored low on this subscale of perfectionism). However, for participants with self-oriented perfectionism, forming implementation intentions actually improved goal progress. A similar result has been found in the meta-analysis on procrastination by Steel[53] that revealed a (weak) relationship between socially prescribed perfectionism and procrastination ($r = 0.18$) but no such relationship for self-oriented perfectionism or for perfectionism in general ($r = -0.03$). Socially prescribed perfectionism not only represents a risk factor for procrastination but also moderates the effectiveness of implementation intentions, such that a high level of this subtype of perfectionism impedes their effectiveness. It seems important, therefore, to find out why socially prescribed perfectionists do not benefit from implementation intentions so that these problems can be circumvented.

A second line of research examined *conscientiousness*.[54] In an experimental study using undergraduate students, attendance in class was determined to be a function of conscientiousness, openness to experience, goal intentions, and implementation intentions. Results replicated previous findings that a lack of conscientiousness (low or moderate scores on the conscientiousness subsets of self-control, distractibility, organization, and achievement motivation) generally put people at risk for procrastination,

---

51. Powers, Koestner, and Topciu, "Implementation Intentions."
52. E.g., Powers, Zuroff, and Topciu, "Covert and Overt Expressions."
53. Steel, "Nature of Procrastination," 76.
54. Webb, Christian, and Armitage, "Helping Students."

whereas a high level of conscientiousness represented a protection factor.[55] While class attendance of highly conscientious students was not changed by forming implementation intentions as it already was at a high level (ceiling effect), low and moderately conscientious students significantly benefited from planning when, where, and how they would attend class (increasing their previously low class attendance rates).

In summary, the ability to resist procrastination and the effectiveness of implementation intentions are expected to be strongest when a person is highly committed to the goal (strong goal intentions), believes in his or her ability to enact the action required to produce the desired outcomes (high self-efficacy), and does not have the tendency to evaluate his or her behavior according to high standards set by others (socially prescribed perfectionism). A lack of strong goal intentions, low self-efficacy, and high levels of socially prescribed perfectionism not only are directly associated with procrastination but also limit the effectiveness of implementation intentions. In contrast, while low levels of conscientiousness are also positively associated with procrastination, it is those individuals with low and moderate levels of conscientiousness who especially benefit from implementation intentions to counter procrastination.

## EVIDENCE THAT IMPLEMENTATION INTENTIONS HELP OVERCOME PROCRASTINATION

As the problems of forgetting one's intentions and not recognizing an opportunity to act on one's goals do not qualify as procrastination issues, we will not discuss research on the effectiveness of implementation intentions in overcoming these problems.[56] Not all studies analyzing goal striving ask participants for their reasons for having delayed action. Therefore, we cannot be entirely sure in these studies whether participants actually procrastinated or, rather, simply pursued other goals that were more important at the time. However, this criticism does not apply to laboratory experiments in which the time to get started on a focal experimental task is assessed. Moreover, participants' goal intentions as well as their goal progress dependent on the implementation-intention manipulation were measured in all reported studies. Although some of these studies used a quasi-experimental approach (classifying groups based on preexisting differences), most studies applied experimental designs (randomly assigning participants to conditions) that allow for causal inferences from the experimental factors to differences in the dependent variables. Two kinds of implementation intentions were used in the presented studies: implementation intentions in an *if-then* format and implementations in

55. Steel, "Nature of Procrastination," 78.
56. E.g., Achtziger, Bayer, and Gollwitzer, "Committing Oneself."

alternative formats. Although implementation intentions specifying when, where, and how one intends to act on a goal in an *if-then* format are more effective than implementation intentions without the *if-then* format, both types of implementation intentions successfully enhance goal attainment.[57]

Procrastination generally occurs as the consequence of a complex interaction of diverse causes. In some cases, it may be driven primarily by situational characteristics or task characteristics. In other cases, personal characteristics might be the predominant factor. In the following sections, we will review studies in accordance to their main focus: as situation-related, task-related, or individual-related delay.

## Getting Started

As an example of strong situational influences on the postponement of intended actions, a person would be more likely to procrastinate on a goal at times when other important goals or social norms are competing for his or her attention. For instance, in one study, German participants voluntarily committed themselves to the goal of writing an essay on how they spent their Christmas Eve by December 26 (also a holiday in Germany).[58] To test whether implementation intentions improved participants' goal achievement, half of the sample additionally supported the goal intention with an implementation intention: when, where, and how they intended to write the essay. German Christmas holidays are a time in which any kind of work-related activity is normatively banned in favor of socializing and spending time with family and friends. Thus, participants had to overcome a situational influence (social norms) to pursue their goal. Results revealed that participants who formed implementation intentions were three times more likely to actually write the report (i.e., to procrastinate less) than mere goal-intention participants. They wrote the reports 2.3 days after Christmas, compared with 7.7 days in the control condition, and sent them in 4.9 days after Christmas, compared with 12.6 days in the control condition. Moreover, 71 percent of the participants in the implementation-intention condition sent in their essays, as opposed to 32 percent of those in the control condition. Implementation intentions successfully reduced participants' procrastination even in a situation in which social norms endangered their goal.

Similarly, a person would be expected to be more likely to procrastinate at times when substantial changes are taking place in his or her environment. For example, in a study by Brandstätter et al.,[59] the effect of implementation intentions on getting started in difficult situations was

---

57. Chapman, Armitage, and Norman, "Comparing Implementation Intention Interventions."
58. Gollwitzer and Brandstätter, "Implementation Intentions," study 2.
59. Brandstätter et al., "Goals Need Implementation Intentions."

tested in the area of continuing education after the German reunification. Participants were chosen who indicated their interest in continuing education. The interview questions were "What are your plans for the near future with regard to your professional career?" and "Have you ever thought of continuing your education?" To assess whether participants formed an implementation intention, they were asked if they had already committed themselves to when, where, and how they would start to act on the goal to continue their education. Interviews conducted two years later indicated that participants who had formed an implementation intention were more successful in participating in vocational retrainings than those who did not specify when and where they would start to act. Thus, even in times of dramatic change (the first years after reunification), implementation intentions helped the participants to not procrastinate on their goal to continue their education.

Whereas situational factors might have played a primary role in triggering procrastination in the above cases, task-related factors (such as the negative evaluation of actions required to pursue a goal, also called task aversiveness) seem to be mainly responsible for procrastination in other instances.[60] A person might value being physically fit but still put off starting regular physical exercise because he or she simply does not like exercising. Do implementation intentions help people get started even on aversive tasks? Indeed, numerous studies demonstrate the beneficial effects of implementation intentions on getting started even when an initial reluctance to act has to be overcome.[61] One study on doing weekly math homework (over a period of one month) examined the question of whether implementation intentions specifying the when and how of the intended behavior differed in their effects from implementation intentions using an *if-then* format.[62] In this study, participants were provided with computer disks containing a series of tedious arithmetic tasks. Half of the participants formed *if-then* plans specifying when and how they were planning to act on the goal: "If it is Wednesday at 8:30, then I will perform as many arithmetic tasks as possible." The other half formed implementation intentions detailing when and how by stating: "I will perform as many arithmetic tasks as possible each Wednesday at 8:30." To measure procrastination, the time participants started to work on the arithmetic tasks each week was recorded, and the mean deviation from the intended starting time was computed. When participants formed *if-then* plans, they deviated 1.5 hours from their intended starting time; in contrast, when the implementation intentions were not in an *if-then* format, they procrastinated an average of 8.0 hours. Implementation intentions in an *if-then* format thus helped participants reduce their procrastination behavior on assigned learning goals (performing arithmetic tasks within a certain time

60. Steel, "Nature of Procrastination," 75.
61. Gollwitzer and Sheeran, "Implementation Intentions."
62. Oettingen, Hönig, and Gollwitzer, "Effective Self-Regulation," study 3.

frame) above and beyond implementation intentions that specify the when and how of the intended behavior not using the *if-then* format.

Other examples of the effectiveness of implementation intentions in helping people to overcome initial reluctance and get started with aversive tasks include health goals, such as starting regular physical exercise, conducting breast self-examinations as a cancer-prevention strategy, resuming functional activity after joint-replacement surgery, and eating healthily. Implementation intentions also helped people with their environmental goals, such as using public transport and purchasing organic food, and their professional goals, such as promoting workplace health and safety.[63] In essence, implementation intentions have been shown to be an efficient self-regulatory strategy to overcome procrastination in many parts of life.

Staying on Track

A strong predictor of procrastination is insufficient self-control.[64] An important function of self-control is to ward off potential distractions and temptations during goal striving. We assume that insufficient shielding of one's goals also contributes to procrastination (see above). A classic test for a person's ability to shield an ongoing task from distractions is the resistance-to-temptation paradigm.[65] In this paradigm, participants work on a tedious task while tempting distractions are presented. Four studies have investigated the effects of implementation intentions on resistance to temptation. In the first three studies, participants worked on a strenuous Concentration Achievement Test, in which arithmetic problems had to be solved while clips of award-winning commercials were simultaneously shown.[66] Before the task began, various intention conditions were realized. Participants either worked directly on the task (control condition), formed a goal intention to not let themselves get distracted (goal-intention condition), or supported this goal intention either with an implementation intention to work harder in the face of distractions (task-facilitative *if-then* plan) or with an implementation intention to simply ignore the distraction (temptation-inhibiting *if-then* plan). Task-facilitative implementation intentions only improved goal achievement when participants' motivation to perform well on the task and to ignore the distractions was low. However, participants who formed temptation-inhibiting implementation intentions outperformed the other groups in all three studies, independent of participants' motivation to perform well on the task and to ignore the distractions.

63. Gollwitzer and Sheeran, "Implementation Intentions."
64. Steel, "Nature of Procrastination," 78.
65. E.g., Patterson and Mischel, "Effects of Temptation-Inhibiting."
66. Gollwitzer and Schaal, "Metacognition in Action."

In the fourth study, the effectiveness of *if-then* implementation intentions at shielding goal striving from temptations was tested in six-year-old children.[67] When children start attending school, it is crucial that they learn to not be easily distracted. To improve goal striving, the strategy to ignore distractions seems to be quite effective.[68] To test whether even very young children can automate their action control with *if-then* implementation intentions, children either formed an *if-then* implementation intention ("If I see a distraction, then I will ignore it") or a control intention ("I will ignore distractions") before attempting to ignore funny cartoon pictures or movie clips while working on a repetitive animal or vehicle categorization task. Reaction times in the categorization task were faster for children who formed *if-then* implementation intentions, indicating that such intentions helped even six-year-old children to not procrastinate during goal striving.

## Disengaging from Bad Means and Goals

Procrastination can also endanger successful self-regulation after the phase of getting started or staying on track, when the planned course of action is failing and a person needs to disengage but instead stays committed to the goal. The goal may have become a personal rule, which, in turn, may have motivated misperceptions that encourage continuation of a failing course of action, as people may fear that exceptions will undermine their ability to exert self-control when similar situations arise in the future.[69]

But implementation intentions not only may be used to prevent getting derailed from striving smoothly and effectively toward a goal; they can also be used to solve the problem of calling a halt to a faulty goal striving. People often fail to readily relinquish chosen means and goals that turn out to be faulty because of a strong self-justification motive ("I chose this goal or means, so it must be good"). Such escalation phenomena (also referred to as "throwing good money after bad") can be controlled, however, by the use of implementation intentions that specify when and how to consider a switch to a different means or a different goal. For instance, Henderson, Gollwitzer, and Oettingen asked participants who had chosen a certain strategy for a given task goal to form an implementation intention that specified a simple action response ("If I receive disappointing feedback, then I'll switch my strategy") or merely set the goal to always use the best strategy available.[70] They observed that this implementation intention facilitated disengagement as a response to experienced failure. Interestingly, there was a third condition in which participants specified a complex reflection response in their implementation intention ("If I

67. Wieber et al., "If-Then Planning Helps School-Aged Children to Ignore Attractive Distractions."
68. For an overview, see Metcalfe and Mischel, "A Hot/Cool-System Analysis."
69. Ainslie, *Picoeconomics*.
70. Henderson, Gollwitzer, and Oettingen, "Implementation Intentions."

receive disappointing feedback, then I will think about how things have been going with my strategy so far"). In contrast to participants who had specified the simple implementation intention ("then I'll switch my strategy"), those with the more reflective implementation intentions integrated information about recent improvement in forming their relinquishment decision (they were less willing to relinquish their strategy when things were improving). This finding shows that implementation intentions can be used to curb the escalation of behavioral commitment commonly observed when people experience failure with a chosen strategy of goal striving. Using more reflective implementation intentions even allows for flexible relinquishment of a goal-striving strategy in the sense that recent turns to the better are respected in the decision to switch (or not) to a different goal-striving strategy.

### Preventing Ego-Depletion Effects

According to the resource model of self-regulation,[71] when self-regulatory resources are depleted, performance on subsequent tasks that tax these resources should be impaired. Two studies have tested whether the automatic nature of the effects of implementation intentions enables people to effectively self-regulate despite depleted self-regulatory resources. In the first study, participants' self-regulatory resources were depleted by having them control their emotions during a humorous movie (the ego-depletion condition) or not (the control condition).[72] Subsequently, they either supported the goal intention to solve as many anagrams as possible with the implementation intention "If I solve an anagram, then I will immediately start to work on the next" or did not, before working on an anagram task. In a replication of the classic ego-depletion effect, participants whose self-regulatory resources were depleted solved fewer anagrams than the two other groups. But, more important, participants who formed implementation intentions solved as many anagrams as participants whose self-regulatory resources were not depleted. Implementation intentions thus enabled participants to successfully strive for their goals even when their self-regulatory resources were depleted.

In the second experimental study, participants either were ego-depleted (from counting down in sevens from 1,000 while standing on the weaker leg) or not (counting to 1,000 in fives while standing normally).[73] Next, they formed the goal intention to read the ink color of words presented in one of four different colors (Stroop task) as quickly as possible; they either supported this goal intention with the implementation intention "As soon as I see the word, then I will ignore its meaning [e.g., by concentrating on

---

71. Baumeister et al., "Ego Depletion."
72. Gollwitzer, Bayer, and McCulloch, "Control of the Unwanted."
73. Webb and Sheeran, "Can Implementation Intentions Help."

the second letter only] and name the ink color it is printed in" or formed no implementation intention. Forming implementation intentions improved the Stroop task performance of participants who had been ego-depleted in the initial task up to the level of the nondepleted control group. Both of these studies support the hypothesis that implementation intentions counteract ego-depletion effects.

## Curbing Bad Habits

As noted above, implementation intentions have been demonstrated to have features of automaticity. Automatic processes are required for successful self-regulation in at least two situations: when no self-regulatory capacities remain for resource-demanding self-regulation (in other words, ego depletion) and to keep other unwanted automatic processes in check. The previously discussed research demonstrates that implementation intentions lead to effective action control even when self-regulatory resources are depleted. The effectiveness of implementation intentions to curb the influence of unwanted automatic responses (bad habits) on the ongoing intended goal striving has also been examined. For example, in a study on recycling behavior, the effectiveness of implementation intentions in replacing well-established habits with new recycling habits was tested.[74] The recycling behavior of 109 employees of a telecommunications company was observed by measuring the actual amount of paper and the number of plastic cups in their personal wastebaskets before and after an implementation intention manipulation. Over a period of two months, implementation intentions helped participants to overcome their old recycling habits and to recycle as much as a condition in which an eye-catching facility was used to promote paper-recycling behavior and significantly more than control conditions. In addition to situations in which automatic behavioral responses limit goal striving, automatic cognitive responses such as stereotyping and inappropriate automatic emotional responses can also be successfully regulated with implementation intentions. Moreover, implementation intentions were found to improve goal attainment even when intellectual capabilities or competitive opponents limited goal striving.[75]

## Attenuating Chronic Problems of Self-Control

To this point, we have reviewed research in which procrastination was conceptualized as a state procrastination (namely, as a function of the situation or the task or the individual during the pursuit of one goal). But research has also taken into account the stability of individual procrastination

---

74. Holland, Aarts, and Langendam, "Breaking and Creating Habits."
75. For an overview, see Gollwitzer, Gawrilow, and Oettingen, "Power of Planning."

behavior, as some people may procrastinate not only occasionally but also chronically. Trait procrastination is characterized by the relatively stable tendency over time to postpone actions that are necessary to reach a goal.[76]

To test the relationship between behavioral intentions and behavioral enactment (the intention-behavior gap) in trait procrastinators and whether implementation intentions would help chronic procrastinators to attend a scheduled experiment at their university, an experiment was conducted with the help of 152 college students.[77] In a separate first session, participants filled in a questionnaire on their procrastination behavior, to identify self-reported high- or low-level trait procrastinators. Students then received handouts during class about the opportunity to earn extra credit from a study with 10 possible appointment times. Half of the handouts contained instructions to support the goal intention to attend the session with an implementation intention. ("You are more likely to keep your appointment if you commit yourself to arriving at the assigned room at one of the times listed above. Select now the time at which you plan to come for the second experiment, write it at the bottom of the second page, and return that page to your instructor.") As a measurement of procrastination, participants' actual attendance at the additional study session was measured. Participants whose self-reports indicated high trait procrastination kept the scheduled appointment less often than those whose self-reports revealed low trait procrastination. In addition to these differences, low as well as high trait procrastinators benefited equally from forming implementation intentions: implementation intentions increased the attendance rates from 8.3 to 51.4 percent in high trait procrastinators and from 27.5 to 71.8 percent in low trait procrastinators. Thus, even people with a chronic tendency to procrastinate benefited from forming implementation intentions as much as low procrastinators did (with 40 percent enhancement).

Implementation intentions have also been found to help other critical samples known to have problems with action control. For example, opiate addicts in withdrawal are known to have problems getting started on their goals.[78] During opiate withdrawal, people often do not realize their goals, as they are preoccupied with suppressing the automatic and conscious processes that favor the intake of the drugs. It was predicted, however, that even people in withdrawal would benefit from forming implementation intentions. To test this hypothesis, former heroin users at a German hospital were approached during a workshop on how to find and apply for jobs. Patients were asked to voluntarily participate in a study on how young adults master the task of composing a curriculum vitae. At 10:00 A.M.,

---

76. Schouwenburg, "Procrastination in Academic Settings."
77. Owens, Bowman, and Dill, "Overcoming Procrastination."
78. Brandstätter, Lengfelder, and Gollwitzer, "Implementation Intentions."

patients were shown a model CV and then were asked to form the goal to create their own CVs before 5:00 P.M. on the same day. Half of the participants supported this goal with irrelevant implementation intentions: when, where, and how they wanted to have lunch. The other half supported it with goal-directed implementation intentions: when, where, and how they wanted to write their CV. Whereas irrelevant implementation intentions did not help participants under withdrawal to realize this goal (none of the 10 participants in this condition handed in a CV at 5:00 P.M.), goal-directed implementation intentions did (eight of the participants in this condition handed in a CV at 5:00 P.M.). When using relevant implementation intentions, people procrastinate less, even when suffering from conditions of high cognitive load (in this study, being occupied by controlling the urge to use drugs).

In line with these findings, people suffering from schizophrenia and patients with frontal-lobe injuries were found to perform well on difficult executive-function tasks (e.g., *go/no go* tasks) when using implementation intentions.[79] In addition, children with attention-deficit/hyperactivity disorder (ADHD) benefited from forming implementation intentions in executive-function tasks (e.g., Stroop task) as well as in more real-life self-control tasks (e.g., delay-of-gratification paradigm).[80]

## CONCLUSION

Procrastination, understood as the voluntary delay of an intended course of action despite having the opportunity to act and expecting to be worse off for the delay, is a widespread phenomenon. Whereas previous research discussed procrastination mainly in relation to the failure to get started, we extend this notion to all stages of goal striving. People might not get started to act on an intended goal, might not continue pursuing a goal, might not disengage from goal intentions that became unattainable, or might procrastinate after overextending themselves (in the case of ego depletion). To fight procrastination, implementation intentions are suggested as an easily applicable self-regulatory strategy. Implementation intentions refer to specific plans in which people specify when, where, and how they intend to pursue a goal, preferably in the form of an *if-then* plan. Research shows that implementation intentions help people overcome procrastination with respect to various problems of goal striving, improve goal attainment in situations where goal striving is handicapped (e.g., by bad habits, lack of skills, or competitors), and even improve results in populations known to have chronic problems of action control.

---

79. Brandstätter, Lengfelder, and Gollwitzer, "Implementation Intentions, study 2; Lengfelder and Gollwitzer, "Reflective and Reflexive Action Control."
80. Gollwitzer, Gawrilow, and Oettingen, "Power of Planning."

An important precondition for implementation-intention effects to occur is that strong goal intentions are in place. Future research should therefore develop implementation-intention interventions that are backed up by interventions geared at creating strong goal intentions. For example, protection-motivation interventions[81] or the goal-setting strategy of mental contrasting could precede the formation of implementation intentions as a reinforcement strategy. In a longitudinal study on exercising,[82] participants not only formed self-set implementation intentions—determining when, where, and how they planned to overcome an obstacle; deciding how to prevent an obstacle from occurring; and specifying a good opportunity to act—but also first elaborated positive outcomes of regular exercising and contrasted them with possible obstacles (engaged in mental contrasting). An increase in exercising was observed as an immediate consequence of this intervention; more impressively, this increase held up over the extensive time period of two years. This line of research is most promising, and we hope it continues to highlight the efficacy of implementation intentions, especially as they relate to procrastination.

## ACKNOWLEDGMENTS

We would like to thank Chrisoula Andreou and Mark White for organizing the CSMN workshop and editing this volume. The inspiring discussions at the workshop helped us to pinpoint the thief of time from an interdisciplinary perspective and to thereby advance our understanding of how procrastination might be curbed by implementation intentions. We are also grateful to Olav Gjelsvik and Jennifer Hornsby, as well as the Centre for the Study of Mind in Nature for sponsoring the CSMN workshop.

---

81. Milne, Orbell, and Sheeran, "Combining Motivational and Volitional Interventions."
82. Stadler, Oettingen, and Gollwitzer, "Effects of a Self-Regulation Intervention."

# 12

# Coping with Procrastination

*Chrisoula Andreou*

I am not one of those people who get a big rush out of exercising. My reason for exercising is more along the lines of "I don't want to get osteoporosis and break a hip later on in life, so I'd better be good now." Like many who do not get a big rush out of exercising, I am easily distracted from my exercising goals. For instance, when I first became a faculty member, my busy days made it easy to excuse the fact that the closest I got to regular exercise was carting my loaded backpack from my office to the seminar room. But after a few months, I thought, "It's about time I got back in shape. I really must start exercising a few times a week." Still, the workout-free weeks continued. At some point, I thought, "That's it. If I don't exercise for 20 minutes five times a week, I can't have my usual Friday night dinner out." Strangely, playing this little game did the trick, and I finally started working out. There were occasional lapses, which were punished on Friday, though there was no outside authority supervising the system.

Like procrastination, the strategy for coping with it just described is peculiar yet familiar. It has not, however, been analyzed in the literature on coping with procrastination, which has focused instead on analyzing strategies involving the formation of implementation intentions, the internalization of "bundling" rules, or the arrangement of external incentives and constraints. My aim in this chapter is to analyze the strategy I have illustrated in a way that highlights how it differs from the strategies that have already been studied. An implication of my reasoning is that insofar as we can and do employ this strategy, we take advantage of the possibility that poor self-control can be a local trait rather than a robust character trait. Otherwise put, we take advantage of the possibility that one can exhibit poor self-control in some domains while exhibiting a great deal of self-control in others.

## PROCRASTINATION

According to the notion of procrastination with which I am here concerned, it involves leaving too late or putting off indefinitely what one should, relative to one's goals and information, have done sooner.[1] Because procrastination involves self-imposed frustration, it can be quite puzzling. Why neglect one's own goals? Indeed, how is this even possible? Well, achieving certain goals can be a complicated business. Consider, for example, long-term goals such as saving for a decent retirement, losing weight, or getting in shape. Normally, temporarily failing to contribute to the realization of these goals will not make or break one's chances of achieving them. It is thus tempting to make today an "exception" and keep putting off until tomorrow what would be a burden to get to right away. As long as the goal is still feasible, one can make today an exception without abandoning the goal, and yet if the exception becomes the rule, the goal will never be achieved.

Structurally, procrastination (of the sort just described) seems to be an intertemporal free-rider problem. In the traditional, inter*personal* free-rider problem, one prefers that all or most contribute to maintaining a valuable collective resource rather than that none or few do, but one also prefers not contributing oneself, since the contribution of a single individual is negligible. If each person follows his preference not to contribute, then the valuable collective resource is not maintained, and all are worse off than if all contributed. One can face an interpersonal free-rider problem even if one cares about and identifies with others. By hypothesis, the contribution of a single individual is negligible, so one can fail to contribute without compromising the well-being of the others involved.

Now, consider the procrastinator's situation: At each point in time, the procrastinator prefers to consistently or usually stay on task rather than to never or rarely stay on task, but she also prefers not to stay on task now. If she repeatedly acts on this latter preference, she is bound to rarely stay on task and thus to fail to achieve her long-term goal. And she can face this intertemporal free-rider problem even if she cares about and identifies with herself in the future (or with her future self, if you prefer); for she may correctly see her current decision about whether or not to stay on task as negligible relative to her long-term goal and to her future well-being.

Like other situations in which free-riding is an issue, procrastination can lead to terrible results, including poor health, inadequate savings, and the distress of warranted regret. Because procrastination can have extremely negative consequences, we often seek strategies for coping with the temptation to procrastinate. I turn now to reviewing the main strategies that have been analyzed in the literature on procrastination and goal achievement, highlighting their advantages and disadvantages. I will then

---

1. For more elaborate discussion concerning the relevant notion of procrastination, see Silver and Sabini, "Procrastinating," and Andreou, "Understanding Procrastination", and "Environmental Preservation and Second-Order Procrastination." For a discussion of some subtleties that are glossed over in the rough and partial characterization provided here, see the introduction to this volume as well as the chapters by Sarah Stroud (chapter 3) and Christine Tappolet (chapter 7).

compare these strategies to the neglected strategy illustrated above. I do not mean to put this neglected strategy forward as the best strategy but only as an alternative that is worth considering, particularly when other strategies are not working or are out of place. Furthermore, I see each of these strategies as a crutch aimed at instilling habits that become second nature, initiating actions automatically, as does the habit of brushing one's teeth before bed.

## IMPLEMENTATION INTENTIONS AND BUNDLING RULES

In some cases, the temptation to put off initiating action with respect to an important goal can be dealt with via the formation of an *implementation intention*, which specifies the "when, where, and how" of goal-directed responses.[2] Suppose, for example, that one has the goal of staying in shape. One can, other things being equal, improve one's chances of performing goal-directed actions if one forms an implementation intention such as the following: "From now on, I'm going to walk home from work." This implementation intention, which sets a rule that applies to a bundle of choice points, draws some bright lines. While there remain many ways to get in shape, once one has decided to get in shape by walking home from work, taking the bus home clearly violates a standard or rule one has set for oneself and so is, psychologically, quite significant. If one permits oneself to take the bus home, one will presumably experience some cognitive dissonance if one has nothing to say about why one is abandoning or suspending one's implementation intention. If there is nothing unexpected to appeal to, the failure to stick to one's implementation intention can take a toll on one's confidence that one has the self-control necessary to achieve one's goal, which can, in turn, take a toll on one's self-esteem.

There are a couple of dangers associated with this sort of strategy. As George Ainslie stresses in his work on self-control, while magnifying the significance of carrying out or failing to carry out a certain action can provide one with the motivation one needs to initiate goal-directed action, it can also prove dangerously demoralizing when lapses occur.[3] Suppose, for example, that one decides to lose weight by eating only what comes in the breakfast, lunch, and dinner boxes that one receives from Diet Guru X. Although one is very tempted to eat outside the box and although a single instance of eating outside the box is negligible relative to one's long-term goal of losing weight, one manages to stay on course by investing eating

---

2. Brandstätter, Lengfelder, and Gollwitzer, "Implementation Intentions," 947; see also Frank Wieber and Peter Gollwitzer's chapter 11 in this volume.
3. Ainslie, "Dangers of Willpower" and *Breakdown of Will*.

outside the box with a great deal of significance. "Eating outside the box would be a terrible failure," one convinces oneself; "it would show a complete lack of resoluteness and self-control." Here, one takes advantage of the fact that "the threat of losing one's expectation of future self-control can marshall [sic] a great deal more motivation than depends on the single case at hand."[4] Still, at some point, one finally gives in to temptation, thinking, "What's the point? This is too hard. There's no hope." Depressed and in accordance with one's shattered confidence in one's ability to control oneself, one binges on every treat in sight. According to Ainslie, this dynamic is behind "the 'first-drink' phenomenon," which is such "a conspicuous cause of alcoholics' loss of sobriety."[5] The unwilling alcoholic may "stake such importance on a single lapse that, if it ever occurs, it will lead him to helpless surrender."[6] "A lapse suggests that his will is weak, a diagnosis that [can] actually weaken his will."[7] This is the risk of casting every relevant choice as a crucial "test case."[8]

There is also the danger of becoming compulsive.[9] The desire to avoid lapses and the resulting demoralization may lead one to cultivate a pathologically inflexible commitment to staying on course. And while staying on course is a good thing, it would, presumably, make sense to be concerned about someone who managed to never, ever eat outside the box. It is, however, hard to be appropriately flexible if one seriously doubts one's credibility. Complete failure or complete rigidity might seem like the only options.

## EXTERNAL INCENTIVES AND CONSTRAINTS

The other strategy for coping with procrastination analyzed in the literature is that of arranging for external incentives and constraints.[10] As studies by Dan Ariely and Klaus Wertenbroch show, procrastinators are sometimes willing to impose binding deadlines on themselves even when failure to meet these deadlines will result in significant, externally enforced penalties.[11] In their studies, students were given the option of making all of their papers officially due on the last day of class or setting earlier deadlines with late penalties enforced by the instructor. Although they could

---

4. Ainslie, "Dangers of Willpower," 69.
5. Ainslie, "Dangers of Willpower," 85–86.
6. Ainslie, "Dangers of Willpower," 85.
7. Ainslie, "Dangers of Willpower," 71.
8. Ainslie, "Dangers of Willpower," 85.
9. Ainslie, "Dangers of Willpower" and *Breakdown of Will*.
10. For a discussion of this strategy in relation to self-control problems in general, see Elster, *Ulysses and the Sirens* and *Ulysses Unbound*. See also Becker on side bets in "Notes on the Concept of Commitment."
11. Ariely and Wertenbroch, "Procrastination, Deadlines, and Performance."

have chosen to submit their papers according to private deadlines, which would allow them greater flexibility, especially if something unexpected occurred, students commonly chose the externally enforced deadlines. They seemed to anticipate procrastination and to rely on the more demanding grade-reducing penalty system to keep them on track.

The advantage of relying on external incentives and constraints is that, with the right arrangements in place—and, in particular, with severe enough and immediate enough sanctions—one can virtually guarantee that one will not procrastinate. There are also, however, significant disadvantages. One serious disadvantage is that arranging for external incentives and constraints may be extremely costly or impractical. For example, although one may want to exercise regularly, one may not want to incur the costs, which may or may not be financial, associated with having a monitor make sure that one exercises regularly. Another disadvantage is that, even when it's effective, this strategy may keep one on course by diminishing one's freedom rather than increasing one's self-control. Take the students in Ariely and Wertenbroch's studies who opted for the early deadlines backed by externally enforced penalties. They did not, in handing their papers in early, demonstrate greater discipline; they simply responded to the *external* pressures and constraints that they set up to counter their weak wills.

It may be that one can improve on this strategy by combining externally enforced penalties (or externally binding obligations) with a less costly, internal monitoring system. Suppose, for example, that you bet your friend that you will exercise five times a week or else owe him five dollars for every lapse. Suppose that this friend agrees, collects a returnable deposit from you, and trusts you to honestly report your activities at the end of each week. If you are honest, then this arrangement may solve your problem. For, assuming you know that you are honest, you will also know that your lapses will be more costly than they otherwise would be, and this may prove to be enough to discourage them. If this strategy is a genuine possibility, and if honesty and self-control are genuine virtues, then we must, it seems, reject the familiar philosophical doctrine of the unity of the virtues, according to which the virtues are so deeply interconnected that to have one is to have them all. If it is possible to use one's honesty to help deal with (and in a sense compensate for) a lack of self-control, then presumably, one can be perfectly honest while seriously lacking in self-control.

It might be objected that one could never use one's honesty to help deal with a lack of self-control, since being honest when this is costly presupposes self-control; in particular, it requires resisting the temptation to lie. Although my aim is not to defend the possibility of the strategy just described, I think the objection under consideration can be addressed by some of the reasoning in the next section concerning the strategy of leveraging control. It is this latter strategy, which has one relying less on others and more on oneself, that I am particularly interested in here.

## LEVERAGING CONTROL

Let us return to the opening example. I want to get in shape but keep putting off goal-directed action. At some point, I say, "That's it. If I don't exercise for 20 minutes five times a week, I can't have my usual Friday night dinner out." Playing this little game does the trick, and I finally start working out. There are, of course, lapses. But these are punished on Fridays, though there is no outside authority supervising the system.

A key feature of the strategy employed in this case is that the self-imposed rule is set up so that if one lapses and fails to perform the goal-directed actions one should be performing, one can remain in good standing relative to one's self-imposed rule by accepting the penalty that is built into the rule. (Readers who feel that the penalty must be more immediate can change the example accordingly.)

Of course, if the penalty is not severe enough, one may prefer accepting the penalty over performing aversive goal-directed actions, in which case the desired result of avoiding procrastination will not be achieved. (However, in many cases, the penalty need not be particularly severe, only significant enough to eliminate the idea that the cost of failing to act in this instance is utterly negligible.) Moreover, the penalty cannot be so severe that one would never actually exact it. So, care must be taken in crafting the rule. And one must take advantage of what one knows about oneself.

Now, it might be objected that if one's poor self-control has led to a lapse, one cannot be counted on to penalize oneself for this failure. I will put aside this objection for the moment and get back to it shortly. Suppose, for now, that, given a well-crafted rule, one can be counted on to penalize oneself for lapses. Then this strategy has some significant advantages. Because lapses are not strictly forbidden, their occurrence does not count as a failure to stick to a self-imposed rule. If one accepts the penalty, then one remains in good standing relative to the rule one has set for oneself. Furthermore, because the penalty is self-enforced, its realization requires self-control and so confirms one's ability to control oneself. Also, because the penalty for lapses is self-enforced, one need not pay the often high costs associated with arranging for external incentives.

Although I will continue talking in terms of a penalty system, one might favor a reward system instead. One might, for example, adopt a rule such as "If I exercise for 20 minutes five times a week, I can treat myself to a massage on the weekend." What matters, for my purposes, is that when a lapse occurs, the withholding of the reward is self-enforced. (Because we tend to be more wary of incurring a loss than of not gaining a potential reward, the magnitude of potential rewards might have to be much greater than the magnitude of potential punishments.)

Now, return to the objection that if one's poor self-control has led to a lapse, one cannot be counted on to penalize oneself for this failure. The strategy under consideration seems to presuppose precisely what is lacking: self-control. This suggests that, unlike the preceding strategies considered, which merely have significant disadvantages, this strategy could never work. And yet, as many of us know from first-hand experience, it does work. What is going on?

This puzzle dissolves if one notices a possibility that has recently received a significant amount of attention in moral psychology, namely that the so-called personality traits studied by psychologists and the so-called character traits evaluated by ethicists need not be robust.[12] We often attribute robust personality or character traits to agents—saying, for example, that A is generous or B is cruel or C is conscientious. We also, however, allow for the possibility of local traits—saying, for example that A is extremely conscientious when it comes to X but not at all conscientious when it comes to Y.

The possibility of local traits (given familiar trait taxonomies) allows for and is supported by the possibility that one can solve a self-control problem in one area of one's life by relying on one's high degree of self-control in another area of life. Perhaps as a result of force of habit and/or self-image, self-control is often second nature in certain areas of one's life. If one has a high degree of self-control in some area, then, as long as the penalty one settles on takes advantage of one's self-control in that area, the threat that one will apply the penalty if one lapses is credible (even if one is not compulsive when it comes to applying the penalty), and so the threat may prevent one from lapsing. There is, in short, room for leveraging control. The self-control that comes easily can help with the self-control that does not.

I may, for example, have very poor self-control when it comes to exercising but a great deal of self-control when it comes to spending money on treats. In particular, I may very much enjoy eating out but have cultivated the sensible habit of eating out only occasionally and as a treat (just as one might very much enjoy watching TV but have trained oneself to never turn on the TV in the daytime, while one is supposed to be working in one's home office). If so, then playing the sort of game I've described might work very well for me.

And it is likely to work better than a closely related sort of game we are sometimes tempted to play. This is the game of making the penalty not so much a punishment but an alternative way of achieving the relevant goal. I might, for example, threaten to penalize myself for not exercising today by having to exercise twice as long tomorrow. This may seem like a more rational strategy, since the penalty helps me attain my goal of keeping fit rather than just making me suffer for my lapse; but here it really does seem that one is counting on precisely the sort of self-control one is lacking. The typical result is that the penalties just stack up until one is faced

---

12. For a recent discussion that helped bring this possibility and its potential implications for ethics to center stage, see Doris, *Lack of Character*. I here leave open the question of whether Doris's views concerning the significance of local traits for ethics, and for virtue theory in particular, are on the right track.

with a completely unrealistic task (e.g., eight hours of exercise today or sixteen tomorrow) and abandons the game altogether.

## THE PSYCHOLOGY OF SELF-CONTROL

I have described a strategy for dealing with procrastination and argued that insofar as we can and do employ this strategy, we take advantage of the possibility that poor self-control can be a local trait rather than a robust character trait. In this section, I will relate the idea that poor self-control can be a local trait to two important strands of empirical research on self-control.

One strand of research suggests that while self-control may, like a muscle, be strengthened with exercise, it is also, like a muscle, subject to short-term exhaustion.[13] In particular, engaging in effortful self-control leads to poorer performance in closely following self-control tasks. Relatedly, conserving self-control strength improves performance in closely following self-control tasks. It may, therefore, make sense to save one's self-control strength for certain tasks.

Although this research allows that self-control need not be a robust trait, it might be interpreted as implying that even if one can rely on one's high degree of self-control in one area of one's life to back up a threat that makes even single lapses significantly costly and so less tempting, nothing is really gained because counting on a high degree of self-control will invariably involve counting on a great deal of self-control energy, and if this self-control energy is available, it can be employed to directly stop one from lapsing. But, as at least some proponents of the self-control strength model seem to recognize, this is not quite right, since it cannot be assumed that all self-control processes are "equally expensive."[14] If one's high degree of self-control in some areas is, perhaps as a result of training, habit, or self-image, fairly effortless, then relying heavily on that self-control does not require allotting it a great deal of self-control energy.

I am assuming that how much effortful self-control it takes to do something can vary with the rewards and costs associated with performing or omitting the action. For example, while I may typically need a significant amount of willpower to get myself to jump up and put my weights away properly, virtually no willpower is necessary if I see that I have left my weights precariously balanced and that my precious pet is at risk. And it's not just because of the pull of my pet's sweet face. I would also be in no way tempted to continue lying around if, for some strange reason, there was a million-dollar reward for jumping up and putting my weights away properly.

---

13. See, for example, Muraven, Baumeister, and Tice, "Longitudinal Improvement of Self-Regulation"; Muraven and Shmueli, "Self-Control Costs"; and Muraven, Shmueli, and Burkley, "Conserving Self-Control Strength."

14. Gailliot et al., "Self-Control," 334.

Another strand of research aims to uncover connections between poor self-control and other traits such as low conscientiousness.[15] Although this research often seems to assume that self-control and the so-called personality traits associated with it are robust traits, this assumption is unnecessary. The correct question to ask may be not "What is going on with people who lack self-control?" but "What is going on when someone lacks self-control in some domain?" Although it is often tempting to describe some people as undisciplined and unconscientious, a closer look at their lives might lead one to a more complex description. One's procrastinating student may also be an amazingly disciplined weight-trainer.

It might be objected that if one's procrastinating student is also an amazingly disciplined weight-trainer, she doesn't have a self-control problem at all—she just doesn't care all that much about doing well in school. But what if she laments her susceptibility to watching TV instead of doing her homework? And what if she believes that registering for classes is a waste of her time and money if she does not do well? And what if, given the opportunity, she is willing to impose binding deadlines on herself even when failure to meet these deadlines will result in significant, externally enforced penalties? I would say she has a self-control problem when it comes to studying, though she has trained herself well when it comes to exercising.

The idea that one's self-control can vary from domain to domain is consistent with the idea that some have more serious, more pervasive, or more wide-ranging self-control problems than others. For example, typically, a full-time student who has a procrastination problem when it comes to studying has a more serious problem than a full-time student who has a procrastination problem when it comes to shopping to replace worn-out clothes and shoes. The former procrastination problem is likely to be more serious from both a social perspective and a personal perspective. Relatedly, one would expect someone with the former problem to be characterized and to characterize himself as a procrastinator more readily than someone with the latter problem.

The idea that one's self-control can vary from domain to domain is also consistent with the hypothesis that there is a biological or genetic component to procrastination. According to Piers Steel, this hypothesis has emerged as quite plausible given recent empirical research.[16] Apparently, one of the specific findings behind the general conclusions concerning leadership in the workplace published by Richard D. Arvey et al. is that identical twins provided more similar responses than fraternal twins when each twin was asked to indicate the degree to which he or she is a procrastinator.[17] This suggests that genetics contributes to one's procrastinating

---

15. Some relevant research focused specifically on procrastination, understood as "quintessential self-regulatory failure," is reviewed in Steel, "Nature of Procrastination."
16. Steel, "Nature of Procrastination."
17. Arvey et al., "Determinants of Leadership Role Occupancy"; Richard D. Arvey, personal correspondence, July 5, 2007; Steel, "Nature of Procrastination."

tendencies. One cannot, however, conclude, as Steel does, that procrastination has substantial cross-situational stability and so figures as a (robust) personality trait.[18] The responses can be interpreted as relative to the domain that, in the context, was most salient—namely, the workplace. And even if respondents assume that they are being asked about their procrastinating tendencies in general, in indicating that one is a procrastinator to a high degree, one may be attributing to oneself serious and wide-ranging procrastination problems rather than a uniformly high degree of procrastination across all domains of action. Similarly, in indicating that one is a procrastinator to a low degree, one may be attributing to oneself only a few, not particularly serious procrastination problems rather than a uniformly low degree of procrastination across all domains of action. Consider again the student with a procrastination problem when it comes to shopping to replace worn-out clothes and shoes. Although his procrastination problem in that domain may be persistent, and although he may recognize this, he may not consider himself to be much of a procrastinator in general.

## CONCLUSION

My aim has been to analyze an important coping strategy that has been overlooked in the literature on procrastination: the strategy of leveraging control. Although one must know oneself quite well to use it, it has some significant advantages and so is worth considering, particularly when other strategies are not working or are out of place. Its main advantages are that it can be used even when no external incentives or constraints are conveniently available, and it avoids the dangers associated with magnifying the significance of lapses by casting every relevant choice as a crucial test of one's self-control. Theoretically, the strategy is initially somewhat puzzling, since it seems to rely on having a significant amount of self-control when such self-control is, it seems, precisely what is lacking. The puzzle dissolves once one recognizes the possibility that self-control can figure as a local trait rather than a robust character trait.

## ACKNOWLEDGMENTS

My thanks to Ron Mallon, Elijah Millgram, Sarah Stroud, Christine Tappolet, Mark D. White, Mike White, the participants in the CSMN workshop, and audiences at Syracuse University, University of California–Riverside, University of Montreal, University of Rochester, and University of San Francisco for their helpful comments on earlier drafts of this chapter.

    18. Steel, "Nature of Procrastination."

# 13

# Resisting Procrastination
Kantian Autonomy and the Role of the Will

*Mark D. White*

Procrastination may be the most common and widespread instance of weakness of will.[1] Many of us, if not most of us, procrastinate with respect to particular tasks some of the time, and some of us persistently procrastinate at certain tasks most of the time. Common cases of weakness of will can also be understood to incorporate features of procrastination; one component of the failure to control one's eating, for instance, can be considered procrastination with regard to starting a diet or exercise program.

Economists, psychologists, and philosophers—including many of the contributors to this book—have written extensively and brilliantly on the causes of procrastination. But I would argue that they have dealt with only one side of the problem. They have described, often in excruciating detail (especially the economists), the reasons procrastination is attractive to us at the time we choose it: salience, hyperbolic discounting, and so on. But how do they recommend that people combat the urge to procrastinate? It is the same remedy they offer for any other case of weakness of will: manipulate the relevant costs and benefits, often through changes made in the choice environment, so that the akratic action is no longer the action picked by (myopic) rational deliberation. But this does not solve weakness of will as much as it avoids or sidesteps it altogether. Someone who locks her refrigerator to block late-night binges has not exhibited a strong will; she has merely accounted for the weak will she will have later by changing the payoffs now, before temptation strikes (and when her will seems stronger).

---

1. As George Ainslie states in chapter 1 of this book, procrastination is the "basic impulse" and is "as fundamental as the shape of time." However, the identification of procrastination with weakness of will must be qualified in light of Sarah Stroud's chapter 3, which is a detailed conceptual analysis of procrastination and how it does and does not fit into various philosophical understandings of weakness of will and akrasia.

While such scholars can explain why agents do or do not have incentives or preferences to procrastinate, they cannot explain why agents sometimes resist the urge to procrastinate—because they do not recognize the existence of the will as a faculty of choice independent of preferences or desires. While most philosophers, in the spirit of Gilbert Ryle's "ghost in the machine" remark, do not see any reason to posit a will, economists have almost completely ignored the concept.[2] The resulting deterministic model of choice denies the "agent" any true choice or agency at all. If the agent's payoffs are such that procrastination maximizes their utility, then that agent *must* procrastinate, almost by definition. In this model, there can be no choice contrary to the result of one's calculation of utility-maximizing action; the only thing the agent can do is to take another action preemptively to manipulate the relevant payoffs, because there is no way she can resist them once they are "active."

In contrast to traditional economic and philosophical theories of decision making, I posit an active faculty of choice, a will, through which the agent makes a final choice in any decision-making situation. By incorporating the will into the economic model of choice, I refute the psychological determinism inherent in mainstream models, and allow for choices that contradict the agent's best considered reasons for action. Taken in a Kantian context, I consider these true choices to be a function of strength of will or character, emphasizing the ethical aspect of choice itself (regardless of the ethical nature of the options among which the agent is choosing).

Relying on this conception of choice, I hope to provide an alternative to the various coping strategies suggested in other chapters in this book (and elsewhere).[3] Rather than circumvent or account for her weakness of will, the agent can exercise her strength of will; simply put, she can *try harder*. In the same way that modern labor-saving devices have made us physically weaker (and heavier) compared with previous generations, I argue that the proliferation of coping mechanisms has made our wills weaker. This is not entirely a negative thing, of course; technological and institutional developments that economize on effort can be very beneficial, but only if they allow effort to be redirected to a more productive use. Most of us have little need for significant physical strength in our everyday lives; those of us who exercise do so primarily to improve our health or appearance. But we have no gyms or health clubs for our will, and I would argue that in the modern world, we have occasion to need strength of will more often than muscular strength. If we ever lose access

---

2. One prominent exception is Don Ross ("Introduction"), who, like Ryle, disputes the existence of an independent will. Other treatments of the will in economics include Brennan, "Voluntary Exchange"; Cooter, "Lapses, Conflict, and Akrasia"; and Kim, "Hyperbolic Discounting" (discussed below).

3. See Joseph Heath and Joel Anderson's chapter 14 in this book for more on external coping mechanisms.

to our coping mechanisms, our willpower is all we have to fall back on, and we will be sorely disappointed if we find it missing as a result of sustained neglect.

In this chapter, I will reinterpret the phenomenon of procrastination using a Kantian-economic model of choice (incorporating a concept of the will) that I developed elsewhere.[4] This model is broadly consistent with much of the previous work on procrastination by economists and philosophers, in that it includes this work as a special case and expands on it. (My contention is not that this other work is incorrect, but rather incomplete.) I begin by surveying some of the work on procrastination by economists, pointing out its strength and weaknesses. Next, I summarize the work of volitionist philosophers who maintain the existence of an independent will or faculty of choice, before explaining my Kantian-economic model of choice based on volitionism. I then explain how procrastination is understood in the context of the Kantian-economic model, compare it with similar approaches, and conclude with limitations of the exercise of willpower.

## ECONOMISTS' PERSPECTIVES ON PROCRASTINATION

Previous work on procrastination by economists has focused on the structure of preferences that leads to such behavior, and they have analyzed a fair range of possible circumstances in which procrastination will arise.[5] The first prominent economist to address procrastination directly was George Akerlof, who based his understanding of procrastination on the salience, or vividness, of the costs of the arduous present task: "Procrastination occurs when present costs are unduly salient in comparison with future costs, leading individuals to postpone tasks until tomorrow without foreseeing that when tomorrow comes, the required action will be delayed yet again."[6] Akerlof emphasizes the costs of delaying the task, resulting from the exaggerated weight given the salient costs.

In a series of papers since 1999, Ted O'Donoghue and Matthew Rabin have offered the most extensive analysis of procrastination on the part of economists. To explain procrastination, they focus on *present-biased preferences*, which they consider "a more descriptive term for the underlying human characteristic that hyperbolic discounting represents"[7] and functionally equivalent to Akerlof's salience (with less implication that they

---

4. See White, "Does *Homo Economicus* Have a Will?"; "Multiple Selves"; "Can *Homo Economicus* Follow Kant's Categorical Imperative?"
5. See Don Ross's chapter 2 in this book for a more detailed examination of prominent economic models of procrastination.
6. Akerlof, "Procrastination and Obedience," 1.
7. O'Donoghue and Rabin, "Doing It Now or Later," 103n. 2.

are not "real" preferences). Consistent with hyperbolic discounting, "when considering trade-offs between two future moments, present-biased preferences give stronger relative weight to the earlier moment as it gets closer."[8] In another 1999 paper, they analyze principals' options for countering their agents' tendencies to procrastinate, basically arguing that penalties for delay must be increased for such agents to counteract their present-bias effects.[9] In a later paper, they elaborate on their basic model by introducing multiple tasks and tasks of varying importance.[10] They argue that introducing a new option (a new task) with higher long-run benefit may prompt the agent to switch to that one, but the new option may also have high present costs, which will lead one to procrastinate. This is based on the observation that task choice and timing choice are made differently and can counteract each other. Also, more important projects, which may require higher up-front costs, may incite more procrastination. Most recently, they discuss procrastination in multistage projects, claiming, for instance, that projects with high start-up costs but lower finishing costs never get started (because of procrastination), while projects with low start-up costs but high finishing costs get started but not finished (again, because of procrastination).[11]

In "Read This Paper Later," Carolyn Fischer eschews time inconsistency, developing a model of procrastination with time-consistent preferences, using simple marginal analysis of the work/leisure trade-off.[12] Given a fixed amount of time to perform a task (such as writing a paper) and a (time-consistent) preference for present leisure, the agent will postpone the task until there is just enough time to finish it. Furthermore, this is utility-maximizing. The problem, however, lies in interpreting this behavior as procrastination, rather than rational time-allocation (based on time preference), as a later paper of Fischer's acknowledges.[13] In that paper, she utilizes time-inconsistent preferences instead, focusing on hyperbolic discounting and "differential discounting," by which the utility from leisure is discounted at a higher rate than returns from work. (She links this to Akerlof's salience, as well as arguing that preferences based on differential discounting can appear hyperbolic.)

This is just a sampling of economists' work on procrastination, but I think it represents the dominant approach to studying the phenomenon. The problem with all of these explanations is that they focus on preferences or utility; in these models, it is the conflict among different sets or types of preferences that leads to the self-control problem. These models provide truly fascinating insights into the motivations behind procrastination,

---

8. O'Donoghue and Rabin, "Doing It Now or Later," 103.
9. O'Donoghue and Rabin, "Incentives for Procrastinators."
10. O'Donoghue and Rabin, "Choice and Procrastination."
11. O'Donoghue and Rabin, "Procrastination on Long-Term Projects."
12. Fischer, "Read This Paper Later."
13. Fischer, "Read This Paper Even Later."

but they cannot escape the tyranny of preferences and therefore cannot explain how the agent may resist the pull of his preferences and *choose* not to procrastinate. For that, we need a model that acknowledges that agents can somehow override their preferences—for instance, by exerting willpower.

## KANTIAN-ECONOMIC MODEL OF WILL

### Volitionism and Economics

The standard economic model of choice can best be described as constrained preference satisfaction (given information that may have been acquired rationally or provided exogenously). The economic agent chooses the option (among those available) that satisfies the highest-ranked preference within her constraints and given her information. It is in this sense that the economic agent has no true choice or agency; her decision is determined wholly by her preferences, constraints, and information. This resembles the basic Humean desire-belief model in philosophy, in which desires and beliefs determine choice (and action). J. David Velleman describes it as follows: "There is something that the agent wants, and there is an action that he believes conducive to its attainment. His desire for the end, and his belief in the action as a means, justify taking the action, and they jointly cause an intention to take it, which in turn causes the corresponding movements of the agent's body. Provided that these causal processes take their normal course, the agent's movements consummate an action, and his motivating desire and belief constitute his reasons for acting."[14]

While fairly standard among philosophers (albeit in much more elaborate versions), nonetheless some prominent philosophers reject this model. R. Jay Wallace calls it the "hydraulic interpretation of human motivational psychology," which is ultimately grounded in psychological determinism, leaving "no room for genuine deliberative agency. Action is traced to the operation of forces within us, with respect to which we as agents are ultimately passive, and in a picture of this kind real agency seems to drop out of view."[15] Velleman also criticizes the standard conception of choice for the passivity it implies on the part of agents; he argues that it "fails to include an agent—or, more precisely, fails to cast the agent in his proper role. In this story, reasons cause an intention, and an intention causes bodily movements, but nobody—that is, no person—does anything. Psychological and physiological events take place inside a person, but the person serves merely as the arena for these events: he takes no

---

14. Velleman, "What Happens," 461. (In its modern form, the Humean model is normally attributed to Donald Davidson; see his *Essays on Actions and Events*.)
15. Wallace, *Normativity and the Will*, 174.

active part."[16] On a more positive note, as a supplement to the standard model, Richard Holton posits a "distinct faculty of will-power," emphasizing that it is a faculty "that the agent actively employs," and further explores the concept of strength of will (see below).[17]

John Searle, in *Rationality in Action*, refers to the Humean picture as "the Classical Model," which he claims "represents human rationality as a more complex version of ape rationality" (referring to experiments that showed apes to be rational decision makers).[18] Searle argues that rationality requires a true act of choice or agency, and he locates this agency in "gaps" in the decision-making process, one of which exists "between the reasons for making up your mind, and the actual decision that you make."[19] In other words, the gap "occurs when the beliefs, desires, and other reasons are not experienced as causally sufficient conditions for a decision,"[20] a description reminiscent of Wallace and Velleman's criticisms of psychological determinism.[21] But obviously, the activity in the gap is not itself reducible to desires, beliefs, or other reasons, so Searle asks, "What fills the gap? Nothing. Nothing fills the gap: you make up your mind to do something, or you just haul off and do what you are doing to do."[22] In Searle's view, an "irreducible notion of the self" is necessary for understanding "our operation in the gap," "a self that combines the capacities of rational and agency," where agency implies "consciously try[ing] to do something."[23]

In the spirit of the scholars cited above, I incorporate true agency or will into the economic model of choice. This involves modeling the activity of the will as choosing between two (or more) alternatives, which may be defined as simple options, lotteries, or preference rankings; in the interest of generality, let us refer to the options as "paths" among which the agent chooses. In interesting choice situations, these paths will be in some sort of conflict, with the two paths having qualitatively different allures. For instance, one path may be to pursue a giving life characterized by a nonegoistic moral code, while the alternative path may be one of pursuing one's narrowly defined self-interest. One path may represent living a

---

16. Velleman, "What Happens," 461.
17. Holton, "How Is Strength of Will Possible?" 48–49.
18. Searle, *Rationality in Action*, 5.
19. Searle, *Rationality in Action*, 14. Other gaps occur between decision and action and between the initiation of an action extended in time and its continuation or completion—both of which have relevance to procrastination, but I will concentrate primarily on the first gap (that between reasons and decision).
20. Searle, *Rationality in Action*, 62.
21. Searle reminds us of Velleman when he supposes a world in which our actions were determined by our intentions: "if that were how the world worked in fact, we would not have to *act on* our intentions; we could, so to speak, wait for them to act by themselves. We could sit back and see how things turned out. But we can't do that, we always have to act" (*Rationality in Action*, 232–233).
22. Searle, *Rationality in Action*, 17.
23. Searle, *Rationality in Action*, 74, 83, 95.

healthy lifestyle of proper diet and exercise, and the other may be an easier life of sloth and gluttony. Or one path may involve long-range planning and commitment to one's chosen goals, while the other may represent myopia and impulsive action.

We assume that the agent has a metapreference or second-order preference over the two paths, but the specific nature of that metapreference is not of concern here. However, we can imagine that in the pairings above, the agent would normally prefer to follow the first path, but the second path nonetheless has its own appeal; otherwise, there would be no conflict of interests. Most people would rather be altruistic, healthy, and resolute than the alternatives, but behaving so is a matter of willpower; one has to be able to avoid the more immediate, salient pull of the "lesser" path.

We can represent an agent's strength of will with a simple probability distribution, in which $p_H$ is the likelihood that the agent will choose the "higher" or preferred path, while $p_L \equiv 1 - p_H$ is the likelihood that the agent will choose the "lower" path. (Again, the designation of paths as higher or lower is a personal matter, not imposed from the outside, and generally speaking not necessarily a moral distinction; it is more an issue of the agent setting goals and aspirations for herself.) It is very important to note that the use of a probability distribution should not be taken to imply that the agent's choice is random, though it may appear that way to the outside observer (or behaviorist). Rather, this technique is necessary because there is no way to model the operation of the will in a deterministic fashion—it is a matter of truly free choice.[24] As Searle writes, "What makes the action a psychologically free action is precisely that the antecedent psychological causes were not sufficient to cause it."[25] According to this framework, we would expect a person with $p_H$ = 80 percent to choose the better path four times out of five and the lesser path one time out of five. Once again, this does not describe a stochastic process; rather, this person's will is such that she simply fails to choose to do the "better" thing 20 percent of the time.

## Kant and Heteronomy

What does it mean when someone fails to follow her (chosen) higher path? In precisely what way has she failed? If we take the higher path to be one consistent with the moral law, then, in Kantian terms, we would say the person has been *heteronomous* or has allowed inclination to affect her moral decisions. This stands in opposition to *autonomy*, the ideal of

---

24. Free choice, as I use the term, should not be confused with free will in the metaphysical sense; I am rejecting psychological determinism only, not (necessarily) physical determinism. In a sense, the agent is determining her choice through her will, but there is no antecedent psychological cause (such as desires or preferences) affecting the working of her will; the agent is the determinant through her volition. (I thank Chrisoula Andreou for emphasizing the last point.)

25. Searle, *Rationality in Action*, 73.

making moral choices according to (and out of respect for) duty, with no undue influence from inclinations or desires (much less external authority). Every person, because of her rationality, has the capacity for autonomy (or inner freedom), but her strength or virtue in this regard can vary: "For while the capacity to overcome all opposing sensible impulses can and must be simply *presupposed* in man on account of his freedom, yet this capacity as *strength* is something he must acquire."[26] In the Kantian-economic model described in the last section, $p_H$ represents this strength of character, or virtue, which Kant defines as "the strength of a human being's maxims in fulfilling his duty."[27]

There are several ways in which a person can be heteronomous. One is "the general weakness of the human heart in complying with the adopted maxims, or the frailty of human nature."[28] I will henceforth call this *simple weakness*, which describes the person who is generally of strong will but occasionally lapses in her moral duty. Consider the person who cheats on his diet once in a while (assuming dieting accords with duty) but for the most part sticks to it.[29] As the term implies, this is merely weakness, resulting from the imperfect rationality and morality of human beings and the constant, relentless pull of inclination, which no person can resist all of the time (although some are more successful—stronger—than others). As Kant writes, "I incorporate the good (the law) into the maxim of my power of choice; but this good, which is an irresistible incentive . . . is subjectively the weaker (in comparison with inclination) whenever the maxim is to be followed."[30] More precisely, this weakness does not imply any viciousness on the part of the agent but "only a lack of virtue . . . which indeed can coexist with the best will."[31] In such cases, inclination has not influenced the determination of the person's maxim but has only interfered with executing the maxim itself.

The other version of heteronomy is more troubling; this is the case of the *impure will*, which describes the person who allows consideration of inclination to influence her deliberations over maxims.[32] Impurity of the

---

26. Kant, *Metaphysics of Morals*, 397. (All citations from Kant's works will list the Academy pagination.) On Kant's theory of virtue as strength, see Gregor, *Laws of Freedom*, 70–75; Guyer, *Kant on Freedom*, 306–311; and Engstrom, "Inner Freedom" (and references therein, especially 290, n. 5).
27. Kant, *Metaphysics of Morals*, 394.
28. Kant, *Religion*, 29.
29. See below on how sticking to one's plans, such as dieting, may be seen as following the duty of self-respect.
30. Kant, *Religion*, 29.
31. Kant, *Metaphysics of Morals*, 408.
32. Technically, having an impure will involves mixing inclination with duty for otherwise moral ends, while depravity (or the "corruption of the human heart") involves putting aside the moral law altogether. (See Kant, *Religion*, 29–30.) Since I am not concerned here with the ultimate ends of the agent, I will use impurity of the will to refer to any influence of inclination on the determination of maxims (for whatever end).

will involves a conscious choice to be heteronomous, a surrender in the endless fight against inclination, as opposed to simple weakness, which represents merely a temporary loss of control. Since an impure will allows inclination to participate in the determination of maxims (and, through them, actions), such a person is much less virtuous than the merely weak one, sliding dangerously close to vice and letting inclination take over completely (threatening to drive $p_H$ to zero).[33]

Kant emphasizes the distinction between simple weakness and impurity of the will in his discussions of affect and passion. To Kant, affect (sometimes translated as "emotion") is more akin to a momentary impulse, "feelings" that, "preceding reflection," are temporarily powerful enough to interfere with the execution of our maxims but then pass quickly ("this tempest quickly subsides").[34] Passion, on the other hand, is a "sensible *desire* that has become a lasting inclination" and therefore more stable and long-lasting.[35] Simple weakness can be understood as an agent succumbing to affect (such as a sudden, irresistible craving for chocolate or a burst of anger), which overwhelms her action, while the impure will is based on a strong, persistent taste or passion (such a lifelong love of chocolate or perpetual anger), which she admits—even welcomes—into the determination of her maxims.[36] In other words, while affect overwhelms our rational faculties, passions become an intrinsic part of them, corrupting the very process rather than just the result. The impure will involves a deliberate submission, a choice to admit the influence of inclination—as Kant writes, "the calm with which one gives oneself up to it permits reflection and allows the mind to form principles upon it"—and is therefore more blameworthy than simple weakness (which nonetheless must be fought).[37]

In the context of the Kantian-economic model, both of these types of heteronomy contribute to a lower $p_H$, but I argue they do so in different ways, which will prove important for the upcoming discussion of procrastination. The degree to which an agent is "simply weak," insofar as this is a determinant of $p_H$, would seem to be more stable, since the impulses (affects) that trigger it are transitory and do not necessarily signal a significant change in the agent's strength of character or her process of moral

---

33. Kant, *Metaphysics of Morals*, 408.
34. Kant, *Metaphysics of Morals*, 407–408.
35. Kant, *Metaphysics of Morals*, 408.
36. As Stephen Engstrom notes, "passions directly interfere with our choice of ends, rather than of actions," and affects "directly interfere with our choice of actions rather than of ends" (Engstrom, "Inner Freedom," 309n. 22).
37. Kant, *Metaphysics of Morals*, 408. To Kant, the ideal "state of health in the moral life," deriving from the ancient Stoics, is "moral apathy," which disregards affect (and rejects extreme passions) to achieve a "tranquil mind," which is thereby the "true strength of virtue" (*Metaphysics of Morals*, 409). See also Kant, *Religion*, 253–254; Gregor, *Laws of Freedom*, 72–73; Engstrom, "Inner Freedom," 307–308, 310n. 24; and Seidler, "Kant and the Stoics."

deliberation. Nevertheless, maintenance of a certain $p_H$ involves effort even in the face of mere weakness, and any relaxation of moral resolve can result in more frequent lapses and a lower $p_H$. To use the dieting example again, the strong-willed person will not give in to every craving he experiences. With a $p_H$ of 80 percent (based only on simple weakness), he will only give in to temptation one time out of five. This does take an exertion of will—without it, he would give in every time—but it is his "baseline" exertion of will, or what he has become used to. As Kant says, strength of will develops through practice (as well as contemplation), so if one can avoid temptations nine times out of 10, we would say his will has strengthened, and his $p_H$ will have risen to 90 percent. Character is only as strong as the obstacles it overcomes, which we can safely interpret as frequency, as well as degree, of temptation.[38]

Compared with simple weakness, impurity of will poses a more serious threat to strength of character, based on its essential corruptive nature. To some extent, impurity (based on the influence of passions) overrules— and eventually lowers—an agent's strength of will or $p_H$. (Not for nothing does Kant refer to passions as "cancerous stores for pure practical reason.")[39] The deliberate consideration of inclination in decision making weakens the separation of the higher and lower paths. In a sense, rather than represent a probability, $p_H$ may become more of a linear combination term, such as in computing expected utility; the agent may construct his maxim on a linear combination of the two paths (rankings, "utility" functions, etc.), and in that way incorporates inclination from the lesser path into his deliberation. To the extent that the impure will allows inclination to matter, it is as if the agent is choosing the lesser path more often, which implies a lower $p_H$.

While affect "produces a momentary loss of freedom and self-control," passion "surrenders both, and finds pleasure and satisfaction in a servile disposition."[40] So, a simpler way of thinking of the workings of the impure will is that it simply gives up or submits to inclination, not even exerting willpower, and clearly diminishing $p_H$. As strength "can be recognized only by the obstacles it can overcome, and in the case of virtue these obstacles are natural inclinations, which can come into conflict with the human being's moral resolutions," an act of an impure will would be one that lacks strength, because it does not even try to restrict the obstacle of temptation by passion.[41]

---

38. However, the strength of the temptation should not matter, as this is a sensuous matter. But insofar as weakness implies allowing inclination into decision making, even temporarily, it may trigger greater weakness, and resistance may, in turn, signal a strengthening of character.
39. Kant, *Anthropology*, 266.
40. Kant, *Anthropology*, 267.
41. Kant, *Metaphysics of Morals*, 394.

Finally, regarding virtue or strength, Kant writes "if it is not rising, [it] is unavoidably sinking."[42] As soon as the agent stops trying to resist inclination, it expands its grasp on him, and the $p_{11}$ thereby falls as he is more likely to succumb to temptation in the future. But by the same token, his will can also be made stronger, and Kant says that "the way to acquire [strength] is to enhance the moral *incentive* (the thought of the law), both by contemplating the dignity of the pure rational law in us and by *practicing* virtue."[43] Thereby, the effect of exertions of willpower are cumulative, which will help explain the persistence of procrastination (while also previewing the willpower-as-muscle theory discussed below).

## PROCRASTINATION

For the purposes of this chapter, I regard procrastination as a temporally oriented variation of weakness of will or akrasia, in which an agent is likely to put off performing (relatively) disagreeable tasks, against her better judgment, rather than enduring the displeasure now.[44] As summarized above, economists also see procrastination as a variation of weakness of will, representing it as a self-control problem and explaining it by detailing the nature of the preferences that make procrastination attractive to the agent. Either their choice situation leads them to procrastinate or it does not—if it does, then they can manipulate the choice situation ahead of time such that they are no longer led to procrastinate when the time comes. But none of these scholars (with one qualified exception noted below) incorporates the role of the will in their models of procrastination, and therefore none of them can explain how people, while facing these strong incentives to procrastinate, nonetheless sometimes resist the urge to do so.

### Application of the Kantian-Economic Model

In the context of the Kantian-economic model of choice, procrastination (with respect to a generic task or goal) takes the form of the lesser path, and timely action is the higher path. If this distinction between higher and lesser paths were purely prudential, this would not be controversial, but I am claiming that procrastination is an issue of character and therefore moral in nature. For this purpose, I follow Thomas E. Hill in maintaining

---

42. Kant, *Metaphysics of Morals*, 409.
43. Kant, *Metaphysics of Morals*, 397.
44. I follow Andreou's definition: "those cases of delaying in which one leaves too late or puts off indefinitely what one should—relative to one's ends and information—have done sooner" ("Understanding Procrastination," 183). But again, see Stroud's chapter 3 in this volume for a discussion of the temporal nature of procrastination and the problems this poses for an interpretation of procrastination as weakness of will.

that procrastination—as with weakness of will in general—represents a failure of self-respect, a violation of duty to oneself, insofar as one fails to follow through on one's goals and plans (at the appropriate time) as previously deliberated upon.[45]

Understood this way, the model implies that an agent has a certain likelihood of resisting procrastination based on her strength of will, virtue, or character. Regardless of the incentives she faces, procrastination still represents the lesser path, the choice favoring inclination (to delay performing the task) over duty (to honor one's plans and not to procrastinate), and therefore the perfectly autonomous agent would never choose to procrastinate. Even if circumstances change to make procrastination more attractive, the ideal autonomous agent would not be tempted, although the heteronomous agent might be. (This assumes that those incentives do not change enough to make delay the overall best choice, both prudentially and ethically; if so, the nature of higher path itself would change, and choosing delay would no longer qualify as procrastination but, rather, would be prudent delay.)

And indeed, as Kant was well aware, none of us is a perfectly autonomous agent, for we are all at least weak to some degree, if not impure of will. All of us at times succumb to momentary impulse—an interesting television show is on, the task at hand just seems unbearable at the moment, and so forth. If our $p_H$ is high, this will occur only occasionally, and it will happen more often if the will is weaker. And if the "rational" incentives to procrastinate do not enter into our decision making formally, simple weakness is all there is to it. The agent still has a duty to strengthen her will, character, or virtue, but she is not a bad person for her weakness.

However, deliberate rational consideration of the incentives to procrastinate—the factors identified in so much detail by economists—would signal an impure will, for these elements would never be considered by an autonomous agent (even a merely weak one) in determining one's maxim.[46] Admittedly, if an agent with an impure will can manipulate her environment in such a way as to render procrastination less attractive, she will procrastinate less, and no one can deny that this is a good outcome.

---

45. See Hill, "Weakness of Will." This assumes that the task in question is not contrary to duty itself; if it were, procrastination in performance of the task would compound one violation of duty on top of another and therefore still show a lack of character, despite any beneficial effects from delaying the wrongful act. (I thank Chrisoula Andreou for pointing out this possibility and prompting me to clarify the ethical status of procrastination in this section.)

46. I am not ruling out "rational reconsideration," as long as the factors reconsidered are not the same ones that motivated the need for self-control in the first place. For example, recalling how tasty doughnuts are is not a good reason to reconsider a resolution to avoid doughnuts in the interest of one's health, given that the wonderful taste of doughnuts was the original motivation for the resolution. (See Holton, "How Is Strength of Will Possible?")

Kant's description of an impure will focuses on one whose inclinations are oriented toward good, in which case inclination and duty lead to the same action. But the danger remains, as with any instance of mixed motivation, that inclination will sometimes dominate choice and will not always correspond to duty. So, ethically speaking, it is better in the long run to resist procrastination through an act of will than to rely on one's inclination based on deliberate manipulation of the choice environment. A person's character, will, or virtue (as fortitude) is more essential to her "self" and less contingent on the details of a particular situation or environment, and exerting her strength of character will further develop it, so future exertions will come more naturally (though taking the same effort).[47]

So far, we have only discussed single incidents of procrastination, which are troubling enough. But of even greater concern is persistent procrastination, the type that we find so hard to combat and to dig out from under. There are two ways to explain persistent procrastination within the context of the Kantian-economic model. The simpler theory is to posit a simply weak will. Someone with a $p_{11}$ of 75 percent will procrastinate in one-quarter of the relevant choice situations, independent of whether she procrastinated previously (or how often). Suppose such an agent faces the possibility of procrastination today and succumbs to it with 25 percent probability. If the decision arises again tomorrow, she will procrastinate then, also with 25 percent probability, regardless of her decision the day before. Looked at from the beginning, the likelihood of a longer procrastination diminishes, of course—two subsequent days of procrastination occur 25 percent × 25 percent, or 6.25 percent, of the time. But the important thing is that persistent procrastination is not necessarily symptomatic of anything more elaborate than a simply weak will that occasionally manifests itself in "runs" of repeated procrastination. Nonetheless, the longer the procrastination keeps up, the less likely simple weakness is the culprit—there is probably something else going on.

It strikes us as very intuitive that procrastination one day increases the chance of procrastination in the future; in fact, this is a standard finding in the psychological literature.[48] In the context of the Kantian-economic model, this would be the case if succumbing to procrastination in one situation would lower one's $p_{11}$ before encountering the next similar situation (for example, putting off grading exams to watch one TV show leads to higher chances of doing it with the next show, and possibly even the next time exams need to be graded). For the merely weak person, it seems unlikely that this would occur. Such a person may repeatedly exhibit weakness, as described above, and may even experience a "slide" in strength of will or character as a result of an increase in the incidence of procrastination.

---

47. This is similar to strengthening a muscle; see the discussion of willpower as muscle below.
48. See the references in Kim, "Hyperbolic Discounting."

But I have argued that insofar as $p_H$ is caused by weakness, it should be fairly robust, since it is less corruptible by outside factors. Therefore, it is less likely to be affected by a single incident of procrastination in such a way as to lead to increased likelihood of procrastination the following times.

However, if the procrastination is based on the influence of an impure will on $p_H$, and an impure will corrupts itself, then we would expect $p_H$ to fall as the agent continues to procrastinate, leading to a procrastination trap. Recall that the impure will represents laxity in resolve; the will (which is to say, the agent herself) simply gives up trying to resist the pull of inclination and instead admits its influence into her decision making at the level of maxim formation. In other words, impurity of the will implies that the influences identified by economists hold sway—influences that, as described above, may lead to less procrastination but for reasons that will disappear if the incentives change for the worse.

In either case, in the context of the Kantian-economic model, the agent still has a way out of the procrastination trap, no matter how long she has been in it: she can choose to break it through an act of will or volition. She can exercise her autonomy, her "inner freedom" or virtue, and choose to resist the increasingly strong temptation to continue to procrastinate. This is bound to happen eventually, since as long as $p_H$ does not diminish completely, there is always some willpower left, some reserve of strength the agent can summon up to resist inclination and follow the dictates of duty. But obviously, the sooner she does this, the less time she will spend in a procrastination trap, and the easier it will be to dig out of it.

## Similar Views

There are several scholars whose analyses of procrastination (or weakness of will in general) have much in common with the ideas presented herein. Psychiatrist George Ainslie argues that willpower properly refers to the ability of agents to link their present actions to their future ones, so that procrastination today will be seen to lead to repeated procrastination in the future through a process of recursive self-prediction.[49] Rather than rely on external manipulation of the choice situation, Ainslie advocates an internal restructuring of the relevant costs and benefits of acting at the prudent time rather than procrastinating.[50] The formation of personal rules—preferably with bright lines precisely demarcating approved and disapproved behavior—is one example: a person establishes a rule for herself, which motivates her to resist the temptation to violate it if she believes that failing to resist this time will make future resistance less likely. If I believe that a doughnut eaten today, in violation of a personal

---

49. Ainslie, *Breakdown of Will*, chap. 7, and his chapter 1 in this present volume.
50. For a recent formalization of this idea, see Bénabou and Tirole, "Willpower and Personal Rules."

rule against eating doughnuts, will lead to eating doughnuts every day thereafter, I vest today's decision with the enormous consequences of perpetual failure and will more likely pass up the doughnut today.

Insomuch as Ainslie recommends that agents reassess their incentives internally, rather than relying on manipulation of external cues, in order to achieve some degree of self-control, he is in agreement with the model presented in this chapter, as well as the general thesis regarding self-control. However, it falls short of the Kantian ideal, because the agent is still making decisions based on her incentives or inclinations, albeit manipulated, rather than making choices based on duty alone. Granted, the internal reconceptualization of incentives may have been conducted out of duty—as, too, may be external manipulations—but this is an indirect way to act out of respect for the moral law. Such effort would not have to be invested in manipulation of incentives, whether internal or external, if agents would increase their strength of will or volition and thereby their capacity to transcend the impact of incentives and inclinations altogether.

Among economists, Jeong-Yoo Kim is unique in that he does employ a version of willpower to explain resistance to procrastination, as well as the persistence of procrastination when resistance fails.[51] He posits an "unconscious working of will, an automatic process of pre-programmed mechanism (will) that tends to resist yielding to temptation," a mechanism that "is like a machine that only responds stochastically" to incentives to procrastinate.[52] This fixed measure of willpower, together with a person's perception of her own willpower, contributes to a probability function, the random draw from which determines the actual choice (what I would call her "operative willpower"). Because of this understanding, "the actual choice cannot be viewed as the result of a conscious mental process" but is instead simply stochastic.[53] Therefore, whether one procrastinates or resists is just a matter of luck, and also has an effect on the probability of success in the future through a change in her perception of her strength of will.

While the model presented in this chapter does present the actual choice as a conscious, free one—a difference of more interest to philosophers than to economists—Kim's explanation of perpetual procrastination bears significant similarity to mine, in that both of our models depict a progressive decline in willpower. Where I differ from Kim is in the nature of willpower; he regards the basic measure of willpower as fixed but the agent's operative willpower as influenced also by her self-perception. As a result, her operative willpower can be stronger or weaker than her actual willpower, which never changes. While I recognize (though have

---

51. Kim, "Hyperbolic Discounting."
52. Kim, "Hyperbolic Discounting," 346, 349.
53. Kim, "Hyperbolic Discounting," 350.

not yet emphasized) the possible relevance of self-perception in the operation of the will, I would argue that any influence of it would be on a person's willpower itself; in other words, I see no relevant distinction between actual and operative willpower. If a person loses faith in her willpower, her willpower declines, period. As she succeeds in exerting her willpower, her belief in herself grows, and her willpower grows as well. But I see no reason Kim's model could not be modified to make the effect in willpower more direct in this way.

## CONCLUSION AND A REMAINING QUESTION

It has been my contention that procrastination, like weakness of will in general, results from a lack or insufficient exertion of willpower. Procrastination can be avoided, therefore, not only by indirect measures, such as externally manipulating the choice environment or internally reconceptualizing the costs and benefits of acting now, but also directly by exerting one's willpower. Not only is one's willpower an omnipresent force, but its exercise will strengthen it for future use and will make us less reliant on costly external coping mechanisms.

But a practical question remains: Can we reasonably do this? Even if we accept the existence of an independent faculty of choice, surely the willpower behind it is not unlimited; it may be omnipresent, but surely it is not omnipotent. Among those scholars who acknowledge the existence of the will, some compare willpower to a muscle, which can be strengthened over time through repeated use but has limited efficacy at any one given time and can therefore be exhausted (until replenished with time). Richard Holton is the leading advocate of this view among philosophers, repudiating the Humean model for phenomenological as well as empirical reasons, arguing that explaining strength of will by strength of desire does not correspond to our experiences during periods of resoluteness: "It certainly doesn't feel as though in employing will-power one is simply letting whichever is the stronger of one's desires or intentions have its way. It rather feels as though one is actively doing something, something that requires effort."[54]

The empirical aspect of Holton's claim is based in large part on the work of psychologist Roy Baumeister, who, with various colleagues, has studied the exertion of self-control in a number of laboratory situations and is credited with developing the concept of "willpower as muscle." In a survey of the psychological research, Baumeister and Mark Muraven write that "controlling one's own behavior requires the expenditure of some inner, limited resource that is depleted afterward" but also "shows long-term improvement, just as a muscle gets stronger through exercise . . .

---

54. Holton, "How Is Strength of Will Possible?" 49.

gaining strength with practice,"[55] to which Heatherton and Baumeister add, "which if left alone becomes flaccid."[56] This theory complements the Kantian analysis above in that it provides psychological support for the dynamics of strength of will, in particular that the will can be strengthened with continued use.

Other aspects of this literature resemble the analysis of the will herein. For instance, Baumeister and Heatherton write of "acquiescence," of persons giving in to undesirable impulses rather than fighting them, similar to the actions of an impure will versus simple weakness (using procrastination as one example, based on the observation that procrastinators are normally not "compelled" to put tasks off but instead actively choose to do so).[57] In the same paper, the authors also write of "transcendence . . . a matter of focusing awareness beyond the immediate stimuli (i.e., transcending the immediate situation)," which may be considered analogous to the Kantian/Stoic concept of moral apathy (or, more generally, autonomy).[58] These parallels suggest that the Kantian model of will can fruitfully be integrated with the research deriving from Baumeister's work.

Regardless of the precise dynamics or nature of this type of strength or resolve, it seems undeniable that there are limits to the amount of willpower we can exert in any given situation or over time. In such cases of insufficient resolve, we must rely on clever coping mechanisms and manipulation of the choice environment, such as most economists, philosophers, and psychologists recommend. But we must also recognize that sometimes these extrapsychic tools are not available, feasible, or cost-effective. It is then that we find we must rely on our willpower, but if we have let our "muscles" wither through neglect, we will find them lacking when we need them most.

## ACKNOWLEDGMENTS

For helpful comments and criticism, I would like to thank the participants in the CSMN workshop, particularly Chrisoula Andreou, George Ainslie, Christine Tappolet, Sergio Tenenbaum, and Frank Wieber, as well as those who attended the Philosophy Forum at the College of Staten Island, where an early version of this chapter was discussed.

---

55. Muraven and Baumeister, "Self-Regulation," 247, 254. A more recent paper proposes that general decision making (not just self-control situations) draws on this same limited psychological resource, resulting in "decision fatigue"; see Vohs et al., "Making Choices."
56. Heatherton and Baumeister, "Self-Regulation Failure," 93.
57. Baumeister and Heatherton, "Self-Regulation Failure: Overview," 6–9.
58. Baumeister and Heatherton, "Self-Regulation Failure: Overview," 4.

# 14

# Procrastination and the Extended Will

*Joseph Heath & Joel Anderson*

Less than a decade ago, "rational-choice theory" seemed oddly impervious to criticism. Hundreds of books, articles, and studies were published every year, attacking the theory from every angle, yet it continued to attract new converts. How times have changed! The "anomalies" that Richard Thaler once blithely catalogued for the *Journal of Economic Perspectives* are now widely regarded not as curious deviations from the norm, but as falsifying counterexamples to the entire project of neoclassical economics. The work of experimental game theorists has perhaps been the most influential in showing that people do not maximize expected utility, in any plausible sense of the terms *maximize*, *expected*, or *utility*. The evidence is so overwhelming and incontrovertible that by the time one gets to the end of a book such as Dan Ariely's *Predictably Irrational*,[1] it begins to feel like piling on. The suggestion is pretty clear: not only are people not as rational as decision and game theorists have traditionally taken them to be, but they are not even as rational as they themselves take themselves to be.

This conclusion, however, is not self-evident. The standard interpretation of these findings is that people are irrational: their estimation of probabilities is vulnerable to framing effects, their treatment of (equivalent) losses and gains is asymmetric, their choices violate the "sure thing" principle, they discount the future hyperbolically, and so on. Indeed, after surveying the experimental findings, one begins to wonder how people manage to get on in their daily lives at all, given the seriousness and ubiquity of these deliberative pathologies. And yet most people do manage to get on, in some form or another. This, in itself, suggests an alternative interpretation of the findings. What experimental game theorists may have demonstrated is not that people are systematically irrational but that human rationality is heavily *scaffolded*. Remove the scaffolding, and we do not do very well. People are able to get on because they "offload" an enormous amount of practical reasoning onto their environment. As a result, when they are put in novel or unfamiliar environments, they perform very poorly, even on apparently simple tasks.

1. Ariely, *Predictably Irrational*.

This observation is supported by recent empirically informed shifts in philosophy of mind toward a view of cognition as (to cite the current slogan) "embodied, embedded, enactive, extended." Andy Clark, for example, has argued that "advanced cognition depends crucially on our ability to *dissipate* reasoning: to diffuse achieved knowledge and practical wisdom through complex social structures, and to reduce the loads on individual brains by locating those brains in complex webs of linguistic, social, political and institutional constraints."[2] Clark and others have made a very plausible case for the idea that a proper assessment of human cognitive competence must include environmental components. To limit our attention to what lies within the skin-skull boundary is, in effect, to miss the big story on human rationality. Insofar as we are rational, it is often because of our ingenuity at developing "work-arounds" to the glitches in the fast-and-frugal heuristic problem-solving capabilities that natural selection has equipped us with.[3] And these work-arounds often involve a detour through the environment (so-called offloading of cognitive burdens). This is an instance of the now widely accepted view that the evolutionary success of humans is the result of adaptations not merely in our biological endowment but also—and perhaps more significantly—in our linguistic, social, and material culture.

When it comes to practical rationality, things are no different. Yet in many discussions of "the will," there is still a tendency to put too much emphasis on what goes on inside the agent's head. For example, the self-controlled person is usually seen as one who has a capacity to exercise tremendous willpower, not as one who is able to organize his life in such a way that he is never called upon to exercise tremendous willpower. This internalist and mentalist bias is liable to make the various "glitches" in the structure of the will—such as the temporary preference reversals induced by hyperbolic discounting—seem much more threatening to the coherence of the agent's plans than they actually are. For example, everyone procrastinates on occasion. Yet only 15 to 20 percent of adults describe themselves as "chronic procrastinators" or find that the tendency to procrastinate interferes with their ability to achieve major life goals.[4] This is actually lower than one might expect, simply from looking at the psychological literature on discounting.

Our objective in this chapter is to articulate this conception of "the extended will" more clearly, using the strategies that people employ to overcome procrastination for the central set of examples. Procrastination, in our view, constitutes a particular type of self-control problem, one that is particularly amenable to philosophical reflection, not only because of the high volume of psychological research on the subject but

---

2. Clark, *Being There*, 180. See also, e.g., Norman, *Things That Make Us Smart*.
3. Marcus, *Kluge*.
4. Steel, "Nature of Procrastination," 65.

also because of the large quantity of "self-help" literature in circulation—a literature that provides an invaluable perspective on the everyday strategies that people use in order to defeat (or, better yet, circumvent) this type of self-defeating behavior pattern. In general, what we find is that the internalist bias that permeates discussions of the will gives rise to a set of practical recommendations that overemphasize changing the way one *thinks* about a task, while ignoring the much richer set of strategies that are available in the realm of environmental scaffolding. In the concluding section, we highlight some of the policy implications of this, particularly regarding social trends involving the dismantling of support structures.

## FROM EXTENDED MIND TO EXTENDED WILL

To begin with a familiar example, most of us can do multiplication "in our heads" with numbers up to 10 but cannot go beyond that—despite the fact that we have all mastered a procedure (so-called long multiplication) that transforms the larger problem into a set of smaller problems, each of which we are capable of solving in our heads (e.g., to multiply 43 by 87, first you multiply 7 by 3, then you multiply 7 by 4, and so forth). We can easily solve each of these subproblems in our heads, but the reason we cannot solve the problem as a whole is that the solution to the four subproblems must be kept in working memory in order to resolve the final subproblem, which involves addition of the four products. Most of us are simply not able to remember four multiple-digit numbers in order to perform a final operation on them.

The most common form of offloading that we perform is to transfer segments of our working memory onto the environment: We write things down. Obviously, the ability to encode things symbolically for this purpose constitutes the major mechanism through which language (and a number-writing system) enhances our innate cognitive abilities. Indeed, when trying to characterize human beings as computational systems, the difference between "person" and "person with pencil and paper" is vast. It is only when we are embedded in our familiar system of artifacts that we can do even moderately sophisticated arithmetic.

In this respect, the offloading metaphor is slightly misleading. When we "dump" the contents of our working memory onto the environment (e.g., by writing things down), we are not just doing so for purposes of storage. We park them in a form in which we are still capable of performing computations on them. Thus, features of the environment in which this information is embodied become an active component of our cognitive system. Of course, once we become properly habituated to using an external system, it may become internalized, so that we can perform the relevant transformation inside our heads, much in the way children learn first to speak out loud and only later become capable of thinking things through silently, in their heads.[5] For example, older Chinese merchants who have been trained in the use of an abacus are often able to do extensive computations without the benefit of the device—although you can often see them moving their fingers slightly. Having used the abacus for so long, they are able to picture it clearly in their minds and feel the position of the beads with their fingers so well that they no longer need the actual piece of equipment. The movement of the fingers is the vestigial trace of the external origins of the cognitive competence. The scaffolding is not so much removed as absorbed.

The abacus actually provides a wealth of examples of ways external artifacts can be used to provide work-arounds or "kluges" that help us to circumvent limitations of what lies within the skin-skull boundary. First, there are the beads; as physical objects, these have the attractive property of staying put. Thus, when arranged into a configuration that represents a number, they can overcome limitations in our working memory (the central problem of which being that so little stays put there). The second major feature is that it allows the operator to replace the set of primitive arithmetic computations with a set of finger movements. Adding and subtracting become like positioning one's fingers on the frets of a guitar in order to produce a note, something that quickly becomes second nature and can be accomplished with little or no attention. Finally, the "uprights" or bars are used to represent orders of magnitude, making it possible to perform operations such as "carrying the 1" in a very simple, tactile way. This provides an easy way to deal with the rather unintuitive character of the notation that we use for numbers, namely the "base" numbering system. (Think of how a bank teller counting out a large sum in 20-dollar bills will count out five bills, then make a stack, count out five more bills, make a second stack, and so on.)

In each case, the inventor of the device has taken a cognitive operation that we find very demanding and, through clever colonization and manipulation of objects in the environment, replaced it with one that we find relatively easy (or that can become quite easy through habituation). In particular, cognitive operations that must be performed consciously are mapped onto a set of physical motions that can, with practice, be performed without paying attention. Computational outcomes that must be represented linguistically are mapped onto configurations of objects that can be visualized. All of this amplifies our cognitive abilities. But it also means that when thinking about these abilities, it is important not to focus too narrowly on what happens in our brains. The central lesson of the literature on the "extended mind" is that we should not think of these external artifacts as merely aids to cognition; they are often a proper part of the cognitive system. They are, in this respect, more like prosthetics than tools.

---

5. Vygotsky, *Thought and Language*; see also Bruner, *Acts of Meaning*, and Wertsch, *Mind as Action*.

And, as has often been remarked in the case of the blind person's cane—the tip of which is actually the terminus of the person's sense of touch—many prostheses are so well integrated into how one makes one's way through the world that we can say we "use" them only in the sense that we can say that we "use" our fingers to type. In fact, we simply type. Similarly, we simply "add the numbers," whether in our heads or on paper.

## THE CASE OF PROCRASTINATION

When it comes to tasks such as arithmetic, the limitations of our cognitive system are so obvious and solved in such familiar ways that no one dwells on the remarkable fact that most of us are unable to remember a set of four double-digit numbers for long enough to carry out long multiplication. Our dependence on environmental prosthetics is self-evident. When it comes to practical rationality, on the other hand, many theorists have either ignored or denied the presence of any systematic defects. Rational-choice theorists have been front and center in this campaign. Gary Becker's analysis of addiction as a consequence of straightforward, unproblematic utility maximization represents perhaps the apogee of this tendency.[6] This is partly a result of the noncognitive (or subjectivist) conception of preference that typically informs rational-choice theories, which results in practical rationality being held to a lower standard than theoretical rationality. After all, if one puts no constraints at all on the content of preferences, then it becomes possible to construe any action as rational (in a rather undemanding sense of the term) simply by positing a preference for doing it.[7]

Yet even if one says nothing at all about the content of preferences, there are still defects in our practical reasoning that can be specified at a purely formal level. The most obvious examples involve self-control problems, where individuals, upon due reflection, formulate an intention to perform some action, fail to perform it when the time comes, and subsequently regret this failure. What makes this type of situation noteworthy and problematic is the subsequent regret. It is not merely that the agent fails to follow through on the intention—this could be described simply as a change of mind. It is the fact that the agent subsequently regrets the failure that suggests that she maintains a constant preference, in some sense, for the initially intended action throughout.

An example of this is the everyday phenomenon of procrastination. A quick definition of procrastination would be to say that it occurs when

1. an agent delays initiation of an action that is associated with some level of disutility, even though

---

6. Becker and Murphy, "Theory of Rational Addiction."
7. Heath, *Following the Rules*.

2. the agent knows now that doing so will increase the level of disutility at the time the act must ultimately be performed, and
3. the agent has reason to believe that she will subsequently regret having delayed the action.

This definition is intended to capture the sense in which the procrastinating agent chooses the larger, later evil over the smaller, sooner evil (procrastination is thus the converse of intemperance, in which the agent chooses the smaller, sooner good over the larger, later good). The qualifications are there in order to exclude a couple of cases in which the agent delays initiation of an aversive task but where this is not genuine procrastination. First, it is not procrastination to put something off when something else comes up that one considers genuinely more important and must be attended to first. In that case, the agent has no reason to regret, ex post, the choice he made. Second, even when one has nothing more urgent to do, merely delaying a task is not procrastination, unless things can be expected to get worse somehow as a result of the delay. Sometimes we put things off just because we do not feel like doing them now, and from a certain rigorist standpoint, this might be thought to be a failing of some sort. But if the delay has no significant repercussions, it is hard to see how it merits the label of procrastination, since it lacks the quality of perverseness that has made procrastination seem mysterious to so many people. Finally, it should be noted that it is the reasonable expectation of future regret that is the important element of procrastination. Whether the agent actually regrets the task later does not matter (e.g., sometimes unpleasant tasks actually do just go away when they are deferred for long enough, even though we have no reasonable expectation that they will).

A simple example of procrastination would be leaving the dishes to stack up in the sink, even though it is easier to clean them right away, before the muck on them hardens. The behavior induces regret because when the individual finally does settle down to perform the task, he will be aware that it is now more unpleasant or difficult than it would have been had he done it right away. A more serious example would be someone who puts off having a colonoscopy and therefore may miss having colon cancer diagnosed at an early stage. In this case, the colonoscopy does not become any more unpleasant as a result of the delay, but the individual's anticipated health outcome becomes worse (and thus the delay "makes things worse").

If *utility* is defined in terms of payoffs—with respect to how much satisfaction or dissatisfaction a sequence of events ultimately generates for the individual—procrastination foreseeably fails to maximize the individual's achieved utility level (i.e., as seen from an ex post perspective). It is because the delay in some sense makes things worse that the agent can expect to subsequently regret the delay and therefore can be said to suffer a failure of self-control. However, one of the most noteworthy features of procrastination is that the agent does not suffer from any loss of intentional control throughout this period. Thus, the individual who fails to do the dishes promptly is nevertheless *choosing* not to do the dishes at the time at which he forgoes the opportunity to do them. He is not the same as someone who gets drunk or angry or into some other state in which executive function is impaired and does something that he subsequently regrets. People often procrastinate under that description (i.e., if you ask them why they have not done something yet, they will say, "I'm procrastinating"). This is one of the reasons a hyperbolic discounting model provides the most perspicuous representation of the phenomenon: It offers a rationalizing account of procrastination yet one that is still able to account for the preference reversal and regret that characterize such failures of self-control.

The hyperbolic discounting model has two central components. The first claim is that agents not only have preferences with respect to various events that can occur but also have a time preference that (all things being equal) leads them to experience delay as aversive when it intervenes between the present and a positively valued event and as attractive when it intervenes between the present and a negatively valued event.[8] The common way of expressing this is to say that individuals *discount* future satisfaction. The second component is the claim that there is a "warp" in this aversion toward delay, such that agents find a delay of a given length less aversive, the farther removed it is from the present, above and beyond what can be attributed to the mere fact that the experience of this delay is delayed.[9] This is typically expressed by saying that individuals discount future satisfaction in a way that is highly exaggerated in the near term—hence "hyperbolic" discounting.

The most important feature of hyperbolic discounting is that it leads individuals to rank near-term and long-term events very differently. Hyperbolic discounters have a preference ordering of distant events that is almost exactly the same as the atemporal ranking that could be derived from the "payoff" value of these events, but their ranking of more proximate events frequently deviates quite significantly from a strictly payoff-based ranking. As a result, the passage of time can lead individuals to change their preference ordering, in such a way as to make smaller, sooner payoffs more attractive than larger, later ones. This subsequently induces regret, at the time at which the larger, later reward could have been obtained. ("If only I had waited," the agent will say.) When the payoffs are negative, the same phenomenon occurs in reverse. Long before the dishes are dirty, the agent may see that it makes sense to wash them right away,

---

8. The most important exception is dread, which occurs when the delay of an aversive event is also experienced aversively. This can lead people to want to "get it over with" sooner rather than later, a phenomenon that is capable of generating the opposite of procrastination. Consider a patient who opts to have a painful dental procedure done right away by a less experienced practitioner, rather than later by a more experienced one.

9. Ainslie, *Breakdown of Will*.

thereby minimizing the negative payoff. Yet she waits, only to regret the decision later, once the disutility of the payoff has grown. ("If only I had done this sooner," she will say.)

Two things should be noted about this in passing. First, hyperbolic discounting is introduced here as a *model* that can be used to represent the dynamics of procrastination, not as an *explanation* for why individuals procrastinate. Indeed, a variety of theories seek to explain the psychological underpinnings of hyperbolic discounting, particularly why there is the warp in our attitude toward delay. For our purposes, it does not matter *why* there is a warp, only *that* there is this warp.

The second thing to notice about the hyperbolic discounting model is that it provides an account of procrastination and other forms of giving in to temptation without invoking what philosophers call strict akrasia or intentional counterpreferential choice.[10] Although there is a whiff of irrationality about the dynamic inconsistency in the agent's preferences, the fact remains that at the time at which she acts, she is acting in accordance with her occurrent subjective preferences—not contrary to them. Formally speaking, there is no logical inconsistency in changing one's preferences over time or in changing them back. Indeed, there are occasions on which we might quite easily sympathize with the agent's "intemperate" self, the one who wants to change the decision, even knowing that he will subsequently regret having done so.[11] Given how wide open our eyes typically are about what we are doing when we procrastinate, it seems unlikely that the most effective strategies for reducing procrastination will focus on simply understanding how counterproductive it is. Rather, we are likely to be helped most by kluges, work-arounds, and scaffolding.[12]

## SELF-CONTROL STRATEGIES

In some cases, avoiding procrastination is a matter of just buckling down and doing it, a straightforward exercise of willpower.[13] An agent who opts for such a strategy simply resolves to perform a certain action and holds

---

10. Mele, *Irrationality*.

11. Consider Jay Christensen-Szalanski's "Discount Functions and the Measurement of Patients' Values," a study of the behavior of pregnant women who had chosen, prior to labor, to refrain from using any pain control. He found that a majority reversed this decision after active labor pains had begun. He also found, however, that almost all of those who reversed their position drifted back to their original view—that pain control was undesirable—within three months postpartum. Thus, their standing preference was for childbirth without pain control, and it was only when they were actually experiencing the pain that they fully appreciated the merits of pain control. In this case, one might easily identify with the preference at the moment of decision and suspect that there is an element of self-deception in the standing preference.

12. For a related discussion, see Heath, *Following the Rules*, 228–234.

13. See chapter 13 by Mark D. White in this volume for more on the exercise of willpower.

steadfastly to that intention, resisting whatever inclinations may arise to revise his or her plans (along the lines of a New Year's resolution). We often describe people who are able to do this as having a lot of "self-discipline." There is no doubting that individual willpower, whatever it turns out to be, is a good thing to have in the struggle to avoid making unpleasant tasks worse by delaying them. The more complex and individualized societies become, the more individuals will need self-discipline if they are not to suffer disadvantages in both competitive and noncompetitive contexts.

But there are reasons to doubt that "simply buckling down" will be enough to solve many pathologies of the will—or, indeed, that it ever has been enough. To begin with, there are many unanswered empirical questions about how such self-discipline is possible and what the limits of it are. Several recent studies suggest that although willpower is like a muscle and can be trained, it can also become exhausted. In experimental studies, Roy Baumeister and colleagues have shown that (human) subjects who resisted a temptation for a period of time were less able than control-group members to resist a temptation that followed closely thereafter.[14] If the demands of individuals for processing decisions and resisting various temptations is on the rise in increasingly complex societies, these individual capacities might easily become overtaxed—if pure willpower were all that people could rely on. It is, however, unclear to what extent the average person actually relies on individual self-discipline to avoid or to limit procrastination. Our suspicion is that its role is greatly exaggerated. Much of the time, what looks like sheer willpower is the result of more or less well-orchestrated attempts by individuals to arrange their lives in such a way as to *economize* on willpower, by avoiding situations that call for its exercise. We refer to this as *distributed willpower*, since it involves individuals creating more than one locus of self-control.[15]

Self-control strategies can usefully be thought of under four general categories, as part of a progression that involves movement away from the purely psychological toward the environmental.

### Direct Psychological Strategies

Many effective strategies involve shifts in one's cognitive approach to an aversive task. These are ways of reconceptualizing or reframing tasks so as to inhibit negative tendencies or, more often, to help individuals tap into motivational resources that would be otherwise uninvolved. The system of "mental accounts" that many people use to control household spending (distinguishing retirement savings from rent money and spending money, for instance) is a well-known example of this.[16] These sorts of psychological

---

14. Muraven and Baumeister, "Self-Regulation."
15. The parallel here is with "distributed cognition" within cognitive science discussions. See, e.g., Hutchins, *Cognition in the Wild*, and also Ross et al., *Distributed Cognition*.
16. Thaler, "Mental Accounting" and "Saving."

techniques differ from "pure willpower" in that the individual is not simply forcing herself to do something but is somehow modifying the construal of the task in such a way as to decrease the level of forcing that is required. We refer to such techniques as *strategic reframing*.

A general approach to the analysis of such strategies can be found in "temporal motivation theory" (which is, essentially, an approach to procrastination derived from the hyperbolic discounting model).[17] This model identifies three items as central to the dynamic of preference change and hence procrastination: expected utility, delay, and sensitivity to delay. Thus, one way in which individuals can avoid their own tendency to procrastinate is to manipulate one (or more) of these three variables.

To begin with, take the (dis)utility associated with boredom. People are most likely to procrastinate before performing boring tasks (and people who are easily bored are more likely to procrastinate).[18] The natural explanation is that boredom increases the aversiveness of a task (thus diminishing expected utility). One way to avoid procrastination is, therefore, to try to find something interesting about the task or to embed it within some larger construct that makes it more appealing (e.g., turning it into a game or timing one's performance and then trying to beat that time). One might think of this as the Mary Poppins strategy: "For every job that must be done, there is an element of fun. Find the fun and, snap, the job's a game." In some cases, a mere redescription of a task can be effective in enhancing motivation, since preferences regarding actions have been shown to be sensitive to the language in which the action (or associated outcome) is described.[19]

Similarly, to overcome the tendency to put off initiating a task with a distant payoff, one can set a sequence of intermediate goals. This strategic reframing involves the tried-and-true time-management strategy of breaking down an intimidating task into its component parts, each of which is much more doable. By shifting one's focus from the ultimate goal to specific intermediate steps, one not only turns an intimidating mountain into a series of doable molehills, but one also reduces the delay between effort and reward (whether that reward is an intermediate treat or simply the confidence-building sense of accomplishment). So, while the reward of having written a book may be so far off as to have little motivational pull, the satisfaction associated with having written a chapter or, better yet, having met one's target of three pages per day is likely to be much more effective. Empirical support for this reframing strategy is found in research on "implementation intentions" by Peter Gollwitzer and his colleagues. In one study, it was shown that "difficult goal intentions were completed about 3 times more often when participants had furnished them with

---

17. Steel, "Nature of Procrastination."
18. Steel, "Nature of Procrastination."
19. Trope and Libennan, "Temporal Construal."

implementation intentions."[20] For related reasons, techniques involving visualizing the steps to be taken tend to create the impression that the results are even more proximate.

Self-Management Strategies

The reframing techniques described above are still relatively direct in the sense that when they're successful, they actually fix the problem by eliminating the underlying tendency to procrastinate. A person who persuades himself that cleaning up the dishes is fun is no longer tempted to procrastinate, because he no longer finds the task aversive. He may have engaged in all sorts of artful self-manipulation in order to convince himself that it is fun, yet the end result is an actual elimination of the inclination to procrastinate.

Apart from these direct strategies, there are also numerous psychological "kluges" that people employ. Rather than trying to resolve or eliminate the underlying problem, here the individual simply tries to work around it. In many cases, this involves taking some other defect in our nature and using it to counteract the defect that leads us into temporary preference reversals. For example, a major limitation of the reframing strategies just discussed is that they require quite a bit of active purposefulness, such as maintaining conscious attention, and this is often precisely what individuals are lacking in cases of procrastination. As a result, individuals may find it useful to develop automatic processes that are set up in advance and can channel their behavior in cases where their attention lapses. The classic example of this is good habits; in a sense, if you have good habits, you do not need willpower.

Closely related to this is the strategy of "psychological bundling" of tasks. The idea here is to take something that you do not particularly like doing and combine it with something that you do like. Singing while you work is perhaps the best example of this, although, unfortunately, it is a technique that only works well with manual labor. Another example would be keeping track of how much money you are making as you perform some employment-related task. (This is particularly effective when working on piece rates.) Once the two activities become habitually conjoined, then the psychological bundling may diminish the aversiveness of the package. And since a daily routine can itself become a source of gratification, building the performance of certain chores into a routine can amount to a form of psychological bundling.

A related strategy involves recruiting strong preferences from another domain to motivate self-control in a problematic domain. Many self-reward schemes exploit the fact that we are usually capable of different levels of self-control in different areas of life. A person who is rather

---

20. Gollwitzer and Brandstätter, "Implementation Intentions." See also chapter 11 by Frank Wieber and Peter Gollwitzer in this volume.

miserly, for instance, may find it easy to refrain from spending money. He might coax himself into performing an unpleasant task by promising to buy himself something he has long wanted once the task is complete. In this case, the willpower he is able to exercise in one domain is "leveraged," through the self-reward strategy, into self-control in another.[21]

Another example of self-management is known as "structured procrastination."[22] The basic idea here is to use one's own capacity for self-deception as a way of combating procrastination. Most people, when they procrastinate, do not choose simply to sit idle. A person who is putting off doing the dishes, for instance, typically will not just stare at the wall but will do something else, such as watch television. John Perry has observed, however, that many people, instead of performing the highly aversive task that is being avoided, will perform some other mildly aversive, perhaps even marginally useful, task. Thus, a person who hates a particular household chore may put it off by doing some other chore, one that is somewhat less useful but at the same time less unpleasant (e.g., light dusting).[23] Structured procrastination involves intentionally choosing an ambitious goal that one is unlikely to pursue, then doing what one should have been doing all along as a way of avoiding the more ambitious goal. Thus a person who has trouble washing the dishes might persuade himself that he really ought to clean the oven, then put this off by washing the dishes.

## Environmental Strategies

Many of the examples given so far involve a certain degree of cleverness and manipulation on the part of the individual. In part, this is a reflection of the relative poverty of the psychological resources that are available to us when it comes to dealing with self-control problems. When we turn to environmental strategies, by contrast, the field of possibilities opens up considerably. The use of environmental manipulation by individuals as a technique for enhancing self-control is absolutely routine and ubiquitous; indeed, it is so commonplace that we are often in danger of overlooking it completely. (In the same way, when it comes to overcoming weaknesses in our memory, the mnemonist's bag of tricks seems quite exotic and recherché, when compared with the simple expedient of writing things down.)

Looking at someone's office, kitchen pantry, bedroom, or even computer monitor, what one sees is an entire structure of cognitive and

---

21. See Chrisoula Andreou's chapter 12 in this volume and also Ainslie, *Breakdown of Will*.
22. Perry, "Structured Procrastination."
23. In many cases, this is undoubtedly connected to the fact that the temporary preference reversal associated with procrastination is rationalized; see Sjoberg and Johnson, "Trying to Give Up Smoking." This rationalization is easier to sustain if one is doing something mildly unpleasant as opposed to straightforwardly pleasurable; see Perry, "Structured Procrastination."

volitional scaffolding, a system that this person uses in order to accomplish (with varying degrees of success) routine tasks. Many aspects of the way this environment is organized are intended to facilitate self-control. People who are good at environmental manipulation try to organize their affairs in such a way as to make certain activities easier and others harder. We can distinguish three general types of environmental kluges: triggers, chutes, and ladders. Each represents features of the environment that either assist or discourage one from initiating and persevering in an intended task. They may have emerged by more or less adaptive happenstance, or they may have been intentionally designed, whether by the individual or by someone else.

*Triggers* are environmental cues that, when appropriately placed, set automatic processes in motion (or bring them to a stop). Suppose that you intend to go running first thing every morning, but once you have poured yourself a cup of coffee and opened up the morning paper, the idea of a run seems like an unpleasant interruption. Putting your running shoes in front of the coffee maker can trigger the intended routine of going for a run before other routines kick in. Triggers can also work in tandem with other strategies—for example, by periodically reminding one of various promised rewards—thereby activating those motivational resources. In addition, triggers can function as warnings, alerting one to impending temptations or calling for a quick check of whether one is on track (such as nag screens that pop up every time one switches to one's browser).[24]

Many environmental features help with task completion by making certain desirable courses of action particularly smooth and effortless. These *chutes* are setups that make it easier to slide into doing something. To take a variation on the early-morning run case: by laying out, the evening before everything one needs, the threshold to "just doing it" is lowered. You step out of bed, the chute takes over, and the next thing you know, you are running out the door. Another example comes from the literal design of one's environment. The architect Gerrit Rietveld's premier 1924 "Schröder Huis" includes, next to the entrance, a fold-down chair and a desk with storage for stationery, pens, envelopes, and postage, so that Frau Schröder could answer mail immediately upon opening it, without even leaving the entryway.

Just as chutes lower the threshold to doing the right thing, *ladders* can be positioned to raise the threshold to undertaking wasteful actions, especially when it comes to procrastination. By structuring one's environment effectively, one can reduce the distractions and temptations behind much procrastination. Again, it is often sufficient just to introduce a delay in the initiation of the time waster. If e-mail, instant messaging, solitaire, or Web surfing is a source of procrastination, then simply removing bookmarks

---

24. See, e.g., Merlin Mann's "Right now, what are you doing?" nag screen at http://www.43folders.com/2008/09/01/what-are-you-doing.

and other shortcuts or regularly shutting down the programs may provide enough of a threshold to keep one from "just checking" too often. A more extreme option is to install a product called Software Time Lock, which allows the user to "set blocks of time during which you cannot access the Web, set blocks of time during which specific programs cannot be used, set blocks of time during which you cannot use the computer at all, set limits on how long you can access the Web each day," and so forth.[25]

Given that distractibility and impulsiveness are strongly correlated with procrastination, this sort of environmental management is crucially important. Even something as simple as closing the office door or working in an environment without an Internet connection, telephone, or cell-phone reception can dramatically improve task performance.

## Social Strategies

The most obvious way to exercise self-control in the event of an anticipated failure of willpower is simply to preauthorize some other person either to act on your behalf or to impose control upon you. The locus classicus for this strategy is Ulysses' ordering his sailors to tie him to the mast and then to ignore his subsequent instructions. There are, however, a multitude of far more subtle strategies that we use, in order to offload (or perhaps one should say outsource) our self-control onto other people.

When it comes to procrastination, the most obvious example of this is the social institution of deadlines. By accepting a deadline, the individual essentially makes a commitment to another person that a particular task will be accomplished by a certain time. It is often not the case that this deadline coincides with any objective requirement; that is, nothing bad actually happens if the deadline is missed, other than that the deadline is missed. And yet deadlines are often motivationally quite effective, even when everyone is aware of their artificiality. A closely related strategy is the time-honored technique of overcommitment. If Parkinson's Law is correct—that work expands to fill the time available for its completion—then the best way to ensure that one is working at a reasonably high intensity level is to take on too much. This makes it easier to meet deadlines, in part because it deprives one of certain rationalizations that are often used to excuse procrastination. "I'll get to it tomorrow" becomes far less persuasive if the workload is such that there is literally no slack in the schedule (so that leaving it until tomorrow is as good as not doing it at all).

Teamwork is another closely related strategy. Like deadlines, working on a task jointly with other people brings a variety of social motives (such as the individual's norm-conformative disposition, desire to avoid disapproval, unwillingness to "let down the side," concern over social status) into alignment with his or her instrumental work objectives. Many people find that they can only bring themselves to exercise by playing team

---

25. See http://leithauserresearch.com/software_time_lock.html.

sports. In the same way, many people work far more effectively in groups. Many of the direct psychological strategies outlined above are also far more effective and much easier to implement when carried out in a social context. "Making a game of it" can require considerable imagination, when carried out in solitude. But in a social context, it is always possible to make a game out of any task, often quite literally. The most obvious way is by introducing a competitive structure, such as by giving a prize to the person who performs best (think of how companies give out bonuses or "employee of the week" awards). In a social context, it is possible to change the incentives governing a particular task in a way that is often not possible at a purely individual level. Relatively feeble "self-rewards" can be replaced by actual rewards.

People in long-term intimate relationships often develop a very advanced division of labor between themselves. This extends both to cognitive tasks, such as remembering names, and to practical, volitional ones. One can often see a division of self-control tasks in the way household labor is divided up (e.g., the person least likely to buy junk food is the one who does the grocery shopping, the one who is most likely to pay the bills on time is the one who looks after the finances, and so on). More informally, couples may employ the "license to nag," whereby they essentially authorize each other to complain, criticize, and even punish them for failures of willpower. They may also begin to rely on the other person's complaints as a cue for initiating action.

Perhaps the most subtle mechanism of self-control is selective association. Imitation and conformity provide very powerful motives. In particular, we rely on imitation to establish what Ap Dijksterhuis and John Bargh refer to as "default social behavior."[26] Thus, one way to avoid self-control failures of a particular sort is to avoid the company of those who suffer from such failures. Being around prompt, hardworking high achievers is one of the best ways of becoming prompt and hardworking as well, while associating with slackers is a good way of becoming a slacker.

Even from this quick survey of the available set of strategies, it is evident that they become richer and more numerous as one proceeds down the list. There is not all that much we can do, using our "onboard" resources, when it comes to controlling procrastination. When one moves into the domain of the environment, on the other hand, especially the social environment, the set of available strategies becomes less restricted. The latter seems to be limited primarily by human imagination, not any inherent limitations of the medium.

The importance of these environmental strategies can be seen in the phenomenon of college procrastination, the fact that college students, particularly during their first and second years, experience much higher levels of problem procrastination than the general public. What is

---

26. Dijksterhuis and Bargh, "Perceptual-Behavior Expressway." See also Bargh and Chartrand, "Unbearable Automaticity of Being."

particularly interesting about this phenomenon is that it has little predictive significance when it comes to determining work habits in other contexts.[27] From an internalist perspective, this is perhaps mysterious, but when seen from the perspective of environmental scaffolding, it is entirely unsurprising. College students are given a fairly high degree of autonomy when it comes to determining a plan of work for themselves, yet they are deprived of all of the scaffolding they have used in the past to offload motivational resources. Often, they are living away from home for the first time and so are missing whatever system they had developed for the timely completion of tasks. For example, merely studying in the same location has been shown to decrease procrastination among college students.[28] This is a habit that many high-school students would have but could easily be lost in the transition to college. Furthermore, they are no longer under direct parental supervision and are cut free from what has typically been their most important social self-control mechanism.

## BEYOND MENTALISTIC, INDIVIDUALISTIC, AND VOLUNTARISTIC ASSUMPTIONS ABOUT RATIONAL ACTION

One could view the foregoing discussion of "externalist" strategies simply as elements in a diverse toolbox for reducing procrastination. But we believe that coming to appreciate the prevalence of distributed willpower has wider implications for understanding rational human agency. According to what one might call the standard model, strategies for avoiding irrationality are largely understood in mentalistic, individualistic, and voluntaristic terms. Being rational, in this view, is a matter of correct thinking, engaged in by individuals, along with the ability to exert one's will decisively. But looking at how we are able to avoid procrastination suggests that rationality is achieved rather differently.

Traditional-time management advice has been mentalistic in assuming that solutions will come from individuals thinking more rationally about how best to achieve their goals. The focus is on cognitive accomplishments that are within the intentional control of the mind; they are, indeed, operations of the mind that are thought to flow directly into action. Much of the self-help literature also focuses on internal psychological factors, such as fear of failure, that may discourage people from working as effectively as they might; for example, one popular book claims that

---

27. Moon and Illingworth, "Exploring the Dynamic Nature," 307. For a sample of the voluminous literature on college students and procrastination, see Kachgal, Hansen, and Nutter, "Academic Procrastination Prevention/Intervention"; Pychyl, Morin, and Salmon, "Procrastination and the Planning Fallacy"; and Solomon and Rothblum, "Academic Procrastination."

28. Ziesat, Rosenthal, and White, "Behavioral Self-Control."

"procrastination may be protecting a fragile sense of self-worth that is shaken by threats of judgment, control, closeness or distance."[29] Rather than restructuring the temporal dynamics of choice or changing their external incentives, individuals are encouraged simply to focus more clearly on the goals they hope to attain and the negative consequences of delay.[30]

Consider, for instance, the following list of "tips" for overcoming procrastination:

- Figure out what has the biggest payoff, and do that first.
- Be your own biggest fan.
- Start sooner.
- Stop busywork.
- Set aside hopelessness and other forms of negative thinking.
- Forgive previous mistakes and expect new ones.[31]

While this author does eventually get around to making environmental recommendations, these typically occur last, after a lengthy set of purely psychological recommendations. There is no offloading here, nothing that reduces the motivational burden on the individual; rather, these are all either direct psychological or else self-management strategies. As we have emphasized throughout, however—and as the empirical data suggest—avoiding procrastination is typically not achieved through these forms of cognizing.

This idea is beginning to be reflected in some approaches to time management. It is highly instructive, for example, to consider that the approach that has gained perhaps the most significant following among knowledge workers and other professionals, found in David Allen's *Getting Things Done*,[32] is resolutely externalist in its orientation. At the core of the system of personal organization and time management is the insistence that absolutely everything that is not immediately being worked on be offloaded into an external physical system that one trusts and preprocessed into "next action" chunks that are easily initiated, in response to contextual cues. Getting things done becomes then a decidedly nonmentalistic matter of turning amorphous responsibilities into a much less intimidating pile of "widgets to be cranked."

Even approaches to avoiding procrastination that understand the importance of material scaffolding still tend to focus rather individualistically on personal tools and habits. While these are important, we have seen how many of the supports that enable us to avoid procrastination are part of the social and built environment. This is clearest in the breach. As traditional offices, with their doors for shutting out distractions, have been

---

29. Burka and Yuen, *Procrastination*, 83.
30. Burka and Yuen, *Procrastination*, 119.
31. Lively, *Procrastinator's Guide*, 20–27.
32. Allen, *Getting Things Done*. For a fascinating analysis of the parallels between Allen's approach and empirical psychology, see Heylighen and Vidal, "Getting Things Done."

replaced with open offices of cubicles, people have come to realize how much harder they have to work to keep on task in the face of constant distractions.[33] These and other aspects of the built environment have changed in the past few decades, in a way that has forced individuals to rely ever more upon their onboard resources. Much the same can be said for the social environment, where freelancers and telecommuters find that working out of the home office leaves them without the supportive peer pressure of colleagues who will notice when they linger in the cafeteria or turn on a TV. What becomes clear is that in such cases, being self-disciplined is a contextualist property—not simply a personality trait but, rather, a feature of persons as they are in particular contexts, with the requisite scaffolding. The further implication of this is that, although individual differences in personalities and skill sets clearly make a difference, some of the most important resources for overcoming procrastination are not portable, individual assets but are shared goods—and goods that are being dismantled even as individual competition becomes more cutthroat.

A related but perhaps more controversial point can be made about the assumption of voluntarism, the view that what is needed for avoiding forms of counterproductive behavior is a matter of our setting up systems, adopting practices, arranging our environments, and so on. The reality is that many of the most effective support structures—especially the social ones—are not built by us but are built for us, part of an institutional and material heritage. And they are much more difficult to bring about intentionally than to dismantle. When a traditional institution such as the relatively early "last call" for drinks at British pubs is abolished, it is, of course, possible for people to institute, perhaps with friends, various strategies for avoiding procrastinating about getting to bed on time. But such arrangements are typically effortful and fragile relative to taken-for-granted structures. To take just one example, consider the sleep deprivation that has become a source of complaint in our society, which can plausibly be attributed, at least in part, to a tendency to procrastinate about going to bed on time.[34] It used to be the case that TV stations would end their broadcasts at around midnight, bars and restaurants would close, subways and buses would stop running—the clear message being sent was "It is time to go to bed." These institutional arrangements also made it much easier to go to bed on time, since there was little else to do after a certain hour. Now, individuals must exercise more self-control about when to go to bed.

There is, we acknowledge, a danger of this point being seen as licensing paternalistic, authoritarian, or traditionalist approaches. There are complex challenges here regarding how to balance a commitment to autonomy and freedom with the recognition that there are often real benefits of volitional supports being unchosen. And these complexities come into

---

33. Steel, "Nature of Procrastination," 82.
34. On bedtime procrastination, see Ainslie, *Breakdown of Will*, 41.

particularly sharp focus as one looks at the effects of their dismantling on those who have the fewest resources for handling the new individual responsibilities. This brings us to some concluding remarks about the political and public-policy implications of this more externalist understanding of how to counter irrational human tendencies.

## CONCLUDING REMARKS: ACCESS TO SCAFFOLDING AS AN ISSUE OF PUBLIC POLICY

Procrastination, like weakness of will, is a fascinating philosophical and psychological puzzle. Equally fascinating, we have suggested, is our extraordinary ingenuity in recruiting our environment to solve our standard gaps in self-control.

It remains the case, however, that chronic procrastination has real and often devastating consequences. This is not just about last-minute Christmas shopping or birthday cards getting sent late. When they put things off, people lose their jobs, their insurance, and their homes; their health suffers; and they tend to be "more miserable in the long term."[35] Our externalist account of procrastination suggests that this has potentially important political implications. To the extent to which we can assume (1) that certain social and economic developments in modern societies place increasingly high demands on the capacities that make up our ability to avoid procrastination,[36] (2) that current trends toward individualization and liberalization involve the dismantling or abandonment of traditional forms of unchosen scaffolding, and (3) that the impact of the two preceding effects will be especially devastating for those who are already most vulnerable (think of the difficulties that the homeless have in taking advantage of environmental supports), then procrastination becomes not just an issue of individual psychology but also an issue of social justice. If people's life chances are significantly shaped (perhaps along lines of class, race, degree of disability, and so forth) by their access to scaffolding and if many forms of scaffolding are being dismantled or rendered inadequate as the result of social processes that could be addressed (at least to some extent) by public policy, then the negative consequences of procrastination are not just the result of people failing to cognize appropriately as individuals but are partly the result of decisions and dynamics over which individuals have little control.

Does this mean that "society" should be responsible for people not paying their taxes on time or putting off a visit to the doctor? Not quite. But to the extent that public-policy decisions affect the availability of and access to the relevant scaffolding and that these decisions can potentially affect individual life chances, a collective concern with individual welfare

---

35. For an overview of these costs, see Steel, "Nature of Procrastination," 65.
36. This is convincingly portrayed by Beck in *Risk Society*.

or the reduction of vulnerability or inequalities entails a concern for procrastination, along with an obligation to avoid dismantling the scaffolding that enables people, standardly, to keep procrastination in check. Once this concern is raised, of course, very controversial differences in social and political theory emerge regarding the best way to approach these deficits and their distribution. Will an approach geared toward the development of new forms of social solidarity and ego-psychological development be able to address these deficits?[37] Or do the arguments we have been making here point, rather, in the direction of a more paternalist, even if only "nudge paternalist," direction?[38] These are complicated issues, but as a society, we should not put off addressing them.

## ACKNOWLEDGMENTS

We would like to thank the Social Sciences and Research Council of Canada for financial support, CSMN for sponsoring the New York workshop, Ida Momennejad and Bas Kops for research assistance, and Chrisoula Andreou and Mark White for helpful suggestions as well as the social scaffolding needed to bring our chapter and this book to completion.

37. Habermas, "Individuation through Socialization."
38. Thaler and Sunstein, *Nudge*. See also, critically, Anderson, "Autonomy Gaps," and White, "Behavioral Law and Economics."

# 15

# Procrastination and the Law

*Manuel A. Utset*

Some legal rules prohibit people from acting, while others require them to do something by a particular date. Repeated procrastination can significantly affect the operation and effectiveness of these two types of legal rules. People routinely procrastinate completing onerous tasks, such as saving for retirement, starting exercise regimes, or quitting smoking. From a long-term perspective, they conclude that they would be better off acting by a specified date, but when the time to act arrives, they give added weight to the immediate disutility of acting and choose to delay instead. Law and economics models begin with the simplifying assumption that people have perfect self-control and thus do not procrastinate. However, there is a large literature in behavioral economics finding that people routinely override their long-term preferences because of the pull of immediate gratification.[1] With this in mind, this chapter develops a simple model of repeated procrastination and uses it to examine the extent to which such behavior affects the decision-making process of actors subject to legal rules.

Repeated procrastination can lead to large aggregate welfare losses, both for the procrastinator and for those affected by her actions. This point is important, because one role of legal rules is to deter people from overindulging in behavior that harms third parties. Those who oppose legal intervention to prevent a procrastinator from self-harm should not be bothered by this more traditional use of government regulation. Given the evidence on people's propensity to procrastinate, it follows that lawmakers should, at the very least, consider how repeated procrastination affects the overall effectiveness of legal rules. As I show in this chapter, people with a preference for immediate gratification may engage in socially suboptimal levels of misconduct. In some cases, they may violate the law even though they have a long-term preference not to do so. In addition to this sort of *time-inconsistent misconduct*, the model developed

---

1. For instance, see Frederick, Loewenstein, and O'Donoghue, "Time Discounting," 192–210.

in this chapter also leads to a counterintuitive result: a person who from a long-term perspective believes that violating the law is economically worthwhile may nonetheless repeatedly procrastinate following through with the planned misconduct. This sort of *time-inconsistent obedience* helps explain an important puzzle in the criminal law literature: the fact that people routinely obey the law even though the expected benefits of disobedience greatly exceed the expected sanctions. For example, given the low probability of detection, we might predict that people would cheat on their taxes much more than they do. While this observed overcompliance can be explained in part as the product of a norm of obeying the law, time-inconsistent obedience is an equally likely explanation and one that relies on a more intuitive motivation.

The phenomenon of time-inconsistent obedience has implications beyond the problem of unintended overdeterrence. In particular, I argue that lawmakers who are sufficiently aware of the self-control problems of citizens can take advantage of them by creating legal rules that lead them to repeatedly procrastinate doing otherwise legal activities. In particular, I argue that a lawmaker who wants to deter people from doing A and who does not want to bear the political consequences of prohibiting A can create legal obstacles that impose sufficiently high immediate costs to provide them with an incentive to procrastinate doing A. For example, a lawmaker who believes that divorce is immoral but who knows that a majority of the electorate would oppose a bald prohibition can create costly legal hurdles that cause a subset of people whose long-term preference is to get a divorce to repeatedly procrastinate following through. I refer to this strategy as *stealth regulation* and show how, as an example, even relatively low hurdles for getting abortions can have a much larger impact on reducing the number of abortions than one would expect if one were to assume that people have perfect self-control. Additionally, I extend the concepts of time-inconsistent obedience and stealth regulation to interactions between private parties, such as co-conspirators, corporate participants, and spouses.

The first part of the chapter develops a general model of procrastination. The second part applies this model to the problems of time-inconsistent misconduct and obedience, and the third develops a model of stealth regulation.

## PROCRASTINATION: THE GENERAL PROBLEM

An intertemporal decision is one in which the costs and rewards that flow from the decision are not all incurred or received in the same time period.[2] The relative timing of costs and rewards matters because, as a

---

2. Loewenstein and Thaler, "Anomalies," 181.

general matter, people are impatient in that they prefer to receive benefits as early as possible and delay incurring costs until future periods. Early work in formalizing intertemporal choice used an exponential discount function, which, while easier to use, has an important (but, in hindsight, undesirable) side effect: it implies that actors have a constant level of impatience.[3] In short, an exponential discounter will never give added weight to immediate costs and rewards and thus will always act in a time-consistent manner.[4] But, as mentioned above, there is a large body of empirical evidence showing that people routinely exhibit time-inconsistent preferences, because of a short-term preference for immediate gratification that leads them to override their long-term preferences.[5] As we will now see, it is this asymmetry between long-term and short-term impatience that leads people to procrastinate.

## A Simple Model of Procrastination

A rational intertemporal decision maker will choose her behavior to maximize the sum of her current and future welfare, which, in turn, requires her to take into account how her current actions may affect her future behavior.[6] I will say that an action at time $t$ is *intertemporally worthwhile* if, given an actor's beliefs about how she plans to act in the future, the action in question maximizes her current *and* future well-being.[7]

From a long-term perspective, when all of the costs and benefits flowing from an action are in the future, time-consistent and time-inconsistent actors value those payoffs in the same manner and thus make identical long-term utility-maximizing decisions.[8] I will say that doing A at time $\tau$ is *long-run worthwhile* if, from the detached, long-term perspective of time $t$, an actor has determined that such a course of action would maximize her current and future well-being. This means that intertemporal decision makers have a preference to engage in behavior that is long-run worthwhile.

---

3. Frederick, Loewenstein, and O'Donoghue, "Time Discounting," 162–168.
4. Frederick, Loewenstein, and O'Donoghue, "Time Discounting," 166–167, 170, which states that the exponential function is the only one that ensures that actors will exhibit constant levels of impatience, which, in turn, "implies that a person's intertemporal preferences are *time-consistent*, which means that later preferences 'confirm' earlier preferences."
5. Frederick, Loewenstein, and O'Donoghue, "Time Discounting," 192–210; Bickel and Johnson, "Delay Discounting," 422 ("Exponential discounting . . . has *not* been empirically supported by behavioral research" conducted in humans and animals).
6. O'Donoghue and Rabin, "Doing It Now," 106.
7. O'Donoghue and Rabin, "Choice and Procrastination," 128, for a general model in which people act with reasonable beliefs about future actions and choose current actions to maximize preferences in light of those beliefs.
8. Since from a long-term perspective, time-consistent and time-inconsistent actors use the same exponential discount function, I will assume throughout that there is no long-term discounting; this makes it easier to focus on the short-term preferences that motivate time-inconsistent behavior.

When time τ arrives, the decision maker will have to decide whether or not to follow through with her original decision to do A. The actor will do A immediately only if she determines it is *short-run worthwhile*, in the sense that, from the perspective of period τ, it would maximize her intertemporal utility. In order to model how an actor's preference for immediate gratification affects this short-term cost-benefit analysis, it is helpful to introduce a short-term *immediacy multiplier* that becomes operative whenever that actor makes a decision involving immediate costs or benefits. For example, an actor with an immediacy multiplier of 2.00 gives twice as much weight to immediate costs and benefits, while one with a multiplier of 1.25 gives them 25 percent greater weight. By definition, a time-consistent actor has an immediacy multiplier of 1.00.

I will assume that doing A requires the actor to incur an immediate cost, but some or all of the benefits flowing from that action are delayed until some future period. If an actor has determined that doing A at time τ is long-run worthwhile, then it must be the case that if she delays doing A until time τ + 1, she will incur some sort of welfare loss.[9] Nonetheless, at time τ, the actor perceives some benefit from delaying—avoiding the heightened immediate costs of acting. It follows that an actor will determine that procrastination is short-run worthwhile only if the incremental gain from delay is greater than the incremental welfare loss.

A person procrastinates when her deliberation process and behavior meet two conditions. First, her long-term cost-benefit analysis at time *t* leads her to conclude that doing A at time τ is long-run worthwhile. Second, when time τ arrives, the actor's cost-benefit analysis leads her to conclude that it is short-run worthwhile to delay doing A until some future period. Moreover, she concludes this solely as a result of the fact that she gives sufficient added weight to the immediate costs of executing the task, such that the incremental benefit from avoiding that immediate disutility is greater than the incremental loss from delay.[10] Finally, as we will see below, in the case of criminal misconduct, the immediate costs that motivate procrastination include not just out-of-pocket expenses but any other type of disutility, such as harming others, violating moral strictures, or exerting physical or mental effort.

It is natural to take a person's long-term preferences as her "preferred preferences," given that they are free of the transient distortions brought about by the prospect of experiencing immediate gratification.[11] Suppose that in period τ, the actor chooses to procrastinate until period τ + 1. Then

---

9. In other words, it must be that the net benefits of acting in the following period are lower; if not, the actor would have made a long-term decision to act then instead of at time τ.

10. This eliminates cases in which an actor overrides her original decision because of long-run justifiable reasons, such as the acquisition of new information.

11. See Utset, "Hyperbolic Criminals," 632–633, for an argument regarding an actor's "preferred" preferences.

the incremental welfare loss from this one instance of procrastination is the difference between the net benefit that she would have received if she had kept to her original decision and the net benefit from acting in period $\tau + 1$. While a one-period delay will produce relatively small welfare losses, as we will see below, what ultimately matters are the aggregate welfare losses incurred by an actor who repeatedly procrastinates.

Recall that in deciding whether or not an action is intertemporally worthwhile, a decision maker will take into account her beliefs about how she will act in the future. These beliefs are important because at time $\tau$, a person is more likely to put off doing A until the following period if she believes that she will, in fact, follow through at that time. The economic literature on procrastination has focused on three types of beliefs about an actor's future behavior.[12] A person has *naive* beliefs if each time she makes a short-term decision, she believes incorrectly that she will have perfect self-control in the future. On the other hand, a person has *sophisticated* beliefs if she correctly predicts her future temptation to procrastinate. However, most people fall somewhere in between complete naiveté and sophistication; a *partially naive* actor is one who knows that she will have an incentive to procrastinate in the future but holds incorrect beliefs about the magnitude of the immediacy multiplier that she will use when time $\tau$ arrives.

If a person has a long-term preference to do task A at time $\tau$ and is aware that at time $\tau$, procrastination will be short-run worthwhile, then a *commitment device* is any mechanism adopted ahead of time to ensure that she does not procrastinate. Commitment devices are costly to implement, and even if they were available at zero cost, people are reluctant to restrict their ability to act freely unless they believe that precommitment is otherwise worthwhile.[13] Nonetheless, commitment devices are common in many types of contexts. For example, people with long-term preferences to eat healthily, exercise, and lose weight join health clubs and go to special weight-loss spas, both of which require costly up-front commitments. The fact that people find precommitment valuable is evidence that people have self-control problems and that they have some awareness of their predicament.

In order to deter an actor from repeatedly putting off completing a long-run worthwhile action, a commitment device would have to manipulate one or more of the factors underwriting her decision to procrastinate:

---

12. O'Donoghue and Rabin, "Choice and Procrastination," 126–127.

13. One cost of commitment is that people generally value their autonomy and find disutility in having their wills constrained unnecessarily; see Fried, *Contract as Promise*, 13–14. In addition, psychologists have found that individuals often prefer changeable decisions because they predict, sometimes incorrectly, that they will not be satisfied with the choices they made. See, e.g., Gilbert and Ebert, "Decisions and Revisions," 510–511, which finds that although the individuals who were given the choice to change their minds about which photography prints to keep liked their choices less than those individuals who had no ability to change, individuals still preferred having the option to change.

(1) her immediacy multiplier, (2) the immediate costs of acting, (3) the incremental loss from a one-period delay, and (4) her awareness of the true magnitude of her self-control problems. I will assume that the actor's preference for immediate gratification will remain fixed, at least over relatively short periods. As a result, there are three general strategies for foreclosing an actor's incentive to procrastinate. The first approach is to sufficiently reduce the immediate costs of doing A, such that the gain from delay (after applying the immediacy multiplier) is less than the incremental loss from delay. The second would require increasing the incremental loss from delay by a sufficient amount so that procrastination is no longer short-run worthwhile. Finally, the actor can be made aware of her actual propensity to procrastinate and, thus, of the value of using commitment devices.

## A Numerical Example

Suppose that Mary is making a decision regarding task A, which she is able to complete in one of four periods. Acting in periods 1 through 4 would requires her to incur immediate costs of 60, 100, 160, and 260 utils, respectively. Moreover, if Mary completes the task, she will receive a benefit of 1,000 utils in the following period. I will assume that Mary has an immediacy multiplier of 2.00.

While the benefits of doing A always exceed the costs, Mary will want to complete the task in the period with the lowest costs. Table 15-1, showing the perceived disutilities in each period, indicates that from the long-term perspective of period 0, Mary will conclude that completing task A in period 1 is intertemporally worthwhile and will form an intention to do so. In period 1, Mary's immediacy multiplier of 2.00 will lead her to perceive an immediate disutility from acting as 120 (instead of 60). She will compare this with the period 2 (delayed) costs of 100 and have an incentive to procrastinate. As can be seen, Mary's immediacy multiplier is sufficiently high that, in each period, she will have an incentive to procrastinate until the following period.

Whether or not Mary actually procrastinates depends on her belief about her future behavior, which, in turn, will depend on her beliefs about her future willpower. If Mary has naive beliefs, she will procrastinate until the last period.[14] Notice that in each period, Mary has an incentive to procrastinate only until the following period. For example, in period 1, she prefers to wait until period 2, because she prefers the delayed costs of 100 to the immediate costs of 120; at the same time, when she compares the (delayed) period 2 and period 3 costs of 100 and 160, respectively, she will conclude that it is intertemporally worthwhile to complete the task in period 2. The reason for this is that a naive Mary believes incorrectly

---

14. As can be seen in the table, each period in which a naive Mary makes a decision, she will conclude that the following period (the one in bold) is the intertemporally worthwhile period to complete the task.

**Procrastination and the Law**   259

**Table 15-1** An illustration of incentive to procrastinate repeatedly

|          | When Decision Is Made |          |          |          |
|----------|----------|----------|----------|----------|
|          | Period 0 | Period 1 | Period 2 | Period 3 |
| Period 1 | 60       | 120      |          |          |
| Period 2 | 100      | 100      | 200      |          |
| Period 3 | 160      | 160      | 160      | 320      |
| Period 4 | 260      | 260      | 260      | 260      |

that in period 2, she will use a multiplier of 1.00 and surely complete the task. By definition, a naive Mary will always make the same mistakes about her future willpower. This will lead her to procrastinate again in periods 2 and 3 and complete the task in the final period. Mary's repeated procrastination causes her to incur a welfare loss of 200 utils, which is the difference between the net benefit that she would have received if she had kept to her long-term preference to do A in period 1 and the net benefits from acting in period 4.

A sophisticated Mary correctly predicts the magnitude of the immediacy multiplier that she will use in each period. Working backward, she will first determine that if she were to wait to complete the task until period 3, she would definitely have an incentive to procrastinate until period 4. She also knows that in period 2, she would, at least in theory, prefer to delay until period 3; however, since delaying until period 3 is equivalent to delaying until period 4, her short-term cost-benefit analysis in period 2 would lead her to act immediately—she prefers the period 2 costs of 200 over the period 4 costs of 260. With this in mind, she correctly concludes that if she were to procrastinates in period 1, she would definitely complete the task in period 2. Since, from a long-term perspective, completing the task in period 2 creates a disutility of 100 (instead of the cost of 60 in period 1), this one-period delay will cause a sophisticated Mary to suffer a relatively small welfare loss of 40 utils.[15]

More generally, the welfare losses from procrastinating just one period will be bounded. To see this, we can change the facts and suppose that the effort cost in period 2 is 121 instead of 100. Now, both a sophisticated and a naive Mary will conclude that completing the task in period 1 is short-run worthwhile—from the perspective of period 1, the heightened immediate costs are 120, which are lower than the delayed period 2 costs of 121. It follows that given the period 1 costs of 60 and Mary's immediacy multiplier of 2.00, the maximum welfare loss from procrastinating in

---

15. A partially naive Mary knows that in the future, she will use a multiplier of more than 1.00 but believes incorrectly that it will be lower than its true magnitude of 2.00. In this instance, if Mary believes that her multiplier is greater than 1.59, she will act in the same manner as a fully sophisticated actor; but if she believes that it is below that, she will repeatedly procrastinate until period 4, just as if she were fully naive.

period 1 cannot exceed 60 utils.[16] Although the welfare losses from procrastinating just one period are bounded, a naive (or sufficiently partially naive) actor can incur large aggregate welfare losses by procrastinating repeatedly. For example, suppose that Mary had two additional periods in which to complete the task, periods 5 and 6, at a cost of 510 and 999, respectively. Then a naive Mary will procrastinate until period 6 and incur an aggregate welfare loss of 939 utils.

## PROCRASTINATION AND LEGAL BEHAVIOR

The economics literature has focused on the role of benevolent lawmakers whose aim is to help deter actors from engaging in repeated procrastination.[17] However, commentators have overlooked an important fact: a non-benevolent lawmaker who wants to prohibit people from doing A without bearing the full political cost of enacting a bald prohibition can design legal rules that will exacerbate people's incentive to repeatedly procrastinate doing A. The lawmaker can do so by adopting legal rules that either increase the immediate costs of doing A or decrease the delayed loss from procrastinating for one period. I refer to this phenomenon, in which lawmakers exploit the self-control problems of regulated actors, as stealth regulation. This section develops a model of time-inconsistent misconduct and time-inconsistent obedience, showing that the optimal criminal sanctions of economics theory will, depending on the context, either systematically underdeter or overdeter time-inconsistent actors. The next section will develop a model of stealth regulation.

### Time-Inconsistent Misconduct

### The General Model

I will assume that both time-consistent and time-inconsistent offenders have a long-term preference to violate the law if and only if it is long-run worthwhile: if from a long-term perspective, the benefits from the crime are greater than the expected sanctions (the gross sanctions times the offender's subjective probability that she will be caught and convicted).[18] However, what ultimately matters is an offender's behavior when she is presented with the opportunity to commit a crime. Misconduct is short-run

---

16. This is assuming that if Mary is indifferent, she will procrastinate. If one assumes that an indifferent Mary will complete the task, then the maximum welfare loss is 59 utils. All other things being equal, an actor with a higher preference for immediate gratification than Mary would incur higher welfare losses from procrastinating just one period; e.g., someone with an immediacy multiplier of 3.00 would have a maximum loss of 180 or 179, respectively.
17. See, e.g., O'Donoghue and Rabin, "Doing It Now," 120.
18. For a standard treatment, see Posner, *Economic Analysis of Law*, 219–220.

worthwhile whenever the immediate benefits—as magnified by an actor's immediacy multiplier—are greater than the delayed expected sanctions. Since a time-consistent offender has a multiplier equal to 1.00, all other things being equal, she will conclude that a crime is short-run worthwhile only if it is also long-run worthwhile. On the other hand, time-inconsistent offenders will sometimes commit crimes that are not long-run worthwhile. They will engage in this sort of time-inconsistent misconduct whenever the immediate benefits, as magnified by the immediacy multiplier, exceed the (delayed) expected sanctions.

There are two principal types of time-inconsistent misconduct. First, an offender may take a prohibited action that provides him with an immediate reward, such as embezzling funds, discharging pollutants into a stream, or making a false disclosure in a securities filing. An offender may "overconsume" crimes of this sort in the same manner that a person with a long-term preference not to smoke or overeat may repeatedly succumb to temptation. We can refer to this type of serial misconduct as *nibbling opportunism*. Moreover, once an offender has embarked on a course of misconduct, the immediate costs of reverting back to a lawful path may lead him to repeatedly delay leaving the criminal life. This means that a repeat offender may set out on a path of long-run worthwhile misconduct and will continue violating the law, even when doing so is no longer long-run worthwhile.[19]

Second, many laws and regulations require regulated parties to do something by a specific date, such as filing tax returns, making corporate disclosures, and complying with environmental regulations. A required-action rule is thus one that punishes regulated parties whenever they fail to do A by time $\tau$. However, in order to do A, a regulated party will have to exert effort and, in most cases, incur other immediate costs. For example, managers who own company stock or have been awarded stock options may delay making a required disclosure to the extent that it would lead to an immediate decline in the price of the stock. A time-inconsistent offender who has a long-term preference to do A no later than time $\tau$ will have an incentive to procrastinate in each period in which these immediate costs, as magnified by his immediacy multiplier, are greater than the incremental delayed sanction of waiting one more period. Each time the offender delays, he engages in an instance of *compliance procrastination*.

*Optimal Deterrence and Time-Inconsistent Offenders.* All punishment theories provide some account of why society should punish offenders and prescriptions for choosing the type and magnitude of criminal sanctions. The neoclassical economic model of criminal misconduct posits that the

---

19. See, e.g., Sanders, "Becoming an Ex-Sex Worker," 75–76, which describes studies finding that women delay leaving the sex trade because of the immediate costs of exit, such as the costs of discontinuing (or finding an alternative source of funds for) drug use and the lack of available alternative work.

sole aim of punishment is to maximize social welfare.[20] Suppose that a lawmaker has determined that doing A produces a social harm $h$. Under the neoclassical approach, the aim is to deter offenders from engaging in behavior that produces greater social harm than benefits, not necessarily to foreclose all criminal activity. Some crimes, such as murder, rape, and armed robbery, require total deterrence; however, there are a series of less harmful offenses, including regulatory crimes that, while serious, do not necessarily call for total deterrence—at least, not from an economics standpoint.

As a result, when crimes call for total deterrence, the lawmaker will set the expected sanctions high enough to effectively foreclose all violations. But in all other cases, it would set them equal to the harm of the illegal behavior.[21] Under such a penalty scheme, a rational offender will violate the legal rule only when it produces a net social gain; that is, only when his net benefits (after taking the expected sanctions into account) are at least as great as the social harm. Since, by definition, an offender's preferred preferences are his long-term preferences, it follows that committing a crime is socially worthwhile only if it is long-run worthwhile.

For example, if discharging pollutants into a stream produces a harm of $1,000, and there is a 50 percent probability that an offender will be detected and punished, then the optimal fine under the neoclassical approach is $2,000. This will ensure that the expected sanctions and harm both equal $1,000 and that a utility-maximizing offender will pollute if and only if it is socially worthwhile. However, suppose that a time-inconsistent offender has an immediacy multiplier of 2.00, and polluting would provide him with an immediate benefit of $750. While polluting is not long-run worthwhile and thus would produce a net social harm, a lawmaker who assumes that such an offender has time-consistent preferences will adopt suboptimal sanctions. That is, the lawmaker will adopt sanctions that are too low to deter the polluter's time-inconsistent misconduct. More generally, if the expected sanction is lower than $1,500, the time-inconsistent offender will be underdeterred. Moreover, if a lawmaker who adopts the standard time-consistency assumption observes this person violating the law, notwithstanding the expected sanctions of $1,000, the lawmaker will incorrectly conclude that the offender is actually getting a benefit from misconduct that is greater than the social harm that he is producing.

*Procedural Paternalism.* An offender who engages in time-inconsistent misconduct will incur a welfare loss equal to the amount by which the

---

20. Becker, "Crime and Punishment," 181–185.

21. As a general matter, suppose that an offense produces a harm $h$, and the probability of detection is $p$. If the sanction $s$ is discounted by $p$ (resulting in an expected sanction of $p \times s$), and we set $p \times s = h$, then the optimal sanction is reached by multiplying the harm by the probability multiplier $1/p$. Therefore, the optimal sanction is $h/p$.

expected sanctions triggered by the misconduct exceed the actual benefits. A benevolent lawmaker can engage in *procedural paternalism* by providing sophisticated offenders with default commitment devices or adopting detection and punishment schemes that will deter time-inconsistent misconduct without at the same time deterring socially beneficial misconduct.[22]

As with default rules generally, default commitment devices can provide value whenever a large number of offenders face the same type of time-inconsistent misconduct scenarios. However, offenders who are sufficiently naive regarding their future self-control problems will see no harm in opting out of these default devices. One way to address this problem is to erect costly hurdles, setting them low enough so that sophisticated actors will opt out if they have better forms of commitment but high enough so that naive actors will repeatedly procrastinate and never opt out.

## Time-Inconsistent Obedience

One empirical puzzle of the standard economic approach to criminal sanctions is that, in the real world, people routinely fail to engage in misconduct that is clearly long-run worthwhile; in short, they obey the law more than they "should" (if one assumes that they are rational, utility-maximizing actors). This puzzle can be explained once one allows for the possibility that offenders have a preference for immediate gratification. The general intuition is straightforward: many types of criminal activity require offenders to incur immediate costs, which, if sufficiently great, can lead them to repeatedly procrastinate engaging in the planned, long-run worthwhile misconduct. Because such an offender has a long-term preference to engage in misconduct, I refer to this phenomenon as time-inconsistent obedience.

Various types of immediate costs can lead an offender to engage in time-inconsistent obedience. First, offenders have to acquire information about possible crimes and determine whether they are worthwhile. Second, in order to execute a crime and avoid detection, an offender will have to exert effort and may have to incur out-of-pocket expenses.[23] The avoidance activity of repeat offenders will require even greater planning and coordination—greater levels of deception, anxiety, and greater effort to keep their stories straight over time. Third, a number of intangible costs are associated with criminal misconduct. For example, an offender may experience the immediate disutility that often flows from moral conflicts and the recognition of one's ethical shortcomings. Even when moral strictures are not sufficient to deter criminal activity, they can still create

---

22. Utset, "Hyperbolic Criminals," 657–661, discusses various types of detection and penalty schemes that have these characteristics.
23. Sanchirico, "Detection Avoidance," 1352–1361.

sufficiently large internal moral discord to produce time-inconsistent obedience. While some criminals are morally bankrupt, or at least moral agnostics, one can plausibly assume that some offenders give weight to moral norms or at least deliberate in their shadow.

*The General Model.* Suppose that in order to execute a crime, an offender has to incur one or more immediate costs (execution costs) and that the benefits from misconduct are not received until the following period. At time $t$, an offender will conclude that engaging in misconduct at time $\tau$ is long-run worthwhile if the benefits are greater than the sum of the expected sanctions and the execution costs. For example, suppose that the crime will provide the offender with a delayed benefit of $100; moreover, the expected sanctions are $50, and the execution costs are $30. Also suppose that a time-inconsistent offender has an immediacy multiplier of 2.00. From the perspective of time $t$, committing the crime is long-run worthwhile, but when time $\tau$ arrives, the offender will have an incentive to procrastinate. This is because misconduct is short-run worthwhile only if the delayed benefits are greater than the sum of the expected sanctions and the *heightened* immediate execution costs, which in this case are $60. As a result, the offender will conclude that the aggregate costs of misconduct ($50 + $60 = $110) exceed the delayed benefits ($100). At the same time, from the perspective of period $\tau$, he will conclude that engaging in misconduct in the following period is long-run worthwhile and will form an intention to do so.

Whether or not an offender repeatedly procrastinates will depend on his awareness of his future willpower. Thus, sophisticated offenders who want to make sure that they follow through with their planned misconduct may adopt commitment devices. This type of commitment device is more common than may initially appear; for instance, certain criminal organizations and gangs use formal initiation rites, such as killing someone, and other institutional strategies that act as commitment devices.[24] These features of criminal organizations are usually explained as devices that group members adopt to make sure that *other* group members do not defect. However, offenders may also independently value them as a way of committing to a path of long-run worthwhile misconduct.

*Time-Inconsistent Obedience and Criminal Conspiracies.* Whenever individuals (such as co-conspirators) come together to form a group, they need to incur organizational costs that, if high enough, can lead to collective action problems.[25] If the immediate costs of forming a group are sufficiently great, it is possible that every potential group member believes that it is long-run worthwhile to form the group, and yet they never do so

---

24. Having group members engage in murder is a particularly powerful commitment device because there is no statute of limitations.
25. Hardin, *Collective Action*, 38–49.

due to their repeated procrastination. It follows that overcoming collective action problems will be more difficult than predicted by the standard account, because, even when a sufficient number of potential members are willing to contribute to produce a public good, their preference for immediate gratification may get in the way. This means, moreover, that policymakers can positively or negatively affect the formation of groups by subsidizing or increasing organizational costs.

One can interpret the legal rules governing conspiracies as being of this sort. Under the law, conspiracies come into existence with an explicit or implicit "agreement" between two or more individuals to carry out an unlawful act (or a lawful act through unlawful means), even if the actors have not taken any other actions in furtherance of the conspiracy.[26] This makes sense from a deterrence point of view, since it increases the immediate costs of organizing conspiracies. For example, a potential co-conspirator may want to limit her interactions with others until she is sure that it is worthwhile to join the conspiracy.

More generally, crimes involving multiple offenders will have higher execution costs, given that offenders must coordinate their behavior and monitor one another to prevent defections.[27] As a result, each potential co-conspirator will have to incur screening costs before they agree to join a conspiracy, including acquiring information about the skill sets and trustworthiness of the others. Additionally, they will have to delineate the group's goals and identify the extent to which their intentions intersect. Finally, members must also agree on how to divide tasks and allocate costs and surpluses. While organizational costs are incurred immediately, the rewards to the members are necessarily delayed, given that a group must first be formed before a surplus can be produced and distributed. This means that, even when each potential co-conspirator believes that forming a conspiracy will provide her with positive expected returns, if the immediate costs of agreeing to conspire are sufficiently great, they each may have an incentive to repeatedly delay getting the process started. This, in turn, exacerbates the problem since it increases the search and coordination costs that co-conspirators have to incur to form the conspiracy.

## STEALTH REGULATION AND DEMOCRATIC ACCOUNTABILITY

As we saw above, an actor engages in time-inconsistent obedience whenever doing an illegal act is long-run worthwhile, but the immediate execution

---

26. See *Pettibone v. United States*, 148 U.S. 197, 203 (1893), which defines conspiracy as "a combination of two or more persons, by concerted action, to accomplish a criminal or unlawful purpose or some purpose not in itself criminal or unlawful by criminal or unlawful means."

27. Katyal, "Conspiracy Theory," 1350–1353.

costs lead her to repeatedly procrastinate violating the law. While this allows benevolent lawmakers to economize on the costs of deterring offenders, the same strategy can be used by nonbenevolent lawmakers to enact de facto prohibitions of certain types of behavior without having to bear the full political costs of doing so.

## Stealth Regulation

Citizens delegate to legislators, judges, and agency administrators the power to adopt and enforce legal rules. The ability of citizens to observe the behavior of these lawmakers is the first step in holding them accountable through the voting process.[28] I will say that an action by a lawmaker is *transparent* to a citizen if each of its material characteristics is directly or indirectly observable by that citizen; moreover, a characteristic is *material* if a reasonable voter would consider it important in determining how to vote. I will limit the analysis of transparency to one practical characteristic of legal rules: the lawmaker's intentions in adopting the rule.[29]

In this regard, one can distinguish between two types of rule-making intentions. A *majoritarian* intention is one that a majority of citizens would not disapprove of (in the sense that if they knew the intention, they would either vote for the lawmaker or not take it into account when deciding how to vote). On the other hand, a *minoritarian* intention is one that would lead a majority of citizens to vote against the lawmaker or at least consider it to be a material characteristic of the legal rule in question. The underlying assumption here is that citizens care not just about the actual consequences of a legal rule but also about the justification that, if asked, the lawmaker would give for adopting the rule. Although this is ultimately an empirical question, it is a plausible account of the deliberation process underwriting the voting decisions of citizens.[30]

A lawmaker who wants to adopt a minoritarian legal rule to prohibit A and who believes correctly that regulated parties in fact have time-inconsistent preferences can adopt a rule that allows people to do A but only after they make an up-front investment, such as having to purchase a license. This will lead a subset of parties (those who are sufficiently naive) with a long-term preference to do A to repeatedly procrastinate. The lawmaker can, in essence, deter a subset of time-inconsistent actors

---

28. The discussion below is limited to the accountability of elected officials and of other lawmakers who are indirectly accountable, at least in part, through the voting process.

29. I explicitly refer to a lawmaker's intention (as opposed to motive) to capture the mental state's forward-looking nature at this point in the lawmaker's decision-making process. Relatedly, I use the term *intention* to refer both to the lawmaker's ultimate goal and to the course of action that she deploys to meet that goal. See Kenny, *Metaphysics of Mind*, 63, on the distinction between forward-looking intentions and backward-looking motives.

30. Even a committed consequentialist would care about the intentions of lawmakers, since they provide evidence regarding the types of legal rules they are likely to adopt in the future.

from doing A without explicitly prohibiting the behavior. However, in order for this strategy to work, voters have to be sufficiently mistaken about the lawmaker's actual intentions.

I will say that a legal rule is the product of *stealth regulation* if it is based on minoritarian intentions but citizens incorrectly believe that it is based on majoritarian ones. Moreover, a legal rule is based on *antipaternalism* assumptions to the extent that it reflects an intention of lawmakers to treat regulated parties as either (1) perfectly rational actors with no self-control problems or (2) fully autonomous actors, who may have self-control problems but not of the sort that would warrant the state's taking away their freedom to act as they wish. Finally, a legal rule is *long-term directed* if it evinces an intention by lawmakers to maximize the long-term intertemporal utility of regulated parties. A necessary condition for a rule being long-term directed is that it does not take advantage of people's short-term preference for immediate gratification.

Assume that a legal rule provides that parties can do A only if they purchase a license costing $100 first and that Mary believes that doing A is long-run worthwhile but repeatedly procrastinates. If Joe observes that Mary never does A, and he believes that she has time-consistent preferences, he will conclude that the value to Mary of doing A is less than $100. Suppose, instead, that Joe knows that Mary is procrastinating due to her time-inconsistent preferences; and that he also incorrectly believes that the legal rule requiring the license is based on antipaternalism assumptions and is long-term directed. A person who holds these two beliefs will conclude that the lawmaker intends to dissuade people from doing A only in cases in which action A is not long-run worthwhile. Therefore, even though Joe knows that Mary is procrastinating, he does not hold the lawmaker accountable for this fact. It follows that an important cost of misattributing the antipaternalism assumption (when coupled with the lack of transparency about the true intentions of lawmakers) is that it makes it easier for lawmakers to engage in stealth regulation and thus to avoid full democratic accountability.

## Abortion and Stealth Regulation

Let us apply this logic to the example of abortion law. I will assume that a woman will decide to get an abortion only if she believes that it would maximize her long-term welfare. Nonetheless, a woman with time-inconsistent preferences who has concluded that getting an abortion is long-run worthwhile may make repeated short-term decisions to delay having the procedure. This means that some women will carry their pregnancies to term solely because they procrastinated past the period in which abortions are legally allowed.

The benefits from an abortion are usually received over relatively long periods of time following the abortion. On the other hand, the procedure itself involves a variety of immediate costs, including the effort required to arrange for the abortion and to follow through with it; the immediate toll in emotions, anxiety, and internal moral conflict at the time of getting the abortion; legal obstacles that increase the time, effort, and cost of the abortion; the disutility from encountering protesters outside a clinic; and the financial resources required to pay for the abortion.

The Supreme Court has held that a state cannot prohibit a woman from having an abortion prior to the viability of the fetus,[31] nor can it, during that period, impose "a substantial obstacle in the path of a woman seeking an abortion."[32] What exactly is being protected by these rulings? At the very least, *Roe v. Wade* and its progeny protect a woman's right to *carry out* a decision to terminate her pregnancy. A state-provided obstacle that has the effect of preventing a woman from following through with her decision to terminate a pregnancy is presumably "substantial" in nature. A bald prohibition would be one example; but what else would constitute a substantial obstacle?

A lawmaker with an intention to prevent women from getting abortions and who is constrained by either public opinion or the Constitution can nonetheless decrease the number of abortions merely by creating obstacles that require women to experience additional immediate disutility at the time of the abortion or during the deliberation process. Assume that a majority of citizens believe that a woman should have a right to choose whether or not to get an abortion and that if they knew of the lawmaker's minoritarian intentions, they would hold him or her accountable. The lawmaker will be able to engage in stealth regulation to the extent that citizens incorrectly believe that the legal rule erecting these obstacles is based on antipaternalism assumptions and is long-term directed.

Moreover, if the Supreme Court adopts the standard economics assumption that people have time-consistent preferences and would never procrastinate, it is more likely to conclude that state-imposed obstacles to abortions are benign. For example, the Supreme Court has upheld state laws that prohibit doctors from performing abortions unless they have given patients information about the nature and health risks of the procedure.[33] The Court has also upheld state laws that impose a 24-hour waiting period between the time the patient receives this information and the procedure itself. On their face, these two requirements appear to be relatively harmless—they seem to impose a relatively small cost on women who have already made a decision to get an abortion. However, these costs are immediate in nature and can lead a subset of these women to repeatedly procrastinate. For example, while the required disclosures can help with a woman's deliberation process, they also increase the immediate

---

31. *Roe v. Wade*, 410 U.S. 113 (1973).
32. *Planned Parenthood v. Casey*, 505 U.S. 833, 877–878 (1992).
33. *Planned Parenthood v. Casey*, 833, 882–883.

disutility or anxiety of getting an abortion. Moreover, suppose that a woman has determined to get an abortion and has endured the immediate anxiety, other psychic disutility, and effort of getting to a clinic, where she is told that the doctor is required by law to wait 24 hours before performing the procedure. When the woman returns to the clinic, she will have to bear the same type of immediate costs as before, and while familiarity may have reduced some of them, others may have been magnified by the information that she received during the first visit. The procrastination model developed in the first part of this chapter predicts that, given these immediate costs, a subset of women who go to the clinic intent on having an abortion and are forced to wait 24 hours will procrastinate with regard to returning to the clinic. As a result, they will either get the abortion later than they had originally intended, or, if they procrastinate past the viability deadline, they will carry the pregnancy to term, notwithstanding their beliefs that the abortion is long-run worthwhile.

Finally, while the immediate costs of getting an abortion will lead to the potential of repeated procrastination, all other things being equal, the existence of a salient viability deadline will have the effect of *increasing* the number of abortions that are actually performed. This is a counterintuitive result, given that proponents of choice generally favor removing such a deadline, while opponents of abortions want to retain it. To see the general intuition, suppose that there is no viability deadline but that there is a biological one: a woman who has repeatedly procrastinated may, after some point in time, decide that the pregnancy is so advanced that it is no longer worthwhile to get an abortion (or possible, since at an extreme, the deadline would be the birth of the child). The biological deadline may vary among women and, in any case, is not easy for them to identify ex ante. As a result, it is possible that some women will procrastinate past their biological deadline but would get the abortion if they were faced by a salient legal viability deadline.[34]

## Generalizing the Concept of Stealth Regulation

Whenever two actors are bound to each other in some sort of long-term relationship, they may be able to influence each other's behavior by taking advantage of their self-control problems. Therefore, the intuitions behind time-inconsistent obedience and stealth regulation apply more generally to any context in which two or more actors are bound in a codependent relationship, as is the case in criminal conspiracies, corporations, and romantic relationships.

---

34. As a general matter, a deadline with a penalty can act as a commitment device by increasing the delayed loss of procrastinating past the deadline; see Utset, "Hyperbolic Criminals," 637.

*Defecting from Conspiracies.* I argued above that even when an offender wants to deviate from a path of criminal misconduct, she will have an incentive to delay if the immediate costs of exit are sufficiently high. One implication of this fact is that the punishment needed for conspiracy leaders to keep members from defecting, if immediate enough, will be *lower* than those predicted by standard collusion models. In other words, the punishment only has to be sufficiently high and immediate to cause co-conspirators with a long-run preference to exit to repeatedly procrastinate. More generally, it follows that, once formed, hate groups, gangs, cartels, and criminal organizations will be more cohesive than standard economic theory predicts. As a result, a lawmaker who wants to cause group members to defect will need to adopt policies that decrease the immediate costs of exit or, alternatively, that increase the immediate or delayed rewards from leaving the group—for example, immediate monetary rewards for defectors and whistle-blowers or delayed benefits such as reductions in sentences and witness protection for defectors and their families.

*Management Misconduct and Gatekeeper Oversight.* The ability of corporate managers to engage in self-dealing and become entrenched will depend on the level of monitoring and disciplining activities by activist shareholders, the board of directors, creditors, regulators, lawyers, and accountants; let us call these monitoring parties gatekeepers. Given the procrastination model, it follows that a manager who is sufficiently aware of the time-inconsistent preferences of gatekeepers would want to adopt strategies that increase the immediate costs that they have to incur in order to identify and punish managerial misconduct. This entrenchment argument can be generalized to other types of institutional changes. For example, once corporate cultures and other institutional rules are established, they may gather path dependence, even though the costs of making institutional changes are relatively low. In other words, even if each member of an institution is willing to incur the full costs of making these changes, each may repeatedly procrastinate. Moreover, an actor who opposes institutional change can exacerbate this procrastination problem by adopting strategies that increase the immediate costs of making these changes.

One can interpret a number of provisions in the Sarbanes-Oxley Act as helping to reduce procrastination by gatekeepers. A manager who wants to prevent board members and auditors from challenging the accuracy of financial statements may try to pressure them into not challenging the financials by threatening to punish defectors. Sections 301 and 303 of Sarbanes-Oxley help reduce the ability of managers to impose immediate costs on gatekeepers by, among other things, requiring that audit committees be wholly composed of nonmanagement directors and punishing attempts by managers to pressure auditors.[35] Additionally, section 307

---

35. Sarbanes-Oxley Act of 2002, §§301, 303.

addresses procrastination by corporate counsel by reducing the immediate costs of confronting managers engaged in misconduct and increasing the delayed penalty for lawyers who procrastinate with regard to disclosing ongoing illegal activity.

Finally, lawmakers can take advantage of time-inconsistent *obedience* of gatekeepers by increasing the immediate costs of engaging in negligent or illegal monitoring activity. One such approach is to adopt gatekeeper schemes in which gatekeepers not only engage in their usual monitoring activities but also police each other. One example is section 404 of Sarbanes-Oxley, which requires (1) managers to make representations regarding the company's internal control procedures and (2) auditors "to attest to, and report on, the assessment made by the management."[36] This two-step requirement, in turn, leads accounting firms to hire lawyers to help prepare their attestations. While section 404 imposes potentially high compliance costs, critics have overlooked the fact that this sort of cross-monitoring scheme can help reduce the overall cost of deterring misconduct by fostering time-inconsistent obedience by managers and auditors.

*Leaving Abusive Relationships.* Spousal abuse is a leading cause of injury to women.[37] The abuse may be physical or psychological and may be directed at both the woman and her children. In a common spousal-abuse scenario, a woman is abused by her husband in repeated, albeit intermittent fashion over a long period of time. The abuse occurs in cycles in which a period of abuse is followed by one of nonabusive interactions.[38] As a general matter, abused spouses remain in relationships longer than appears rational to outside observers. While a number of explanations have been offered for this observed delay in terminating these relationships, one that has been overlooked by commentators is that the immediate costs of exit may lead abused spouses to repeatedly procrastinate with regard to following through with a planned exit.

As with the other types of exit decisions discussed above, a batterer who wants to cause a spouse to continue in the relationship can either increase the immediate cost or decrease the delayed benefits from ending the relationship. The benefits from leaving a batterer will be greatest during periods of abuse, but this is also the point in time at which the immediate costs of exit—in the form of potential violence or withholding economic support—are most salient. A woman who believes that exit is long-run worthwhile may thus stay in the relationship longer than she herself believes rational. This fact helps explain why battered women's shelters are effective. Since shelters only provide temporary economic support and protection against violence, they are unlikely to supply a

---

36. Sarbanes-Oxley Act, §404(b).
37. Mahoney, "Legal Images," 10–11.
38. Koons, "Gunsmoke and Legal Mirrors," 671.

sufficiently high benefit to lead a woman who believes that staying in the abusive relationship is long-run worthwhile to conclude otherwise. However, shelters help reduce the immediate costs of executing a planned exit and therefore help reduce the incentive to procrastinate.

Recognizing the role played by time-inconsistent preferences in battered-spouse relationships is important for another reason. A number of states have adopted legal rules that require police officers answering domestic-violence calls to arrest the batterer, as well as "no-drop" policies, which prevent complaining spouses from dropping spousal-abuse charges. While these two types of rules address some important concerns, they can increase the immediate costs of reporting batterers, which may again deter women from taking actions that are long-run worthwhile—that is, reporting the abuse. To see this, note that when the battered spouse's choice not to press for an arrest or a prosecution is taken away, the reporting spouse loses a valuable option: to wait until later to see if she really wants to exit the relationship or trigger legal proceedings. On the other hand, if the police cannot be trusted to arrest batterers who may harm the reporting spouse, it would lead to an increase in the immediate cost of exit and greater procrastination. However, a better policy is to give the police greater discretion but under stricter guidelines regarding what types of scenarios should trigger an arrest.

## CONCLUSION

This chapter has argued that repeated procrastination can have important effects on the way legal rules operate and their overall efficacy. In particular, it develops a simple model of procrastination that builds on the empirical findings that people routinely exhibit short-term preferences for avoiding immediate costs. In order to capture this preference for immediate gratification, I introduced an immediacy multiplier that does not affect an intertemporal decision maker's long-term decisions but leads her to give added weight to the immediate costs of executing a planned action. As a result, a person can be said to procrastinate whenever at time $t$, she concludes that doing A at time $\tau$ is long-run worthwhile, but when time $\tau$ arrives, her immediacy multiplier leads her to conclude that doing A in that period is not short-run worthwhile.

The second and third parts of the chapter applied this model to a number of legal areas. In particular, the model predicts that offenders who conclude that violating the law is not long-run worthwhile may nonetheless engaged in repeated time-inconsistent misconduct. Using a similar reasoning, the model predicts that in some cases, a person who has a long-term preference to violate the law may repeatedly procrastinate with regard to following through with the planned, value-maximizing misconduct. While benevolent lawmakers may adopt legal rules that help to properly deter time-inconsistent misconduct, a nonbenevolent lawmaker may try to exploit the phenomenon of time-inconsistent obedience. In particular, a lawmaker who wants to prohibit people from doing A but who believes that such a policy would encounter opposition from the electorate may, instead, adopt a legal rule that allows people to do A but imposes sufficiently high immediate cost to doing so that it leads a subset of actors with a long-term preference to do A to never follow through. To the extent that citizens incorrectly believe that lawmakers would not take advantage of their self-control problems, lawmakers will be able to engage in stealth regulation, effectively prohibiting certain types of behavior without bearing the full political cost of those prohibitions.

## ACKNOWLEDGMENTS

I would like to thank participants in the CSMN workshop for their comments during the conference and particularly Mark White and Chrisoula Andreou for their helpful written comments.

# Bibliography

Aarts, Henk, Ap Dijksterhuis, and Cees Midden. "To Plan or Not to Plan? Goal Achievement of Interrupting the Performance of Mundane Behaviors." *European Journal of Social Psychology* 29 (1999): 971–979.

Achtziger, Anja, Ute C. Bayer, and Peter M. Gollwitzer. In press. "Committing Oneself to Implementation Intentions: Attention and Memory Effects for Selected Situational Cues." *Motivation and Emotion*.

Achtziger, Anja, Peter M. Gollwitzer, and Paschal Sheeran. "Implementation Intentions and Shielding Goal Striving from Unwanted Thoughts and Feelings." *Personality and Social Psychology Bulletin* 34 (2008): 381–393.

Adams, Henry. *The Education of Henry Adams*. Ed. by Ernest Samuels. Boston: Houghton Mifflin, 1973.

Ainslie, George. *Breakdown of Will*. Cambridge: Cambridge University Press, 2001.

———. "Can Thought Experiments Prove Anything about the Will?" In *Distributed Cognition and the Will: Individual Volition and Social Context*, ed. by Don Ross, David Spurrett, Harold Kincaid, and G. Lynn Stephens, 169–196. Cambridge, Mass.: MIT Press, 2007.

———. "The Dangers of Willpower: A Picoeconomic Understanding of Addiction and Dissociation." In *Getting Hooked: Rationality and Addiction*, ed. by Jon Elster and Ole-Jørgen Skog, 65–92. Cambridge: Cambridge University Press, 1999.

———. "The Core Process in Addictions and Other Impulses: Hyperbolic Discounting versus Conditioning and Cognitive Framing." In *What Is Addiction?* ed. by Don Ross, Harold Kincaid, David Spurrett, and Peter Collins, 211–245. Cambridge, Mass.: MIT Press, 2010.

———. "Impulse Control in Pigeons." *Journal of the Experimental Analysis of Behavior* 21 (1974): 485–489.

———. "Motivation Must Be Momentary." In *Understanding Choice, Explaining Behaviour: Essays in Honor of Ole-Jørgen Skog*, ed. by Jon Elster, Olav Gjelsvik, Aanund Hylland, and Karl Moene, 9–24. Oslo: Unipub Forlag/Oslo Academic Press, 2006.

———. *Picoeconomics: The Strategic Interaction of Successive Motivational States within the Person*. Cambridge: Cambridge University Press, 1992.

———. "Pleasure and Aversion: Challenging the Conventional Dichotomy." *Inquiry*, 52 (2009): 357–377.

———. "Précis of *Breakdown of Will*." *Behavioral and Brain Sciences* 28 (2005): 635–673.

———. "Specious Reward: A Behavioral Theory of Impulsiveness and Impulse Control." *Psychological Bulletin* 82 (1975): 463–496.

Ainslie, George, and John Monterosso. "Building Blocks of Self-Control: Increased Tolerance for Delay with Bundled Rewards." *Journal of the Experimental Analysis of Behavior* 79 (2003): 83–94.

Ajzen, Icek. "The Theory of Planned Behavior." *Organizational Behavior and Human Decision Processes* 50 (1991): 179–211.

Akerlof, George. "Procrastination and Obedience." *American Economic Review* 81, no. 2 (1991): 1–19.

Allen, David. *Getting Things Done: The Art of Stress-Free Productivity*. New York: Penguin, 2001.

Andersen, Steffan, Glenn Harrison, Morten Lau, and E. Elisabet Rutstrom. "Eliciting Risk and Time Preferences." *Econometrica* 76 (2008): 583–618.

Anderson, Joel. "Autonomielücken als soziale Pathologie. Ideologiekritik jenseits des Paternalismus" ["Autonomy Gaps as Social Pathology: *Ideologiekritik* without Paternalism"], trans. R. Celikates and E. Engels. In *Sozialphilosophie und Kritik*, ed. by Rainer Forst, Martin Hartmann, Rahel Jaeggi, and Martin Saar, 433–453. Frankfurt: Suhrkamp, 2009.

Anderson, John R. *The Architecture of Cognition*. Cambridge, Mass.: Harvard University Press, 1983.

Andreou, Chrisoula. "Environmental Damage and the Puzzle of the Self-Torturer." *Philosophy and Public Affairs* 34 (2006): 95–108.

———. "Environmental Preservation and Second-Order Procrastination." *Philosophy and Public Affairs* 35 (2007): 233–248.

———. "Going from Bad (or Not So Bad) to Worse: On Harmful Addictions and Habits." *American Philosophical Quarterly* 42 (2005): 323–31.

———. "Instrumentally Rational Myopic Planning." *Philosophical Papers* 33 (2004): 133–145.

———. "Making a Clean Break: Addiction and Ulysses Contracts." *Bioethics* 22 (2008): 25–31.

———. "Temptation and Deliberation." *Philosophical Studies* 131 (2006): 583–606.

———. "Understanding Procrastination." *Journal for the Theory of Social Behaviour* 37 (2007): 183–193.

Annas, Julia. *The Morality of Happiness*. New York: Oxford University Press, 1995.

Anscombe, G. E. M. *Intention*, 2nd ed. Ithaca, N.Y.: Cornell University Press, 1985.

———. "Modern Moral Philosophy." In *Virtue Ethics*, ed. by Roger Crisp and Michael Slote, 26–44. Oxford: Oxford University Press, 1997.

Ariely, Dan. *Predictably Irrational: The Hidden Forces That Shape Our Decisions*. New York: HarperCollins, 2008.

Ariely, Dan, and Klaus Wertenbroch. "Procrastination, Deadlines, and Performance: Self-Control by Pre-Commitment." *Psychological Science* 13 (2002): 219–224.

Aristotle. *Nicomachean Ethics*. Trans. by David Ross. Oxford: Oxford University Press, 1998.

Arkes, Hal R., and Catherine Blumer. "The Psychology of Sunk Cost." *Organizational Behavior and Human Decision Processes* 35 (1985): 124–140.

Arpaly, Nomi. "On Acting Rationally against One's Best Judgment." *Ethics* 110 (2000): 488–513.

Arvey, Richard D., Maria Rotundo, Wendy Johnson, Zhen Zhang, and Matt McGue. "The Determinants of Leadership Role Occupancy: Genetic and Personality Factors." *Leadership Quarterly* 17 (2006): 1–20.

Asheim, Geir B. "Procrastination, Partial Naiveté, and Behavioral Welfare Analysis." Memorandum 02/2007, Department of Economics, University of Oslo, revised August 2008. Available at http://folk.uio.no/gasheim/procra02.pdf (accessed August 17, 2009).

Audi, Robert. "Weakness of Will and Rational Action." *Australasian Journal of Philosophy* 68 (1990): 270–281.

Augustine. *The Confessions of Saint Augustine*. Trans. by Edward B. Pusey. New York: Random House, 1949.

Bacharach, Michael. *Beyond Individual Choice*. Princeton: Princeton University Press, 2006.

Bain, Alexander. *The Emotions and the Will*. New York: Appleton, 1859/1886.

Bandura, Albert. *Self-Efficacy: The Exercise of Control*. New York: Freeman, 1997.

Bargh, John A. "Conditional Automaticity: Varieties of Automatic Influence in Social Perception and Cognition." In *Unintended Thought*, ed. by James Uleman and John A. Bargh, 3–51. New York: Guilford, 1989.

Bargh, John A., and Kimberly Barndollar. "Automaticity in Action: The Unconscious as Repository of Chronic Goals and Motives." In *The Psychology of Action: Linking Cognition and Motivation to Behavior*, ed. by Peter M. Gollwitzer and John A. Bargh, 457–481. New York: Guilford, 1996.

Bargh, John A., and Tanya L. Chartrand. "The Unbearable Automaticity of Being." *American Psychologist* 54 (1999): 467–468.

Baumeister, Roy F., Ellen Bratslavsky, Mark Muraven, and Dianne M. Tice. "Ego Depletion: Is the Active Self a Limited Resource?" *Journal of Personality and Social Psychology* 74 (1998): 1252–1265.

Baumeister, Roy F., and Todd Heatherton. "Self-Regulation Failure: An Overview." *Psychological Inquiry* 7 (1996): 1–15.

Baumeister, Roy F., Todd Heatherton, and Dianne M. Tice. *Losing Control*. Burlington, Mass.: Academic Press, 1994.

Baumeister, Roy F., and Kathleen Vohs, eds. *Handbook of Self-Regulation: Research, Theory and Applications*. New York: Guilford, 2007.

Bayer, Ute C., Anja Achtziger, Peter M. Gollwitzer, and Gordon Moskowitz. "Responding to Subliminal Cues: Do If-Then Plans Cause Action Preparation and Initiation without Conscious Intent?" *Social Cognition* 27 (2009): 183–201.

Becerra, Lino, Hans C. Breiter, Roy Wise, R. Gilberto Gonzalez, and David Borsook. "Reward Circuitry Activation by Noxious Thermal Stimuli." *Neuron* 32 (2001): 927–946.

Beck, Ulrich. *Risk Society: Towards a New Modernity*. London: Sage, 1992.

Becker, Gary S. "Crime and Punishment: An Economic Approach." *Journal of Political Economy* 76 (1968): 169–217.

Becker, Gary S., and Kevin Murphy. "A Theory of Rational Addiction." *Journal of Political Economy* 96 (1988): 675–700.

Becker, Howard S. "Notes on the Concept of Commitment." *American Journal of Sociology* 66 (1960): 32–40.

Bénabou, Roland, and Jean Tirole. "Willpower and Personal Rules." *Journal of Political Economy* 112 (2004): 848–886.

Benhabib, Jess, and Alberto Bisin. "Modeling Internal Commitment Mechanisms and Self-Control: A Neuroeconomics Approach to Consumption-Saving Decisions." *Games and Economic Behavior* 52 (2004): 460–492.

Bernheim, B. Douglas, and Antonio Rangel. "Addiction and Cue-Triggered Decision Processes." *American Economic Review* 94 (2004): 1558–1590.

Berns, Gregory S., C. Monica Capra, and Charles Noussair. "Receptor Theory and Biological Constraints on Value." *Annals of the New York Academy of Sciences* 1104 (2007): 301–309.

Berridge, Kent C. "Motivation Concepts in Behavioral Neuroscience." *Physiology and Behavior* 81 (2004): 179–209.

Bickel, Warren K., and Matthew W. Johnson. "Delay Discounting: A Fundamental Behavioral Process of Drug Dependence." In *Time and Decision: Economic and Psychological Perspectives on Intertemporal Choice*, ed. by George Loewenstein, Daniel Read, and Roy F. Baumeister, 419–440. New York: Russell Sage Foundation, 2003.

Boice, Robert. "Quick Starters: New Faculty Who Succeed." *New Directions for Teaching and Learning* 48 (1991): 111–121.

Boice, Robert. *Procrastination and Blocking: A Novel, Practical Approach*. Westport, Conn.: Praeger, 1996.

Brandstätter, Veronika, Dörte Heimbeck, Juliane T. Malzacher, and Michael Frese. "Goals Need Implementation Intentions: The Model of Action Phases Tested in the Applied Setting of Continuing Education." *European Journal of Work and Organizational Psychology* 12 (2003): 37–59.

Brandstätter, Veronika, Angelika Lengfelder, and Peter M. Gollwitzer. "Implementation Intentions and Efficient Action Initiation." *Journal of Personality and Social Psychology* 81 (2001): 946–960.

Bratman, Michael E. *Faces of Intention: Selected Essays on Intention and Agency*. Cambridge: Cambridge University Press, 1999.

———. *Intention, Plans, and Practical Reason*. Cambridge, Mass.: Harvard University Press, 1987.

———. "Planning and Temptation." In *Faces of Intention: Selected Essays on Intention and Agency*, 35–57. Cambridge: Cambridge University Press, 1999.

———. "Temptation Revisited." In *Structures of Agency: Essays*, 257–282. Oxford: Oxford University Press, 2007.

Brennan, Timothy J. "Voluntary Exchange and Economic Claims." *Research in the History of Economic Thought and Methodology* 7 (1990): 105–124.

Brockner, Joel. "The Escalation of Commitment to a Failing Course of Action: Toward Theoretical Progress." *Academy of Management Review* 17 (1992): 39–61.

Broome, John. "Does Rationality Consist in Responding Correctly to Reasons?" *Journal of Moral Philosophy* 4 (2007): 349–374.

———. *Ethics out of Economics*. Cambridge: Cambridge University Press, 1999.

———. "Reasoning with Preferences?" In *Preferences and Well-Being*, ed. by Serena Olsaretti, 183–208. Cambridge: Cambridge University Press, 2006.

Bruner, Jerome. *Acts of Meaning: Four Lectures on Mind and Culture*. Cambridge, Mass.: Harvard University Press, 1992.

Buehler, Roger, Dale Griffin, and Michael Ross. "Exploring the Planning Fallacy." *Journal of Personality and Social Psychology* 67 (1994): 366–81.

Burge, Tyler. "Individualism and the Mental." *Midwest Studies in Philosophy* 4 (1979): 73–121.

Burka, Jane B., and Lenora M. Yuen. *Procrastination: Why You Do It, What to Do about It*. Cambridge, Mass.: Da Capo, 1990.

Butler, Joseph. "Of Personal Identity." In *Personal Identity*, ed. by John Perry, 99–105. Berkeley: University of California Press, 1975.

Carroll, Lewis. *Through the Looking Glass*. In *Complete Works*, 131–272. New York: Vintage/Random House, 1976.

Carver, Charles S., and Michael Scheier. "Principles of Self-Regulation: Action and Emotion." In *Handbook of Motivation and Cognition: Foundations of Social Behavior*, Vol. 2, ed. by E. Tory Higgins and Richard M. Sorrentino, 3–52. New York: Guilford, 1990.

Chapman, Janine, Christopher J. Armitage, and Paul Norman. "Comparing Implementation Intention Interventions in Relation to Young Adults' Intake of Fruit and Vegetables." *Psychology and Health* 24 (2009): 317–332.

Christensen-Szalanski, Jay. "Discount Functions and the Measurement of Patients' Values: Women's Decisions during Childbirth." *Medical Decision Making* 4 (1984): 47–58.

Cicero. *Philippics*. Trans. by Walter C. A. Ker. Suffolk, U.K.: St. Edmundsbury, 1926.

Clark, Andy. *Being There: Putting Brain, Body, and World Together Again*. Cambridge, Mass.: MIT Press, 1997.

Conti, Regina. "Competing Demands and Complimentary [sic] Motives: Procrastination on Intrinsically and Extrinsically Motivated Projects." *Journal of Social Behavior and Personality* 15, no. 5 (2000): 47–60.

Cooter, Robert D. "Lapses, Conflict, and Akrasia in Torts and Crimes: Towards an Economic Theory of the Will." *International Review of Law and Economics* 11 (1991): 149–164.

Damasio, Antonio. *Descartes' Error*. New York: Putnam, 1994.

Davidson, Donald. *Essays on Actions and Events*. Oxford: Clarendon Press, 1980.

———. "How Is Weakness of the Will Possible?" In *Essays on Actions and Events*, 21–42. Oxford: Clarendon Press, 1980.

———. "Intending." In *Essays on Actions and Events*, 83–102. Oxford: Clarendon Press, 1980.

Delaney, Liam, Carolyn Rawdon, Kevin Denny, Wen Zhang, and Richard Roche. "Event-Related Potentials Reveal Differential Brain Regions Implicated in Discounting in Two Tasks." Working Paper 200811, Geary Institute, University College Dublin. Available at http://ideas.repec.org/p/ucd/wpaper/200811.html.

Deluty, Martin Z. "Self-Control and Impulsiveness involving Aversive Events." *Journal of Experimental Psychology: Animal Behavior Processes* 4 (1978): 250–266.

Deluty, Martin Z., Wayne G. Whitehouse, Mark Millitz, and Phillip N. Hineline. "Self-Control and Commitment involving Aversive Events." *Behavior Analysis Letters* 3 (1983): 213–219.

Dennett, Daniel. *Consciousness Explained*. Boston: Little, Brown, 1991.

———. "Why You Can't Make a Computer That Feels Pain." In *Brainstorms: Philosophical Essays on Mind and Psychology*, 190–229. Cambridge, Mass.: Bradford, 1978.

Dijksterhuis, Ap, and John A. Bargh. "The Perceptual-Behavior Expressway: Automatic Effects of Social Perception and Social Behavior." In *Advances in Experimental Social Psychology*, Vol. 30, ed. by M. Zanna, 1–40. New York: Academic Press, 2001.

Dodd, Dylan. "Weakness of Will as Intention-Violation." *European Journal of Philosophy* 17 (2009): 45–59.

Doris, John M. *Lack of Character: Personality and Moral Behavior*. Cambridge: Cambridge University Press, 2002.

Dreier, James. "Humean Doubts about Categorical Imperatives." In *Varieties of Practical Reasoning*, ed. by Elijah Millgram, 27–47. Cambridge, Mass.: MIT Press, 2001.

Dweck, Carol. "Motivational Processes Affect Learning," *American Psychologist* 41 (1986): 1040–1048.

Edwards, Jonathan. "Procrastination or the Sin and Folly of Depending on Future Time." Available at http://www.biblebb.com/files/edwards/procrastination.htm (accessed February 28, 2009).

Ellis, Albert, and Williams J. Knaus. *Overcoming Procrastination*. New York: Signet, 1977.

Elster, Jon. *Alchemies of the Mind: Rationality and the Emotions*. Cambridge: Cambridge University Press, 1999.

———. *Explaining Social Behavior*. Cambridge: Cambridge University Press, 2007.

———. *Solomonic Judgements: Studies in the Limitations of Rationality*. Cambridge: Cambridge University Press, 1989.

———. *Ulysses and the Sirens: Studies in Rationality and Irrationality*. Cambridge: Cambridge University Press, 1984.

———. *Ulysses Unbound: Studies in Rationality, Precommitment, and Constraints*. Cambridge: Cambridge University Press, 2000.

———. "Urgency." *Inquiry* 52 (2009): 399–411.

———. "Weakness of Will and Preference Reversals." In *Understanding Choice, Explaining Behaviour: Essays in Honor of Ole-Jørgen Skog*, ed. by Jon Elster, Olav Gjelsvik, Aanund Hylland, and Karl Moene, 57–73. Oslo: Unipub Forlag/Oslo Academic Press, 2006.

Engle, Randall. "What Is Working Memory Capacity?" In *The Nature of Remembering: Essays in Honor of Robert G. Crowder*, ed. by Henry Roediger III and James Nairne, 297–314. Washington, D.C.: American Psychological Association, 2001.

Engstrom, Stephen. "The Inner Freedom of Virtue." In *Kant's Metaphysics of Morals: Interpretative Essays*, ed. by Mark Timmons, 289–315. Oxford: Oxford University Press, 2002.

Epictetus. *Handbook of Epictetus*. Trans. by Nicholas White. Indianapolis: Hackett, 1983.

Epicurus. "Letter to Menoeceus 121–135." In *Voices of Ancient Philosophy: An Introductory Reader*, ed. by Julia Annas, 338–340. New York: Oxford University Press, 2000.

Ferrari, Joseph R. "Procrastination as Self-Regulation Failure of Performance: Effects of Cognitive Load, Self-Awareness, and Time Limits on 'Working Best under Pressure.'" *European Journal of Personality* 15 (2001): 391–406.

Ferrari, Joseph R., and John F. Dovidio. "Examining Behavioral Processes in Indecision: Decisional Procrastination and Decision-Making Style." *Journal of Research in Personality* 34 (2000): 127–137.

Ferrari, Joseph R., Judith L. Johnson, and William G. McCowen. *Procrastination and Task Avoidance: Theory, Research, and Treatment*. New York: Springer, 1995.

Ferrari, Joseph R., and T. Patel. "Social Comparisons by Procrastinators: Rating Peers with Similar or Dissimilar Delay Tendencies." *Personality and Individual Differences* 37 (2004): 1493–1501.

Ferrari, Joseph R., and Timothy Pychyl, eds. *Procrastination: Current Issues and New Directions*. Corte Madera, Calif.: Select, 2000.

Fischer, Carolyn. "Read This Paper Even Later: Procrastination with Time-Inconsistent Preferences." Working paper. 1999. Available at http://www.rff.org/documents/RFF-DP-99-19.pdf.

———. "Read This Paper Later: Procrastination with Time-Consistent Preferences." *Journal of Economic Behavior and Organization* 46 (2001): 249–69.

Franklin, Benjamin. *Autobiography*. New Haven, Conn.: Yale University Press, 1976.

Frederick, Shane, George Loewenstein, and Ted O'Donoghue. "Time Discounting and Time Preference: A Critical Review." In *Advances in Behavioral Economics*, ed. by Colin F. Camerer, George Loewenstein, and Matthew Rabin, 162–222. New York: Russell Sage Foundation, 2004.

Fried, Charles. *Contract as Promise: A Theory of Contractual Obligation*. Cambridge, Mass.: Harvard University Press, 1981.

Fudenberg, Drew, and David Levine. "A Dual Self Model of Impulse Control." Harvard Institute of Economic Research, Discussion Paper No. 2112. Available at http://papers.ssrn.com/sol3/papers.cfm?abstract_id=888752.

Gailliot, Matthew T., Roy F. Baumeister, C. Nathan DeWall, Jon K. Maner, E. Ashby Plant, Dianne M. Tice, Lauren E. Brewer, and Brandon J. Schmeichel. "Self-Control Relies on Glucose as a Limited Energy Source: Willpower Is More Than a Metaphor." *Journal of Personality and Social Psychology* 92 (2007): 325–336.

Garner, D. M., and S. C. Wooley. "Confronting the Failure of Behavioral and Dietary Treatments of Obesity." *Clinical Psychology Review* 11 (1991): 729–780.

Garvey, Andrew J., Taru Kinnunen, Zandra N. Quiles, and Pantel S. Vokonas. "Smoking Cessation Patterns in Adult Males Followed for 35 Years." Poster presented at Society for Research on Nicotine and Tobacco Annual Meetings, Savannah, Ga., 2002 (http://www.hsdm.harvard.edu/pdf-files/Dr._Garvey.pdf).

Gauthier, David. "Resolute Choice and Rational Deliberation: A Critique and Defense." *Noûs* 31 (1997): 1–25.

Gibbon, John. "Scalar Expectancy Theory and Weber's Law in Animal Timing." *Psychological Review* 84 (1977): 279–325.

Gilbert, Daniel T., and Jane E. J. Ebert. "Decisions and Revisions: The Affective Forecasting of Changeable Outcomes." *Journal of Personality and Social Psychology* 82 (2002): 503–514.

Gjelsvik, Olav. "Are There Reasons to Be Rational?" In *Homage à Wlodek: Philosophical Papers Dedicated to Wlodek Rabinowicz*, ed. by T. Rønnow-Rasmussen, B. Petersson, J. Josefsson, and D. Egonsson. 2007. Available at http://www.fil.lu.se/hommageawlodek.

Glimcher, Paul, Joe Kable, and Kenway Louie. "Neuroeconomic Studies of Impulsivity: Now or Just as Soon as Possible?" *American Economic Review* 97(2) (2007): 142–147.

Gollwitzer, Peter M. "Implementation Intentions: Strong Effects of Simple Plans." *American Psychologist* 54 (1999): 493–503.

Gollwitzer, Peter M., Ute Bayer, and Kathleen McCulloch. "The Control of the Unwanted." In *The New Unconscious*, ed. by Ran R. Hassin, James S. Uleman, and John A. Bargh, 485–515. Oxford: Oxford University Press, 2005.

Gollwitzer, Peter M., and Veronika Brandstätter. "Implementation Intentions and Effective Goal Pursuit." *Journal of Personality and Social Psychology* 73 (1997): 186–199.

Gollwitzer, Peter M., Caterina Gawrilow, and Gabriele Oettingen. "The Power of Planning: Self-Control by Effective Goal-Striving." In *Self-Control in Society, Mind, and Brain*, ed. by Ran R. Hassin, Kevin N. Ochsner, and Yaacov Trope, 279–296. Oxford: Oxford University Press, 2010.

Gollwitzer, Peter M., Elisabeth J. Parks-Stamm, Alexander Jaudas, and Paschal Sheeran. "Flexible Tenacity in Goal Pursuit." In *Handbook of Motivation Science*, ed. by James Y. Shah and Wendi L. Gardner, 325–341. New York: Guilford, 2008.

Gollwitzer, Peter M., and Bernd Schaal. "Metacognition in Action: The Importance of Implementation Intentions." *Personality and Social Psychology Review* 2 (1998): 124–136.

Gollwitzer, Peter M., and Paschal Sheeran. "Implementation Intentions and Goal Achievement: A Meta-Analysis of Effects and Processes." *Advances in Experimental Social Psychology* 38 (2006): 69–119.

Goncharov, Ivan. *Oblomov*. New York: Penguin, 1978.

Green, Leonard, and Joel Myerson. "A Discounting Framework for Choice with Delayed and Probabilistic Rewards." *Psychological Bulletin* 130 (2004): 769–792.

Gregor, Mary. *Laws of Freedom*. Oxford: Basil Blackwell, 1963.

Griffin, James. *Well-Being*. Oxford: Oxford University Press, 1988.

Gul, Farouk, and Wolfgang Pesendorfer. "The Simple Theory of Temptation and Self-Control." Working paper. Available at http://www.princeton.edu/~pesendor/finite.pdf.

———. "Temptation and Self-Control." *Econometrica* 69 (2001): 1403–1436.

Guyer, Paul. *Kant on Freedom, Law, and Happiness*. Cambridge: Cambridge University Press, 2000.

Habermas, Jürgen. "Individuation through Socialization: On George Herbert Mead's Theory of Subjectivity." In *Postmetaphysical Thinking: Between Metaphysics and the Critique of Reason*, 149–204. Cambridge, U.K.: Polity, 1994.

Hall, Brandon L., and Daniel E. Hursch. "An Evaluation of the Effects of a Time Management Training Program on Work Efficiency." *Journal of Organizational Behavior Management* 3 (1982): 73–96.

Hardin, Russell. *Collective Action*. Baltimore: Johns Hopkins University Press, 1982.

Hariri, Ahmed, Sarah Brown, Douglas Williamson, Janine Flory, Harriet de Wit, and Stephen Manuck. "Preference for Immediate over Delayed Rewards Is Associated with Magnitude of Ventral Striatal Activity." *Journal of Neuroscience* 26 (2006): 13213–13217.

Harriott, Jesse, and Joseph R. Ferrari. "Prevalence of Chronic Procrastination among Samples of Adults." *Psychological Reports* 73 (1996): 873–877.

Heath, Joseph. *Following the Rules*. New York: Oxford University Press, 2008.

Heatherton, Todd F., and Roy F. Baumeister. "Self-Regulation Failure: Past, Present, and Future." *Psychological Inquiry* 7 (1996): 90–98.

Helzer, John E., Audrey Burnham, and Lawrence T. McEvoy. "Alcohol Abuse and Dependence." In *Psychiatric Disorders in America: The Epidemiologic Catchment Area Study*, edited by Lee N. Robins and Darrel A. Regier, 81–115. New York: Free Press, 1991.

Henderson, Marlone D., Peter M. Gollwitzer, and Gabriele Oettingen. "Implementation Intentions and Disengagement from a Failing Course of Action." *Journal of Behavioral Decision Making* 20 (2007): 81–102.

Herrnstein, Richard J. "The Evolution of Behaviorism." *American Psychologist* 32 (1977): 593–603.

———. *The Matching Law*. Cambridge, Mass.: Harvard University Press, 1997.

———. "Melioration as Behavioral Dynamism." In *Quantitative Analyses of Behavior, Volume II: Matching and Maximizing Accounts*, ed. by Michael Commons, Richard J. Herrnstein, and Howard Rachlin, 433–458. Cambridge, Mass.: Ballinger, 1982.

———. "Relative and Absolute Strength of Response as a Function of Frequency of Reinforcement." *Journal of the Experimental Analysis of Behavior* 4 (1961): 267–272.

Herrnstein, Richard J., and Drazen Prelec. "A Theory of Addiction." In *Choice over Time*, ed. by George Loewenstein and Jon Elster, 331–361. New York: Russell Sage Foundation, 1992.

Heylighen, Francis, and Clément Vidal. "Getting Things Done: The Science behind Stress-Free Productivity." *Long Range Planning* 41 (2008): 585–605.

Hill, Thomas E. "Weakness of Will and Character." In *Autonomy and Self-Respect*, 118–137. Cambridge: Cambridge University Press, 1991.

Hoch, Stephen, and George Loewenstein. "Time-Inconsistent Preferences and Consumer Self-Control." *Journal of Consumer Research* 17 (1991): 492–507.

Holland, Rob W., Henk Aarts, and Daan Langendam. "Breaking and Creating Habits on the Work Floor: A Field Experiment on the Power of Implementation Intentions." *Journal of Experimental Social Psychology* 42 (2006): 776–783.

Holton, Richard. "How Is Strength of Will Possible?" In *Weakness of Will and Practical Irrationality*, ed. by Sarah Stroud and Christine Tappolet, 39–67. Oxford: Oxford University Press, 2003.

———. "Intention and Weakness of Will." *Journal of Philosophy* 96 (1999): 241–262.

Hursthouse, Rosalind. *On Virtue Ethics*. Oxford: Oxford University Press, 1999.

Hutchins, Edwin. *Cognition in the Wild*. Cambridge, Mass.: MIT Press, 1995.

James, William. *Principles of Psychology*. New York: Holt, 1890.

Jaspers, Karl. *General Psychopathology*. Baltimore: John Hopkins University Press, 1997.

Johansen, Leif. *Lectures on Macroeconomic Planning*. Amsterdam: North-Holland, 1977.

Johnson, Robert. "Virtue and Right." *Ethics* 113 (2003): 810–834.

Johnston, Mark. "Human Concerns without Superlative Selves." In *Reading Parfit*, edited by Jonathan Dancy, 149–179. Oxford: Blackwell, 1997.

Kachgal, Mera M., L. Sunny Hansen, and Kevin J. Nutter. "Academic Procrastination Prevention/Intervention: Strategies and Recommendations." *Journal of Developmental Education* 25 (2001): 14–25.

Kahneman, Daniel, and Amos Tversky. "Prospect Theory." *Econometrica* 47 (1979): 263–91.

Kant, Immanuel. *Anthropology from a Pragmatic Point of View*. Trans. by Victor Lyle Dowdell. Carbondale, Ill.: Southern Illinois University Press, 1978.

———. *The Metaphysics of Morals*. Trans. by Mary Gregor. Cambridge: Cambridge University Press, 1996.

———. *Religion within the Boundaries of Mere Reason*. In *Religion within the Boundaries of Mere Reason and Other Writings*, ed. by Allen Wood and George di Giovanni, 33–191. Cambridge: Cambridge University Press, 1998.

Katyal, Neal Kumar. "Conspiracy Theory." *Yale Law Journal* 112 (2003): 1307–1398.

Kenny, Anthony. *The Metaphysics of Mind*. New York: Oxford University Press, 1992.

Kim, Jeong-Yoon. "Hyperbolic Discounting and the Repeated Self-Control Problem." *Journal of Economic Psychology* 27 (2006): 344–359.

Kind, Amy. "The Metaphysics of Personal Identity and Our Special Concern for the Future." *Metaphilosophy* 35 (2004): 536–553.

Kirby, Kris N. "Bidding on the Future: Evidence against Normative Discounting of Delayed Rewards." *Journal of Experimental Psychology: General* 126 (1997): 54–70.

Kirby, Kris N., and Barbarose Guastello. "Making Choices in Anticipation of Similar Future Choices Can Increase Self-Control." *Journal of Experimental Psychology: Applied* 7 (2001): 154–164.

Knaus, William. "Procrastination, Blame, and Change." In *Procrastination: Current Issues and New Directions*, ed. by Joseph R. Ferrari and Timothy A. Pychyl, 153–166. Corte Madera, Calif.: Select, 2000.

Koons, Judith. "Gunsmoke and Legal Mirrors: Women Surviving Intimate Battery and Legal Doctrines." *Journal of Law and Policy* 14 (2006): 617–693.

Korsgaard, Christine. "The Normativity of Instrumental Reason." In *Ethics and Practical Reason*, ed. by Garrett Cullity and Berys Gaut, 215–254. Oxford: Oxford University Press, 1997.

Kruglanski, Arie, and Donna Webster. "Motivated Closing of the Mind: 'Seizing' and 'Freezing.'" *Journal of Personality and Social Psychology* 103 (1996): 263–283.

Kuhl, Julius. "A Functional-Design Approach to Motivation and Self-Regulation." In *Handbook of Self-Regulation*, ed. by Monique Boekaert, Paul Pintrich, and Moshe Zeidner, 111–169. San Diego, Calif.: Academic Press, 2001.

Laibson, David. "A Cue-Theory of Consumption." *Quarterly Journal of Economics* 66 (2001): 81–120.

———. "Golden Eggs and Hyperbolic Discounting." *Quarterly Journal of Economics* 62 (1997): 443–477.

———. "Life-Cycle Consumption and Hyperbolic Discount Functions." *European Economic Review* 42 (1998): 861–871.

Laibson, David, Andrea Repetto, and Jeremy Tobacman. "Self-Control and Saving for Retirement." *Brookings Papers on Economic Activity* 1 (1998): 91–196.

Lay, Clarry H. "Trait Procrastination, Agitation, Dejection, and Self-Discrepancy." In *Procrastination and Task Avoidance: Theory, Research, and Treatment*, ed. by Joseph R. Ferrari, Judith L. Johnson, and William G. McCown, 97–112. New York: Springer, 1995.

Lay, Clarry H., and Rosemarie Brokenshire. "Conscientiousness, Procrastination, and Person-Task Characteristics in Job Searching by Unemployed Adults." *Current Psychology* 16 (1997): 83–96.

Lay, Clarry H., and Stuart Silverman. "Trait Procrastination, Anxiety, and Dilatory Behavior." *Personality and Individual Differences* 21 (1996): 61–67.

Lazarus, Arnold. "Phobias: Broad-Spectrum Behavioral Views." *Seminars in Psychiatry* 4 (1972): 85–90.

Lea, Stephen E. G., and Paul Webley. "Money as Tool, Money as Drug: The Biological Psychology of a Strong Incentive." *Behavioral and Brain Sciences* 29 (2006): 161–209.

LeDoux, Joseph. *The Emotional Brain*. New York: Simon & Schuster, 1996.
Lengfelder, Angelika, and Peter M. Gollwitzer. "Reflective and Reflexive Action Control in Patients with Frontal Brain Lesions." *Neuropsychology* 15 (2001): 80–100.
Levy, Neil. "Self-Deception and Responsibility for Addiction." *Journal of Applied Philosophy* 20 (2003): 133–142.
Levy, R. A. "Failure to Refill Prescriptions: Incidence, Reasons and Remedies." In *Patient Compliance in Medical Practice and Clinical Trials*, ed. by Joyce Cramer and Bert Spilker, 11–18. New York: Raven, 1991.
Lively, Lynn. *The Procrastinator's Guide to Success*. London: McGraw-Hill, 1999.
Loewenstein, George. "Out of Control: Visceral Influences on Behavior." *Organizational Behavior and Human Decision Processes* 65 (1996): 272–292.
———. "A Visceral Account of Addiction." In *Getting Hooked: Rationality and Addiction*, ed. by Jon Elster and Ole-Jørgen Skog, 235–264. Cambridge: Cambridge University Press, 1999.
Loewenstein, George, and Richard H. Thaler. "Anomalies: Intertemporal Choice." *Journal of Economic Perspectives* 3, no. 4 (1989): 189–193.
Lynn, Steven J., and Judith W. Rhue. "Fantasy Proneness: Hypnosis, Developmental Antecedents, and Psychopathology." *American Psychologist* 43 (1988): 35–44.
MacIntosh, Duncan. "Buridan and the Circumstances of Justice (On the Implications of the Rational Unsolvability of Certain Co-ordination Problems)." *Pacific Philosophical Quarterly* 73 (1992): 150–173.
———. "Prudence and the Reasons of Rational Persons." *Australasian Journal of Philosophy* 79 (2001): 346–365.
Mahoney, Martha R. "Legal Images of Battered Women: Redefining the Issue of Separation." *Michigan Law Review* 90 (1991): 1–71.
Marcus, Gary. *Kluge: The Haphazard Construction of the Human Mind*. London: Faber and Faber, 2008.
Maunsell, John H. R. "Neuronal Representations of Cognitive State: Reward or Attention?" *Trends in Cognitive Sciences* 8 (2004): 261–265.
Maxwell, Bruce. *Professional Ethics Education: Studies in Compassionate Empathy*. Dordrecht: Springer, 2008.
Mazur, James E. "An Adjusting Procedure for Studying Delayed Reinforcement." In *Quantitative Analysis of Behavior Vol. 5: The Effect of Delay and of Intervening Events on Reinforcement Value*, ed. by Michael Commons, James Mazur, John Nevin, and Howard Rachlin, 55–73. Hillsdale, N.J.: Lawrence Erlbaum, 1987.
———. "Hyperbolic Value Addition and General Models of Animal Choice." *Psychological Review* 108 (2001): 96–112.
———. "Procrastination by Pigeons: Preference for Larger, More Delayed Work Requirements." *Journal of the Experimental Analysis of Behavior* 65 (1996): 159–171.
———. "Procrastination by Pigeons with Fixed-Interval Response Requirements." *Journal of the Experimental Analysis of Behavior* 69 (1998): 185–197.
McClennen, Edward F. "Pragmatic Rationality and Rules." *Philosophy and Public Affairs* 26 (1997): 210–258.
———. *Rationality and Dynamic Choices: Foundational Explanations*. Cambridge: Cambridge University Press, 1990.

McClure, Samuel, David Laibson, George Loewenstein, and Jonathan Cohen. "Separate Neural Systems Value Immediate and Delayed Monetary Rewards." *Science* 306 (2004): 503–507.

McDowell, John. *Mind, Value, and Reality*. Cambridge, Mass.: Harvard University Press, 1998.

———. "Reductionism and the First Person." In *Reading Parfit*, ed. by Jonathan Dancy, 230–250. Oxford: Blackwell, 1997.

McIntyre, Alison. "Is Akratic Action Always Irrational?" In *Identity, Character, and Morality: Essays in Moral Psychology*, ed. by Owen Flanagan and Amélie Oksenberg Rorty, 379–400. Cambridge, Mass.: MIT Press, 1993.

———. "What Is Wrong with Weakness of Will?" *Journal of Philosophy* 103 (2006): 284–311.

Mele, Alfred. *Irrationality: An Essay on Akrasia, Self-Deception and Self-Control*. New York: Oxford University Press, 1987.

Metcalfe, James, and Walter Mischel. "A Hot/Cool-System Analysis of Delay of Gratification: Dynamics of Willpower." *Psychological Review* 106 (1999): 3–19.

Millgram, Elijah. *Ethics Done Right: Practical Reasoning as a Foundation for Moral Theory*. Cambridge: Cambridge University Press, 2005.

———. *Practical Induction*. Cambridge, Mass.: Harvard University Press, 1997.

———. "Williams' Argument against External Reasons." *Noûs* 30 (1996): 197–220.

Milne, Sarah, Sheina Orbell, and Paschal Sheeran. "Combining Motivational and Volitional Interventions to Promote Exercise Participation: Protection Motivation Theory and Implementation Intentions." *British Journal of Health Psychology* 7 (2002): 163–184.

Mirrlees, James A. "The Optimal Structure of Incentives and Authority within an Organization." *Bell Journal of Economics* 7 (1976): 105–131.

Monterosso, John, and George Ainslie. "Beyond Discounting: Possible Experimental Models of Impulse Control." *Psychopharmacology* 146 (1999): 339–347.

Monterosso, John, George Ainslie, Pamela Toppi-Mullen, and Barbara Gault. "The Fragility of Cooperation: A False Feedback Study of a Sequential Iterated Prisoner's Dilemma." *Journal of Economic Psychology* 23 (2002): 437–448.

Moon, Simon M., and Alfred J. Illingworth. "Exploring the Dynamic Nature of Procrastination: A Latent Growth Curve Analysis of Academic Procrastination." *Personality and Individual Differences* 38 (2005): 297–309.

Moore, G. E. *Principia Ethica*. Amherst, Mass.: Prometheus, 1988.

Muraven, Mark, and Roy F. Baumeister. "Self-Regulation and Depletion of Limited Resources: Does Self-Control Resemble a Muscle?" *Psychological Bulletin* 126 (2000): 247–259.

Muraven, Mark, Roy. F. Baumeister, and Dianne M. Tice. "Longitudinal Improvement of Self-Regulation through Practice: Building Self-Control Strength through Repeated Exercise." *Journal of Social Psychology* 139 (1999): 446–457.

Muraven, Mark, and Dikla Shmueli. "The Self-Control Costs of Fighting the Temptation to Drink." *Psychology of Addictive Behaviors* 20 (2006): 154–160.

Muraven, Mark, Dikla Shmueli, and Edward Burkley. "Conserving Self-Control Strength." *Journal of Personality and Social Psychology* 91 (2006): 524–537.

Murray, E. J., and F. Foote. "The Origins of Fear of Snakes." *Behavior Research and Therapy* 17 (1979): 489–493.

Myerson, Joel, and Leonard Green. "Discounting of Delayed Rewards: Models of Individual Choice." *Journal of the Experimental Analysis of Behavior* 64 (1995): 263–276.

Neurath, Otto. "*Die Verirrten des Cartesius und das Auxiliarmotiv (Zur Psychologie des Entschlusses)*." *Jahrbuch der Philosophischen Gesellschaft an der Universität zu Wien* (1913): 45–59.
Nichols, Shaun. *Sentimental Rules: On the Natural Foundations of Moral Judgment*. Oxford: Oxford University Press, 2004.
Norman, Donald A. *Things That Make Us Smart: Defending Human Attributes in the Age of the Machine*. New York: Basic Books, 1993.
Nussbaum, Martha. *Hiding from Humanity: Disgust, Shame, and the Law*. Princeton, N.J.: Princeton University Press, 2004.
O'Doherty, John P. "Reward Representations and Reward-Related Learning in the Human Brain: Insights from Neuroimaging." *Current Opinion in Neurobiology* 14 (2004): 769–776.
O'Donoghue, Ted, and Matthew Rabin. "Doing It Now or Later." *American Economic Review*, 89 (1999): 103–124.
———. "Choice and Procrastination." *Quarterly Journal of Economics* 116 (2001): 121–160.
———. "Incentives for Procrastinators." *Quarterly Journal of Economics* 114 (1999): 769–816.
———. "Procrastination in Preparing for Retirement." In *Behavioral Dimensions of Retirement Economics*, ed. by Henry Aaron, 125–156. Washington, D.C.: Brookings Institute and Russell Sage Foundation, 1999.
———. "Procrastination on Long-Term Projects." *Journal of Economic Behaviour and Organization* 66 (2008): 161–175.
Oettingen, Gabriele, and Peter M. Gollwitzer. "Goal Setting and Goal Striving." In *Intraindividual Processes, Volume I of the Blackwell Handbook in Social Psychology*, ed. by Abraham Tesser and Norbert Schwarz, 329–347. Oxford: Blackwell, 2001.
Oettingen, Gabriele, Gaby Hönig, and Peter M. Gollwitzer. "Effective Self-Regulation of Goal Attainment." *International Journal of Educational Research* 33 (2000): 705–732.
Owens, Shane G., Christine G. Bowman, and Charles A. Dill. "Overcoming Procrastination: The Effect of Implementation Intentions." *Journal of Applied Social Psychology* 38 (2008): 366–384.
Pap, Arthur. 1961. "Determinism, Freedom, Moral Responsibility, and Causal Talk." In *Determinism and Freedom in the Age of Modern Science*, ed. by Sidney Hook, 200–205. New York: Collier, 1961.
Parfit, Derek. "Personal Identity and Rationality." *Synthese* 53 (1982): 227–241.
———. *Reasons and Persons*. Oxford: Clarendon Press, 1984.
Patterson, Charlotte J., and Walter Mischel. "Effects of Temptation-Inhibiting and Task-Facilitating Plans of Self-Control." *Journal of Personality and Social Psychology* 33 (1976): 209–217.
Perry, John. "The Importance of Being Identical." In *The Identities of Persons*, ed. by Amélie Oksenberg Rorty, 67–90. Berkeley: University of California Press, 1976.
———. "Structured Procrastination." Available at http://www.structuredprocrastination.com (accessed February 28, 2009).
Pettit, Philip. "Preferences, Deliberation and Satisfaction." In *Preferences and Well-Being*, ed. by Serena Olsaretti, 131–154. Cambridge: Cambridge University Press, 2006.
Phelps, Edmund, and Robert Pollack. "On Second-Best National Saving and Game Equilibrium Growth." *Review of Economic Studies* 35 (1968): 201–208.

Posner, Richard A. *Economic Analysis of Law*, 6th ed. New York: Aspen, 2003.
Powers, Theodor A., Richard Koestner, and Raluca A. Topciu. "Implementation Intentions, Perfectionism, and Goal Progress: Perhaps the Road to Hell Is Paved with Good Intentions." *Personality and Social Psychology Bulletin* 31 (2005): 902–912.
Powers, Theodor A., David C. Zuroff, and Raluca A. Topciu. "Covert and Overt Expressions of Self-Criticism and Perfectionism and Their Relation to Depression." *European Journal of Personality* 18 (2004): 61–72.
Prelec, Drazen, and Ronit Bodner. "Self-Signaling and Self-Control." In *Time and Decision*, ed. by George Loewenstein, Daniel Read, and Roy Baumeister, 277–298. New York: Russell Sage Foundation, 2003.
Putnam, Hilary. "The Meaning of 'Meaning.'" In *Mind, Language and Reality*, 215–271. Cambridge: Cambridge University Press, 1975.
Pychyl, Timothy A., Richard W. Morin, and Brian R. Salmon. "Procrastination and the Planning Fallacy: An Examination of the Study Habits of University Students." *Journal of Social Behavior and Personality* 15 (2000): 135–152.
Quinn, Warren. "The Puzzle of the Self-Torturer." In *Morality and Action*, 198–209. Cambridge: Cambridge University Press, 1994.
Rachlin, Howard. *The Science of Self-Control*. Cambridge, Mass.: Harvard University Press, 2000.
Rand, Ayn. "What Is Capitalism?" In *Capitalism: The Unknown Ideal*, 11–31. New York: Penguin, 1967.
Read, Daniel. "Is Time-Discounting Hyperbolic or Subadditive?" *Journal of Risk and Uncertainty* 23 (2001): 5–32.
Rocochnick, David. "Aristotle's Account of the Vicious: A Forgivable Inconsistency." *History of Philosophy Quarterly* 24 (2007): 207–220.
Ross, Don. *Economic Theory and Cognitive Science: Microexplanation*. Cambridge, Mass.: MIT Press, 2005.
———. "Integrating the Dynamics of Multi-Scale Economic Agency." In *The Oxford Handbook of Philosophy of Economics*, ed. by Harold Kincaid and Don Ross, 245–279. Oxford: Oxford University Press, 2009.
———. "Introduction: Science Catches the Will." In *Distributed Cognition and the Will: Individual Volition and Social Context*, ed. by Don Ross, David Spurrett, Harold Kincaid, and G. Lynn Stephens, 1–16. Cambridge, Mass.: MIT Press, 2007.
Ross, Don, David Spurrett, Harold Kincaid, and G. Lynn Stephens, eds. *Distributed Cognition and the Will: Individual Cognition and Social Context*. Cambridge, Mass.: MIT Press, 2007.
Ross, Stephen. "The Economic Theory of Agency: The Principal's Problem." *American Economic Review* 63, no. 2 (1973): 134–139.
Ryle, Gilbert. *The Concept of Mind*. Chicago: University of Chicago Press, 1949/1984.
Sanchirico, Chris William. "Detection Avoidance." *New York University Law Review* 81 (2006): 1331–1391.
Sanders, Teela. "Becoming an Ex-Sex Worker: Making Transitions Out of a Deviant Career." *Feminist Criminology* 2 (2007): 74–95.
Sani, Fabio. "Introduction and Overview." In *Self-Continuity: Individual and Collective Perspectives*, ed. by Fabio Sani, 1–19. New York: CRC Press/Taylor and Francis Group, 2008.
Scanlon, T. M. *What We Owe to Each Other*. Cambridge, Mass.: Belknap, 1998.

Schelling, Thomas. "Economics, or the Art of Self-Management." *American Economic Review* 68, no. 2 (1978): 290–294.

———. "The Intimate Contest for Self-Command." *Public Interest* 60 (1980): 94–118.

———. "Self-Command in Practice, in Policy, and in a Theory of Rational Choice." *American Economic Review* 74, no. 2 (1984): 1–11.

Schouwenburg, Henri C. "Academic Procrastination: Theoretical Notions, Measurement, and Research." In *Procrastination and Task Avoidance: Theory, Research, and Treatment*, by Joseph R. Ferrari, Judith L. Johnson, and William G. McCown, 71–96. New York: Springer, 1995.

———. "Procrastination in Academic Settings: General Introduction." In *Counseling the Procrastinator in Academic Settings*, ed. by Henri C. Schouwenburg, Clarry Lay, Timothy A. Pychyl, and Joseph Ferrari, 3–17. Washington, D.C.: American Psychological Association, 2004.

Schouwenburg, Henri C., and Jan T. Groenewoud. 2001. "Study Motivation under Social Temptation: Effects of Trait Procrastination." *Personality and Individual Differences* 30: 229–240.

Schouwenburg, Henri C., Clarry H. Lay, Timothy A. Pychyl, and Joseph R. Ferrari. *Counseling the Procrastinator in Academic Settings*. Washington, D.C.: American Psychological Association, 2004.

Searle, John. *Rationality in Action*. Cambridge, Mass.: MIT Press, 2001.

Seidler, Michael. "Kant and the Stoics on the Emotional Life." *Philosophy Research Archives* 7 (1981): 1–56.

Seneca. "On Anger." In *Seneca: Moral and Political Essays*, ed. by John M. Cooper and J. F. Procopé, 1–116. Cambridge: Cambridge University Press, 1995.

Shafir, Eldar, Itamar Simonson, and Amos Tversky. "Reason-Based Choice," *Cognition* 49 (1993): 11–36.

Shah, James Y., Rose Friedman, and Arie W. Kruglanski. "Forgetting All Else: On the Antecedents and Consequences of Goal Shielding." *Journal of Personality and Social Psychology* 83 (2002): 1261–1280.

Sheeran, Paschal. "Intention-Behavior Relations: A Conceptual and Empirical Review." *European Review of Social Psychology* 12 (2002): 1–36.

Sheeran, Paschal, Thomas L. Webb, and Peter M. Gollwitzer. "The Interplay between Goal Intentions and Implementation Intentions." *Personality and Social Psychology Bulletin* 31 (2005): 87–98.

Shoemaker, David W. "Caring, Identification, and Agency." *Ethics* 114 (2003): 88–118.

———. "Personal Identity and Ethics." In *Stanford Encyclopedia of Philosophy*, ed. by Edward N. Zalta. Available at http://plato.stanford.edu/entries/identity-ethics/ (accessed February 28, 2009).

———. "Personal Identity and Practical Concerns." *Mind* 116 (2007): 316–357.

Shoemaker, Sydney. "Comments." In *Perception and Personal Identity: Proceedings of the 1967 Oberlin Colloquium in Philosophy*, ed. by Norma Care and Robert Grimm, 107–127. Cleveland: The Press of Case Western Reserve University, 1969.

Shope, Robert. "The Conditional Fallacy in Contemporary Philosophy." *Journal of Philosophy* 75 (1978): 397–413.

Sidgwick, Henry. *The Methods of Ethics*, 7th ed. London: Macmillan, 1907.

Sigall, Hal, Arie Kruglanski, and Jack Fyock. "Wishful Thinking and Procrastination." *Journal of Social Behavior and Personality* 15 (2000): 283–296.

Silver, Maury, and John Sabini. "Procrastinating." *Journal for the Theory of Social Behavior* 11 (1981): 207–221.

Sjoberg, Lennart, and Tommy Johnson. "Trying to Give Up Smoking: A Study of Volitional Breakdowns." *Addictive Behaviors* 3 (1978): 149–164.

Skog, Ole-Jørgen. "Hyperbolic Discounting, Willpower, and Addiction." In *Addiction: Entries and Exits*, ed. by Jon Elster, 151–168. New York: Russell Sage Foundation, 1999.

Smart, R. G. "Spontaneous Recovery in Alcoholics: A Review and Analysis of the Available Research." *Drug and Alcohol Dependence* 1 (1975): 277–285.

Solomon, L. J., and E. D. Rothblum. "Academic Procrastination: Frequency and Cognitive-Behavioral Correlates." *Journal of Counseling Psychology* 31 (1984): 503–509.

Sorenson, Roy. "Originless Sin: Rational Dilemmas for Satisficers." *Philosophical Quarterly* 56 (2006): 213–223.

Spellecy, Ryan. "Reviving Ulysses Contracts." *Kennedy Institute of Ethics Journal* 13 (2003): 373–392.

Sreenivasan, Gopal. "Errors about Errors: Virtue Theory and Trait Attribution." *Mind* 111 (2002): 48–68.

Stadler, Gertraud, Gabriele Oettingen, and Peter M. Gollwitzer. "Effects of a Self-Regulation Intervention on Women's Physical Activity." *American Journal of Preventive Medicine* 36 (2009): 29–34.

Steel, Piers. "Case Studies." Available at http://www.procrastinus.com (accessed February 28, 2009).

———. "The Nature of Procrastination: A Meta-Analytic and Theoretical Review of Quintessential Self-Regulatory Failure." *Psychological Bulletin* 133 (2007): 65–94.

Steel, Piers, Thomas Brothen, and Catherine Wambach. "Procrastination and Personality, Performance, and Mood." *Personality and Individual Differences* 30 (2001): 95–106.

Strotz, Robert. "Myopia and Inconsistency in Dynamic Utility Maximization." *Review of Economic Studies* 23 (1956): 165–180.

Stroud, Sarah. "Weakness of Will." In *Stanford Encyclopedia of Philosophy*, ed. by Edward N. Zalta. Available at http://plato.stanford.edu/entries/weakness-will/ (accessed February 28, 2009).

Stroud, Sarah, and Christine Tappolet. "Introduction." In *Weakness of Will and Practical Irrationality*, ed. by Sarah Stroud and Christine Tappolet, 1–16. Oxford: Oxford University Press, 2003.

Sully, James. *Outlines of Psychology*. New York: Appleton, 1884.

Tenenbaum, Sergio. "Intention and Commitment." Working paper.

———. "Speculative Mistakes and Ordinary Temptations: Kant on Instrumental Conceptions of Rationality." *History of Philosophy Quarterly* 20 (2003): 203–223.

Thaler, Richard H. "Mental Accounting and Consumer Choice." *Marketing Science* 4 (1985): 199–214.

———. "Saving, Fungibility and Mental Accounts." *Journal of Economic Perspectives* 4 (1990): 193–205.

Thaler, Richard H., and Cass Sunstein. *Nudge: Improving Decisions about Health, Wealth and Happiness*. New Haven: Yale University Press, 2008.

Thompson, Michael. *Life and Action*. Cambridge, Mass.: Harvard University Press, 2008.

Tice, Dianne M., and Roy F. Baumeister. "Longitudinal Study of Procrastination, Performance, Stress and Health: The Costs and Benefits of Dawdling." *Psychological Science* 8 (1997): 454–458.

Trope, Yaacov, and Nira Libennan. "Temporal Construal and Time-Dependent Changes in Preference." *Journal of Personality and Social Psychology* 79 (2000): 876–889.

Utset, Manuel A. "Hyperbolic Criminals and Repeated Time-Inconsistent Misconduct." *Houston Law Review* 44 (2008): 609–677.

Van Eerde, Wendelien. "A Meta-Analytically Derived Nomological Network of Procrastination." *Personality and Individual Differences* 35 (2003): 1401–1418.

———. "Procrastination: Self-Regulation in Initiating Aversive Goals." *Applied Psychology* 49 (2000): 372–389.

Velleman, J. David. *The Possibility of Practical Reason*. Oxford: Clarendon Press, 2000.

———. "What Happens When Someone Acts?" *Mind* 101 (1992): 461–481.

Verplanken, Bas, and Suzanne Faes. "Good Intentions, Bad Habits, and Effects of Forming Implementation Intentions on Healthy Eating." *European Journal of Social Psychology* 29 (1999): 591–604.

Vogler, Candace. "Anscombe on Practical Inference." In *Varieties of Practical Reasoning*, ed. by Elijah Millgram, 437–464. Cambridge, Mass.: MIT Press, 2001.

———. *Reasonably Vicious*. Cambridge, Mass.: Harvard University Press, 2002.

Vohs, Kathleen D., Roy F. Baumeister, Brandon J. Schmeichel, Jean M. Twenge, Noelle M. Nelson, and Dianne M. Tice. "Making Choices Impairs Subsequent Self-Control: A Limited-Resource Account of Decision Making, Self-Regulation, and Active Initiative." *Journal of Personality and Social Psychology* 94 (2008): 833–898.

Vygotsky, Lev S. *Thought and Language*, rev. ed. Cambridge, Mass.: MIT Press, 1986.

Wallace, R. Jay. *Normativity and the Will: Selected Essays on Moral Psychology and Practical Reason*. Oxford: Oxford University Press, 2006.

Webb, Thomas L., Julie Christian, and Christopher J. Armitage. "Helping Students Turn Up for Class: Does Personality Moderate the Effectiveness of an Implementation Intention Intervention?" *Learning and Individual Differences* 17 (2007): 316–327.

Webb, Thomas L., and Paschal Sheeran. "Can Implementation Intentions Help to Overcome Ego-Depletion?" *Journal of Experimental Social Psychology* 39 (2003): 279–286.

———. "Does Changing Behavioral Intentions Engender Behavior Change? A Meta-Analysis of the Experimental Evidence." *Psychological Bulletin* 132 (2006): 249–268.

———. "Mechanisms of Implementation Intention Effects: The Role of Goal Intentions, Self-Efficacy, and Accessibility of Plan Components." *British Journal of Social Psychology* 47 (2008): 373–395.

Weber, Max. *The Protestant Ethic and the Spirit of Capitalism*. New York: Charles Scribner's Sons, 1958.

Wegner, Daniel M. *The Illusion of Conscious Will*. Cambridge, Mass.: MIT Press, 2002.

———. *White Bears and Other Unwanted Thoughts: Suppression, Obsession, and the Psychology of Mental Control*. New York: Penguin, 1989.

Weinberger, Jerry. *Ben Franklin Unmasked: On the Unity of His Moral, Religious, and Political Thought*. Lawrence: Kansas University Press, 2008.

Wertsch, James V. *Mind as Action*. New York: Oxford University Press, 1998.

White, Mark D. "Behavioral Law and Economics: The Assault on Consent, Will, and Dignity." In *New Essays on Philosophy, Politics & Economics: Integration and Common Research Projects*, ed. by Gerald Gaus, Christi Favor, and Julian Lamont, 203–223. Stanford, Calif.: Stanford University Press, 2010.

———. "Can *Homo Economicus* Follow Kant's Categorical Imperative?" *Journal of Socio-Economics* 33 (2004): 89–106.

———. "Does Homo Economicus Have a Will?" In *Economics and the Mind*, ed. by Barbara Montero and Mark D. White, 143–158. London: Routledge, 2007.

———. "Multiple Selves and Weakness of Will: A Kantian Perspective." *Review of Social Economy* 64 (2006): 1–20.

Whiting, Jennifer. "Friends and Future Selves." *Philosophical Review* 95 (1986): 547–580.

Wieber, Frank, Georg Odenthal, and Peter M. Gollwitzer. "Self-Efficacy Feelings Moderate Implementation Intention Effects." *Self and Identity* 9 (2010): 177–194.

Wieber, Frank, and Kai Sassenberg. "I Can't Take My Eyes Off of It: Attention Attraction Effects of Implementation Intentions." *Social Cognition* 24 (2006): 723–752.

Wieber, Frank, Antje von Suchodoletz, Tobias Heikamp, Gisela Trommsdorff, and Peter M. Gollwitzer. "If-Then Planning Helps School-Aged Children to Ignore Attractive Distractions." *Social Psychology* 42 (2011): 39–47.

Williams, Bernard. *Ethics and the Limits of Philosophy*. Cambridge, Mass.: Harvard University Press, 1985.

———. "Internal and External Reasons." In *Moral Luck*, 101–113. Cambridge: Cambridge University Press, 1982.

———. "Persons, Character and Morality." In *Moral Luck*, 1–19. Cambridge: Cambridge University Press, 1982.

———. "Replies." In *World, Mind and Ethics: Essays on the Ethical Philosophy of Bernard Williams*, ed. by J. E. J. Altham and Ross Harrison, 185–224. Cambridge: Cambridge University Press, 1995.

Winter, Sidney. "Economic 'Natural Selection' and the Theory of the Firm." *Yale Economic Essays* 4 (1964), 225–272.

Wolf, Susan. "The Meanings of Lives." In *Introduction to Philosophy: Classical and Contemporary Readings*, 4th ed., edited by John Perry, Michael Bratman, and John Martin Fischer, 62–73. New York: Oxford University Press, 2006.

———. "Self-Interest and Interest in Selves." *Ethics* 96 (1986): 704–720.

Wray, Ian, and Mark G. Dickerson. "Cessation of High Frequency Gambling and 'Withdrawal' Symptoms." *British Journal of Addiction* 76 (1981): 401–405.

Zauberman, Gal, and John G. Lynch. "Resource Slack and Discounting of Future Time versus Money." *Journal of Experimental Psychology: General* 134 (2005): 23–37.

Ziesat, Harold A., Jr., Ted L. Rosenthal, and Glenn M. White. "Behavioral Self-Control in Treating Procrastination of Studying." *Psychological Reports* 42 (1978): 59–69.

# Index

Aarts, Henk, 191n32, 202n74
abortion law, 267–269
abusive relationships, 271–272
Achtziger, Anja, 189n23, 193, 196n56
Adams, Douglas, 165n
Adams, Henry, 159
affect (Kantian), 224–226
Ainslie, George, 29–50, 89, 101–102, 104, 123n29, 143n16, 146, 188n21, 190n28, 200n69, 208–209, 216n, 229–230, 239–240, 244n21, 250n34. *See also* hyperbolic discounting; picoeconomics
Ajzen, Icek, 186n8
Akerlof, George, 29–31, 89n4, 101–105, 113–114, 185n3, 218–219
akrasia. *See* weakness of will
Allen, David, 249
Andersen, Stefan, 48n
Anderson, Joel, 217n3
Anderson, John R., 193n42
Andreou, Chrisoula, 21n38, 51–52, 57n13, 68–85, 120n23, 121, 123–124, 136n13, 146n18, 226n44, 244n21
Annas, Julia, 178n
Anscombe, G. E. M., 153n5, 162–163
appetite, 24–26
Ariely, Dan, 15n13, 28n2, 209–210, 233
Aristotle, 144, 152, 153n5, 157, 173–181
Arkes, Hal R., 95n30, 189n24
Armitage, Christopher J., 195n54, 197n57
Arpaly, Nomi, 121n26
Arvey, Richard D., 214–215
Asheim, Geir, 100

assurance game, 35–38
Audi, Robert, 121n26
Augustine, 3, 17
automatic responses, 202
autonomy (Kantian), 222–223

Bacharach, Michael, 30, 34–38
Bain, Alexander, 18n30
Bandura, Albert, 187n14, 190n27, 194n47
bargaining
 interpersonal 18
 intertemporal 18, 34
Bargh, John A., 190n28, 192n34, 193n41, 247
Barndollar, Kimberly, 190n28
Baumeister, Roy F., 3n3, 15n16, 17–18, 40n, 89n8, 187n16, 189n26, 201n71, 213n13, 231–232, 241
Bayer, Ute C., 192n36, 193, 196n56, 201n72
Becerra, Lino, 23n47
Beck, Ulrich, 251n36
Becker, Gary S., 15n20, 237, 262n20
Becker, Howard S., 209n10
behavioral economics, 28, 233, 253–273
Bénabou, Roland, 44, 229n50
Benhabib, Jess, 47–50
Bernheim, B. Douglas, 12n2
Berns, Gregory S., 12n3
Berridge, Kent C., 23n45
better-than relation, 108–112
Bible, Holy, 171n18
Bickel, Warren K., 255n5
Bisin, Alberto, 47–50
Blumer, Catherine, 95n30, 189n24
Bodner, Ronit, 44n35
Boice, Robert, 167–168, 174

293

Bowman, Christine G., 194n46, 203n77
Bowman, Margaret, 163n
Brandstätter, Veronika, 192n35, 192n37, 197–198, 203n78, 204n79, 208n2, 242–243
Bratman, Michael E., 15n17, 61–62, 103n10, 130n, 133n5
Brennan, Timothy J., 217n2
bright lines, 18, 229–230
Brockner, Joel, 189n25
Brokenshire, Rosemarie, 187n11
Broome, John, 107–109, 112n20, 113
Brothen, Thomas, 187n12
Bruner, Jerome, 236n
Buehler, Roger, 90n10, 95n29
bundling
 of rewards, 16, 91, 208–209
 of tasks, 243
Burge, Tyler, 157n8
Buridan's ass, 80–81
Burka, Jane B., 249n29–30
Burkley, Edward, 213n13
Burnham, Audrey, 18n31
Butler, Joseph, 117n8

calculative reasons, 162–163
Capra, C. Monica, 12n3
Carroll, Lewis, 154
Carver, Charles S., 187n14
Chapman, Janine, 197n57
character traits, 211–215
Chartrand, Tanya L., 247n
Chesterton, G. K., 158n
Christensen-Szalanski, Jay, 240n11
Christian, Julie, 195n54
chutes, 245
Cicero, 87
Clark, Andy, 234
closure, decisional and cognitive, 90–91
cognitive biases, 94–95
commitment, 193–194, 257–258
conditional fallacy, 152–153
conscientiousness, 195–196, 214
conspiracy, criminal, 264–265, 270
Conti, Regina, 89n8
Cooter, Robert D., 217n2
coping strategies
 environmental, 244–246
 in general, 128–129, 185–215, 233–252
 social, 246–248

Damasio, Antonio, 92–93
Davidson, Donald, 55–56, 60n19, 69n, 220n14
deadlines, 246
Delaney, Liam, 42–43
delay
 excused, 68–69
 irrational (*see* procrastination, as irrational delay)
 prudent, 69
Deluty, Martin Z., 14, 15n12
democratic accountability, 265–272
Dennett, Daniel, 37, 119n16
Descartes, René, 117
desire-belief model (Hume), 220–221
Dickerson, Mark G., 11n1
Dijksterhuis, Ap, 191n32, 247
Dill, Charles A., 194n46, 203n77
discounting, time, 103–106, 113, 146. *See also* hyperbolic discounting; quasi-hyperbolic discounting
disengagement from failing plans, 189, 200–201
distraction, resisting, 188–189, 199–200
Dodd, Dylan, 53n7
Doris, John M., 212n12
Dovidio, John F., 169n
Dreier, James, 160n12
dual self model (of impulse control), 38–40
dummy goals, 159–62
Dweck, Carol, 166n3, 168n10
dynamic inconsistency. *See* preference, time-inconsistent

Ebert, Jane E. J., 257n13
economic models. *See* procrastination, economic models of
*Education of Henry Adams, The*, 159
Edwards, Jonathon, 171
ego depletion, 201–202
Ellis, Albert, 185n2
Elster, Jon, 69n, 103–106, 209n10
emotion
 procrastination in emotional reward, 21–26

**Index**

as reward-seeking processes, 22–24
as source of procrastination, 90–94
virtue and, 179–180
Engle, Randall, 42n26
Engstrom, Stephen, 223n26, 224n36–37
Epictetus, 179
Epicureans, 175–181
Epicurus, 179
ethical theory, 165–181
evaluative footprint, 157
ever-better problems, 79–81
excuses, credible, 17–20
experiments, psychological
  animals, with, 14–16
  criticism of, 89–90
  in general, 13–16, 166–169, 185–205, 213–215
extended mind, 235–237
external incentives/constraints, 209–210

Faes, Suzanne, 193n39
false beliefs, 177–181
Fee, Ronda L., 92
Ferrari, Joseph R., 89n6–7, 167, 169, 177, 185n1, 185n4
Fischer, Carolyn, 219
Fisher, Irving, 31
fMRI data, 42–43
Foote, F., 22n43
Franklin, Benjamin, 169–172
Frederick, Shane, 253n, 254–255
free-rider problems. *See* procrastination, as free-rider problem
free will, 222n24
Fried, Charles, 257n13
Friedman, Rose, 189n23
Fudenberg, Drew, 38–41, 48–50
Fyock, Jack, 95n31

Gailliot, Matthew T., 213n14
Garner, D. M., 18n32
Garvey, Andrew J., 18n31
Gault, Barbara, 18n30
Gauthier, David, 133n5, 135n8, 143n17
Gawrilow, Caterina, 188n19, 202n75, 204n80

Gibbon, John, 12n3
Gilbert, Daniel T., 257n13
Gjelsvik, Olav, 122n27
Glimcher, Paul, 42
goal(s)
  implementation intentions and, 191–192
  setting, 186–187
  striving, 187–190
Gollwitzer, Peter M., 208n2, 242–243
Goncharov, Ivan, 115
Green, Leonard, 13n4, 32n13
Gregor, Mary, 223n26, 224n37
Griffin, Dale, 90n10, 95n29
Griffin, James, 158n
Groenewoud, Jan T., 13n6, 19n34
Guastello, Barbarose, 16
Gul, Farouk, 43–44
Guyer, Paul, 223n26

Habermas, Jürgen, 252n37
habit, 202
Hall, Brandon L., 181n29
Hamlet, 94
Hansen, L. Sunny, 248n27
Hardin, Russell, 264n25
Hariri, Ahmed, 42n28
Harriott, Jesse, 185n1
Heath, Joseph, 217n3
Heatherton, Todd F., 15n16, 40n, 232
Helzer, John E., 18n31
Henderson, Marlone D., 200–201
Herrnstein, Richard J., 25n50, 31–33
heteronomy (Kantian), 222–229
Heylighen, Francis, 249n32
Hill, Thomas E., 226–227
Hoch, Stephen, 43n31
Holland, Rob W., 202n74
Holton, Richard, 60–66, 221, 227n46, 231
Hönig, Gaby, 198n62
Hursch, Daniel E., 181n29
Hursthouse, Rosalind, 151n1
Hutchins, Edwin, 241n15
hyperbolic discounting, 12–15, 31–34, 41–42, 89–92, 101–102, 104, 146, 239–240

identity. *See* personal identity
Illingworth, Alfred J., 248n27

implementation intentions, 185–205, 208–209, 242–243
impulses, 11–12
instrumentalism, 147–150, 162–163
intention-behavior gap, 187
intentions, 60–66, 186–187
intransitivity. *See* preferences, intransitivity
irrationality. *See* procrastination, as irrational delay; procrastination, as rational failing
irresoluteness, 60–66

James, William, 15n17
jam-yesterday-jam-tomorrow structure, 154–156
Jaspers, Karl, 119n18
Johansen, Leif, 95–96
Johnson, Judith L., 89nn6–7, 167n6
Johnson, Matthew W., 255n5
Johnson, Robert, 153n5
Johnson, Samuel, 94
Johnson, Tommy, 244n23
Johnston, Mark, 117n6

Kable, Joe, 42
Kachgal, Mera M., 248n27
Kafka, Franz, 119
Kahneman, Daniel, 93n23, 95n29
Kant, Immanuel, 222–229. *See also* will, Kantian-economic theory of
Katyal, Neal Kumar, 265n27
Kenny, Anthony, 266n29
Kim, Jeong-Yoon, 217n2, 228n48, 230–231
Kind, Amy, 119n16
Kirby, Kris N., 13n4, 16
Knaus, Williams J., 185n2
Koestner, Richard, 195n51
Koons, Judith, 271n38
Korsgaard, Christine, 147–150
Kruglanski, Arie W., 91n14, 95n31, 189n23
Kuhl, Julius, 187n14

ladders, 245–246
Laibson, David, 12n2, 27n55, 41–43
Langendam, Daan, 202n74
law and economics, 253–273
Lay, Clarry H., 92, 185n4, 187n11

Lazarus, Arnold, 22n43
Lea, Stephen E. G., 22n42
LeDoux, Joseph, 90n13
Lengfelder, Angelika, 192n37, 203n78, 204n79, 208n2
leveraging control, 211–213, 243–244
Levine, David, 38–41, 48–50
Levy, Neil, 18n33
Levy, R. A., 166n2
Libennan, Nira, 242n19
Lively, Lynn, 249n31
Locke, John, 117n8
Loewenstein, George, 12n2, 27n55, 43–44, 253n, 254–255
Louie, Kenway, 42
Lynch, John G., 20n35
Lynn, Steven J., 22n41

Mahoney, Martha R., 271n37
management misconduct, 270–271
Mann, Merlin, 245n24
Marcus, Gary, 234n3
matching law, 32–33
Maunsell, John H. R., 23n48
Maxwell, Bruce, 128n39
Mazur, James E., 13n4, 14n7–8, 32, 41, 48
McClennen, Edward F., 15n17, 143n17
McClure, Samuel, 42
McCowen, William G., 89nn6–7, 167n6
McCulloch, Kathleen, 201n72
McDowell, John, 117n6, 151n1, 152
McEvoy, Lawrence T., 18n31
McIntyre, Alison, 52n2, 60–66, 121n26
means-end reasoning, 162–163
Mele, Alfred, 240n10
melioration, 32–33, 38–40
Metcalfe, James, 200n68
Midden, Cees, 191n32
Milne, Sarah, 205n81
Mirrlees, James A., 20n37
Mischel, Walter, 199n65, 200n68
misconduct (legal). *See* time-inconsistent misconduct
modality, 25
money pump arguments, 75–76, 104–112

# Index

Monterosso, John, 16n24, 16n27, 18n30
Moon, Simon M., 248n27
Moore, G. E., 158
moral apathy, 224n37, 232
Morin, Richard W., 89n6, 89n9, 248n27
Muraven, Mark, 17n29, 213n13, 231–232, 241
Murphy, Kevin, 15n20, 237
Murray, E. J., 22n42
muscle (theory of will). *See* will, as muscle
Myerson, Joel, 13n4, 32n13

nag screen, 245n24
naive/sophisticated reasoning, 258–260
Neurath, Otto, 92n24
nibbling opportunism, 261
Nichols, Shaun, 128n39
Norman, Donald A., 234n2
Norman, Paul, 197n57
Noussair, Charles, 12n3
Nussbaum, Martha, 170n14
Nutter, Kevin J., 248n27

obedience (to the law). *See* time-inconsistent obedience
Oblomov, 115
Odenthal, Georg, 194n48
O'Doherty, John P., 23n47
O'Donoghue, Ted, 5n6, 28n1, 42n24, 45–50, 89n4, 90n11, 101–102, 104, 134n, 218–219, 253n, 254–255, 257n12, 260n17
Oettingen, Gabriele, 186n7, 188n19, 198n62, 200–201, 202n75, 204n80, 205n82
opportunity costs (of decision-making), 93–94
Orbell, Sheina, 205n81
organic wholes, 158
Owens, Shane G., 194n46, 203n77

pain, 23
Pap, Arthur, 15n17
Paradox of Hedonism, 161n14
Parfit, Derek, 52n2, 117–118, 125
passion (Kantian), 224–226
Patel, T., 167n5

paternalism, 252, 262–263
Patterson, Charlotte J., 199n65
penalties for lapsing, 212–213
perfectionism, 92, 94, 178–179, 195
Perry, John, 116, 118–119, 244
personal identity
  Cartesian ego and, 117
  Lockean theory of, 117n8
  procrastination and, 115–129
  psychological continuity accounts of, 117–119, 127–128
  special concern and theories of, 116–120
personal rules, 20–21, 34–35, 229–230
Pesendorfer, Wolfgang, 43–44
*Pettibone v. United States*, 265n26
Pettit, Phillip, 109
picoeconomics, 30–50. *See* also hyperbolic discounting
Phelps, Edmund, 41
*Planned Parenthood v. Casey*. *See* abortion law
planning, 64–66, 130–150, 185–205
pleasure, 24
policies, intermediate, 139–143
Policy-as-Action model (PAM), 130–134
Pollack, Robert, 41
Poor Richard's Almanac. *See* virtue, Poor Richard theory of
Posner, Richard A., 260n18
Powers, Theodor A., 195n51–52
practical judgment
  correlative vice of, 144–145
  virtue, as, 138–145
Practical Tortoise, 160n12
Prelec, Drazen, 31–32, 44n35
preference
  global versus local, 70, 74–77
  intransitive, 68–85, 104–113, 137
  momentary, 135–136
  time-inconsistent, 12–15, 31–34, 38–48, 101–102, 104, 146, 218–220, 239–240, 255–260
  transitive, 106–107
preference reversal. *See* preference, time-inconsistent
premature action, 90–91
principal-agent problems, 20–21
prisoner's dilemma, 33–38

proceduralization, 193
procrastination
  actions versus tasks, 87
  as akrasia, 55–59, 173–175
  as basic impulse, 11–27
  bedtime, 250
  behaviors associated with, 167–168
  biological or genetic component of, 214–215
  blind, 121
  buck-passing model of, 124–125
  chronic, 202–204
  clear-eyed, 120–121, 125–126
  cognitive biases as source of, 94–95
  compliance, 261
  costs of, 166–167
  definitions of, 3–6, 11, 51–53, 68–69, 99–101, 120–122, 185–186, 207n, 237–238
  dual self model of, 38–40
  economic models of, 28–50, 68–85, 218–220, 255–260
  emotion as source of, 90–94
  as free action, 120
  as free-rider problem, 123, 207
  immoral, 123
  implementation intentions and, 185–205
  imprudent, 123–126
  as inaction, 63
  as instrumental irrationality, 139
  instrumentalism and, 147–150
  intransitivity model of, 68–85
  as irrational delay, 87–96, 99–103, 120–121
  Kantian-economic model of, 226–229
  as lack of concern for future selves, 115–129
  legal issues with, 253–273
  long-term, 134–138
  persistent, 228–229
  personal identity and, 115–129
  political considerations of, 251–252
  practical judgment and, 130–150
  principled, 160
  as putting off, 53–54, 154
  as rational failing, 51–54
  recurrent or repeated, 28–29, 253–273
  resisting, 216–232, 240–241
  and self-respect (failure of), 226–227
  strategies for coping with (see coping strategies)
  structured, 244
  task aversiveness and, 188
  task initiation, with respect to, 197–199
  temporal motivation theory of, 242–243
  trait, 202–204
  as vice, 130–150, 173–175
  virtue ethics and, 165–181
  as weakness of will, 51–66, 226
  will (or willpower) and, 17–21, 216–232
prospect theory, 93
psychological determinism, 222n24
punishment, 261–262
Putnam, Hilary, 157n8
Pychyl, Timothy A., 89nn6–7, 89n9, 248n27

quasi-hyperbolic discounting, 41–43, 45–47
Quinn, Warren, 70–72

Rabin, Matthew, 5n6, 28n1, 42n24, 45–50, 89n4, 90n11, 101–102, 104, 134n, 218–219, 255n6–7, 257n12, 260n17
Rachlin, Howard, 15n18, 31
Rand, Ayn, 171–172
Rangel, Antonio, 12n2
rationalization, 17
rational reconsideration, 227n46
Read, Daniel, 43
regulation. *See* stealth regulation
Repetto, Andrea, 42n24
resolution, 143–144
reward
  emotional, 21–26
  versus rewards, 21
rewards
  bundling of, 16
  versus reward, 21
  smaller-sooner and larger-later (*see* hyperbolic discounting)
  visceral, 12, 43–44

**Index**

Rhue, Judith W., 22n41
Rietveld, Gerrit, 245
risk aversion, 26n53
Rocochnick, David, 174n25
*Roe v. Wade. See* abortion law
Rosenthal, Ted L., 248n28
Ross, Don, 188n21, 217n2, 218n5, 241n15
Ross, Michael, 90n10, 95n29
Ross, Stephen, 20n37
Rothblum, E. D., 99–100, 248n27
Ryle, Gilbert, 14, 217

Sabini, John, 3, 51–55, 56n13, 57n14, 59n15, 99–100, 120–122, 207n
salience, 29–30, 218–219
Salmon, Brian R., 89n6, 89n9, 248n27
Sanchirico, Chris William, 263n23
Sanders, Teela, 261n
Sani, Fabio, 119
Sarbanes-Oxley Act, 270–271
Sassenberg, Kai, 191n33
satisficing, 81
scaffolding
 built aspects of, 249–250
 environmental aspects of, 244–246, 249–250
 institutional aspects of, 250–251
 policy aspects of, 251–252
 of rationality, 233–252
 social aspects of, 246–248
Scanlon, T. M., 52n2
Schaal, Bernd, 193n38, 193n41, 199n66
Scheier, Michael, 187n14
Schelling, Thomas, 30n, 31
Schouwenberg, Henri C., 13n6, 19n, 89n6, 187n13, 203n76
Searle, John, 221–222
Seidler, Michael, 224n37
selective association, 247
self-control as muscle. *See* will, as muscle
self-deception, 159–162
self-efficacy, 194
self-help literature, 248–249
self-management, 243–244
self-prediction, recursive, 17, 34, 229–230
self-regulation, resource model of. *See* will, as muscle

self-signalling, 44
self-torturer, puzzle of the, 70–73, 78–81
Seneca, 87
sex trade, delaying leaving, 261n
Shafir, Eldar, 93–94
Shah, James Y., 189n23
Shakespeare, 94
Sheeran, Paschal, 187n9, 187n15, 188n18, 189n23, 191n30–31, 193, 194n49, 198n61, 199n63, 201n73, 205n81
Shmueli, Dikla, 213n13
Shoemaker, David W., 116n4, 117n7, 118n9
Shoemaker, Sydney, 119n16
Shope, Robert, 152–153
Sidgwick, Henry, 117n8, 118, 146
Sigall, Hal, 95n31
Silver, Maury, 3, 51–55, 56n13, 57n14, 59n15, 99–100, 120–122, 207n
Silverman, Stuart, 185n4
Simonson, Itamar, 93–94
Sjoberg, Lennart, 244n23
Skog, Ole-Jørgen, 91n16
Smart, R. G., 18n31
Software Time Lock, 246
Solomon, L. J., 99–100, 248n27
Sorenson, Roy, 81n12
Spellecy, Ryan, 161n13
Sreenivasan, Gopal, 167
Stadler, Gertraud, 205n82
stealth regulation
 abortion law and, 267–269
 in general, 265–272
Steel, Piers, 54n, 100, 114, 165n, 186, 187n10, 187n12, 188n20, 188n22, 193n43, 194n50, 195, 196n55, 198n60, 199n64, 214–215, 234n4, 242, 250n33, 251n35
Stoics, 175–181, 224n37, 232
strategic reframing, 241–243
Strotz, Robert, 30n, 89
Stroud, Sarah, 69n, 114n, 120n20, 207n, 216n, 226n44
Sully, James, 16
Sunstein, Cass, 28n2, 252n38
Supreme Court of the United States, 267–269
symmetry-breaking techniques, 80–81

Tangney, June P., 92
Tappolet, Christine, 207n
team reasoning, 34–38
teamwork, 246–247
Thaler, Richard H., 28n2, 241n16, 252n38, 254n
Thompson, Michael, 131n3, 162n15
*Through the Looking Glass*, 154
Tice, Dianne M., 3n3, 17n29, 40n, 89n8, 213n13
time-inconsistent misconduct, 260–263
time-inconsistent obedience, 263–265
time-inconsistent preferences. *See* hyperbolic discounting
Tirole, Jean, 44, 229n50
Tobacman, Jeremy, 42n24
Topciu, Raluca A., 195n51–52
Toppi-Mullen, Pam, 18n30
transitivity. *See* preferences, transitive
triadology, 156–158
triggers, 245
Trope, Yaacov, 242n19
Tversky, Amos, 93–94, 95n29

urgency, 90

vagueness, 81–84, 137–138
Van Eerde, Wendelien, 185n4, 187n17, 188n20
Velleman, J. David, 158, 220–221
Verplanken, Bas, 193n39
vice, 144–145, 165–81
Vidal, Clément, 249n32
virtue
  as character or strength, 222–226
  Poor Richard theory of, 170–172, 179–180
  procrastination and, 138–145, 151–181
  traditional, 175–176
Vogler, Candace, 162n15–16
Vohs, Kathleen, 40n, 232n55
volitionism, 220–222
Vygotsky, Lev S., 236n

Wallace, R. Jay, 220–221
Wambach, Catherine, 187n12
weakness of will
  classic understanding (as akrasia), 55–59
  procrastination as, 51–66, 69, 226
  revisionist understanding, 60–66
  simple, 223–226
  synchronic versus diachronic phenomenon, 59, 61, 63
Webb, Thomas L., 191n31, 193, 194n49, 195n54, 201n73
Weber-Fechner law, 12
Weber, Max, 171
Webley, Paul, 22n42
Webster, Donna, 91n14
Wegner, Daniel M., 14, 24n
Weinberger, Jerry, 170n15
Wertenbroch, Klaus, 15n13, 209–210
Wertsch, James V., 236n
White, Glenn M., 248n28
White, Mark D., 240n13, 252n38
Whiting, Jennifer, 116n5, 118n9, 118n11
Wieber, Frank, 208n2, 242–243
will
  distributed willpower, 241
  economic treatments of, 217n2, 230–231
  extended, 233–252
  impure, 223–226
  Kantian-economic theory of, 220–226
  as muscle, 15, 17–18, 201–202, 213, 231–232, 241
  against procrastination, 17–21, 216–232, 240–241
  strength of, 222, 224–229
  theories of, 15–16
  weakness of (*see* weakness of will)
Williams, Bernard, 104n12, 115n2, 121n24, 152–153
Winter, Sidney, 95n32
Wolf, Susan, 119, 173
Wooley, S. C., 18n32
Wray, Ian, 11n1

Yuen, Lenora M., 249n29–30

Zauberman, Gal, 20n35
Ziesat, Harold A., Jr., 248n28
Zuroff, David C., 195n52

Printed in Great Britain
by Amazon